# The School Counselor's Desk Reference and Credentialing Examination Study Guide

*The School Counselor's Desk Reference and Credentialing Examination Study Guide, Second Edition* is the only study guide and desk reference on the market that covers the latest ASCA School Counselor Competencies and ASCA Mindsets and Behaviors, CACREP Standards, and the CAEP and NBPTS Standards. It effectively prepares students for the Praxis II Professional School Counseling exams (5421 & 0420), NBPTS School Counseling National Certification exam, School Counselor Preparation Comprehensive Exams, and state-specific certification/licensure exams for the professional practice of school counseling. This revised volume is designed to build knowledge and skills through end-of-chapter practice tests, a full-length practice exam with exam answers and rationales, guided reflections, and case studies. Additional resources include a glossary of important terms and a list of commonly used acronyms within the profession.

**Rita Schellenberg, PhD, LPC, NCC, NCSC, ACS,** is a professor and the chair of the school counseling program at Liberty University in Virginia. She was recognized by the American School Counselor Association (ASCA) as one of the top 15 school counselors in the nation and honored "Outstanding Graduate" in her PhD program in Counselor Education and Supervision at Regent University. Dr. Schellenberg has authored many successful publications on professional school counseling including, most recently, *A New Era in School Counseling* (Rowman & Littlefield Publishers, 2013). You can learn more about Dr. Schellenberg, her consulting services, and other published works by visiting her professional website, *Cultivating Performance* at www.CultivatingPerformance.com.

Dr. Rita Schellenberg covers the breadth of contemporary school counseling topics and content to help master's candidates and the highly motivated practitioner to prepare for national and state credentialing exams. Each of the eight chapters provides simulations, case conceptualization, and reflections that frame critical concepts. Additionally, Dr. Schellenberg skillfully uses ASCA's position statements to illustrate and provide direction to challenging school counseling situations. From clear descriptions and web links for each exam, to standards alignment and integration of the ASCA National Model, this second edition successfully removes the fear factor that causes most of us to shy away from the challenges of national credentialing.

**Carol Dahir**, **Ed.D.** *is a professor and chair of the School Counseling Department at the New York Institute of Technology*

# The School Counselor's Desk Reference and Credentialing Examination Study Guide

## Second Edition

### Rita Schellenberg

Routledge
Taylor & Francis Group

NEW YORK AND LONDON

Second edition published 2018
by Routledge
711 Third Avenue, New York, NY 10017

and by Routledge
2 Park Square, Milton Park, Abingdon, Oxon, OX14 4RN

*Routledge is an imprint of the Taylor & Francis Group, an informa business*

© 2018 Taylor & Francis

*Library of Congress Cataloging-in-Publication Data*
Names: Schellenberg, Rita Cantrell, author.
Title: The school counselor's desk reference and credentialing examination study guide / Rita Schellenberg.
Other titles: School counselor's study guide for credentialing exams
Description: Second edition. | New York : Routledge, 2017. | Preceded by The school counselor's study guide for credentialing exams / Rita Schellenberg. 2012. | Includes bibliographical references and index.
Identifiers: LCCN 2017024164| ISBN 9781138681873 (hardcover : alk. paper) | ISBN 9781138681880 (pbk. : alk. paper) | ISBN 9781315545523 (e-book)
Subjects: | MESH: Counseling | Child | Adolescent | School Health Services | Child Guidance | United States | Case Reports | Examination Questions
Classification: LCC LB1027.5 | NLM WA 18.2 | DDC 371.4076—dc23
LC record available at https://lccn.loc.gov/2017024164

First edition published 2012 by Taylor & Francis

ISBN: 978-1-138-68187-3 (hbk)
ISBN: 978-1-138-68188-0 (pbk)
ISBN: 978-1-315-54552-3 (ebk)

Typeset in Garamond
by Florence Production Limited, Stoodleigh, Devon

This book is dedicated to all school counselors, school counselor educators, and school-counselors-in-training. May I express my gratitude and applaud your tireless efforts toward positively impacting the lives of millions of children, adolescents, and parents. You have quieted restless minds, calmed distressed souls, and taught forgiveness, acceptance, and an appreciation for all people. Your drive for excellence is shaping our practices and securing a rock-solid future for our profession. You are at the helm of one of the greatest professions in the fleet. Together as shipmates, we are cutting through the sometimes rough seas on what is the voyage of our life!

John, thank you for the support you have shown me these many years. I am grateful for the rations of solitude that you gift me with just as naturally as breathing.

Mom and Dad, thank you for the abundance of unconditional love. Rogerians rejoice in the knowledge of the power of nurturing and encouragement—'cause we sure didn't have money! More precious than dough—Mom, you gave me your strength and your compassionate nature. Dad, you gave me your sense of humor and determination. I love you both beyond words.

Kenny, Teresa, and Ronnie, oh, the journey we've had—we have lived, loved, laughed, and mourned together. I wouldn't trade these years for a lifetime supply of Razzles and Mountain Dew. Kelly and Donna, life has not been the same since Jesus called you home. Our family feels the void every day; but, we are comforted in the promise of eternity with you and Jesus Christ.

Glory to God for the life He breathed into each of us and into this work. Amen.

# Contents

# Foreword to the First Edition

Rita Schellenberg has successfully created a book that serves as a resource and guide for members of the counseling community. In this era of educational reform and accountability, educators are required to be highly skilled and trained. School counselors currently practicing in the field and counselors-in-training recognize the need to demonstrate that they are highly qualified, well-trained professionals in the field of education and counseling. Obtaining national certification is an excellent way to enhance a school counselor's career and provide documentation of highly qualified status.

As with many aspects of her professional life, Dr. Schellenberg recognized a critical need and proceeded forward with a plan to effectively address the need. The creation of this valuable resource was truly a labor of love for Dr. Schellenberg. Her professional goals led her to seek national certification as a counselor. Dr. Schellenberg's enthusiasm for pursuing such a goal was met with the frustration of being unable to find the resources needed to assist her in preparing for the certification process. Before this study guide, a school counselor would have to perform the daunting task of compiling information from several different resources, which requires exhausting hours of research. With the numerous responsibilities and workloads of most practicing school counselors, this search for adequate resources becomes an extraordinary source of frustration and a major hindrance in the pursuit of certification. Dr. Schellenberg has eliminated this barrier, and this book has the potential to encourage more school counselors to pursue national credentials.

As a counselor educator, Dr. Schellenberg also noticed that counselors-in-training lacked a study guide for comprehensive examinations of graduate programs. By writing this book, Dr. Schellenberg provides counselors-in-training with an excellent resource to prepare them for their comprehensive examinations. The unique benefit of this book is that it provides counselors-in-training with a pathway from their comprehensive examination to national certification.

*The School Counselor's Study Guide for Credentialing Exams* bridges the gap between theoretical knowledge, practice, and certification. This book is a valuable resource to any practicing school counselor or counselor-in-training. Regardless of a school counselor's professional aspirations, this book will enhance the counselor's professional development. This comprehensive resource should be included in every professional library.

**Sylinda Gilchrist-Banks, EdD**
*American School Counselor Association, Past President 2012–2013*

# Preface

## Hello, My Name is Rita Schellenberg and I *AM* a Credential Junkie

The growing demand for accountability and enhanced mental health services for children and adolescents has further heightened the need for rigorous credentialing requirements. Virtually every state in this great nation requires a school counselor specialty exam in order to obtain licensure/certification to ensure the that school counselors are fully prepared to provide counseling services to minors in K–12 settings. Optimal preparation is critical; the school counselor is the only counselor a troubled child or adolescent may ever see.

My own experience, paddling through the pool of school counseling exam study guides, quickly became a daunting and exhausting plunge. I searched and searched for one study guide that could be used for any school counseling comprehensive exam—nothing. How was this possible? I could not fathom the nonexistence of a dedicated study guide for such an important discipline. As I plowed through one text after another to identify one resource that would cover all the critical content needed for the comprehensive exam, I became frustrated. Yes, yes I did, I said *frustrated*—and that is exactly how I felt!

So, as they say, necessity being the "father of invention" I created my own study guide, which is now this second edition of *The School Counselor's Desk Reference and Credentialing Examination Study Guide*, formerly *The School Counselor's Study Guide for Credentialing Exams*. I am pleased that my first edition met with extremely positive reviews and more importantly candidates passing a variety of school counseling exams in a multitude of states across the country. Mission accomplished!

I am humbled at how many of you *hunted me down* to thank me and share your positive testing experience. Some of you ask that I continue to update the text so you could use it as a comprehensive desk reference while a practicing school counselor. As clichéd as it is—your wish is my command!

So whether you're bending the pages of this text to pass a school counseling exam or to help you better understand the law and ethics as it applies to the case notes you are writing, thank you for seeking to be the very best school counselor you can be! It is my hope that you never stop seeking to improve your skills and obtain advanced voluntary credentials that set you apart as a professional dedicated to providing optimal counseling services.

My own journey to becoming a *credential junkie* (CJ) has been an exciting life-long expedition of continuous mind, body, and spiritual renewal. With each credential I find myself reenergized with the fervor equivalent to that of Rob Pattinson's childhood mission to save the snails (enchants the heart)! However, I must openly disclose that, due to the ecstasy that envelops me each time I add a new credential to my professional belt, I have to wonder if I could use some counseling myself when something as innocuous as a credential could become the pinnacle of my existence at any moment in time. I can just imagine myself standing up at a *CJ meeting*, saying, "Hello, my name is Rita Schellenberg and I am a credential junkie." Well, there are worse things. So—I wish you all successful school counseling practices, exam triumph, and credential addiction!

# Acknowledgments

I owe a debt of gratitude to countless and sensational colleagues, who, over the years and as a collective, have informed, encouraged, supported, challenged, and propelled me forward. This desk reference and study guide is not the work of one, but of many, as demonstrated by the exhaustive references section.

I am thrilled to acknowledge my students—past, present, and future. Bearing witness to your sincere yearning for knowledge has pushed me to continue learning so that I might continue to have something more to share. It is my hope that I might encourage you to be explorers of your own world while exploring the worlds of others and to live in the world, not just on it.

I would especially like to express my gratitude to Dr. Sylinda Gilchrist-Banks, past president of the American School Counselor Association, for writing the Foreword in support of this text and my work related to professional school counseling. Sylinda, your history of laudable altruistic acts has not gone unnoticed. Your book *Choice Theory: Using Choice Theory and Reality Therapy to Enhance Student Achievement and Responsibility* (2009) reminds us of the power and ability that lie within each of us, all of us, to make change and author our own lives.

Special thanks is extended to the outstanding Routledge/Taylor & Francis team, namely Elizabeth Graber, Editor, Nina Guttapalle, Editorial Assistant, and Chantelle Walker for her marketing expertise. I would also like to thank Howard Rosenthal, EdD, author of the academic bestseller *Encyclopedia of Counseling* (2007) for his review and helpful comments.

**Rita Schellenberg**

# About the Author

**Dr. Rita Schellenberg** is full professor and chair of the school counseling program at Liberty University in Virginia. She also serves on the executive board as School Counseling Representative for the Virginia Association for Counselor Education and Supervision. Dr. Schellenberg received her training in school counseling from the College of William and Mary in Virginia. She was named outstanding graduate in her PhD in counselor education and supervision program completed at Regent University. She is a licensed professional counselor and licensed school counselor. She also holds the credentials of National Certified Counselor, National Certified School Counselor, Approved Clinical Supervisor, Clinical Mental Health Counselor, and Distance Credentialed Counselor. Dr. Schellenberg is also an ASCA-certified School Counseling Legal and Ethical Specialist and a Bully Prevention Specialist.

Dr. Schellenberg has authored many successful publications on the discipline of school counseling and has presented at numerous conferences across the country on topics related to the contemporary practice of school counseling. Notable textbooks include *The New School Counselor: Strategies for Universal Achievement*, *A New Era in School Counseling: A Practical Guide*, and *The School Counselor's Desk Reference and Credentialing Examination Study Guide*. Two of her textbooks include a CD containing interactive action plans and results reports in addition to a multitude of electronic forms and documents specific to the practice of school counseling.

Dr. Schellenberg has over a decade of experience as a school counselor at both the elementary and secondary levels. She has been recognized at the local and national levels for her contributions in education and counseling. In 2010, Dr. Schellenberg was named one of the top 15 school counselors in the nation by the American School Counselor Association.

Dr. Schellenberg was one of six children born to loving parents, who, without high school educations, labored tirelessly to support the family. Dr. Schellenberg did not give up on the college dream. She worked full time while going to college at night to earn her degrees. Her humble beginnings are an inspiration to her students and to others who are overcoming obstacles to achieving the college dream.

You can learn more about Dr. Schellenberg, her work, and consulting services by visiting her professional website at www.Cultivating Performance.com.

# Acronyms

| | |
|---|---|
| AACD | American Association for Counseling and Development |
| AACE | Association for Assessment in Counseling and Education |
| AASA | American Association of School Administrators |
| ACA | American Counseling Association |
| ACES | Association for Counselor Education and Supervision |
| ACT | American College Testing |
| ADA | Americans with Disabilities Act |
| ADHD | Attention-deficit/hyperactivity disorder |
| AMCD | Association for Multicultural Counseling and Development |
| APGA | American Personnel and Guidance Association |
| ASCA | American School Counselor Association |
| ASGW | Association for Specialists in Group Work |
| ASVAB | Armed Services Vocational Aptitude Battery |
| AYP | Adequate yearly progress |
| CACGS | Computer-assisted career guidance systems |
| CACREP | Council for Accreditation of Counseling and Related Educational Programs |
| CAEP | Council for the Accreditation of Educator Preparation |
| CAPTA | Child Abuse Prevention and Treatment Act |
| CBT | Cognitive Behavioral Theory/Therapy |
| CDSCP | Comprehensive Developmental School Counseling Program |
| CIDS | Career information delivery systems |
| CPS | Child Protective Services |
| CSCORE | Center for School Counseling Outcome Research and Evaluation |
| DARE | Drug Abuse Resistance Education |
| ELL | English language learners |
| ESEA | Elementary and Secondary Education Act |

| | |
|---|---|
| ESL | English as a second language |
| FAPE | free appropriate public education |
| FERPA | Family Educational Rights and Privacy Act |
| GATB | General Aptitude Test Battery |
| GED | General equivalency diploma |
| GPA | Grade Point Average |
| HIPAA | Health Insurance Portability and Accountability Act |
| IDEA | Individuals with Disabilities Education Act |
| IEP | Individualized education program/plan |
| KOIS | Kuder Occupational Interest Survey |
| LEP | Limited English proficient |
| MBTI | Myers-Briggs Type Indicator |
| MOS | Microsoft Office specialist |
| MTSS | Multitiered system of supports |
| NBCC | National Board for Certified Counselors |
| NBPTS | National Board for Professional Teaching Standards |
| NCC | National Certified Counselor |
| NCDA | National Career Development Association |
| NCE | National Counselor Examination |
| NCLB | No Child Left Behind |
| NCSC | National Certified School Counselor |
| NCTSC | National Center for Transforming School Counseling |
| NOCTI | National Occupational Competency Testing Institute |
| NRF | National Retail Federation |
| NSCTI | National School Counselor Training Initiative |
| O*NET | Occupational Information Network |
| OOH | Occupational Outlook Handbook |
| PIAT | Peabody Individual Achievement Test |
| PSAT | Preliminary Scholastic Aptitude Test |
| PSC | Professional school counseling |
| PTA | Parent–Teacher Association |
| PTSRCs | Parent–teacher–student resource centers |
| RAMP | Recognized ASCA Model Program |
| REBT | Rational emotive behavior therapy |
| SAT | Scholastic Aptitude Test |
| SCALE | School Counseling Analysis, Leadership, and Evaluation |
| SCOPE | School Counseling Operational Plan for Effectiveness |
| SCORE | School Counseling Operational Report of Effectiveness |
| SDS | Self-directed search |

| | |
|---|---|
| SES | Socioeconomic status |
| SII | Strong interest inventory |
| SOL | Standards of learning |
| SST | Student support team |
| STEPS | Solutions to Ethical Problems in Schools |
| TSCI | Transforming School Counseling Initiative |
| WAIS | Wechsler adult intelligence scale |
| WISC | Wechsler intelligence scale for children |

# Introduction

*The School Counselor's Desk Reference and Credentialing Examination Study Guide* is a comprehensive reference for practicing school counselors and the only school counseling-specific study guide that provides potential examinees with one resource for all state-specific school counseling exams (GACE, ICTS, MTTC, PLACE, NES, OSAT, TExES), Praxis II school counseling exams (5421 and 0420), NBPTS school counseling exam, and preparation program comprehensive school counseling exams.

The exams listed above vary in length and format (e.g., multiple choice, short answer, essay, case simulation, recorded client–counselor interactions). Knowledge gained by the use of this resource, which presents content and inquisitions using a variety of approaches, is transferrable to differing test formats. To learn more about the format and length of each test listed, please visit any of the following links:

- **GACE**: www.gadoe.org
  Georgia Assessments for the Certification of Educators, School Counseling
  Test I
  Test II
  Combined
- **ICTS**: https://www.isbe.net
  Illinois Certification Testing System, School Counselor (181)
- **MTTC**: www.michigan.gov/mde
  Michigan Test for Teacher Certification, School Counselor (051)
- **PLACE**: www.cde.state.co.us/
  Program for Licensing Assessments for Colorado Educators, School Counselor (41)

- **Praxis II**:
  School Counselor Exam (5421): www.praxisprep.com/Counselor
  School Guidance and Counseling Exam (0420):
  www.praxisprep.com/Guidance
- **NBPTS**: www.nbpts.org/
  School Counselor Assessment
- **NES**: www.ped.state.nm.us/ped/index.html
  New Mexico National Evaluation Series, School Counselor (501)
- **OSAT**: http://sde.ok.gov/sde/
  Oklahoma Subject Area Test, School Counselor (039)
- **TExES**: http://tea.texas.gov/
  Texas Examinations of Educator Standards, School Counselor (152).

Each test listed above has been researched by this author to ensure that this text covers discipline-specific content areas noted for each exam. Additionally, this resource covers essential information, concepts, theories, approaches, and techniques for developing school counselor competency in the eight chapters outlined below as defined by:

- The 2016 Council for Accreditation of Counseling and Related Educational Programs (CACREP, 2016) Standards (www.cacrep.org)
- The American School Counselor Association (ASCA, 2012) School Counselor Competencies (www.schoolcounselor.org)
- The National Board for Professional Teaching Standards (NBPTS, 2012) for School Counseling (www.nbpts.org)
- Council for the Accreditation of Educator Preparation (CAEP, 2010) (www.caepnet.org).

# Chapter 1: The Foundations of School Counseling

Chapter 1 focuses on the foundations of school counseling and how we evolved into a specialty of the counseling profession. The chapter includes topics that promote the professional identity of school counselors, including a concise history of the profession, current trends, professional associations, accrediting bodies, voluntary credentials, roles of the school counselor, and the professional, ethical, cultural, and legal aspects of counseling in the schools. The basic principles and theories of human development and learning essential to establishing a solid developmental foundation from which to practice are examined. The following standards and school counselor competencies are addressed in Chapter 1:

- CACREP, School Counseling: G.1, G.2, G.3
- CAEP, Other School Professionals: Standard 1
- ASCA, School Counselor Competencies: I-A1-3, A7-8, II-A1-8, III-A1, A6
- NBPTS, School Counseling Standards: III, X, XI.

## Chapter 2: Counseling, Prevention, and Intervention

Chapter 2 is dedicated to traditional and emerging counseling perspectives, theories, and techniques most appropriate to PK–12 student populations, including career development theories, practices, and instruments. The developmental benefits of play are examined along with play therapy techniques and toys. The practice of school counseling is explored and the three broad developmental domains of comprehensive school counseling programs are examined along with the newly introduced ASCA Mindsets and Behaviors. The role of the school counselor is helping students to handle issues of transition and change, and coping with crisis is explored. Risk factors for school dropout are examined, including violence and bullying. Several key topics impacting youth in our schools are also presented, including Internet safety and cyberbullying, divorce, and substance use, abuse, and addiction. The importance of parenting styles in relation to student development is explored. Methods used by school counselors for delivering school counseling services and curriculum are presented. The following standards and school counselor competencies are addressed in Chapter 2:

- CACREP, School Counseling: G.1, G.2, G.3
- CAEP, Other School Professionals: Standard 1
- ASCA, School Counselor Competencies: I-A2-3, A5, A8-9, II-A1, A8, III-A1-5, A7-8
- NBPTS, School Counseling Standards: I, II, IV, VIII, XI.

## Chapter 3: Diversity and Advocacy

Chapter 3 emphasizes the critical roles of diversity and *advocacy* in school counseling. The importance of advocacy in relation to ensuring that all

students have equitable educational opportunities is discussed.
Advocacy competencies are provided and elements essential to
implementing a social justice approach in school counseling are examined.
Barriers to academic achievement and student *wellness* are explored.
Multicultural competence is defined and applied to the roles of the school
counselor, and the role of *data analysis* in identifying access, attainment,
and *achievement gaps* is examined. Spirituality as a cultural agent and
critical aspect of human development is highlighted as a natural
component for exploration in the school counseling process. The
following standards and school counselor competencies are addressed in
Chapter 3:

■ CACREP, School Counseling: G.2, G.3
■ CAEP, Other School Professionals: Standard 1
■ ASCA, School Counselor Competencies: I-A1, A3, A5-6, A8, III-A6, IV-A2, A5
■ NBPTS, School Counseling Standards: I, II, IV, V, VI, VIII, X, XI.

# Chapter 4: Assessment

Chapter 4 examines instruments and appraisal approaches used in the
educational setting for individual student assessment/appraisal. A
description of formal and informal assessments most widely used in the
schools is provided. Life-saving assessment is highlighted, including
indicators of child abuse/neglect, substance abuse, and self-harm.
The development and implementation of needs assessments and how
information from needs assessments and existing data sources is
used to make programming and service delivery decisions is explored.
Measurement concepts are defined. The *Association for Assessment
in Counseling and Education* (AACE) Competencies in Assessment
and Evaluation for School Counselors are listed. The following
standards and school counselor competencies are addressed in
Chapter 4:

■ CACREP, School Counseling: G.1, G.2, G.3
■ CAEP, Other School Professionals: Standard 1
■ ASCA, School Counselor Competencies: III-A6, IV-A5, V-A3
■ NBPTS, School Counseling Standards: VIII, IX, XI.

# Chapter 5: Research and Evaluation

Chapter 5 describes the roles of research, process, perception, and outcome data, and evaluation in creating accountable and outcome-driven school counseling services and programs. Essential data skills for school counselors are outlined and an exhaustive list of data resources is provided. The issue of dropout and dropout *prevention* is discussed. Methods of program evaluation, including proximal and distal evaluation, most often used in the school setting are described along with results reports for documenting and sharing outcomes with stakeholders. The following standards and school counselor competencies are addressed in Chapter 5:

- CACREP, School Counseling: G.2, G.3
- CAEP, Other School Professionals: Standard 1
- ASCA, School Counselor Competencies: IV-A3-5, V-A1-2, A4
- NBPTS, School Counseling Standards: VIII, IX, XI.

# Chapter 6: Academic Development

Chapter 6 focuses on *academic development*—the domain that sets school counseling apart from other counseling specialties. Crosswalking and response-to-intervention approaches used by school counselors to aid in closing achievement gaps are described and illustrated along with instructional strategies, classroom management, curriculum development, classroom guidance lesson plans, and the development of *action plans*. The school counselor's role in preparing students for standardized tests is examined. The interactive nature of multiple intelligences is examined in relation to curriculum development and student learning. A brief look at *No Child Left Behind* mandates is reviewed along with the new vision for school counseling. Alternative education programs to meet the special needs of diverse student populations are introduced. The following standards and school counselor competencies are addressed in Chapter 6:

- CACREP, School Counseling: G.1, G.2, G.3
- CAEP, Other School Professionals: Standard 1
- ASCA, School Counselor Competencies: I-A1, A3, A5, II-A1-2, III-A7
- NBPTS, School Counseling Standards: I, II, III, V, VIII, X, XI.

# Chapter 7: Collaboration, Consultation, and Referral

Chapter 7 describes approaches used by school counselors to engage in *collaboration* and consultation with stakeholders in order to provide students with a comprehensive school counseling program. Circumstances under which school counselors would generally engage in consultation and collaboration are examined along with the processes for both collaboration and consultation. The stages and phases of consultation are examined. Teambuilding strategies and school and community partnerships are explored. The positive outcomes of peer-to-peer helping programs are highlighted. The use of referral is discussed in relation to scope of practice. The following standards and school counselor competencies are addressed in Chapter 7:

- CACREP, School Counseling: G.1, G.2, G.3
- CAEP, Other School Professionals: Standard 1
- ASCA, School Counselor Competencies: I-A1, A6, IV-A2
- NBPTS, School Counseling Standards: I, V, VI, VII, X.

# Chapter 8: Leadership

Chapter 8 focuses on the many aspects of effective leadership and its importance in establishing and maintaining a comprehensive school counseling program and fostering school administrator–school counselor alliances critical to the success of the school counseling program. The qualities and characteristics of an effective leader are examined along with leadership styles found to be most effective in the practice of school counseling. The role of family and community involvement in promoting student learning and systemic change is discussed. The role of technology is also reviewed as it relates to student learning and professional advocacy. The following standards and school counselor competencies are addressed in Chapter 8:

- CACREP, School Counseling: G.2, G.3
- CAEP, Other School Professionals: Standard 1
- ASCA, School Counselor Competencies: I-A1, A4, A6, II-A2, IV-A1-4, A6
- NBPTS, School Counseling Standards: I, V, VI, VII, VIII, X, XI.

# Using this Resource as a Study Guide

As a study guide this resource covers content areas in relation to the roles and functions of the contemporary school counselor. The practice exams at the end of each chapter and at the end of the study guide are formatted as simulations consisting of three components: scenario, information gathering (IG), and decision making (DM). There are five to seven sections following the scenario requiring a combination of IG and DM responses. A full-length (seven simulated school counseling cases) practice examination will be provided at the end of the text.

Learning is improved when you understand where your thinking may have gone astray. For this reason, responses are provided for chapter practice exams and the end of the text full-length exam. To optimize learning, explanations are provided to support correct responses, and explanations are provided to indicate why incorrect responses are incorrect for both the chapter practice exams and the full-length practice exam.

You will also be presented with case illustrations throughout the study guide that require conceptualization, effective client–counselor interactions, and content knowledge application, which are critical to obtaining a passing score on school counseling exams. Some will require a response in short answer/essay format, while others are formatted as multiple choice. Appropriate responses and explanations for case conceptualizations are provided at the end of each chapter in which the case was presented.

Guided reflection sections at the end of each chapter are grounded in Bloom's taxonomy to test you on a variety of levels: knowledge, comprehension, application, analysis, synthesis, and evaluation. You are encouraged to make use of this section to fully reflect on the material presented in each chapter. All the information you need to answer each item in the guided reflection sections is presented in the corresponding chapter.

Italicized words in this text represent key concepts related to the constructs presented. Those that are not already defined in sufficient detail in the body of the chapter are included in the glossary. The glossary of critical terms is provided to assist you in managing the material presented and to provide you with another learning tool.

This study guide presents the information using empirically supported strategies for enhancing learning and recall and uses a variety of assessment formats in order to promote familiarity with diverse school counseling exam structures.

Chapter practice tests, case illustrations, and guided reflection sections reinforce chapter content in a repetitive manner to aid in memorization. This study guide presents theories and other information in lists, clusters, or manageable pieces of information and charts for mapping main ideas, which isolates key points, thereby promoting movement from short-term memory to long-term memory and aiding in the recall of information.

I would encourage the use of a pencil when completing the practice exams and the guided reflection sections, or I would suggest making copies of those sections of the guide. My best advice is to take each exam repeatedly until perfect scores are achieved and to complete each item of the guided reflection sections until you have nailed it! Remember, writing and rewriting helps to commit information to memory.

## Test-Taking Triumph

Without a doubt, taking and passing school counselor licensure, credentialing, and comprehensive exams are important milestones in your career. The enormity of the information needed to prepare can be overwhelming. Keep in mind, however, that you have already been exposed to this information and in many cases you have already applied it in the school setting and during experiential learning activities in your counselor education preparation program.

To help you prepare for all school counseling exams, consider these study basics and test-taking tips proven to improve your score. Keep in mind that although both triumph and defeat reside within each of us, triumph prevails with hard work, perseverance, and a belief in our ability to be victorious.

## Time Management: A Waste of Time?

Most counselor education programs encourage students to study for certification, licensure, and comprehensive exams over time. While cramming has its value, it is not as effective and lasting as learning that takes place over time and builds on previous knowledge with thoughtful reflection and application.

For this reason, consider designing a timeline that allows you to control your study schedule. When it comes to control, I can help. Both a vice and a virtue, I can micromanage a minute, squeezing every ounce of life out of time. Try breaking up the information into manageable segments and pacing study sessions. Consider mastering one segment before moving on to the next segment, which will allow the information to move from short-term memory into long-term memory. This study guide provides you with multiple practice exams and chapter activities so that you can practice-practice-practice applying the material—repetition is key to retention.

## Making Connections

Association has been linked to successful testing outcomes. Consider associating new information with familiar or easily remembered information. My favorite is using acronyms to represent the first letter of each piece of information. This is exemplified in Lazarus' assessment strategy known as BASIC ID (*B*ehavior, *A*ffect, *S*ensation, *I*magery, *C*ognition, *I*nterpersonal, *D*rugs/Biological). BASIC ID is discussed in Chapter 4.

Concept mapping and cognitive mapping, or mental visualization, promotes learning and recall by connecting pieces of information and illustrating relationships. Isolating key facts and grouping concepts are additional avenues for enhancing memory and recall. This study guide presents critical information using a variety of empirically validated visualization strategies (e.g., charts, tables, figures, checklists) to enhance understanding and to promote success on school counseling exams.

## No Veggie Left Behind

For some, studying is just not a part of their cultural or intellectual DNA. However, since you were unable to major in channel surfing, you can develop strategies to make studying ache less. Pairing study time with more desirable activities and studying in an environment that you find personally motivating and in clothing that is comfortable can make all the difference. For example, you may wish to study in your favorite room in the house with the glow of a scented candle, while wearing your favorite warm slippers and those sweat pants that you have rescued from the trash on multiple occasions. I have found that shamelessly plating up a scrumptious gallery of snacks to nibble on while enduring the permeation of knowledge is quite the positive reinforcer.

Oh, and by the way, studies have found that blueberries and caffeine boost memory. Also, cruciferous veggies (e.g., cabbage, carrots, broccoli, Brussels sprouts, cauliflower, kale) improve cognitive functioning and memory. Just beware and warn others in the vicinity—these delicious little rascals are known to induce gas that in concentration could likely be weaponized! Nonetheless, cook up some of those super-veggies to maximize brain power—*buon appetito*!

## Got Peeps?

Sometimes it's helpful to have other people assist you in studying. Alas, your peeps can't take the test for you, but having another person quiz you after completion of each chapter can be helpful. You might want to consider having your study buddy turn each of the chapter headings and subheadings into questions. Or, after you have responded to the end of chapter guided reflections and checked your responses for accuracy and completeness, have your partner ask each one again and again, noting the concepts/topics you missed each time. Eventually, you will have answered each fully and accurately—voilà!

Flash cards are another great study strategy that you can do with others (or alone). You are encouraged to create flash cards from the glossary of terms provided in this study guide with an emphasis on how you would apply those concepts as a school counselor in a PK–12 school setting.

## The Square Root of Pi

There are some important constants that lend themselves to memorization. The square root of Pi is one of the most familiar and culturally significant of all constants that many have devoted countless hours to memorizing. However, the concepts and information related to school counseling are rarely, if ever, constant. So, keep in mind that while some of the material in this guide lends itself to memorization, much of your exam seeks to apply rather than recite.

With this said, while applying knowledge and skills in the practice of school counseling is paramount, it is also important to be able to identify specific tools, models, theories, and techniques that may be warranted in a specific case for a particular student at a certain grade/developmental level. Oh, by the way, the square root of Pi (3.14) is roughly 1.7725.

## Occam's Razor

As hard as this news may hit you, one of the biggest challenges for test takers is following directions. I believe Freud would agree that in our unconscious attempt to control the test-taking environment, we tend to distort the truth of the written word. Selecting the "single best response" becomes "what does the author want?" As triumphant test takers, we must take a minute to be sure that we understand exactly what it is that is being asked in the question. Then, we must think in terms of what the "best" response is based on school counseling standards, best practices, ethics, law, culture, school counselor roles and functions, and the scope of practice within the school setting. Read and carefully consider every response in these terms before making a selection.

Too often we tend to over-analyze exam questions. For this reason, we then tend to provide a response that is too complex, believing that more information is better. Responses that are unnecessary at a given time in the case simulation or may cost the student and parent time, money, energy, and/or delay in counseling processes/outcomes may cost you points. Consider the logic of Occam's razor—do not make more assumptions than the minimum needed. That is, err on the side of less versus more—simplest versus more complex.

## Less IS More

After reading the test item, examinees should anticipate appropriate responses before looking at the response choices. If the item is essay or short answer, the examinee should briefly study the test item to gain a thorough understanding of exactly what is being asked before writing the response. Consider given scenarios from all angles and what you would realistically do as a school counselor in the moment with that student and within the scope of the practice of school counseling.

Not unlike other counseling specialties, school counselors act in the best interest of their clients. In doing so, are there other relevant individuals or agencies (e.g., parent, child protective services, community counselors) whose involvement may be needed or beneficial when counseling specific minors in a specific situation? What ethical and legal issues may need to be considered? What cultural issues may need to be considered? What developmental issues may need to be considered? Provide responses that are helpful, thorough, and relevant to the specific case presented at that given time in treatment—no more, no less. If you err, err on the side of less is more; but, no hasty choices!

## The Hands of Time

Timed tests have been known to heighten the anxiety experienced by test takers. Do not allow the hands of time to dictate when to move to the next item on the exam. There will be some items on the exam that you will blink right through, while others will leave you wide-eyed, sorting through all the possibilities. Do not allow yourself to become overly concerned with the time spent on each item. In my many experiences with counseling and school counseling exams, I have found the time allotted to be ample, and I am a characteristically slow test taker. Stay focused and just allow yourself to recognize when you are spending an inordinate amount of time on one particular item.

Timed tests often elicit an appropriate amount of stress, which has been shown to improve performance. So, embrace the good stress; but, recognize when you're chewing twine and losing your vertical hold as they say. Even short-term stress impedes recall and cognitive functioning. So allow yourself 2–3 minutes to stop and do some deep breathing exercises and muscle relaxation techniques—yes, right there in the exam chair.

You are not expected to make a perfect score. There is room for error. It is likely that you will not know the answer to every question; and, not every correct response will jump out at you. Like my daddy used to say— you can't always get socks on the rooster!

## Oh, the Places You'll Go

Relaxing and remaining positive about your ability to successfully complete the school counseling exam positively impacts your performance. This has been empirically validated! So, should you find yourself loading the wrong wagon, Aaron Beck might say (and I would concur), "use positive self-talk." I have been known to hold entire conversations with myself—out loud. However, you may want to consider an internal dialogue so as to avoid a clinical enthusiast pegging you as schizophrenic. Of course, in my case that ship has sailed, but there's still hope for you! Affirming self-talk goes a long way, just like the Little Engine that Could—with a twist—I know I can . . . I know I can . . . I know I can.

Also, use those rational emotive behavior therapy (REBT) techniques to debunk negative, irrational thoughts destructive to success on the exam. Positive thinking does more than psych you up for exam success, remaining positive during study time improves memory and recall.

During study time, and while taking the exam, consider what you will gain as a result of passing the exam, like earning your degree, adding a certification to your credentials, and/or becoming a practicing school counselor. Imagery is quite the powerful motivator. So, just sit back for a few seconds and imagine yourself putting those hard-working little fingers on that license—like touching the Shroud of Turin. You'll be ready to charge hell with a bucket of ice water! Lastly, consider the inspirational words of Dr. Seuss—*oh, the places you'll go! ( . . . and the students you'll help!)*.

### Delighted Synapses

Music, my personal favorite, has been found to enhance mood and cognitive abilities. So, consider playing music that is personally enjoyable to give study time a twist (and please exercise your freedom to get up and Dougie if you want to!). There is nothing like the smack of a workout to get the ole cognitive juices flowing. Those delighted synapses will sing harmoniously while those boogying neurons will be firing a rate of a million dancing Oompa-Loompas!

## Using this Resource as a Desk Reference

In the world of school counseling no two days are alike. School counselors find themselves adjusting and readjusting their schedules as the day unfolds. You find yourself in situations where it is necessary to know and understand the law as it pertains to counseling minors in the school. You find yourself in situations that are not black and white, but quite gray, needing a quick reference to the ethical code with relevant case studies. You find yourself pulled between the law and the professional ethical code. You find yourself struggling over which assessment, play technique, theory, or counseling intervention may be best applied to a particular student in a specific situation. You find yourself wishing you had a quick reference to aid in your understanding of the developmental aspect that may be manifesting itself in a particular student at a particular period of time. You find yourself drowning in a mysterious sea of acronyms. You find yourself on a theoretical bridge calculating the best way to cross to get to practical application. As a school counselor, you know that I could go on and on, but I'll spare you that agony. I think you get my point!

Throughout the chapters, you will view ASCA position statements as they relate to the practice of school counseling and the domains of development as defined by the *ASCA National Model* and School Counselor Competencies. The ASCA *Ethical Standards for School Counselors* are also weaved throughout this study guide as applicable to the topic of discussion.

This resource is your personal consultant. The desk reference includes a detailed table of contents, exhaustive list of acronyms and their meaning, as well as a glossary of well-defined terms used in the practice setting. The Appendix includes the most current edition of the *ASCA Ethical Standards for School Counselors*, which includes definitions of terms used and an ethical decision-making model. I hope you will find this resource to be your one touch guide to information *on the fly*.

## Using this Resource as a Tool for Professional Development

If you wake up some morning to the realization that you have been so buried in busyness that you could use a refreshing infusion of professional development, this is your injection tool. Keeping the most current edition of this text on hand as a desk reference will provide you with an update on contemporary trends and best practices in the profession.

## *Carpe Diem!*

It is time to move forward—*carpe diem*!

# Chapter 1

# The Foundations of School Counseling

Some believe that even when we are aware of the past, we are doomed to repeat it; this is part of living. Perhaps this is so; I am no philosopher. True or not, I would postulate that by knowing the mistakes of the past, we are better equipped to avoid those mistakes in the present and into the future. Based on this postulation, it is important to become familiar with the profession's roots, milestones, trends, and current and future direction.

The profession of school counseling has been largely shaped by its multidisciplinary heritage that encompasses both education and counseling. With one foot planted in each applied field, school counseling has slowly, but at times not so steadily, morphed into a profession unique in its own right.

## The First Hundred Years

School counseling began as a vocational and moral curriculum developed by Jesse Davis, a high school principal, in 1907. A year later, Frank Parsons, a man that one might consider a jack-of-all-trades—engineer, university professor, public school teacher, lawyer, author, and social activist— became interested in helping students transition from school to work and established the Vocation Bureau. Parsons' work paved the way for the trait and factor theory of career development and earned him the title of "father of vocational guidance."

In the 1920s and 1930s, guidance in the schools grew and became recognized as an area of specialty using a trait and factor model for identifying vocational direction. Together, the progressive education and mental health movements gave rise to vocational guidance and counseling. In the 1940s, Carl Rogers' focus on a nonmedical model for individual counseling resulted in individual counseling in high schools as a primary function of guidance.

In 1952, the American Personnel and Guidance Association (APGA) was established. The work of APGA was grounded in the philosophies of Carl Rogers (1961, 1969) well into the 1960s. The APGA created two divisions: the American School Counselor Association (ASCA) and the Association for Counselor Education and Supervision (ACES). These divisions provide leadership and promote *standards* for training programs and school counseling practices.

In 1957, Soviet satellite Sputnik took a 98-minute celestial stroll around the earth, catapulting our astounded nation into the space age. The United States, perceiving the launch of Sputnik as a display of educational, technical, and political superiority, passed the National Defense Education Act. This legislation was the steroid that instantly pumped up the muscles of the school counseling profession. Funds were made available to create and enhance existing guidance counseling training programs and to hire more *guidance counselors* (as we were called) to provide career guidance and to identify students with a propensity toward the disciplines of science and math. To meet the volumes of post-World War II baby boomers, hiring more guidance counselors turned into an extreme sports version of recruitment and training. We were on our way; and, like Sputnik, our elliptical path was uncertain as we explored, probed, and sometimes wobbled through a mysterious universe.

Comprehensive developmental school guidance programs began to emerge to meet the needs of K–12 students in the 1960s and 1970s. Developmental guidance became a global phenomenon, and in 1985, the APGA changed its name to the American Association for Counseling and Development (AACD).

The impetus behind the shift in paradigm toward a more holistic focus on student development was prompted by an alarming treatise published in 1987 by the AACD, called "School Counseling: A Profession at Risk." The undeniable realities about a profession that was viewed as nice but not necessary by important *stakeholders* incited immediate and unremitting action on the part of concerned school counselor educators and practitioners.

A few years later, with refocused fortitude, the AACD changed its name to the American Counseling Association (ACA). ASCA, taking paramedic responsibility for the resuscitation of a dying profession, created monographs and position statements, revised program philosophies, clarified roles, and provided a series of recommendations to include school counselors as key players in educational reform. ASCA adopted a National Model (ASCA, 2012a) and *National Standards* (Campbell & Dahir, 1997). These national standards have now become the ASCA *Mindsets and Behaviors for Student Success* (ASCA, 2014). ASCA also changed the title of *guidance counselor* to *professional school counselor* (changed again by ASCA in 2016 to *school counselor*) to more appropriately define renewed roles and practices. These new roles and practices extend beyond the limited functions rooted in vocational guidance and *individual-focused* models, broadening our lens to recognize and include the system both within and outside of the school community and the holistic development of all students. In 1997, the Education Trust, with the support of ASCA, ACES, and the ACA, introduced the *Transforming School Counseling Initiative* (TSCI).

## The Transforming School Counseling Initiative

The TSCI (Education Trust, 1997) was based on the belief that the prevailing and historically predominant individual- and mental health-focused model failed to align school counseling with the mission of schools and demonstrate an impact on academic achievement. TSCI balked at what they believed to be an outdated model responsible for the exclusion of school counselors from educational reform agendas. TSCI further contended that the model's ambiguous focus on academic achievement gave rise to the misconception that school counseling is an ancillary service in the schools.

TSCI, seeking to replace the traditional individual- and mental health-focused paradigm, introduced a new vision for school counseling that emphasizes the importance of school counseling *leadership* and support for a *systems-focused* and *academic-focused* paradigm. TSCI's *new vision school counseling* reflects the school counselor's dual roles of educator and counselor and aligns school counseling more closely with the academic mission of schools.

Changing the paradigm from mental health-focused to academic-focused and individual-focused to systems-focused was a bold move that positioned many within the profession nose-to-nose in opposition. For devout traditionalists and others who are just not hardwired to change, skepticism hit like a ballistic missile, creating an explosive divide. Nonetheless, as Julius Caesar declared to his army, *alea iacta est*: the die is cast.

TSCI, the brave scout, trudged forward blazing a trail so that the next era of school counselors could find their way in an uninhabited new frontier. Partnering with Metropolitan Life Insurance Company (MetLife) to fund the development of the NSCTI and the NCTSC, TSCI developed and distributed four modules to bridge previous thinking with new ways of conceptualizing the profession.

The modules describe how school counselors can contribute to high academic achievement and obtain educational equity for all students through both systemic and individual leadership, advocacy, and collaboration. Toward this end, ASCA, the Council for Accreditation of Counseling and Related Educational Programs (CACREP), and the TSCI emphasized the importance of identifying and addressing systemic inequities using data, accountable practices, technological competence, and cultural sensitivity by promoting the tenets of *social justice*, to be discussed in Chapter 3 (Education Trust, 1997). Some are still chafing against what has now become the contemporary practice of school counseling. Alas, the dinosaurs that continue to practice from what has become a Jurassic model are slowly nearing extinction. Eventually, those dinosaurs will only reemerge as relics in an archeological dig into the proud beginnings of our profession.

We have traveled a great distance and gained much ground over the past century, overpowering the challenges and enduring periods of uncertainty. It says much about the tenacity of the gallant stakeholders of our profession when you consider that we have done more than merely survive, but emerge stronger and with the vigor of 10 Grinches plus two and a renewed vision for every Who in Whoville—the tall and the small.

# School Counselor Preparation Programs

As a spice-of-life consequence to our multidisciplinary profession, school counselors generally take a variety of counseling, school counseling, and education courses. In accordance with CACREP (2016), each school counselor education program accredited by CACREP must be a 60-hour program by the year 2020.

---

## ASCA's Position on School Counselor Preparation Programs

School counselors are best prepared through master's- and doctoral-level programs that align with the philosophy and vision of the ASCA National Model (2012), the ASCA School Counselor Competencies (2012), The ASCA Mindsets and Behaviors for Student Success (2014), and the ASCA Ethical Standards for School Counselors (2010). These programs emphasize training in the implementation of a comprehensive school counseling program promoting leadership, advocacy, collaboration and systemic change to enhance student achievement and success.

*Position statement adopted 2008, revised 2014*

---

## *Counselor Education: CACREP*

Committed to the advancement of counselor education and supervision, Association for Counselor Education and Supervision (ACES) began establishing accreditation standards for counseling programs. ACES's indissoluble efforts to standardize counselor education and training programs laid the foundation for its successor—CACREP.

In 1978, CACREP was formed to standardize training and function as the primary accrediting body for counselor education programs, under the prevailing school counseling pedagogy of the time, which was the mental health-focused model. In 2001, CACREP published standards that reflected the new vision's academic- and systems-focused paradigm.

In 2009 and 2016, CACREP revised those standards to continue reflecting the academic- and systems-focused school counseling paradigm. CACREP standards place a strong emphasis on the professional identity of counselor and on student learning outcome measures, particularly in specialty program areas such as school counseling with assessments tied to specific individual standards.

CACREP provides counselor education programs with unified, minimal competencies for the optimal preparation of school counselors at the graduate level. In addition to requirements specific to school counseling, CACREP requires demonstrated knowledge in eight core areas of counselor education, which are: 1) professional counseling, orientation, and ethical practice, 2) social and cultural diversity, 3) human growth and development, 4) career development, 5) counseling and helping relationships, 6) group counseling and group work, 7) assessment and testing, and 8) research and program evaluation) (CACREP, 2016).

## ASCA's Position on the Use of Non-School Counseling Credentialed Personnel in Implementing Comprehensive School Counseling Programs

School counselors are uniquely qualified and solely eligible to meet the requirements of designing and implementing these programs. School counselors recognize that personnel who do not hold a master's degree in school counseling are not qualified to deliver a comprehensive school counseling program that supports academic, career and social/emotional development and positively affects achievement for all students.

*Position statement adopted 1994; revised 2000, 2006, 2012*

The CACREP Standards (2016) specific to school counseling are covered in the content of this resource, which comprise 34 standards listed under three broad domains: 1) Foundations, 2) Contextual Dimensions, and 3) Practice. CACREP requires school counselor preparation programs accredited by their body to demonstrate where each core counseling and special school counseling standard is covered in the program's curriculum.

The school counseling specialty standards emphasize education and training in developing a data-informed, comprehensive, developmentally appropriate school counseling program using evidence-based prevention and *intervention* practices that meet the needs of diverse and *special needs students*. The standards further underscore the importance of using a program model (e.g., the ASCA National Model) in both school counselor education and school counseling practices. CACREP spotlights the importance of academic outcomes and the use of *data-driven* and data-producing programs as well as *program evaluation* in school counseling practices. Additionally, the standards stress collaboration, consultation, leadership, and advocacy, and the identification and removal of personal and systemic barriers to academic achievement.

CACREP has become a university magnet, with schools across the country seeking its stamp of approval. Indeed, if counselor education were a religion, CACREP would be their Bible, with counselor educators striving to live by the word.

## Teacher Education: CAEP

While CACREP is considered to be the primary accrediting body for counselor education programs, CAEP is considered to be the primary accrediting body for teacher education programs. Because school counselors share the dual roles of educator and counselor, some school counseling programs are accredited by both CAEP and CACREP. Some are not accredited at all—buyer beware! CAEP provides standards that address the knowledge, skills, and professional dispositions required of teachers, administrators, and other school personnel (e.g., school counselors). This study guide addresses both CACREP School Counseling Specialty Standards and CAEP Standards for Other School Personnel (see www.caepnet.org).

# The ASCA National Model

ASCA is a division of ACA with a membership of approximately 30,000 school counseling professionals. ACA is the largest professional counseling association in existence. ASCA is the national *professional association* specifically designed for school counselors and the practice of school counseling. ASCA provides professional development, leadership, advocacy, research, publications, and resources to school counselor educators, preservice school counselors, and school counseling practitioners. In case you have not figured it out yet—when ASCA speaks, we listen!

The ASCA National Model (ASCA, 2012a) defines and unifies the professional identity of school counselors and the practices of school counseling. It is recognized by CACREP, CAEP, and the Department of Education as a framework from which to establish accountable, comprehensive, standards-based, developmental school counseling programs that align with academic achievement missions and emphasize systems-focused service delivery as an integral part of the total education program. Due to the overwhelming support backing ASCA, some schools seek to align their school counseling programs with the ASCA National Model in order to become a Recognized ASCA Model Program (RAMP). The ASCA National Model Implementation Guide (2016b) details how to achieve RAMP status and provides tools toward this end.

ASCA advocates for a balanced approach to school counseling. The balanced approach meets the developmental needs of students, providing both prevention and intervention services that are reflected in the ASCA National Model. To fully implement its model, ASCA recommends a student-to-school counselor ratio of 250:1. However, the most recent data (2013–2014) depicts a national average of 490:1. For this reason, school counselors are encouraged to make use of the manpower that is available and willing to assist, freeing the school counselor to focus more on direct and indirect student services.

## ASCA's Position on the Use of Support Staff in School Counseling Programs

The school counselor understands the value added to a comprehensive school counseling program through the effective use of support staff. Assistance from school counseling program support staff members allows school counselors to use their time more efficiently and use their professional expertise and leadership skills more effectively to meet student needs.

*Adopted 1974; reviewed and reaffirmed 1980; revised 1986, 1993, 1999, 2001, 2008, 2013*

The ASCA National Model has had an epic impact on the profession of school counseling. The model consists of four fundamental components: (1) foundation, (2) management, (3) delivery, and (4) accountability. The importance of school counselor skills and attitudes in promoting leadership, advocacy, collaboration, and systemic change for *universal academic achievement* and total student development is built into each of the four components.

The foundation component represents the first operational level of ASCA's model, addressing the "what" of the school counseling program (ASCA, 2016b, 2012a). The foundation includes the mindsets and behaviors for student success organized under three broad developmental domains (i.e., academic, career, and social/emotional). These mindsets and behaviors provide a sound foundation upon which the school counseling program is built and identify what students will know and be able to do as a result of the school counseling program. Foundation building involves: 1) establishing vision and mission statements, 2) analyzing school attendance, achievement, and behavior data, 3) defining program goals, 4) identifying student mindsets and behavior standards to be met over time, and 5) practicing in accordance with the school counselor competencies and the professional ethical standards. The foundation of your school counseling program must be strong, since it is sitting on the San Andreas Fault that is the scrutiny of our educational climate of accountability.

The management system addresses the "when, why, who, and on what authority" the school counseling program is operating (ASCA, 2016b, 2012a). Key components of the management system include: 1) analyzing use of time—how your time is being spent as a school counselor, 2) creating annual agreements and securing administrative support, 3) establishing an *advisory council*, 4) developing calendars of school counseling events and activities, and 5) creating action plans and lesson plans.

Program delivery speaks to "how" the school counseling program is implemented, consisting of both direct and indirect student services (ASCA, 2012a, 2016b). Direct services are in-person interactions with students. Indirect services are interactions with others on behalf of, or for, students. Direct student services are delivered by way of the school counseling core curriculum, individual student planning, and *responsive services*. Indirect student services are delivered by way of referrals, consultation, and collaboration. School counselors blend these methods of delivery for a balanced approach to service delivery to meet the needs of all students.

*Accountability* processes provide evidence as to "how students are different as a result of the school counseling program" (ASCA, 2012a, 2016b). Accountability systems require program evaluation and data analysis to determine the outcomes of services/programs. This information is used to improve services/programs, to document program effectiveness, and to share program outcomes with stakeholders using *results reports*. The accountability system also includes the assessment of school counselor competencies and school counselor performance appraisal.

## School Counselor Roles and Functions

School counselors are a special breed. In the past, I recall a conversation I had with a counselor educator. She referred to one of her school counselors in training as possessing the inherent qualities of Saint Francis of Assisi. Specifically, that the student did not so much seek to be consoled as to console or to be understood as to understand. I have seen the same in so many school counselors and school counselors in training whose hearts of service and passion for the profession are marked with an altruistic drive to make a difference in the world. You are likely reading this book at this very moment in time.

School counselors absolutely do make a difference in the world and the lives of children and adolescents by integrating their primary role of *counselor* with the role of *educator*. School counselors live by a succinct guiding philosophy that holds the healthy mind as an educable mind. And, we are best ready to serve when we understand that a healthy mind is not necessarily a mind that is free from physical, mental, emotional, social, and environmental distress.

Operating from this philosophy, school counselors recognize that we all have baggage that we haul around—some heavier than others. In other words, we are all merely a rubber band snap away from complete madness. Okay, so I am exaggerating just a bit. The point is we cannot ignore academic needs in order to only address the baggage. School counselors make every effort to meet all needs simultaneously. Ignoring educational needs in the presence of other issues is detrimental to the student's academic success and perpetuates achievement gaps.

School counselors are trained to move fluently between the two roles of educator and counselor for optimal and total student development. Meeting the total development of students often requires that school counselors engage in a host of shared functions including *teaming*, consulting, informing, collaborating, leading, advocating, programming, assessing, referring, teaching, evaluating, coordinating, and reporting. Oh yeah—and counseling.

In unifying our roles and functions, ASCA has created the School Counselor Performance Standards (ASCA, 2012a). In addition, ASCA collaborated with practicing school counselors, district school counseling supervisors, and counselor educators to develop the School Counselor Competencies (2012b; see Appendix II) to promote an adequate understanding of the knowledge, skills, and abilities school counselors should possess. Together, these standards and competencies are being used to enhance the curriculum in counselor education. These standards are widely used in the practice setting to identify school counselor professional development training activities and to create performance evaluation tools specific to school counselors, who have historically been evaluated using teacher evaluation tools.

---

## ASCA's Position on Annual Performance Evaluation

The annual performance evaluation of school counselors should accurately reflect the unique professional training and practices of school counselors working within a comprehensive school counseling program. These written evaluations should use forms and tools specifically designed for school counselors, based on documents such as the School Counselor Competencies and the School Counselor Performance Appraisal from the ASCA National Model.

*Position statement adopted 1978; reaffirmed 1984; revised 1986, 1993, 2003, 2009, 2015; reviewed 1999*

---

## *School Counselor as Educator*

Education and training that distinguishes the school counselor as an educator includes PK–12 program design and delivery, classroom instruction, classroom management, theories of learning, child and adolescent development, career preparation, standardized testing and assessment, use of technology, behavioral theory, disability and exceptional behavior, identifying student competencies and ways to achieve academic competency, identifying and removing barriers to academic achievement, and developing effective learning environments, *needs assessment*, and educational program evaluation. School counselors work closely with stakeholders, namely teachers, engaging their skills as educators to provide the finest services to students and parents and to accomplish the academic mission of schools.

As educators, school counselors engage in instruction by way of classroom guidance lessons using *research-based* or research-supported curriculum that crosswalks academic standards with school counseling standards. In addition to instruction, functions inherent in the school counselor's role of educator include delivering school-wide programs that provide information and resources to all participants, interpreting standardized test score reports, and evaluating the academic needs of students in order to design and deliver needs-based educational programs.

Because fulfillment of the school counselor's role of educator involves instruction, four states (Alabama, Nebraska, Oregon, and Texas) still require a teaching background or what each deems equivalent in order to become a school counselor. Decades of research have examined the question of whether or not school counselors should be teachers prior to becoming school counselors. In summary, many studies indicate that school administrators, school counselor supervisors, and practicing school counselors do not find previous teaching experience necessary in order to be an effective school counselor (Hobson, Fox, & Swikert, 2000; Moyer & Yu, 2012). Research identifies distinct differences between the functions of teachers and school counselors, which necessitates that teachers unlearn previously held dispositions in order to acquire new dispositions that are in some ways contrary in nature to that of the school counselor. For example, the teacher's role is to judge, discipline, and manage. The role of teacher is subject-focused and involves didactic teaching with little or no concern for confidentiality in teacher–student interactions. The school counselor's role is to be nonjudgmental in nature. And, school counselors do not discipline students. The role of the school counselor is facilitative and change-focused and ensures confidentiality in school counselor–student interactions. Apples and oranges!

## School Counselor as Counselor

Just as in the role of educator, school counselors provide classroom guidance lessons that are preventative in nature and delivered to all students, addressing issues related to career and the personal, social, and emotional well-being of students. In the role of counselor, school counselors meet with students individually and in small groups to provide direct responsive services that promote well-being and remove barriers to academic achievement and holistic development.

School counselors also work with teachers to modify the classroom climate for optimal learning and to develop academic contracts and schedules of *reinforcement*. School counselors consult and collaborate with stakeholders (discussed in Chapter 7) to provide support, information, and referral sources as needed and to promote equity and access to school programs, activities, and rigorous curriculum.

School counselors understand that the relationship between academic success and personal, emotional, social, and physical well-being is a door that swings both ways. As such, school counselors encourage students faced with issues related to personal, social, and emotional health and physical challenges to believe in their ability to change, grow, overcome challenges, and achieve academically. School counselors encourage impaired students to embrace academics as an avenue to a promising, self-directed future.

Academic-focused channeling can be therapeutic, motivational, and build competencies, self-esteem, and psychological *resilience*—epitomizing the specialty of school counseling. Challenges can be our greatest asset, pushing us onward and lifting us up to achieve at higher levels. For this reason, school counselors are dogmatic in their efforts to balance their roles of counselor and educator for optimal student development. While priority is given to the significant role of counselor, counselors embrace and fulfill their dual roles of counselor and educator. After all, this is the role that sets counseling in the schools apart from other counseling specialties and defines our profession.

# NBCC and NBPTS Voluntary School Counseling Credentials

Certification is the recognition that a professional has met specific qualifications to practice in a particular profession, distinguishing professionals as dedicated to the continued pursuit of competence. School counselors are encouraged to secure advanced voluntary credentials and actively seek out opportunities for professional development, embracing a continuous state of learning in order to provide optimal counseling services and to strengthen professional identity.

## *ASCA's Position on Credentialing and Licensure*

ASCA strongly supports a school counselor credentialing or licensing law in each state that includes: a definition of the profession, minimum qualifications for entry into the profession and requirements for continuing professional development. ASCA encourages all state education certification or licensure agencies to adopt the ASCA School Counselor Competencies from the ASCA National Model for school counselor credentialing or licensing.

*Position statement adopted 1990;*
*revised 1993, 1999, 2003, 2009, 2015*

NBCC is the national professional certification board that monitors the certification system for counselors and maintains a national register of certified counselors. In addition to national credentialing, NBCC provides counselors with a code of ethics for guiding professional practices. NBCC examinations are used by more than 48 states to credential professional counselors on a state level. NBCC was created by the ACA, and both organizations work closely to advance the profession of counseling and maintain high standards of excellence.

NBCC administers the Uncle Sam of national general counseling credentials—the National Certified Counselor (NCC) credential. Students who are graduating from CACREP accredited programs are afforded the opportunity to waive the experience requirement and take the National Counselor Exam (NCE) that, when passed, results in acquiring the NCC credential.

NBCC also administers several national specialty counseling credentials such as the National Certified School Counselor (NCSC) credential, first awarded in 1991. School counselors who hold the NCSC have a master's degree and have demonstrated competence in areas specific to contemporary school counseling by way of training and experience. School counselors who earn the NCSC demonstrate a high level of professional commitment that goes beyond required state licensing. The NCSC credential is a result of a collaborative effort with professional counseling associations, counselor educator accrediting bodies, and certification organizations in counseling and is governed by a board of counselors. The NCC credential is a prerequisite to the NCSC credential.

Holding the NCC and the NCSC and other advanced voluntary credentials serves to inspire school and community confidence in the school counselor's clinical ability to meet the personal, social, and emotional needs of their children. This is particularly significant in a charged climate where the public's confidence in our educational system is already wavering if not waning. Parents are questioning not only the ability of public schools to successfully educate their child, but the ability of public schools to identify and effectively intervene in situations with troubled students who threaten the safety of their progeny. Other benefits to certification by the NBCC are outlined on their website at www.nbcc.org.

The NBPTS also offers a national voluntary credential for school counselors along with School Counseling Standards (NBPTS, 2012). Like the NCSC credential, obtaining national teacher board certification in school counseling demonstrates a high level of professional commitment that goes beyond required state licensing. Unlike the NCSC credential, the credential does not require a master's degree, nor is it a collaborative effort with professional counseling associations, counselor education accreditation bodies, and/or certification organizations in counseling. The credential is governed by a board of primarily teachers.

# Ethical, Legal, and Professional Considerations

Personal ethics are moral principles guiding an individual's behavior; codes of ethics and ethical behavior are values that guide an entity with which members of that entity are bound (Remley & Herlihy, 2015; Stone, 2013). Ethical codes for the counseling profession steer the professional practices of counselors to ensure the safety and well-being of clients. Counselors' ethical standards, regardless of specialty, are grounded in five ethical principles (autonomy, nonmaleficence, beneficence, justice, and fidelity), which are described as follows (Kitchener, 1984):

- *Autonomy* refers to the notion of independence, which encourages the client to exercise freedom of choice and behavior when those actions do not infringe upon the rights and beliefs of others. Autonomy is promoted versus dependence upon the counselor.
- *Nonmaleficence* is often defined as "above all do no harm" and viewed by many as the most critical of the five ethical principles. In brief, this concept promotes the idea of avoiding any actions or intentions that may place the client at risk for harm.
- *Beneficence* refers the counselor's responsibility to do good. Counselors contribute to the well-being of clients.
- *Justice* should be conceptualized as treating others equally, but in relation to their individual differences. When treating clients differently in order to meet their unique needs, counselors operate from a sound rationale for such actions.
- *Fidelity* refers to the trusting nature of the therapeutic relationship built upon a demonstrated reliability and authenticity toward the client. Counselors promote fidelity by honoring commitments and obligations to clients.

Primarily, school counselors follow the ASCA *Ethical Standards for School Counselors* (ASCA, 2016a) located in Appendix I. School counselors also refer to the American Counseling Association *Code of Ethics* (ACA, 2014) for additional guidance related to the ethical practice of counseling located at www.counseling.org.

Some ethical guidelines are straightforward, others, well, not so much. There will likely be many times during the course of your life as a school counselor that you will encounter ethically laden situations that require tough decisions. Trust me, some will be real head scratchers and finger drummers—perhaps even paving the way to baldness and chipped nails. For this reason, ACA and ASCA have introduced models for ethical decision making. School counselors will want to be familiar with both models. ACA suggests the following seven-step tried and true ethical decision-making model (Forester-Miller & Davis, 1996):

1. *Identify the problem*: Gather objective information (e.g., facts) and gain clarification of the problem.
2. *Apply the ethical standards (ACA and/or ASCA)*: Follow the course of action indicated by the standards or continue this model for more complex dilemmas.
3. *Determine the nature and dimensions of the dilemma*: Examine the problem from all angles and consider:
   a. The five moral principles for guiding ethical practices noted earlier in this section
   b. Professional literature
   c. Consulting with professional colleagues, supervisors, and/or professional associations.
4. *Generate potential courses of action*: Brainstorm possible solutions.
5. *Consider the potential consequences of all options and determine a course of action*: Assess each option and possible consequences to each option and then select the most promising option(s).
6. *Evaluate the selected course of action*: Consider any possible ethical issues associated with your option(s). If your course of action presents ethical issues, then reevaluate the initial problem and original options.
7. *Implement the course of action*: Carry out your plan and follow up on the situation.

ASCA adopted the Solutions to Ethical Problems in Schools (STEPS) model (Stone 2013), which furthered ACA's seven-step model by addressing the specialty of counseling in the school setting. The STEPS model is part of the Ethical Standards for School Counseling Programs (ASCA, 2016a). The STEPS model includes the following nine steps to ethical decision making:

1. Define the problem emotionally and intellectually.
2. Apply the ASCA Ethical Standards and the law.
3. Consider the students' chronological and developmental levels.

4. Consider the setting, parental rights, and minors' rights.
5. Apply the moral principles.
6. Determine your potential courses of action and their consequences.
7. Evaluate the selected action.
8. Consult.
9. Implement the course of action.

---

**THE SAME OR DIFFERENT?**

The school counselor meets with a fifth-grade Caucasian female student, Rita, for issues related to social skills. The school counselor meets with a different fifth-grade student, Regina, an African American female, for issues related to social skills. The school counselor uses a different counseling approach for each student, although both are experiencing issues with social skills. The school counselor is applying which ethical principle in these two students' cases?

a. Fidelity
b. Nonmaleficence
c. Justice
d. Autonomy
e. Beneficence

---

The importance of a school counselor's knowledge of the laws, regulations, and policies related to counseling minors in the schools in order to protect student rights resonates throughout the ASCA *Ethical Standards for School Counselors* (ASCA, 2016a). Protecting the rights of children while those children are in our care during the school day is also emphasized in the common-law doctrine *in loco parentis*.

In addition to ethical guidelines, school counselors must be assiduously mindful of the legal issues related to the population to whom they are providing services—minors. Minors are typically those students who are under the age of 18 and the population generally served by school counselors.

While school counselors follow fairly consistent national ethical standards created by our governing bodies and professional associations, a large variation exists in the law and policy from state to state, city to city, and school division to school division. Such differences necessitate that school counselors become familiar with legislation and policy as it pertains to counseling minors in their state and locality. There are times when division policy, ethical standards, and legal mandates conflict. It is necessary for school counselors to find a way to balance ethical, legal, and school policy requirements as though walking a greased tightrope.

Although school counselors rely on school division policy to guide practices, school division policy does not substitute for knowing and abiding by the law and ethical guidelines for the profession. In cases where ethical guidelines and the law conflict with school division policy, school counselors should advocate for change based on such knowledge. The simple fact is that in some cases school administrators are unaware and unfamiliar with the law as it pertains to school counseling and that which may place school counselors in an unethical situation. And, since principals are vicariously responsible for the actions or inactions of the school counselors in their building, principals more often than not appreciate your expertise in relation to your job. Knowing your stuff may keep your principal from stumbling into bad lighting. Roger that?!

## *Confidentiality*

Confidentiality, the hallmark of a trusting therapeutic relationship, is one of the most common areas of controversy. Perhaps this is why the "Confidentiality" section in the ASCA *Ethical Standards for School Counselors* (ASCA, 2016a) is as long as the Mississippi River. Confidentiality is a concept grounded in ethical principles that refer to a client's right to privacy in the practice of counseling. A related construct, privileged communication, is a legal term that refers to the requirement to protect the privacy between counselor and student (Stone, 2013).

In many states, the school counselor and student relationship is not recognized by law as privileged. School counselors need to know if the state in which they practice recognizes privileged communication between the school counselor and student and under what circumstances. Perhaps privilege exists, but only with specific school counselors in the school (e.g., student assistance counselors).

## *ASCA's Position on Confidentiality*

School counselors recognize their primary obligation for confidentiality is to the student but balance that obligation with an understanding of the family or guardians' legal and inherent rights to be the guiding voice in their children's lives (ASCA *Code of Ethics*, 2010, A.2.d.).

*Position statement adopted 1974; reviewed and reaffirmed 1980; revised 1986, 1993, 1999, 2002, 2008, 2014*

School counselors are ethically and morally obligated to maintain a minor client's confidentiality except in circumstances of harm to self/others, abuse, court order, or when the client has provided written permission to share his or her disclosures made during counseling sessions. Keep in mind that harm to others can include property. Also, there are policies in some school divisions that require school counselors to breach confidentiality, such as engaging in sexual activity, alcohol use, or in cases of student pregnancy. Know your school division's policy.

When counseling minors, the law's perspective is often that counselors are obligated to the parents or guardians of their minor clients with regard to the disclosure of information shared in a counseling session. In short, school counselors have an ethical obligation to the minor client and a legal obligation to the parent or guardian.

On the other hand, if privileged communication exists between school counselors and minors in the state in which the school counselor is practicing, then it is illegal for the school counselor to disclose counseling session information without the consent of the minor student in the absence of clear and imminent danger. Also, some states have minor consent laws in place that allows minors, deemed *emancipated minors*, to enter into counseling relationships and make other decisions without the consent of an adult, which affords those students privileged communication (Remley & Herlihy, 2015; Stone, 2013).

**ORDER IN THE COURT, HERE COMES THE JUDGE**

A school counselor has been subpoenaed to appear in court in a state that does not recognize privileged communication between school counselors and students. The school counselor expresses her reluctance to answer the attorneys' questions regarding the case of Donna, the 15-year-old student that the school counselor has been providing individual counseling services to for the past 4 weeks. When the judge requires that the school counselor answer the attorneys' questions, the school counselor responds by attempting to explain the importance of maintaining counselor–student confidentiality and requesting a withdrawal of the requirement. What are the ethical implications in this case? Are the school counselor's actions in accordance with professional ethical standards?

When confidentiality must be breached, remind the student of the conversation held during the initial session pertaining to the limits to confidentiality. Then, explain the reasoning behind the need to break confidentiality. If it is a situation where the parent needs to be contacted, empower the student to be the one to make contact with the parent in your presence. Another option is to offer to be the one to initiate the communication with the parent in the student's presence. At a minimum, let the student know that you will be contacting the parent as legally/ethically required and discussed in the initial counseling session.

If the issue requires that contact be made to social services or the local police, the school counselor should make contact and keep the student involved as much as is possible or prudent. The school counselor should continue to maintain sensitive and open communication with the student throughout the process. Whether or not it is appropriate or practical to allow the student to be present during mandatory contacts should be considered on a case-by-case basis.

In situations where parent involvement may be helpful to the student's progress, but is not ethically or legally required, the student's consent should be secured. In these cases, it is recommended that school counselors discuss with the student the reasons why parent involvement is desired and let the student know what information will be shared.

The school counselor might encourage the student to be present to hear what is shared and encourage the student to speak freely during the communications. It has been this school counselor's experience that even the most reluctant students come around when they understand the school counselor's reasoning and trust that the school counselor will remain involved and supportive throughout the process.

In the secret-keeping business, a primary and legitimate concern for parents is that counseling sessions will not be kept private. Parents express concern that teachers, staff, and other parents or students may overhear or somehow find out about personal information shared in the counseling session, which may result in harm or embarrassment for their child and/or their family. Having an open discussion with the parent and the student about confidentiality and its limits at the time that counseling is initiated is paramount to helping the parent and student to understand the nature of counseling. I would also advise school counselors to post limits to confidentiality in their offices, in the student–parent handbook, and on parent–teacher counseling referral forms.

If the student will be participating in group counseling, school counselors need to let students and parents know that confidentiality cannot be guaranteed in group counseling sessions. School counselors should also let the parent and student know that there may be times when sharing information with faculty and school administrators is deemed in the best interest of the student in order to provide the student with additional supports and allies during times of stress. During these times, permission will be sought from the student, and perhaps the parent as well, depending upon the developmental level of the student.

The ASCA *Ethical Standards for School Counselors* (ASCA, 2016a) encourages school counselors to recognize the powerful potential alliance between teachers and students in supporting students in times of stress, while filtering confidential information so as to provide these allies only with what they "need to know" in order to advantage the student. Seek *consultation* with other school counseling professionals when in doubt as to what constitutes a need-to-know basis.

Filtered confidential information is considered that which is true and accurate and shared in a sensitive and caring manner (Remley & Herlihy, 2015; Stone, 2013). Information shared that might be construed as an invasion of privacy or defamation of character may place the school counselor in a legally troubling situation that transcends the lunacy of just another day.

**ALLIANCES**

Robert is an elementary school counselor. In an attempt to establish a partnership with parents toward the well-being of their children and to ease parents' concerns about their child having sessions with the school counselor, Robert announces during a Parent–Teacher Association (PTA) meeting that he is happy to share information discussed during counseling sessions with their children. Robert emphasizes the importance of sharing information and working together in order to help students to be successful. What do you think about Robert's approach to promoting positive school counselor–parent relations? Are there ethical concerns to be considered here?

In cases of divorce, make every attempt to provide information to both parents that is objective and respectful unless, of course, explicitly prohibited by court order. The ASCA *Ethical Guidelines for School Counselors* (ASCA, 2016a) avows that in cases of divorce or separation, school counselors make a good-faith effort to keep both parents informed, while not engaging in the support of one parent/guardian over the other. What is Switzerland (for 10 points)?

In the case of guardians and noncustodial parents, school counselors generally provide them with information that the school counselor deems helpful to the student and family with the custodial parent's knowledge. The ASCA *Ethical Standards for School Counselors* (ASCA, 2016a) cautions school counselors with regard to recognizing the diverse rights of both custodial and noncustodial parents, who have vested interest in the well-being of the minor in the eyes of the law. With this said, however, school counselors are well advised to be aware of any restraining orders that may exist, to ensure information is shared only with parents and guardians legally eligible to receive such information.

## Confidentiality of Counseling-Related Electronic Communication

When using technology for counseling and counseling-related communications, and for the transmission of student records, school counselors are careful to consult the ethical guidelines to ensure confidentiality is maintained. Parents and students often request that school counselors provide services via the Internet, e-mail, texting, or other forms of electronic communication. School counselors are in no way required to provide electronic counseling to students, parents, teachers, or other school personnel.

School counselors aflame with the desire to make use of the banquet of avant-garde (you may have to look that one up—got to keep you from falling asleep on me . . .) modalities of communication need to be aware of the school's and the school division's policy on this issue, as well as relevant ethical and legal standards of practice. Even those school counselors who are not intending to provide technologically based counseling services should be aware of the legal and ethical implications involved.

Unintentional electronic counseling may occur disguised simply as e-mail. Do not fall for the old e-mail disguise! E-mail has been considered in legal cases to be an educational record and therefore subject to the proviso of the FERPA of 1974, P.L. 93-380 (United States Department of Education, 2008). See what I mean about the infamous e-mail masquerade? Using technology to communicate with parents/students has advantages; but, bring your A-game!

School counselors should gain an understanding of FERPA, also known as the Buckley Amendment. It is important for school counselors to know how this legislation applies to student records and accessing school counseling case notes. FERPA's arm extends far and wide. It is a legal and ethical mandate to safeguard the rights of students and parents in relation to educational records (ASCA, 2016a).

FERPA is a federal law that applies to all schools that receive funds from the U.S. Department of Education. FERPA protects the privacy of student records and provides parents (or students over 18 and/or postsecondary school students) with rights pertaining to record inspection, correction, copying, and general consent before release. Requests must be made in writing. Schools will provide the parent or student with access to the record within 45 days of the date of the request.

Unless a parent specifically requests a school not disclose directory information about the student, directory information may be disclosed. Directory information may be considered to be the following:

■ Name
■ Address

- Telephone number
- Grade level
- Sports activities
- Weight and height of members of athletic teams
- Enrollment status
- E-mail
- Date and place of birth
- Photograph
- Major field of study and degrees obtained
- Previous schools attended and dates of attendance
- Honors and awards.

While disclosing information that is not considered directory information requires parental consent, like all good rules, there are exceptions to this as well. Consent is not required by the parent to disclose information contained in a student's record under the following circumstances:

- Judicial order/subpoena
- State law (local juvenile justice authority)
- School studies/audit/evaluation
- School safety/health emergency
- Student's financial aid advisor
- School officials with legitimate educational interest
- School transfer

School counseling case notes are not part of the educational record. For this reason, case notes are not accessible under FERPA.

Section A.14.b of the ASCA *Ethical Standards for School Counselors* (ASCA, 2016a) emphasizes the need for school counselors to "take appropriate and reasonable measures for maintaining confidentiality of student information and educational records stored or transmitted through the use of computers, social media, facsimile machines, telephones, voicemail, answering machines and other electronic technology."

NBCC, anticipating the growing trend in technologically driven counseling services, has created a guidance document titled "The Practice of Internet Counseling." This document is available at www.nbcc.org. The document describes the different types of technology-assisted distance counseling tools and methods and provides Internet counseling standards.

With this said, in situations where sharing student information meets the need-to-know ethical guidelines noted previously, school counselors must be mindful of the confidential nature of student information when using technology and electronic storage devices (e.g., CD, DVD, flash drives). In these cases, be sure that which is communicated is free of any identifying information (e.g., student name, social security number, student identification number, photograph) and that it is professional and aligned with the school counselor duties and responsibility to students and parents. A good rule of thumb is to only communicate electronically that which could be shared in a public forum. That is, if the *National Educational Inquirer* intercepted it, there would be no story.

There are also times when the electronic transfer of student information may not be appropriate (e.g., sensitive, personal information that may be linkable to a particular student). In such cases, a plan needs to be developed for the sharing of confidential information between professionals (e.g., school counselor to personal counselor).

## Harm to Self or Others

School counselors have a duty to protect and a duty to warn in cases of harm to self or others (or their property), respectively. This duty requires a breach in confidentiality. When a student names an identifiable other to which they have a plan to do harm, then the school counselor needs to warn the identified victim. This may require more than parent notification, but police officer involvement as well, to be sure protection can be obtained for the intended victim.

School counselors have a duty to protect in cases where students threaten harm to self. In such cases, school counselors should assess for clear and imminent danger. Most school divisions have policy, guidelines, and forms to aid school counselors in making such assessments—know your school division's policy and review assessments and guiding forms used by the school counselors to be sure they accurately reflect current federal and state legislation. If it is believed that the student is at risk for self-harm, the proper authorities must be notified and the student should remain under adult supervision until the appropriate authorities arrive.

Section A.9.d. of the ASCA *Ethical Standards for School Counselors* (ASCA, 2016a) states that school counselors "report to parent/guardians and/or appropriate authorities when students disclose a perpetrated or a perceived threat to their physical or mental well-being." It is important to spotlight "parent/guardians *and*/*or* appropriate authorities" in this statement. Because the student is a minor, the immediate reaction of some may be to contact the parent when a student threatens harm to self. This may not be the appropriate action in some cases.

If the parent is implicated by the student as a factor for suicidal thoughts, the parent would not be the first contact. In fact, the school counselor may not contact the parent at all in such cases. In most states, school counselors would contact CPS, a division of Social Services. The CPS personnel would make contact with the parent at their discretion based on a more detailed investigation and discussion with the student. If parents are not implicated, they should be the first contact.

School counselors should provide parents with a list of resources that provide counseling services to children, adolescents, and families. In some states, if parents indicate in any way that they will not be seeking professional counseling for their child or adolescent who is at risk of suicide or other self-injurious behaviors (e.g., cutting), this is viewed as child neglect. In such cases, generally, CPS would be contacted immediately.

In some cases, school counselors may not deem particular information shared by a student as constituting harm to self or others. In such cases, and where law or policy is not in place, school counselors may decide not to disclose particular information to a parent (e.g., risky behaviors, drug and/or alcohol use, issues related to eating/diet, sexual activity) to avoid a possible negative impact on the counseling relationship. In these situations, school counselors are assuming responsibility for the student's safety and well-being. Should any harm come to the student as a result of

---

### THOUGHTS OF SUICIDE

Patrick, a ninth grader, was referred to you by a teacher who said Patrick expressed suicidal intentions because he is having some personal and family issues. You talk to Patrick long enough to assess that he is at imminent risk of suicide. Understanding that Patrick is a minor, the school counselor contacts the student's parent(s) and prints a resource list of community mental health counselors to give to the parent. Is this the best course of action, ethically and legally, on behalf of this student?

withholding such information, school counselors may be held legally responsible for those inactions. School counselors are strongly encouraged and supported by the ASCA *Ethical Standards for School Counselors* (ASCA, 2016a) to consult, consult, consult with other counselors in the best interest of the student in instances where they may be uncertain about a course of action.

The reverse can also be true, in cases where the school counselor shares information with the parent or guardian that should not have been disclosed even in the absence of privileged communication and in the presence of clear and imminent danger. For example, if a student threatens to commit suicide and implicates their parent or guardian as a reason for their suicidal thoughts, disclosing this information to the parent could result in serious harm to the student at the hand of him- or herself or an abusive parent. In this case, the school counselor may be found negligent and held liable if the law in the state in which they practice requires that school counselors contact CPS when parents are implicated—perhaps even in the absence of such law.

## *Child Abuse and Neglect*

The federal Child Abuse Prevention and Treatment Act (CAPTA) established minimum standards, allowing each state to create its own definition of child abuse and neglect. CAPTA defines *child abuse* and *child neglect* as "any recent act or failure to act on the part of a parent or caretaker which results in death, serious physical or emotional harm, sexual abuse or exploitation, or an act or failure to act which presents an imminent risk of serious harm" (Child Welfare Information Gateway, 2013, p. 2).

All 50 states have passed mandatory child abuse and neglect reporting laws. Legislation imposes penalties to school counselors who do not report suspected child abuse or neglect.

### ASCA's Position on Child Abuse and Neglect

It is the school counselor's legal, ethical and moral responsibility to report suspected cases of child abuse and neglect to the proper authorities. School counselors work to identify the behavioral, academic and social/emotional impact of abuse and neglect on students and ensure the necessary supports for students are in place.

*Position statement adopted 1981;*
*revised 1985, 1993, 1999, 2003, 2015*

As mandated reporters, school counselors must make verbal contact with CPS in cases of suspected child abuse or neglect generally within 48–72 hours. What constitutes abuse or neglect varies from state to state.

Some states still allow corporal punishment in schools. Not having been accused of being a woman of few words, let me say with the greatest conviction that I can muster—corporal punishment in our schools pollutes the very air that we seek to purify. ASCA, too, takes a strong stand, supporting the extermination of corporal punishment in the schools. School counselors remain diligent in reporting suspected child abuse that may be occurring within and outside of the school—not excluding those schools that still practice this archaic form of discipline that is purposeful in its intent to humiliate and inflict physical pain upon children and adolescents.

## ASCA's Position on Corporal Punishment in the Schools

School counselors oppose the use of corporal punishment.

*Position statement adopted 1995;*
*revised 2000, 2006, 2012*

In most states, school counselors need only to have reasonable cause to suspect child abuse and/or neglect and do not need to see bruises, cuts, or marks of any kind in order to request CPS intervention on behalf of a child, adolescent, or the elderly (Child Welfare Information Gateway, 2013). If the school counselor suspects that the student may run or that the student is afraid to go home, this needs to be shared in the initial contact with CPS.

**CHARLIE'S WORLD**

Charlie is a 9-year-old student who went to the school nurse because his back was hurting. The school nurse did not see any visible signs of injury, but asked the school counselor to talk to Charlie because he said that while he was staying with his dad last weekend his dad punched him, so he called his mother crying to come and get him. The school counselor talked to Charlie and found out that his father was very angry and hit Charlie, repeatedly, in the stomach and back about a week ago. Charlie had been out of school for the past week while back with his mother, who told Charlie's teacher that he was playing and fell out of a tree. Since the school counselor knew that Charlie's parents were separated and this happened at the dad's house, the school counselor called the mother. Do you agree with the school counselor's actions in this case? Why or why not?

Together, the school counselor and CPS intake specialist should determine an immediate course of action based on the information provided by the student.

## Scope of Practice

Another area that is potentially problematic for school counselors involves the scope of practice and referrals. School counselors want to be careful not to practice outside of their areas of expertise and training. ASCA supports the use of referrals and a collaborative approach to meet the persistent and long-term needs of these students.

## ASCA's Position on Student Mental Health

School counselors recognize and respond to the need for mental health and behavioral prevention, early intervention and crisis services that promote psychosocial wellness and development for all students. School counselors are prepared to address barriers and to assess ways to maximize students' success in schools, communities and their family structure by offering education, prevention, and crisis and short-term intervention until the student is connected with available community resources.

> *Position statement adopted 1974; reviewed and reaffirmed 1980; revised 1986, 1993, 1999, 2002, 2015*

School counselors do not provide ongoing counseling sessions with students whose issues are so severe, frequent, and enduring that they cannot be sufficiently addressed within the scope of school counseling and within the expertise of the school counselor, as this is in violation of professional ethical guidelines. Section A.6.b. of the *ASCA Ethical Standards for School Counselors* (ASCA, 2016a) requires school counselors to

> provide a list of resources for outside agencies and resources in their community to student(s) and parents/guardians when student need or request additional support. School counselors provide multiple referral options or the district's vetted list and are careful not to indicate an endorsement or preference for one counselor or practice.

There are times when a school counselor and agency counselor may wish to collaborate to help the student. In such instances, all parties

---

**MOONLIGHTING**

Stuart is a school counselor and a licensed professional counselor. Since counseling students for an indefinite period of time and providing diagnoses and therapy is outside of the scope of school counseling services, Stuart has decided to offer his counseling services to students outside of the school day in his private practice setting. This will allow students in his small rural town to get the needed outside counseling services. Since he is the students' school counselor, he is offering a reduced rate. Are there ethical implications to consider here?

involved (i.e., parents, student, both counselors) should agree to the collaborative relationship, which will require the sharing of confidential information, communications, and student records. All parties will need to sign a release of information, which should include a statement that clearly defines and describes the nature of the collaborative relationship between all parties involved.

Another consideration with regard to scope of school counseling practice involves student evaluation, assessment, and interpretation. Psychological and *intelligence testing* by school counselors can be particularly problematic. Testing and assessment of this nature may be acceptable practices for school counselors in some school divisions, while unacceptable in others. Know your school division's policy. I realize by saying this yet again for about the sixth time in one chapter, I am running the risk of your having me committed for echolalia! Just so you know, I am not answering the door to anyone wearing a white coat—although a sanitarium does offer something of a restful appeal.

School counselors only engage in evaluation, assessment, and interpretation when adequately trained. Section A.13.b. of the ASCA *Ethical Standards for School Counselors* (ASCA, 2016a) emphasizes that school counselors "adhere to all professional standards when selecting, administering and interpreting assessment measures and only utilize assessment measures that are within the scope of practice for school counselors and for which they are licensed, certified, and competent."

## *Informed Consent*

School counselors are not legally obligated to obtain parental permission prior to counseling unless there is a federal or state statute to the contrary (Remley & Herlihy, 2015; Stone, 2013). However, many school division policies require that school counselors obtain parental consent, particularly if counseling will extend beyond one or two sessions, as a matter of best practices (Stone, 2013).

School administrators, intent on promoting positive relations and support for the school counseling program, are aware that judicial rulings have historically favored parental rights (Remley & Herlihy, 2015). For this reason, school systems generally have a policy in place with regard to parental consent for individual and small group counseling. Classroom guidance lessons, unless they are of a sensitive nature (e.g., sexual abuse), are viewed as part of the curriculum afforded to all students.

Many school systems include an "opt out" of counseling form in the student handbook. In this case, if a parent does not specifically opt a student out of counseling services, then school counselors are free to provide counseling services to students as needed. School counselors check with division supervisors for school counseling to stay abreast of school division policies pertaining to the provision of school counseling services.

## SENSITIVE TOPICS

In an effort to be proactive in promoting child safety, an elementary school counselor conducted a classroom guidance lesson for all fourth- and fifth-grade students on Internet safety. The school counselor invited a community police officer to talk about a particular case where a boy was lured by a stranger over the Internet, abducted, and killed. The next day, a very upset parent called because their fifth grader, Kirbi, came home in tears as the program reminded her of what had happened to her brother, who had been abducted and killed. The parent said she had not been informed that this program would take place or she would not have allowed her child to participate. Are school counselors required to inform parents about the topics of classroom guidance lessons and school-wide presentations? Should the parent have been informed about this classroom guidance lesson?

Some high schools now have student assistance counselors, student assistance programs (SAPs), and *response to intervention* (RTI) as part of a multitiered system of supports (MTSS). Student assistance counselors are generally school counselors who specialize in working with students in crisis and those who are experiencing varying degrees of personal, social, and emotional distress and behavioral issues. Student assistance counselors often have more specialized and/or advanced counseling credentials (e.g., NCC, NCSC, LPC). In addition to specialized counseling services offered in schools to supplement school counseling services, school counselors collaborate with administrators, community agencies, families, and other school professionals when designing and implementing MTSS.

---

### ASCA's Position on Multitiered System of Supports

School counselors are stakeholders in the development and implementation of a multitiered system of supports (MTSS) including but not limited to response to intervention (RTI) and culturally responsive positive behavioral interventions and supports (CR PBIS). School counselors align their work with MTSS through the implementation of a comprehensive school counseling program designed to improve student achievement and behavior.

*Position statement adopted 2008; revised 2014*

---

Informed consent from parents and guardians should be in writing. It is not necessary to get informed consent in writing from the minor, although it is necessary to obtain agreement, or assent, from minor clients. School counselors use developmentally appropriate language to discuss counseling services so that students can make informed decisions about whether or not they wish to engage in a counseling relationship with the school counselor.

## Student Records and Counseling Case Notes

Documenting counseling session information and storing such information in the form of formal professional case notes is another consideration with regard to maintaining confidentiality. School counselor formal case notes should be kept as a critical part of professional and accountable practices. These notes are not a part of the student's academic record. These case notes are objective in nature and discussed in more detail below. In some states, general counseling case notes may be considered part of the educational record. In those states, school counselors are well advised to have a specific understanding of exactly what is required to be placed in the student's education records. Likely, it is no more than dates that the student visited the school counselor and whether the topic was personal, social, emotional, academic, or career related.

School counselors may also consider creating sole possession records written as a memory aid. Unlike the more objective nature of the official case notes, sole possession records are more subjective in nature, documenting professional opinion and observations. These notes are not accessible or shared verbally or in writing with any other party. Like case notes, the school counselor's sole possession notes are not to be kept in the student's school record, which is accessible to many other educators and could constitute a breach of confidentiality. My best advice is to keep two sets of counseling notes: sole possession records and formal counseling records. This will allow you to capture both objective information and your valuable perceptions/interpretations during counseling sessions.

The advanced voluntary credentialing of school counselors (e.g., NCC, NCSC, LPC) require that they abide by the standards of practice of the credentialing agency. Many advanced voluntary credentials earned by school counselors have placed them in the category of mental health provider. Mental health providers are subject to compliance with HIPAA.

In brief, Health Insurance Portability and Accountability Act (HIPAA) established national standards related to the confidentiality and security of health information. Health records in the school setting are exempt from HIPAA because those are covered under FERPA. However, it is not entirely clear how school counseling-related communications, apart from case notes, which are not accessible under FERPA, would be viewed in the event of litigation when the school counselor holds advanced credentials should there be a mighty clash of the titans—HIPAA versus FERPA. So, as the adage goes, better safe than sorry. Since FERPA has no requirements for, nor jurisdiction over, school counseling case notes, why not use what HIPAA requires of mental health providers? As a school counselor with advanced counseling credentials, not only will you be prepared for a curve ball from HIPAA, you will also have an outline for keeping formal case notes, which is generally not provided in school divisions and would serve double-duty by also meeting the accountability demands of today's society. Formal counseling case notes should include the following factual information:

■ Dates of sessions
■ Number of sessions
■ Assessment data
■ Presenting problem

- Treatment/counseling plan
- Information related to collaboration and consultation with others
- Session notes
- Associated documents (e.g., informed consent, drawings, letters, referrals).

Case notes and sole possession records need to be stored in a secure location (e.g., locked in the school counseling office file cabinet) and maintained for several years and perhaps indefinitely in some cases (Remley & Herlihy, 2015; Stone, 2013). Section A.12.f. of the *Ethical Standards for School Counselors* (ASCA, 2016a) suggests

> shredding sole possession records or deleting electronic sole possession records when the student transitions to the next level, transfers to another school or graduates. School counselors do not destroy sole possession records that may be needed by a court of law, such as notes on child abuse, suicide, sexual harassment or violence without prior review and approval by school district legal counsel.

Case notes can be quite valuable, confirming meeting dates and times, dates of conversations with relevant others, and actions taken. Case notes may demonstrate a school counselor's professional, ethical, and legal actions in a given situation.

Case notes and sole possession records are accessible under a subpoena or court order in the absence of privileged communication statutes (ASCA, 2016a; A.12.d.). If (I should say when) you are subpoenaed to appear in court regarding one of your students and you are uncertain about what to say or what information to provide, seek advice from your school division's attorney. In fact, it is just good practice to touch base with your division's attorney when subpoenaed to court for school-related matters.

There may be times when a parent or guardian demands access to case notes or wants to know exactly what has been communicated in a counseling session. In these cases, first try to persuade the adult by expressing that it would not be in the best interest of their child to reveal such information without their child's knowledge—even better their permission. Explain your ethical obligation to the student as well as your desire to collaborate with the parent on their child's behalf. Reassure the parent that, had anything been shared by the student that the parent should know in order to help the student, you would have requested permission from the student to share that information. Encourage the parent to ask their child about the counseling sessions.

If the parent is still insistent, let the parent know that you would like to request the student's permission to share the session content in order to preserve not just the counselor–student relationship, but the parent–child relationship. If the student would like to maintain confidentiality, then encourage a meeting with the student and the parent to mediate a solution. If the meeting is not productive and you decide not to disclose the information to the parent, ensure that you have administrator support. The parent may decide to legally pursue the matter and may have a legal right to the information.

### WHEN TO SAY NO

Shirley is a school counselor in a very large inner-city school. Her principal has asked her to include a copy of her counseling notes in the student's educational record in file room to ensure they are made available under FERPA, if requested. The principal believes this is the only place those case notes will really be secure and made available to teachers, who may wish to know more about the students' issues to better provide assistance. Shirley politely says "no," sharing that these are official counseling case notes that are not intended to be part of the student's educational record in accordance with ethical guidelines and the law. And, because the case notes are not part of the educational record, they are not accessible under FERPA. Shirley further explains that, should the counseling notes be included in the educational records of students, parents may have grounds for legal action based on a breach of confidentiality in the school counselor–student relationship. Do you agree with the school counselor's actions in this case? Why or why not?

## IDEA and Section 504

The Individuals with Disabilities Education Act (IDEA) is civil rights legislation created to ensure equality in education for students with an identified *disability* under three major types of disorders: physical and neurological disabilities, sensory disabilities, and developmental disabilities (United States Department of Education, 2004). Students who are found eligible for services under IDEA will receive an *individualized education program/plan* (IEP), which entitles the student to accommodations and specialized services as decided upon by the IEP team and included in the student's IEP.

A civil rights law, the *Rehabilitation Act of 1973 (Section 504)*, as amended (United States Department of Education, 2009), includes information about the *Americans with Disabilities Act of 1990* (ADA) and protects the rights of students with disabling conditions that limit one or more major life activities (e.g., vision, hearing, speaking, walking, learning). Students who do not qualify for special education services under IDEA are often eligible for services under Section 504. Students who are found eligible under Section 504 will receive a *504 plan*, which entitles the student to accommodations and specialized services as decided upon by the 504 team and included in the 504 plan.

Together, IDEA and Section 504 of the Rehabilitation Act are powerful tools that school counselors use to advocate for *equity and access* to rigorous and appropriate educational programming and services in the schools for all students. School counselors are often the first person parents, teachers, and administrators involve when a student is struggling. Early intervention coupled with resources is key to ensuring that students' needs are met.

Parents, teachers, administrators, school counselors, and just about anyone can refer a student to the *child study* team or to the 504 committee, if a disabling condition and/or learning disability is suspected. Most schools have an early intervention team that assumes many different names but have a similar purpose, which is to begin a plan of action to help students who are struggling academically, personally, emotionally, socially, physically, and/or behaviorally. School counselors are generally members, even chairs, of these teams that also include the parent, classroom teacher(s), a special education teacher, and, upon invitation, the school psychologist, social worker, and/or educational diagnostician.

The early intervention team develops and monitors an intervention plan. The intervention plan is distributed to all who work with the student and a copy is included in the student's educational record. An early intervention plan may be all a student needs to get back on track or to stay on track. If not, the team refers the student to the child study team or the

504 committee for possible *diagnostic testing* and/or additional intervention assistance.

Many schools are now requiring that teachers refer students to the early intervention team before a referral can be made to the child study team. This helps to reduce the number of students in special education because of an overreliance on IEPs versus other less restrictive forms of intervention. However, a parent who wishes to take their child directly to the child study team has a legal right to do so and is not required to go through the early intervention team first.

## THE 504 PLAN

Kenneth is a third-grade student with a 504 plan. The plan allows Kenneth to have extended time, frequent breaks, and small group instruction and testing. The school counselor is creating a standardized testing schedule for their school for special needs students. Kenneth's teacher tells the school counselor not to worry about pulling Kenneth out of the classroom since she has not really been doing this throughout the school year and Kenneth is doing just fine without those accommodations. The school counselor pulls the student out of the class on the day of statewide standardized testing to adhere to the accommodations listed on the student's 504 plan. What issues do you view as problematic in this case? Do you agree with the school counselor's actions in this case? Do you agree with the teacher's actions in this case? What are the implications for Kenneth?

## Homelessness

The most recent data reported 135,701 homeless youth (United States Department of Housing and Urban Development, 2014). Students who are homeless have a higher incidence of developmental delays, behavioral problems, poor academic performance, and depression, which makes poverty a pervasive risk factor (Grothaus, Lorelle, Anderson, & Knight, 2011). Studies have confirmed that youth who experience homelessness count on informal support systems to enhance reliance; and, enhanced coping skills are associated with spirituality, mental health, and creativity (Cronley & Evans, 2017).

School counselors collaborate with stakeholders to remove the barriers to school success perpetuated by homelessness. School counselors need to be aware of the McKinney-Vento Act of 1987 (United States Department of Education, 2000), which defines homelessness as lacking a fixed, regular, and adequate nighttime residence, and provides federal money for homeless shelters.

## Research

It is important for school counselors to consider the ethical and legal issues associated with conducting research in the schools. Section F.1. of the ASCA *Ethical Standards for School Counselors* (ASCA, 2016a) states that school counselors "conduct appropriate research, and report findings in a manner consistent with acceptable educational and psychological research practices . . . and advocate for the protection of individual students' identities when using data for research or program planning" (p. 6). Issues to consider include:

- Obtaining parental and student informed consent
- Confidentiality of assessment data
- Culture and gender bias in the selection of measures
- Withholding treatment
- Providing treatment for all students in experimental groups.

## Dual Relationships

Maintaining professional distance is sometimes more difficult for the school counselor, as opposed to a private practitioner or community counselor. School counselors are often asked by administrators to take on any number of extracurricular program sponsorship roles, making dual relationships in the world of school counseling inevitable.

When dual relationships are unavoidable, continuously examine your professional and ethical behaviors as a school counselor by asking yourself, "Whose needs are being met by my behaviors?" (Stone, 2013). And, since dual relationships are often about personal gain (e.g., extravagant gifts, money, emotional, personal, or social need, recognition, popularity), ask yourself, "Is my reason for doing this to meet a personal need/desire of mine?" If the answer is yes, then, in the words of our former first lady, Nancy Reagan—*just say no*!

Section A.5.a. of the ASCA *Ethical Standards for School Counselors* (ASCA, 2016a) cautions school counselors to

> avoid dual relationships that might impair their objectivity and increase the risk of harm to students (e.g., counseling one's family members or the children of close friends or associates). If a dual relationship is unavoidable, the school counselor is responsible for taking action to eliminate or reduce the potential for harm to the student through use of safeguards, which might include informed consent, consultation, supervision and documentation.

## Supervision

ASCA recommends that school counselors receive regular supervision in order to maintain and enhance professional and ethical practices. Section B.3.h. of the ASCA *Ethical Standards for School Counselors* (2016a) states that "school counselors seek consultation and supervision from school counselors and other professionals who are knowledgeable or school counselors' ethical practices when ethical and professional questions arise."

Supervision at the division level may be thought of as program supervision and is provided by a division level/central office administrator. The other two types of supervision are administrative and clinical supervision. Administrative supervision is generally provided at the building level by the school counseling director or principal. The director or principal provides the school counselor with general guidance pertaining to the daily operations of the school counseling program and evaluates the school counselor's professional performance.

Clinical supervision provides school counselors with consultation and supervision as it pertains to improving counseling skills and providing needed counseling support, yet it is the least received type of supervision for school counselors. School counselors may obtain clinical supervision from local counselor educators and professional counselors in community agencies and private practice. Individual and group peer supervision or consultation by fellow practicing school counselors is the most commonly used method of school counselor supervision, often using a developmental model or some integrated approach that includes various aspects of the developmental model.

Developmental models of supervision allow school counselors to meet peers where they are in their developmental process as a practicing counselor. Developmental models posit that counselors move through qualitatively different stages that require qualitatively different levels of supervisor involvement (e.g., less, moderate, or highly structured) and roles (e.g., teacher, trainer, colleague, consultant) to meet the unique needs of the supervisee (Bernard & Luke, 2015; Bernard & Goodyear, 2004).

Peer supervision or consultation as a type of clinical supervision aids school counselors in case conceptualization and working through complex ethical and legal issues that often arise when counseling minors, while also providing a medium for shared feedback, exploration of thoughts and emotions, and the validation and support critical to self-care (Page, Pietrzak, & Sutton, 2001).

We do not need Nostradamus to tell us what the future holds for school counselors who do not find ways to destress, reenergize, and maintain well-being. How can we effectively meet the needs of others in the lingering presence of our own unmet needs? School counselors are like the cobbler with no shoes. We get so busy fashioning shoes for all of our students, teachers, and parents that we do not make time to create a pair for ourselves. It is time to design our own shoes. Now, before your heart starts hammering too quickly with excitement, I did not say designer shoes—I said—design our own shoes.

It is our personal and professional responsibility to prevent our own impairment that often results from professional burnout. ACA (2003), recognizing the growing number of counselors suffering from professional burnout, created the Taskforce on Counselor Wellness and Impairment to provide counselors with strategies, self-assessments, and resources to address burnout (www.counseling.org/wellness_taskforce/index.htm).

ACA recognizes burnout as an impairment that may impact our professional counseling ability and result in harm to the client, making it our ethical responsibility to address self-care. ACA provides a long list of strategies to reduce burnout and maintain personal health and well-being that fall into the following categories:

■ Clinical supervision (peer consultation/supervision, supervision by a professional counselor)
■ Involvement in professional associations

- A balanced lifestyle that attends to the holistic self, mind, body, and spirit
- Identifying and maintaining a support system
- Identifying and removing the barriers to self-care
- Making time for fun and socialization.

# Human Development, Learning, and Motivation

Human development, simply stated, is the change that occurs in human beings over the course of the lifespan. The process, however, is not so simple. Human development is multidimensional and complex. For these reasons, it is not appropriate to generalize developmental processes and stages across cultures or ethnicities because some developmental characteristics are socially engineered or thwarted by culturally engendered developmental processes. This section will look at key developmental theories and general developmental characteristics of elementary, middle, and high school students.

Understanding the characteristics and processes of a student's psychological, social, cognitive (including learning, motor skills, and language development), spiritual, and moral development during the school-age years is necessary to distinguishing between what may be considered normal developmental characteristics and minor to serious developmental impediments. Knowledge of the multifaceted aspects of human development is also essential to designing developmentally appropriate strategies for successful intervention with specific populations such as students with physical, mental, and emotional disabilities and/or advanced functioning students.

An understanding of human development across the lifespan enables school counselors to adjust language, approaches, and techniques to meet the unique needs of school-age children. It is also important that school counselors consider those biological and environmental forces that impact human development.

Theorists continue to ponder the impact of nature versus nurture on human development. That is, to what extent do genetic factors (i.e., nature) and environmental factors (i.e., nurture) and their interactions influence human development? To date, the topic has been widely researched, and data indicate that both play a significant role in determining our attitudes, beliefs, and behaviors. For this reason, school counselors are encouraged to consider both nature and nurture when working with children, adolescents, and adults.

The fundamental nature of counseling, thus school counseling, and human development is change. Meeting students where they are when prevention and intervention is needed is critical. School counselors achieve this with an understanding of human development theories. The human development theories discussed in this section are categorized as follows: psychosocial development, cognitive development and learning theories, and moral and spiritual development. Figure 1.1 presents this information in a fashion that aids learning and recall.

## *Psychosocial Development*

Psychosocial development theories seek to explain personality development and the acquisition of social skills and social attitudes. The three primary psychosocial theorists discussed in this chapter are Erik Erikson, Robert Havighurst, and Sigmund Freud. Eric Berne's theory of personality development, transactional analysis (TA), is also considered because it is often applied in the school setting.

Erik Erikson (1950, 1959) is best known for his eight stages of psychosocial development. Erikson postulates that each stage held a developmental task that needed to be successfully resolved in order to experience healthy personality development. When the task was successfully resolved, a psychosocial strength, or virtue, would emerge. Table 1.1 presents Erikson's eight stages, corresponding ages, the conflict to be resolved, and the resulting virtue in a manner that will aid in learning and recall.

Erikson is credited for coining the term identity crisis, which he suggests occurs during adolescence. Identity crisis is used to describe a period of role confusion whereby the individual explores roles, questions authority, strives to find his or her own unique self or identity, and struggles with social relationships and social and moral issues. When the individual commits to an identity, role confusion ends and role achievement is reached. Role diffusion is the result when an individual has not experienced identity crisis or commitment.

Robert Havighurst (1972) applied Erikson's concept of stages of psychosocial development, postulating six different stages and an emphasis on the successful achievement of each task at each stage, which derive from three sources: physical maturation (e.g., motor skills, walking and

**Human Development Theories**

| Product Development | Cognitive Development and Learning Theories | Moral and Spiritual Development |
|---|---|---|
| Explains personality development and the acquisition of social skills and social attitudes | Explains the development of thought, intelligence, and problem-solving abilities | Explains the development of attitudes and behaviors toward others, and the meaning and nature of our existence |

**Erik Erikson**

Development driven by stage-related task resolve
Eight stages of psychosocial development:
Trust vs. Mistrust; Autonomy vs. Shame and
Doubt; Initiative vs. Inferiority; Identity vs.
Confusion; Intimacy vs. Isolation; Generativity vs.
Stagnation; Integrity vs. Despair
Key constructs: identity crisis; virtues

**Robert Havighurst**

Development driven by stage-related task resolve
Six stages of personality development: infancy;
early childhood; middle childhood;
adolescence; early adulthood; middle
adulthood; later maturity
Key constructs: developmental tasks (physical
maturation, personal values, societal pressures)

**Sigmund Freud**

Development driven by sexual pleasures and
interactions of the id, ego, and superego
Five psychosexual stages: oral, anal, phallic,
latent period, and genital stage
Key constructs: conscious, unconscious;
Oedipus and Electra complexes; libido;
fixation; erogenous zones; pleasure principle

**Eric Berne**

Development driven by interactions
Key constructs: strokes, ego states,
transactional stimulus, transactional response

**Jean Piaget**

Development is a continuous process of
achieving balance between assimilation and
accommodation (i.e., equilibrium) and the
resulting modification of schemas.
Four stages of cognitive development:
sensorimotor; preoperational; concrete
operational; formal operational
Key constructs: egocentrism; sociocentrism

**B. F. Skinner**

Learning driven by operant conditioning
Key constructs: behavior modification; stimulus;
response; positive and negative reinforcement
and punishment; schedules of reinforcement

**Lev Vygotsky**

Learning is contextual and driven by culture,
environment, and social interactions.
Key constructs: guided participation; zone of
proximal development; scaffolding; cultural
mediation; internalization

**Albert Bandura**

Learning driven by modeling
Key constructs: motivation; observational
learning; reciprocal determinism

**Jean Piaget**

Moral reasoning develops from cognitive
structure and social relationships in two
stages. Individuals construct/reconstruct
their perceptions of the world based on their
interactions with environment and others.
Key constructs: heteronomy; autonomy;
goodness; evil

**Lawrence Kohlberg**

Moral thinking is developed through an
understanding and exposure to concepts such as
justice, human rights and welfare, and equality.
Three levels containing six stages of moral
reasoning: Level 1 (preconventional), Level 2
(conventional), Level 3 (postconventional).
Key constructs: justice operation; moral
universalism; formalism; relativism

**James Fowler**

Faith development occurs in six stages
and involves cognition, emotion, and
imagination: intuitive-projective; mythic-
literal; synthetic-conventional;
individuative-reflective; conjunctive faith;
universalizing (or enlightenment)
Key construct: transcendence

**Figure 1.1 Human development theories.**

**Table 1.1 Erikson's Eight Stages of Psychosocial Development**

| Stage/Age | Task to be Resolved | Characteristics | Virtue |
|---|---|---|---|
| Infancy/ages 0–1 | Trust vs. mistrust | Need for reliable care (e.g., feeding) from caregiver | Hope |
| Toddler/ages 2–3 | Autonomy vs. shame and doubt | Need for sense of control over physical tasks (e.g., toilet training) | Determinism/will |
| Preschool/ages 3–5 | Initiative vs. guilt | Need for control over environment (e.g., exploration) | Courage/purpose |
| School age/ages 6–11 | Industry vs. inferiority | Need to successfully navigate social and educational demands (e.g., school) | Competence |
| Adolescence/ages 12–18 | Identity vs. role confusion | Need to develop a personal identity and sense of self (e.g., peer relationships) | Loyalty/fidelity |
| Early adulthood/ages 19–40 | Intimacy vs. isolation | Need for intimacy and love (e.g., social relationships) | Love |
| Middle adulthood/ages 40–65 | Generativity vs. stagnation | Need to create and nurture (e.g., work/parenthood) | Caring |
| Late adulthood/ages >65 | Ego integrity vs. despair | Need for a sense of fulfillment (e.g., reflection on life) | Wisdom |

**DEFIANCE**

Kelly is in middle school, and his parents are worried that he is exhibiting defiance that could lead to more serious behaviors. His parents say that he just does not listen to a thing they say or comply with what they ask him to do. His grades are good as well as his relationships with peers. His teachers report that he is respectful but questions everything they ask him to do. Developmentally, what might Kelly be experiencing?

talking, adjusting to menses and menopause), personal values (e.g., spirituality/philosophical beliefs, selecting an occupation), and societal pressures (e.g., learning to be responsible, citizenship). Table 1.2 presents Havighurst's six stages of personality development along with the developmental tasks associated with each stage. Havighurst believed that introducing students to these developmental tasks at the right time creates a teachable moment.

Sigmund Freud believed that personality development was driven by sexual interests or pleasures that focused on specific erogenous zones (i.e., mouth, anus, and genital area) at particular stages of development (Nye, 1975). Like other stage theorists, Freud emphasized the importance of resolving developmental conflicts at each stage. Freud proposes that unresolved conflicts at each stage results in fixation, thereby leaving a part of the child's libido (i.e., psychic energy of the mind) fixed at that stage, impacting personality into adulthood. One wonders at which stage Freud developed his rumored fear of ferns—things that make you go hmmm? Nonetheless, Freud's brilliant mind conceptualized five stages of psychosexual development quite influential to this day. Each stage and the characteristics of each stage are listed in Table 1.3.

Freud further believed that personality was driven by the interactions of the mind, or psyche made up of the id (i.e., primal instinct), ego (i.e., realistic, organized part of the mind), and superego (i.e., moralistic part of the mind). The id is our unconscious and driven by the pleasure principle—if it feels good, do it; if it doesn't, don't do it! The ego, mainly but not entirely conscious, operates on the reality principle, which has us delay gratification and endure necessary pain when needed, meeting the needs of the id in a realistic way. The superego mainly but not entirely

**Table 1.2 Havighurst's Stages of Personality Development**

| Stage/Age | Developmental Tasks |
| --- | --- |
| Infancy and early childhood/ages 0–6 | Learning to talk, crawl, and walk; learning to control bowels; learning concepts; learning gender differences |
| Middle childhood/ages 6–12 | Learning interpersonal skills and daily living concepts; developing attitudes about self, others, social groups, institutions, and society; developing a conscience, values, and morality; learning masculine or feminine social roles; achieving independence/autonomy |
| Adolescence/ages 13–18 | Continued development of independence and relationships with males and females; adjusting to one's physique; securing a job; adjusting to physiological changes |
| Early adulthood/ages 19–30 | Selecting a mate; starting a family; becoming a caregiver; achieving *social responsibility*, values, and morality; selecting an occupation |
| Middle age/ages 30–60 | Achieving occupational satisfaction; developing leisure activities; adjusting to physiological changes; assisting aging parents |
| Later maturity/ages >60 | Adapting to living arrangements and declining physical strength/health; adjusting to retirement and reduced income |

unconscious, seeks perfection, discerns right from wrong, and acts as the conscience.

To illustrate, imagine you are sitting in class and your belly begins to grumble and rumble with hunger. Your immediate instinct is to "go now, seek sustenance" (id). But, before you can stand up, you hear, "Dude, you can't just get up and leave right in the middle of the professor's lecture, but we may be able to leave early and go get three or four tacos and a couple of burrito supremes" (ego). Now, at this point, superego would be the cloaked voice from deep within that chimes in now and says (depending upon our individually developed conscience), "For crying out loud, you can wait until the end of class and then go to Taco Bell."

**Table 1.3 Freud's Stages of Psychosexual Development**

| Stage/Age | Characteristics |
|---|---|
| Oral stage/ages 0–1 | The mouth is the child's primary interaction with the world and derives pleasure from oral stimulation (e.g., sucking and tasting). If gratification is not achieved, fixation on oral stimulus is the result into adulthood (e.g., nail biting, thumb sucking, overeating, smoking) |
| Anal stage/ages 1–3 | The primary focus is on bowel control. Too much emphasis can result in excessive need for organization or order and cleanliness into adulthood, whereas too little emphasis can result in sloppiness and destructive behavior into adulthood |
| Phallic stage/ages 3–6 | The genitals are the child's primary focus. Children develop an attraction to the opposite sex parent. Freud termed this the *Oedipus complex* (boy's attraction to mother) and *Electra complex* (girl's attraction to father) |
| Latent stage/ages 6–11 | The primary focus is on the development of social skills, peer relationships, and values. The superego continues to develop while the id is suppressed |
| Genital stage/ages 11–18 | Physiological changes due to puberty, again create a focus on the genitals, and an interest in the opposite sex develops. Individual continues healthy development if progression through the stages has been successful to this point |

Eric Berne (1961), largely influenced by the work of Freud, is best known for his theory of personality development, transactional analysis, known as TA. According to TA, to understand personality we must analyze the interpersonal interactions. During a personal encounter, one individual will act toward the other in some fashion (*transactional stimulus*) and the other will respond in some manner (*transactional response*). TA holds that individuals take on one of three ego states: parent, adult, or child. In the parent ego state, individuals are either critical or nurturing, acting in a manner consistent with that of their parents. In the adult ego state, individuals act in a manner that illustrates self-discovered thinking and behavior. In the child ego state, individuals act as their true, unencumbered self for better (e.g., endearing) or worse (e.g., disobedient). TA also emphasizes the importance of attention in shaping our personalities and interactional patterns. Attention, or strokes, which can be nonexistent (i.e., no strokes, ignoring), negative (i.e., strokes that feel bad), or positive (i.e., strokes that feel good), impact our thoughts, feelings, and behaviors.

---

**EDDIE'S EGO STATE**

You are the middle school counselor meeting with a group of four seventh-grade males. The students were referred to you because of behavioral problems. Eddie, one of the group members, continued during the first group session to do just as the teacher described observing during class—he put others in the group down with hurtful and unsolicited remarks. Together, the school counselor and the other group members helped Eddie to explore his motivation for those behaviors. Eddie realized that this is how his father interacted with him. According to TA, what ego state is Eddie incorporating when he interacts with others?

---

## Moral and Spiritual Development

Moral and spiritual development theories seek to explain the development of attitudes and behaviors toward the self and others and the meaning and nature of our existence. Morality and spirituality are largely determined by cultural and societal norms and laws and form the foundation on ethical behavior (Matsumoto & Juang, 2016). Three theorists, Jean Piaget, Lawrence Kohlberg, and James Fowler, have made a lasting impact on our understanding of moral and spiritual development.

Jean Piaget (1932), most widely known for his theory of cognitive development, discussed in the next section, suggested that moral thinking develops from cognitive structure and social relationships. Piaget studied the moral development of children using exercises of judgment based on the goodness or evil of storybook characters. Piaget's theory of moral development involves two stages: heteronomy and autonomy. Piaget's stages, ages, and primary characteristics for each stage of moral development are described in Table 1.4.

Lawrence Kohlberg (1967, 1969), inspired by Piaget's work and agreeing with his contention that moral development is a reflection of cognitive

**Table 1.4 Piaget's Stages of Moral Development**

| Stage/Age | Characteristics |
|---|---|
| Heteronom/birth to ages 9 or 10 | Children do not understand rules or morality. Children at this stage depend on those in authority to reinforce or punish what is considered to be right (goodness) or wrong (evil) |
| Autonomy/ages 9 or 10+ | Children begin to understand behaviors of right and wrong and allow principles and ideals to guide behavior, which are largely determined by that which was reinforced during the heteronomy stage and by their own maturing perspectives |

development, expanded on Piaget's stage model of moral development. Kohlberg contended that advanced cognitive functioning was necessary, but not sufficient for advanced moral reasoning.

Kohlberg proposed three sequential levels and six stages of moral reasoning, emphasizing the need to experience each stage—no stage skipping—in order to advance to the subsequent higher level of moral reasoning. The preconventional level (level one) consists of stage one, obedience and punishment (ages 5–7), and stage two, instrumental relativist. The conventional level (level two) consists of stage three, interpersonal relationships or good boy, nice girl orientation, and stage four, law and order. The postconventional level (level three) consists of stage five, social contract and individual rights, and stage six, universal principles. Kohlberg's levels, stages, ages, and characteristics at each stage of moral reasoning are illustrated in Table 1.5.

James Fowler (1981) is credited for his significant contributions toward our understanding of the development of faith. In his model, Fowler views faith not as a particular religion but in terms of one's relationship to the universe and to a transcendent power. Fowler's model, illustrated in Figure 1.2, is hierarchical, with each stage building upon the other. The stages of Fowler's model include undifferentiated, intuitive–projective, mythic–literal, synthetic–conventional, individuative–reflective, conjunctive, and universalizing. Although Fowler believes that all individuals have the capacity for faith development, he points out that not all individuals make it to all stages of the developmental model.

School counselors use a variety of clever strategies to teach morality, including character education activities, *bibliotherapy*, ethical case

**Table 1.5 Kohlberg's Levels and Stages of Moral Reasoning**

| Level | Stage (Age) | Characteristics |
|---|---|---|
| Level One, preconventional | Stage one (ages 5–7), obedience and punishment<br><br>Stage two (ages 8–12), instrumental relativist | Obey rules to avoid punishment/gain reward<br><br>Can break rule for reciprocal gain or to meet needs |
| Level Two, conventional | Stage three (ages 13–16), interpersonal relationships or good boy, nice girl<br><br>Stage four (ages >16), law and order | Actions intended to gain approval of others (be nice)<br><br>Actions intended to please society; follow rules and obey the law; respect authority |
| Level Three, postconventional | Stage five (adult), social contract and individual rights<br><br>Stage six (adult), universal principles | Rules important for an orderly society but should be decided on by all based on differing values/beliefs<br><br>Actions begin to reflect internalized morality even if conflicts with rules and the law |

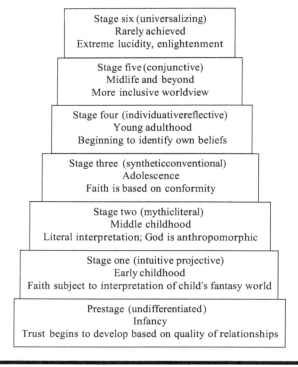

**Figure 1.2 Fowler's stages of faith development.**

discussions, current and past events, positive role models, and role plays to help students to understand the impact of our actions and inactions on others. School counselors promote moral development by encouraging reflection, reasoning, self-esteem, positive social interactions, peaceable schools, respect for others, and appreciation of differences.

## Cognitive Development and Learning Theories

Cognitive development theories seek to explain the development of thought, intelligence, and problem-solving abilities. The most prominent cognitive development theorists include Jean Piaget, B. F. Skinner, Albert Bandura, and Lev Vygotsky. Each of these theorists has contributed significantly to our understanding of learning, information processing, and the development of language and reasoning skills.

Considered to be educators, moreover theorists, Benjamin Bloom and Robert Marzano have also contributed significantly to our understanding of student learning. For this reason, their educational philosophies and instructional strategies widely used in today's educational environments are covered in this section as well.

Piaget (1963) proposed four stages of cognitive development: sensorimotor, preoperational, concrete operational, and formal operational. Piaget's stages encompass birth to adolescence, describing a child's cognitive evolution from egocentrism (i.e., orientation to self) to sociocentrism (i.e., orientation to society). Table 1.6 presents Piaget's stages and the thinking and reasoning characteristics associated with each stage of a child and adolescent's development.

As one of the most influential psychologists of the twentieth century, Skinner's behavioral concepts are still widely used by school counselors in the twenty-first century. This study guide highlights the most salient

### GRANDMA WILL BE BACK

Caryn is an elementary school student whose grandmother just passed away. Caryn is not upset, because she said that her grandmother will wake up and come back over to play with her soon. Which of Piaget's stages of cognitive development is representative of Caryn's thought processes in this situation?

**Table 1.6 Piaget's Stages of Cognitive Development**

| Stage/Age | Thinking and Reasoning Characteristics |
|---|---|
| Sensorimotor/ages birth to 2 | Primarily motor and reflex actions; sucking; grasping; kicking; understands the world through senses; speech is single utterances |
| Preoperational/ages 2–7 | Personifies objects; play important for exploring self and world; present orientation; little perception of time; judgment based on perceptions; egocentric thinking (self the center of all things); egocentric speech (speech said aloud, but to self) to more socialized speech (speech that depicts thought and language as separate functions) |
| Concrete operational/ages 7–12 | More organized, logical thought; good inductive logic (specific to general); sequencing and categorizing; problem solving; understands concept of reversibility; thinking less egocentric and more sociocentric (orientation toward society); socialized speech |
| Formal operational/ages >12 | Ability to understand abstract and hypothetical concepts; good deductive logic (general to specific); socialized speech and vocabulary continue to develop |

concepts of Skinner's behavior modification and learning theory. Skinner contended that our behavior is determined by environmental factors, dismissing the notion of individual freedom (Skinner, 1971; Nye, 1975).

Skinner introduced the process of *operant conditioning*, which is grounded in the belief that behavior is learned. Voluntary behaviors, also referred to as responses, that are followed by a reinforcing stimulus are repeated as the result of desirable consequences and behaviors that are followed by a punishing stimulus and are not repeated as the result of undesirable consequences. The behavior reinforcements or punishments may be *positive* (i.e., applied after the response) or *negative* (i.e., removed after the response). Skinner promoted the use of *schedules of reinforcement* (i.e., multiple reinforcements over time) to modify, or shape, behavior.

School counselors most often use schedules of reinforcement to either increase or decrease the frequency of specific child and adolescent behaviors. This often takes on the form of a *behavior contract* or classroom management strategies in which the school counselor identifies expected behaviors (responses) and consequences based on the removal or application of a punishment or reinforcement (stimulus).

By the way, behavioral counseling, discussed in Chapter 2, is the approach most often used with the growing number of children and adolescents diagnosed with attention-deficit/hyperactivity disorder (ADHD) during the school years. Also, a little piece of trivia to keep in mind: Skinner advocated for reinforcement over punishment unless repeated attempts using schedules of reinforcement were unsuccessful.

---

### DR. CANTHOLDEM

You are a school counselor and a teacher, Dr. Cantholdem, comes to you to ask for guidance. She is having a problem with attendance in her class. You ask her how she feels about exempting students from the final exam if they have perfect attendance. This is an example of:

a. Negative reinforcement
b. Positive reinforcement
c. Positive punishment
d. Negative punishment.

---

Vygotsky (1934, 1978) suggests a sociocultural approach to human development, or social development theory, which holds thought, language, and reasoning development as contextual and driven by culture, environment, and social interactions. Vygotsky's key premise is *cultural mediation* (i.e., interactions between a child and the cultural group as well as individuals of the culture that develops cognitive constructs such as speech patterns, written language, and symbolic knowledge), which occurs during the process of *internalization* (e.g., the acquisition of specific and shared knowledge of a culture).

Vygotsky believed that cognitive development occurs within the *zone of proximal development*, which he defines as the difference between what a child can do without assistance (i.e., actual development) and what a child can do with assistance (i.e., potential development). In the process of assisting the child in mastering new skills, the adult adjusts to the child's level of development, which Vygotsky termed *scaffolding. Guided participation* may be used, whereby students help each other (e.g., peer tutoring) under the general guidance of a teacher.

Bandura (1969, 1977), the originator of social learning theory, believed that behavior was the result of a reciprocal relationship between the world and the person, which he termed *reciprocal determinism*. Bandura postulated that individuals learn through *modeling* (i.e., imitating another), or *observational learning*, driven by a rationalization or perceived reward (e.g., motivation).

Benjamin Bloom (1953) introduced six classifications of learning levels, progressing from the most basic to the most complex in the following hierarchical order: knowledge, comprehension, application, analysis, synthesis, and evaluation. In 2001, Bloom's taxonomy was revised (Anderson & Krathwohl, 2001) to associate specific verbs that represent ways to promote the development of higher-level thinking skills at each level illustrated in Figure 1.3.

Robert Marzano introduced instructional strategies that have been empirically validated as approaches that build background knowledge and improve student achievement across grade levels (Marzano, 2004). These strategies are listed in Table 1.7.

The theory of learning style suggests that individuals have a propensity toward receiving and storing information using one or more of the three sensory modalities: visual (e.g., pictures, written word), kinesthetic (e.g., body movement, tactile), and auditory (e.g., spoken word). It is not only

**Figure 1.3 Bloom's taxonomy and associated verbs.**

**Table 1.7 Marzano's Nine Instructional Strategies**

| Instructional Strategy | Characteristics |
|---|---|
| Identifying similarities and differences | Breaking concepts into similar and dissimilar pieces; representing concepts in graphic forms (e.g., Venn diagrams, charts, analogies) |
| Summarizing and note taking | Conceptualizing presented material then restating it in one's own words; when note taking, more notes are better and allow time to process |
| Reinforcing effort and providing recognition | Show the connection between effort and achievement (e.g., share success stories, underscore student's achievements); recognize individual accomplishments and personalize recognitions |
| Homework and practice | Amount of homework should vary by grade level; homework schedule and setting should be consistent; homework provides practice; provide feedback on homework in a variety of ways |
| Nonlinguistic representations | Use with linguistic representations; nonlinguistic representations stimulate and increase brain activity; use tangible models, physical movement, and apply symbols to represent words/images |
| Cooperative learning | Positive impact on learning; vary group sizes and objectives |
| Setting objectives and providing feedback | Provides direction for learning; students should personalize goals; use contracts; feedback should be timely, specific, and rubric based |
| Generating and testing hypothesis | Use general rules to make a prediction; student should explain their predictions |

important for school counselors to gain an understanding of learning styles and teach to all learning styles but also for students to help identify their learning styles—students learning how to learn.

Generally speaking, individuals also have a preference for particular learning environments and times of day when conditions are optimal for learning. School counselors help students to understand their individual learning preferences and how those preferences can change over time. This self-knowledge enables students to adapt to a variety of teaching environments, selecting a preferred approach to the assigned task.

## *Motivation*

Theories of motivation are often categorized under three broad schools of thought: behavioral, cognitive, and humanistic. In addition to understanding the behavioral, cognitive, and humanistic interpretations of motivation, it is important for school counselors to be familiar with a fourth force—achievement motivation theory and its implications for motivating student learning.

Albert Bandura and B. F. Skinner are considered to be two of the most influential behavioral theorists on the topic of motivation. Both Bandura and Skinner were discussed earlier in some detail. To recap, Bandura holds modeling as having a considerable impact on student learning and motivation. In light of Bandura's suppositions, it is paramount that parents, educators, and important others in a student's life serve as positive role models, illustrating the significance of education and learning. Skinner's behavioral learning theory interprets motivation toward learning as a result of reinforcement. That is, motivation occurs on the basis of extrinsic rewards and punishments.

The cognitive view of motivation, significantly influenced by Jean Piaget, also discussed earlier in this chapter, contends that learning is motivated when dissonance occurs. That is, when students recognize a gap in their knowledge (e.g., inconsistency between newly presented information and what is already known), they experience cognitive discomfort, or disequilibrium, thus motivating them toward learning in order to regain balance, or equilibrium. Sort of like the impact that this study guide may be having on some of you—hey, just keeping it real.

Human *motivation* is believed to be intrinsic and extrinsic. Piaget emphasized the importance of intrinsic motivation. *Intrinsic motivation* rests within the individual, who derives pleasure from accomplishment of the task itself and an interest in the content. Intrinsic motivation is considered to be the highest level of self-regulated behavior, often centered in curiosity that drives individuals to pursue higher learning and new challenges, even when it is not required (Moldovan, 2014). For example, connecting life to academics often piques students' inquisitiveness and interest in learning, perhaps even unearthing a deeply buried and now unremitting passion that takes up permanent residence in the student.

*Extrinsic motivation* rests outside of the individual, driven by reward or threat of punishment. School counselors are careful not to overuse extrinsic rewards (e.g., money, treats, praise), which have often been associated with temporary change and may result in the reduction of intrinsic motivation. School counselors promote learning and holistic student development by applying intrinsic/extrinsic motivation tools and strategies. Research demonstrates that students who view academics as personally relevant to their future are generally more motivated (Moldovan, 2014).

Although research to date demonstrates the superiority of intrinsic motivation on student success, extrinsic rewards such as praise have been shown to produce lasting change when provided in an explicit manner. For example, there is sound research to support the positive impact of praise when the praise is specific and spontaneous and attributes accomplishment to effort. Under these conditions, praise has been found to increase motivation and self-esteem in students. Praise matters—even to adults!

### INTRINSIC MOTIVATION

You are a school counselor conducting a classroom guidance lesson in a second-grade classroom. One of the activities is to draw a picture. While the students are sharing their completed pictures, you are providing praise as a means of recognition. When you get to Ronnie's picture, which of the following statements would be considered specific praise that attributes success to effort?

- Ronnie, what a beautiful picture; you worked really hard!
- Ronnie, you finished your picture so quickly and it is very nice!
- Ronnie, your picture is so beautiful!
- Ronnie, your picture has such a beautiful, yellow, smiling sun, your hard work really shows!

Abraham Maslow's theory of motivation (1970), a humanistic view of motivation, may well be the single most influential theory of motivation to date. Maslow suggests that the most basic human needs must be met before an individual will actively seek out, or be motivated toward, higher levels of need. The simplicity of Maslow's brilliance is undeniable.

Maslow's hierarchy of needs consists of five levels and is illustrated in Figure 1.4. The most fundamental needs are portrayed at the bottom level, with progression up the hierarchy to the top level, which depicts an individual's need to reach his or her full potential. Maslow's levels in order from bottom to top include physiological needs, safety needs, social needs, esteem needs, and self-actualization. Maslow theorizes that a needs deprivation at any level can result in grave consequences. For example, an imbalance of physiological needs can obviously result in death. An imbalance at the safety level may result in a sense of insecurity that will interfere with motivation toward the next level of need. When social needs and/or esteem needs are not met, the intensity can be so overwhelming as to ignore more basic physiological and safety needs. In the absence of feelings of acceptance, intimacy, and belonging, individuals may experience extreme loneliness, anxiety, distress, crippling esteem issues, and feelings of inferiority, resulting in clinical depression, anorexia, and a number of other disorders.

We can understand, then, how the development of disorders at these levels prevents further progression on the hierarchy. We can understand, too, how death can be the ultimate result of imbalances at the higher levels when physiological and safety needs are disregarded. The journey to self-actualization, which might be viewed as meeting one's full potential, is an internally driven human development process. Needs at all the

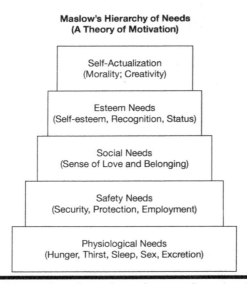

**Figure 1.4 Maslow's hierarchy of needs: a theory of motivation.**

levels must be mastered in order to achieve the uppermost level of self-actualization.

The implications of Maslow's work are clear with regard to student learning. As educators, we must help to ensure, through school and community collaboration, advocacy, counseling, and the promotion of safe and equitable environments, that a student's basic needs are met in order for the student to be available to learn and so that students are motivated to achieve to their full potential.

There are a multitude of family and community issues that may negatively impact a student's need for achievement and their development and functioning, such as abuse, neglect, poor peer relations, divorce, parenting styles, crime, homelessness, and poverty, to name a few. Chapter 2 focuses on counseling theories and school counseling prevention and intervention services delivered by school counselors to mitigate issues related to student development and well-being.

Lastly, achievement motivation theory (McClelland, 1961, 1985) is grounded in the belief that individuals are driven toward success, or avoidance of failure, which is influenced by varying levels of need for achievement and values. Once success is experienced, more success is desired, much like a snowball effect, resulting in self-sustaining desires toward continued achievement (while enhancing self-esteem).

We can understand how the environment in which a student lives and works can either positively or negatively impact a student's need for achievement. Although research is limited, the following areas for attention and training are promising for instilling achievement motivation (i.e., the need for achievement) in both students and adults (McClelland, 1961):

- Provide clear feedback on performance
- Accept responsibility for performance
- Establish realistic and achievable goals
- Provide opportunities whereby the individual can succeed.

## MOTIVATING JOHN

John is an academically average eighth-grade student who has not generally demonstrated evident motivation toward school and learning. John's parents encouraged him to enter his graphic design work in a school competition. John received first place among 100 entries. For the first time that John's parents can recall, John was excited about learning more about digital imagery and graphic design. According to achievement motivation theory, what would be John's parents' next best course of action if they wish to keep John motivated toward learning?

a. Celebrate with John.
b. Work with John's school counselor to get him enrolled in related elective courses for next year (high school) and supporting core courses.
c. Encourage John to enter city- and statewide competitions.
d. Do not get overly excited about John's accomplishment, which might set him up for future disappointment.
e. a, b, and c.
f. b and c.

# Chapter 1: Case Conceptualization Responses

# Ethical Standards and Legal Considerations

*The Same or Different?*
The correct response is "c." The school counselor is applying the ethical principle of justice, meeting the unique needs of each student in relation to individual differences.

## *Confidentiality*

*Order in the Court, Here Comes the Judge*
The school counselor is supported by Section A.2.i. of the ASCA *Ethical Standards for School Counselors* (2016a), when requesting that the court withdraw the requirement to divulge counseling session information without the consent of Donna, the 15-year-old minor client. Respecting the confidential nature of the school counselor and minor client relationship and the information disclosed by the student in counseling sessions adheres to a critical ethical principle—nonmaleficence. Should the judge order disclosure despite the school counselor's request, she should submit to the court order.

*Alliances*
Although school counselors are diligent toward establishing alliances and partnerships with parents and make it clear that they understand and respect parental rights, school counselors do not divulge the content of counseling sessions to parents. Instead, school counselors explain to parents the need for confidentiality in counseling sessions for establishing a trusting relationship with their children, reassuring parents that confidentiality will be breached if needed in order to protect the child or others. Also, sharing with parents that you encourage students during counseling sessions to talk to parents about the issues shared in order to promote family communications and to help students to identify and make use of their support systems.

## Harm to Self or Others

*Thoughts of Suicide*

Patrick's reason for suicidal intentions included his "family," which may indicate that his parent(s) are implicated. The school counselor should explore this area more deeply. If Patrick's parents are implicated, many, if not all, state guidelines would warrant a call to social services instead of a call to Patrick's parents. It would also be important to find out if Patrick was afraid to go home, in which case social services would likely come to the school before the end of the school day to talk with Patrick.

## Child Abuse and Neglect

*Charlie's World*

Since it appears that Charlie's mother knew the truth about what happened to Charlie even though the incident occurred at his father's home, CPS should have been contacted. The school counselor would be wise to directly ask Charlie if he told his mother that his father struck him. If Charlie had said "no" that he did not tell his mother, then asking the student what stopped him from sharing this important information with his mother would be important and could lead to additional critical information (e.g., perhaps both parents are striking the child). Or, perhaps, the child dislikes Dad and is not telling the truth in order to stay with Mom all the time? In either case, however, contacting CPS based on the existing information provided by the child is warranted and essential—err on the side of child safety. Another important piece of information here is that school counselors and school nurses do not have to see scars, bruises, or cuts in order to report suspected child abuse.

## Scope of Practice

*Moonlighting*

Section A.6.h. of the ASCA *Ethical Standards for School Counselors* (2016a) makes it clear that school counselors do not recruit or gain clients for their private practice to gain goods or services. School counselors "ensure there is not a conflict of interest in providing referral resources. School counselors do not refer or accept a referral to counsel a student from their school if they also work in private counseling practice."

# Informed Consent

*Sensitive Topics*

The nature of the school counselor's classroom guidance lesson, while seemingly not so sensitive based on the title of "Internet safety," contained graphic content that is considered to be sensitive in nature, particularly for some students, depending on past experiences. Although school counselors do not generally need to seek parental consent for classroom guidance lessons that are intended to be educational in nature and afforded to all students school-wide, the topic's content warranted informed consent from parents, or at the very least the opportunity for the parent to opt the student out of the classroom guidance lesson by providing information about the program and when it was to occur.

# Student Records and Counseling Case Notes

*When to Say No*

The school counselor's actions are appropriate.

# IDEA and 504 Plan

*The 504 Plan*

The school counselor's actions are appropriate and in compliance with the student's 504 plan—a legal document entitling the student to these *accommodations* as agreed upon by a 504 committee that included the parent/legal guardian. The school counselor would want to discuss their intended actions in advance of testing day, to ensure that the teacher and others involved in testing understand the process and testing arrangements for students with special needs. The school counselor should consult with the teacher to understand why the accommodations are not being followed in the classroom and to encourage either going back to the 504 committee if the teacher believes accommodations are no longer needed or to begin compliance immediately. Another point is to be made here: If a student is not being given the small group testing accommodation outlined in a 504 plan or IEP and is given this accommodation on the day of standardized testing, this could adversely impact the student's performance on the test. Nonetheless, the school counselor is acting in the best interest of the student by following the currently active and legally binding 504 plan.

# Human Development, Learning, and Motivation

## *Psychosocial Development*

### *Defiance*

Kelly is experiencing the developmental stage of adolescence, possibly struggling with identity crisis by resisting authority and questioning adults in an effort to explore and discover his individual self, thoughts, ideas, and behaviors. School counselors can help Kelly's parents to understand this sensitive developmental stage and encourage Kelly's self-development by providing answers to Kelly's questions, which helps to reassure Kelly's sense of self and self-worth. Planned family activities and meal times are great mediums for encouraging exploration of Kelly's own thoughts, ideas, and communications.

### *Eddie's Ego State*

According to TA, Eddie is acting in the parent ego state when he says hurtful things to others. Eddie has discovered during the group process that he is treating others in the same critical manner that his father treats him, while also realizing how he has internalized those influential communications.

## *Cognitive Development and Learning Theories*

### *Grandma Will Be Back*

Caryn is likely between the ages of 2 and 7 years old. According to Piaget's stages of cognitive development for this age, Piaget would consider Caryn to be in the preoperational stage of development since she views death as reversible.

### *Dr. Cantholdem*

The correct response is "a." The school counselor is attempting to apply negative reinforcement in Dr. Cantholdem's class, that is, removal (negative) of the final exam (stimulus) in an effort to increase attendance (desired behavior/response).

# Motivation

*Intrinsic Motivation*
The correct response is "d." The school counselor's praise is attached to a very specific part of the picture. The school counselor also makes it very clear to Ronnie that his success is due to his hard work or effort.

*Motivating John*
The correct response is "e." It is important to celebrate the accomplishments of others, particularly those of your children. According to achievement motivation theory, John's parents should continue to fuel this flame ignited in John by connecting work he enjoys to academics and working. Now is a good time to work with the school counselor to establish a high school academic plan that supports John's talent and interest (e.g., digital photography, graphic art, computer science, multimedia, and web technologies). Also, encouraging John to continue to showcase his talent and enter competitions, whether his workplaces or not, will provide John with additional opportunities to experience successes and to grow from valuable feedback and exposure to others' work.

# Chapter 1: Simulation

# Early Intervention

## Brief Case Description

You, the school counselor, are the chair of the elementary school's early intervention team. The team is meeting today with the parent (biological mother) of a fifth-grade student, Ernesto, who is failing multiple subjects. The teacher also reports a lack of motivation on the part of the student toward school and learning over the past few months. The teacher has not observed any issues socially, that is, the student appears to get along well with peers.

## Section A: Early Intervention

What information would be important to obtain at the beginning of the first meeting of the intervention team to help the committee to gain a greater understanding of Ernesto's case?
    (Select as many as you consider indicated in this section.)

| | |
|---|---|
| _____A—1. | Relationship with peers |
| _____A—2. | Interventions applied previously |
| _____A—3. | Academic history |
| _____A—4. | Psychological history |
| _____A—5. | Subject areas of struggle |
| _____A—6. | Amount of time spent watching television |
| _____A—7. | Interests and hobbies |
| _____A—8. | Information Ernesto has shared with teacher and parent |
| _____A—9. | Amount of time spent on the computer |
| _____A—10. | Recent changes in Ernesto's life |

## Section B: Early Intervention

After sharing a variety of information and gaining some insight into Ernesto's situation, the parent reveals that Ernesto has been crying at home for the past 2–3 months while doing his homework. When she asks him what is wrong, he says that the math is just too hard and he does not understand it. Ernesto's mother expressed her concern because, although Ernesto has experienced many transitions in his young life and struggled with schoolwork before, she has never seen him cry, which was why she was very happy about this academic intervention meeting at school. Which of the following questions might yield the most beneficial information at this time?

(Select as many as you consider indicated in this section.)

| _____B—1. | Has Ernesto reported feeling poorly lately? |
|---|---|
| _____B—2. | What else did Ernesto name as the reason for crying? |
| _____B—3. | What other behaviors have the teacher and parent noticed in the past 3 months? |
| _____B—4. | What has changed in the past 3 months? |
| _____B—5. | How is Ernesto's relationship with his father? |
| _____B—6. | Does Ernesto currently receive tutoring? |

## Section C: Early Intervention

Further communication during the intervention meeting reveals that Ernesto has a good relationship with his father, who has been deployed for the past year. Ernesto's father is very involved in Ernesto's life and, generally, is the parent who attends the school functions and helps in the classroom when he is not deployed. Ernesto has shared with his mother that he misses his father very much, although they write to each other often. At this point in the meeting, what would be the best course of action by the committee?

(Select as many as you consider indicated in this section.)

| _____C—1. | Have the teacher and parent talk alone |
| _____C—2. | Request the assistance of an administrator |
| _____C—3. | Develop an academic intervention plan |
| _____C—4. | Come up with rewards for Ernesto when he completes his classwork and homework |
| _____C—5. | Request that Ernesto join the school counseling small group for students with parents/guardians who are deployed |
| _____C—6. | Table the meeting until Ernesto's father can be present |

## Section D: Early Intervention

Over the next week, the teacher reports to the parent that Ernesto is beginning to push and yell at fellow students, and he gets angry very easily. The parent and teacher agree to send Ernesto to you for individual counseling sessions. During the first session, Ernesto becomes very emotional and shares that he overheard his mother telling his grandmother that she was planning to divorce his father when he returned to the States. Your most immediate courses of action with Ernesto should be:

(Select as many as you consider indicated in this section.)

| _____D—1. | Discuss divorce |
| _____D—2. | Discuss deployment |
| _____D—3. | Work on securing a support system |
| _____D—4. | Discuss involving his mother |
| _____D—5. | Discuss feelings |
| _____D—6. | Work on strategies for managing emotions |
| _____D—7. | Work on strategies for reducing stress |

## Section E: Early Intervention

Ernesto comes to your office first thing in the morning immediately after getting off the bus. He is shaking and crying. As you calm Ernesto and sit down to talk, he reveals that his mother has a boyfriend who has been touching him when mom is not around. He has been telling Ernesto that they are just "wrestling." He said that last night, mom's boyfriend came into his bedroom. Ernesto describes the sexual acts. He said he yelled for his mother, but she did not come into the room. What is the most essential course of action?

(Select ONLY ONE in this section.)

| _____E—1. | Ask questions to determine the mother's knowledge and involvement |
|---|---|
| _____E—2. | Contact the local police |
| _____E—3. | Call the mother |
| _____E—4. | Contact CPS |
| _____E—5. | Request that the school nurse examine Ernesto |
| _____E—6. | Make contact with the father |

## Section F: Early Intervention

Two weeks later, you receive a letter in the mail that says the case is "unfounded." The following week, Ernesto comes to your office, again, right off the bus, shaking and crying, saying that his mother's boyfriend did it again. Ernesto's mother shows up at your door with the principal while Ernesto is in your office. Ernesto's mother very calmly taps on your door and walks in. She said she is there to take Ernesto to a doctor's appointment and that he was not supposed to get on the bus this morning. You express your concern and ask Ernesto if he would like to tell his mother what he just told you. Crying, he nods his head and tells his mother. Calmly, she said, "Ernesto, you know this is a lie, and this is why the social services people dismissed it." What is the best course of action?

(Select as many as you consider indicated in this section.)

| _____F—1. | Call CPS |
|---|---|
| _____F—2. | Contact the local police department |
| _____F—3. | Make contact with the father |
| _____F—4. | Tell the mother that she cannot take Ernesto |
| _____F—5. | Call in the boyfriend and talk with all three (i.e., mother, boyfriend, and Ernesto) |
| _____F—6. | Be stern with Ernesto and ask him for the truth |

# Chapter 1: Simulation Answers

# Early Intervention

## *Brief Case Description*

You, the school counselor, are the chair of the elementary school's early intervention team. The team is meeting today with the parent (biological mother) of a fifth-grade student, Ernesto, who is failing multiple subjects. The teacher also reports a lack of motivation on the part of the student toward school and learning over the past few months. The teacher has not observed any issues socially, that is, the student appears to get along well with peers.

## *Section A: Early Intervention*

What information would be important to obtain at the beginning of the first meeting of the intervention team to help the committee to gain a greater understanding of Ernesto's case?

   (Select as many as you consider indicated in this section.)

| | |
|---|---|
| A—1. | Relationship with peers<br>No<br>Peer relations have already been addressed by the teacher sufficiently at this time. |
| A—2. | Interventions applied previously<br>Yes<br>Knowing what has been done in the past and what has or has not been effective is helpful toward understanding Ernesto's case better. It can also assist in identifying present and future interventions. |
| A—3. | Academic history<br>Yes<br>Gaining a better understanding of past and present academic functioning provides insight into academic change and patterns over time, specific subjects of challenge and strength, and the scope and magnitude of academic problems. |
| A—4. | Psychological history<br>Yes<br>It is a good idea to find out what psychological issues, if any, may be a contributing factor when conceptualizing the student's case. |

| A—5. | Subject areas of struggle<br>Yes<br>Difficulties across subject areas may be indicators of broader issues related to learning disabilities or other special needs (e.g., attention-deficit/hyperactivity disorder). Difficulty in isolated subjects may simply indicate an area of challenge that can be remediated with interventions such as additional study. |
|---|---|
| A—6. | Amount of time spent watching television<br>No<br>The student's struggles are not limited to home. This may be warranted later depending on other information shared. |
| A—7. | Interests and hobbies<br>No<br>This information would not be helpful, at this time, in gaining an insight into Ernesto's struggles. |
| A—8. | Information Ernesto has shared with teacher and parent<br>Yes<br>It is very important to hear what the student identifies as the struggle. |
| A—9. | Amount of time spent on the computer<br>No<br>The student's struggles are not limited to home. This may be warranted later depending on other information shared. |
| A—10. | Recent changes in Ernesto's life<br>Yes<br>This is particularly important considering the teacher's referral to the intervention team is based on changes in the student's academic-related behavior over the past few months. |

## Section B: Early Intervention

After sharing a variety of information and gaining some insight into Ernesto's situation, the parent reveals that Ernesto has been crying at home for the past 2–3 months while doing his homework. When she asks him what is wrong, he says that the math is just too hard and he does not understand it. Ernesto's mother expressed her concern because, although Ernesto has experienced many transitions in his young life and struggled with schoolwork before, she has never seen him cry, which was why she was very happy about this academic intervention meeting at school. Which of the following questions might yield the most beneficial information at this time?

(Select as many as you consider indicated in this section.)

| | |
|---|---|
| B—1. | Has Ernesto reported feeling poorly lately?<br><br>Yes<br><br>It is a good idea to rule out possible medical reasons for Ernesto's lack of motivation toward school and learning. |
| B—2. | What else did Ernesto name as the reason for crying?<br><br>Yes<br><br>Exploring the conversation between Ernesto and his mother may lead to more information about what is particularly related to the student's struggle. |
| B—3. | What other behaviors have the teacher and parent noticed in the past 3 months?<br><br>Yes<br><br>This is particularly important, since the teacher indicates the onset of the academic difficulties as beginning a few months ago. |
| B—4. | What has changed in the past 3 months?<br><br>Yes<br><br>It is important to fully explore this area, particularly since the teacher indicates the onset of the academic difficulties as beginning a few months ago. |
| B—5. | How is Ernesto's relationship with his father?<br><br>Yes<br><br>Exploring Ernesto's relationship with others in the family is important, particularly since his father has not been brought up as of yet, and there is much research on the correlation between family interpersonal relations and academic performance. |
| B—6. | Does Ernesto currently receive tutoring?<br><br>No<br><br>Asking about what interventions may have been successful or unsuccessful in the past is appropriate. However, it is not warranted to specifically target tutoring to elicit information that may provide insight into Ernesto's lack of motivation toward school and learning. |

## Section C: Early Intervention

Further communication during the intervention meeting reveals that Ernesto has a good relationship with his father, who has been deployed for the past year. Ernesto's father is very involved in Ernesto's life and, generally, is the parent who attends the school functions and helps in the classroom when he is not deployed. Ernesto has shared with his mother that he misses his father very much, although they write to each other often. At this point in the meeting, what would be the best course of action by the committee?

(Select as many as you consider indicated in this section.)

| | |
|---|---|
| C—1. | Have the teacher and parent talk alone<br>No<br>This is a committee meeting where the parent and teacher are encouraged to talk openly with the committee so that a plan of action can be created with the team's input in the best interest of the student.<br>If the parent and teacher wish to talk after the meeting, this is encouraged. |
| C—2. | Request the assistance of an administrator<br>No<br>Administrators hire licensed professionals, whom they appoint to interdisciplinary intervention teams to make good informed decisions about the educational needs of students in their absence and, often, outside of their area expertise (e.g., school counselor, school psychologist, nurse). |
| C—3. | Develop an academic intervention plan<br>Yes<br>Now is a good time to establish an intervention plan based on current information. The plan will have progress review dates and be redesigned if it is not being effective or if new information is presented and new developments occur. |
| C—4. | Come up with rewards for Ernesto when he completes his classwork and homework<br>No<br>Ernesto's academic struggles require more than rewards for work completion. A comprehensive action plan with multiple strategies is warranted. Also, extrinsic motivation has been linked to reducing intrinsic motivation and must be used sparingly and carefully and not in the absence of more concrete, research-supported, individualized academic supports. |

| C—5. | Request that Ernesto join the school counseling small group for students with parents/guardians who are deployed<br><br>Yes<br><br>In addition to an academic intervention plan, Ernesto has clearly indicated a need for involvement in small group counseling with other students who experience issues related to parent deployment. |
|---|---|
| C—6. | Table the meeting until Ernesto's father can be present<br><br>No<br><br>School counselors and other educators meet students' needs in the presence and/or absence of parents. Although parental permission and informed consent are required in some circumstances, this is not the case here. |

## Section D: Early Intervention

Over the next week, the teacher reports to the parent that Ernesto is beginning to push and yell at fellow students, and he gets angry very easily. The parent and teacher agree to send Ernesto to you for individual counseling sessions. During the first session, Ernesto becomes very emotional and shares that he overheard his mother telling his grandmother that she was planning to divorce his father when he returned to the States. Your most immediate courses of action with Ernesto should be:

   (Select as many as you consider indicated in this section.)

| D—1. | Discuss divorce<br><br>No<br><br>There is no substantial evidence to support the notion that Ernesto's parents are divorcing. Also, if a school counselor wants to meet with elementary students to discuss parental divorce, parental permission is warranted. This is not to say that the counselor should not listen and validate Ernesto's concern about his belief. |
|---|---|
| D—2. | Discuss deployment<br><br>No<br><br>This is not the topic Ernesto has indicated. Not warranted at this time. |
| D—3. | Work on securing a support system<br><br>Yes<br><br>It is important to help Ernesto to identify important others, particularly adults that he can talk to about what he overheard and his beliefs. |

| D—4. | Discuss involving his mother<br>Yes<br>It is important to help Ernesto to understand the importance of involving his mother, who can talk to him about what he overheard her say to his grandmother. |
|---|---|
| D—5. | Discuss feelings<br>Yes<br>Allow Ernesto to express his thoughts and emotions, and offer validation. |
| D—6. | Work on strategies for managing emotions<br>Yes<br>Helping Ernesto to express his emotions appropriately and to develop an understanding that he does not have to be a puppet to his emotions is an important life skill. |
| D—7. | Work on strategies for reducing stress<br>Yes<br>Helping Ernesto to understand what he is feeling and to teach him strategies for managing the stress he is experiencing. |

## Section E: Early Intervention

Ernesto comes to your office first thing in the morning immediately after getting off the bus. He is shaking and crying. As you calm Ernesto and sit down to talk, he reveals that his mother has a boyfriend who has been touching him when mom is not around. He has been telling Ernesto that they are just "wrestling." He said that last night, mom's boyfriend came into his bedroom. Ernesto describes the sexual acts. He said he yelled for his mother, but she did not come into the room. What is the most essential course of action?

(Select ONLY ONE in this section.)

| E—1. | Ask questions to determine the mother's knowledge and involvement<br>No<br>At this time, it is in the best interest of Ernesto to assume the mother had knowledge of the incident and seek immediate safety for Ernesto. |
|---|---|

| E—2. | Contact the local police<br>No<br>The local police will likely request that you contact CPS, or they will contact CPS. |
|---|---|
| E—3. | Call the mother<br>No<br>The mother may be involved. |
| E—4. | Contact CPS<br>Yes<br>You are suspecting child abuse. Although the suspected sexual abuse is not by a family member, a family member (i.e., the mother) may be involved. The best course of action to protect Ernesto is to call CPS, and they can assess the mother's involvement. |
| E—5. | Request that the school nurse examine Ernesto<br>No<br>This can be humiliating for a child or adolescent (even adults), particularly when care is not taken in the manner in which this may be accomplished. You can report suspected abuse without personally seeing any physical signs or in the absence of physical signs. |
| E—6. | Make contact with father<br>No<br>The father is deployed. Contact CPS. |

## Section F: Early Intervention

Two weeks later, you receive a letter in the mail that says the case is "unfounded." The following week, Ernesto comes to your office, again, right off the bus, shaking and crying, saying that his mother's boyfriend did it again. Ernesto's mother shows up at your door with the principal while Ernesto is in your office. Ernesto's mother very calmly taps on your door and walks in. She said she is there to take Ernesto to a doctor's appointment and that he was not supposed to get on the bus this morning. You express your concern and ask Ernesto if he would like to tell his mother what he just told you. Crying, he nods his head and tells his mother. Calmly, she said, "Ernesto, you know this is a lie, and this is why the social services people dismissed it." What is the best course of action?

(Select as many as you consider indicated in this section.)

| F—1. | Call CPS<br>Yes<br>Again, call CPS with an additional report. |
|------|------------------------------------------------------------------------------|
| F—2. | Contact the local police department<br>No<br>The mother has every legal right at this point to take Ernesto unless she is intoxicated. If so, you may contact the police so that the student is not put in harm's way (e.g., driving under the influence). Police involvement may be warranted, too, if the parent is behaving in a manner that is disruptive in the school. |
| F—3. | Make contact with the father<br>No<br>The father is deployed. The mother, too, is custodial parent and, so, can pick up her child for a doctor's appointment. |
| F—4. | Tell the mother that she cannot take Ernesto<br>No<br>The mother has a legal right to take Ernesto under the current circumstances. |
| F—5. | Call in the boyfriend and talk with all three (i.e., mother, boyfriend, and Ernesto)<br>No<br>Do not involve the boyfriend, who has no legal rights in the case of Ernesto and is the alleged perpetrator. |
| F—6. | Be stern with Ernesto and ask him for the truth<br>No<br>Assume Ernesto is giving you the truth. |

# Chapter 1: Guided Reflection

Identify key events, people, associations, trends, and movements, and discuss their significance in the history of the school counseling profession.

Describe and support the importance of CACREP and CAEP for a school counselor education program.

Explain the purpose of ASCA with regard to the school counseling profession.

Examine and summarize key components of the ASCA National Model and the ASCA *Mindsets and Behaviors for Student Success*.

Identify the dual roles of the school counselor. Then, summarize the functions inherent in each role.

List critical ethical and legal considerations associated with each construct:

Confidentiality

Confidentiality of counseling-related electronic communication

Harm to self or others

Child abuse and neglect

Scope of practice

Informed consent

Student records and counseling case notes

IDEA and Section 504

Homelessness

Research

Dual relationships

Supervision

Match the following theorists to one of the primary categories of human development. It is possible that one theorist could be connected to multiple theories. Then, identify key constructs of the theory, and summarize the theory.

Jean Piaget

Erik Erikson

Lev Vygotsky

James Fowler

Sigmund Freud

Lawrence Kohlberg

B. F. Skinner

Robert Havighurst

Albert Bandura

Support the use of Benjamin Bloom's taxonomy in school counseling.

Discuss the importance of Robert Marzano's nine instructional strategies, and explain how an understanding of those strategies would be useful in school counseling.

Compare and contrast intrinsic and extrinsic motivation. Consider the pros and cons.

Relate the premise of achievement theory by creating a case scenario to illustrate the concept.

Convince me of the importance of Abraham Maslow's theory in relation to student learning and motivation. Use one example in your persuasive argument.

## Chapter 2

# Counseling, Prevention, and Intervention

School counselors engage in prevention and intervention activities for a variety of purposes related to personal, social, emotional, academic, and career development. Prevention is aimed at stopping a problem or problematic situation before it starts, while intervention, also referred to as responsive services, occurs post-onset or after a particular problem or disorder has been identified.

### ASCA's Position on Prevention and Intervention of Behaviors That Place Students at Risk

Professional school counselors work in a leadership role with student service professionals, administrators, faculty, school staff, community members, and parents/guardians to provide comprehensive school counseling programs. Such comprehensive programs identify and prevent behaviors that place students at risk of not completing school and/or harming self or others by promoting student resilience and success.

*Position statement adopted 1989–1990;*
*revised 1993, 1999, 2004, 2011*

Primary prevention, secondary prevention, and tertiary prevention are used by school counselors to promote a safe and preventative school climate that meets the developmental needs of students (Goodman-Scott, Betters-Bubon, & Donohue, 2015). *Primary prevention* focuses on programming for the entire student body using education to ward off any potentially at-risk behavior or problematic situations. *Secondary prevention* is aimed at mediating a specific behavior or problem identified as a potential threat for a specific population deemed at risk. *Tertiary prevention* targets a specific population to reduce or eliminate a problem or behavior that is already occurring. Later in this chapter, all three levels of prevention are illustrated as they relate to substance use, abuse, and addiction. The three levels of prevention are illustrated again in Chapter 7 in relation to consultation and collaboration.

School counselors embrace the proverb "an ounce of prevention is worth a pound of cure," providing students with primary and secondary prevention programs. The school counselor also provides resources and conducts workshops that spotlight at-risk behaviors and teach parents, teachers, and the community what to look for when identifying students who may be contemplating suicide or homicide or both and who are experiencing depression, severe anxiety, or other debilitating conditions.

However, we must be realistic about what we are dealing with here—complex human beings. So, no matter how diligent we are as school counselors, teachers, parents, administrators, and community members, we cannot always head off all problems before onset using primary prevention. For this reason, school counselors engage in tertiary prevention and intervention to meet the needs of students and families using a comprehensive school counseling program.

# Comprehensive School Counseling Programs

The ASCA National Model described in Chapter 1 is the only recognized national comprehensive developmental school counseling program (CDSCP) model that defines our profession. Some states have their own comprehensive, developmental models. Most of these are designed using ASCA's *National Model* as a framework, understanding that school divisions develop programs based on the varying needs of unique school communities.

CDSCPs provide developmentally appropriate prevention and intervention services that support the academic achievement mission of schools. The hallmark of a CDSCP is its focus on providing career, academic, social, and emotional development to all students in addition to support services for teachers, parents, administrators, and the community as an integral part of the educational system.

---

## ASCA's Position on Comprehensive School Counseling Programs

School counselors design and deliver comprehensive school counseling programs that promote student achievement. These programs are comprehensive in scope, preventive in design and developmental in nature. "The ASCA National Model: A Framework for School Counseling Programs" (ASCA, 2012) outlines the components of a comprehensive school counseling program. The ASCA National Model brings school counselors together with one vision and one voice, which creates unity and focus toward improving student achievement and supporting student development.

*Position statement adopted 1988;*
*revised 1993, 1997, 2005, 2012*

---

A meta-analysis of 150 studies revealed the effectiveness of school counseling interventions across all levels—elementary, middle, and high school. Research shows that school counseling interventions result in cognitive, behavioral, and affective improvements, as well as reductions in disciplinary referrals and enhanced problem-solving abilities (Whiston, Tai, Rahardja, & Eder, 2011). To continue to ride the waves of positive student outcomes, careful consideration is given to the varied needs of each developmental level, school community, and student population.

For example, limited language development at the elementary level calls for the use of more expressive approaches such as *play therapy* to communicate and promote interaction between the student and school counselor. I recall one of the first times I engaged in play therapy as a new elementary school counselor. I was sitting with the most adorable first grader on the planet. She was beaming with pure delight while describing her adventures while collecting fireflies in a jar. As we squeezed and manipulated Play-Doh, I could hear the faint sounds of jubilant students singing "We Are the World" completely out of harmony in preparation for that evening's PTA performance. At that wondrous moment in time, I recall thinking, "and they pay me to do this—suckers!" A few days later, the monsoon hit Utopia! Sparing you the details, I recall thinking (I may have even said it under what little breath I had at that moment), "they don't pay me enough to do this—I'm such a stooge." As my esteemed colleagues can attest, this is the ebb and flow of professional school counseling that we would not trade for a million chocolate frogs.

The majority of the elementary school counselor's time is spent facilitating small groups and classroom guidance lessons and responding to students' immediate needs with responsive services strategies and programming. The elementary student's developmental level limits the application of counseling models to the more active approaches that do not require significant insight and self-awareness. Behavioral approaches are more often used at the elementary level while students are beginning to learn appropriate behavioral patterns and expectations.

Students at the elementary level are more closely supervised and sheltered because of their developmental level. Therefore, parents tend to be more actively involved during the elementary school years. Parents are a fabulous resource, and it is important to find ways to involve parents and make them feel welcomed in the classrooms and schools. The school counselor and parent have a major commonality—you both want the best for their children!

During the middle school years, students demonstrate much-improved language skills, heightened individuality, and begin to engage in unparalleled self-exploration. The need to begin high school academic preparation and postsecondary career decision making increases the demand for individual counseling and individual student planning during the middle school years.

Behavioral approaches that may have dominated the school counselor's repertoire at the elementary level are now supplemented with counseling approaches that make use of the more sophisticated cognitive processes developmentally available during adolescence. Adolescents, too, have the relational ability to connect with the counselor and engage in self-analysis.

Counseling approaches that encourage responsible living, decision making, and problem solving, and the impact of cognitions on emotions and behavior, are particularly beneficial for the adolescent.

Developmentally, elementary and middle school students are in two very different places. Although elementary students generally aim to please, treating us like a celebrity when spotted in the grocery store, the adolescent will make every effort to avoid us, as though we are merely annoying creatures to be endured. So, keep in mind the adolescent's unique developmental issues and personal characteristics when selecting counseling approaches and techniques. Developmental constructs are important guides but not all-inclusive, so also be careful not to use a cookie-cutter approach based on widely recognized developmental characteristics and milestones of adolescence.

Parent involvement at the middle school level is often dependent upon the adolescent. Developmentally, adolescents are seeking independence from parents, and may, therefore, be apprehensive about having their parent in the school. Nonetheless, school counselors continue to encourage parents to engage in their adolescent's education both at home and at school, while negotiating responsibility and independence. There is an abundance of research linking parent involvement with improved academic achievement and attendance, as well as reduced dropout rates (Wright & Stegelin, 2002).

The high school counselor spends the majority of his or her time with high school students implementing responsive services and providing individual counseling and student planning. Their primary responsibilities include student scheduling, administration of assessments, providing career and college information, and addressing individual student concerns and assisting with the decision-making process, primarily as it relates to school and postsecondary opportunities.

Generally speaking, high school students will tend to view the school counselor as their friend and equal. Some will even attempt to call us by our first names. Keeping boundaries while maintaining an effective school counselor–high school student relationship can be a challenge, particularly for school counselors from a neighboring generation.

Assuming normal developmental levels, high school students are fully capable of understanding abstract concepts, analyzing, synthesizing, and relating. Advanced developmental levels allow school counselors to apply virtually any counseling approach appropriate to the school setting and fitting to the student and the presenting issue.

Parent involvement is generally low compared with the family's involvement at the elementary and middle school levels. Developmentally, high school students have established their independence, for the most part, and are making many of their own decisions. School counselors are called upon to continue to encourage parent involvement at the high school level because research connecting academic achievement to parent involvement pertains to the high school and college years as well as the earlier school years.

> **THE PARENTS DO NOT TRUST ME**
>
> A school counselor is in a professional development program at his school. A teacher sitting beside him is experiencing her first year at the elementary level. The teacher had just served 5 years at the high school level. The teacher is concerned because she is getting so many visits and calls from parents to help in the classroom. The teacher remarks to the school counselor that perhaps she has done something that has caused the parents not to trust her with their children or perhaps they believe because she came from the high school level that she will not be able to relate to the children. How might you respond to the teacher's concerns?

## Social/Emotional Development

One of the three broad developmental domains of a CDSCP and ASCA's *Mindsets and Behaviors for Student Success* (2014) is *social/emotional development*. School counselors help students to overcome social and emotional challenges so that they can focus on learning, and develop the fortitude for wellness needed to become contributing members of society.

School counselors work collaboratively with other professionals within and outside of the school system to provide optimal services that place the well-being of children first, supporting academic achievement within a climate of safety. School counselors may work with the *school psychologist*, *school social worker*, *school nurse*, special education teachers, resource teachers, and the 504 committee, early intervention team, and child study team to effectively meet the personal and social needs of students.

Collaboration with outside agencies is a growing trend in today's schools. School counselors often partner with community mental health agencies to provide optimal services to students and families. School counselors provide parents with information related to psychosocial development and community resources that include specialized counseling, psychological and psychiatric services, social services, child care services, and support groups.

School counselors implement interventions and consult with teachers and parents to provide strategies for implementation at home and in the classroom. School counselors assist students in identifying support systems to combat unhealthy levels of stress and reduce feelings of isolation. Section A.1.i. of the ASCA *Ethical Standards for School Counselors* (ASCA, 2016a) encourages school counselors to "consider the involvement of support networks, wraparound services and educational teams needed to best serve students."

School counselors, who partner with families, teachers, and community members, are better able to identify supports that strengthen protective factors and enhance resilience, empower students, and help students to discover unique personal strengths (Smith, Beck, Bernstein & Dashtguard, 2014). Developing students' resilience enables them to overcome threats to educational success and to successfully engage life's challenges. CDSCPs that include interventions that place responsibility for success within the student are educational, empowering, and help develop coping skills that can be accessed into adulthood (Gilchrist-Banks, 2009).

School counselors assist teachers, parents, and administrators in developing behavioral interventions and classroom management strategies. School counselors do not engage in the discipline of students (ASCA, 2012b).

## ASCA's Position on Discipline

The school counselor has specialized training and skills in promoting appropriate student behavior and preventing disruptive student behavior. The school counselor is not a disciplinarian but should be a resource for school person- nel as they develop individual and schoolwide discipline procedures. The school counselor collaborates with school personnel and other stakeholders to establish policies encouraging appropriate behavior and maintaining safe schools where effective teaching and learning can take place.

*Position statement adopted 1989;*
*revised 1993, 1999, 2001, 2007, 2013*

Emotional and social needs at the elementary level primarily revolve around the child's egocentric nature, adjustment to the concept of attending school, establishing a sound academic, personal–social, and career development foundation, and the transition to middle childhood. Personal–social programming is generally focused on cooperation, taking turns, making friends, sharing, character education, caring, resolving conflict, and helping.

Classroom guidance and small groups are the primary methods of program delivery at the elementary level. These systems-focused delivery methods are ideal during middle childhood for promoting positive peer interactions and healthy personal development in a social context that is facilitated and closely monitored by the school counselor. The development of social skills and positive peer relationships during middle childhood enhances the likelihood of positive peer relationships during adolescence, which has been identified as critical to prosocial personality development (Schellenberg, 2000).

The middle school years are a time of intense emotions, associated with rapid physical changes and identity development. The adolescent is no longer a child, but not yet an adult, growing away from the family of origin and into the family of man. Peer relationships are extremely influential in the development of identity, self-esteem, and positive interpersonal functioning.

Responsive to this challenging developmental stage, the social/emotional domain of a comprehensive school counseling program focuses programming on the transition to middle school from elementary school and from middle school to high school. The school counseling program also focuses on dealing with bullying, problem solving, responsible decision making, conflict resolution, interpersonal relationships, violence, and Internet safety. In addition, school counselors may include prevention programming that addresses teen dating, teen pregnancy, sexually transmitted disease, and chemical dependency.

Social/emotional programming and counseling services for high school students are a continuation of the areas of focus noted for middle school students. High school counselors continue to focus on a successful transition into high school from middle school, providing services for incoming freshmen to promote social and emotional well-being and academic success in high school, while also continuing to prepare students for postsecondary careers and higher education.

## *Transitioning*

I do not know who said that "the one constant in our lives is change," but I totally agree with this shrewd proclamation that has earned just attention. Change does not sit idle, and the vast number of personal, social, emotional, and physical changes that take place, particularly in the lives of children and adolescents, can be anxiety producing. Even welcomed change upsets homeostasis with some discomfort experienced until balance is regained. Helping clients to change, and to work through change, is the heart of counseling.

Transitioning has been conceptualized in a variety of ways. There are, however, three common points of agreement among specialists in transitioning theory: (1) transition involves grieving the loss of the old and finding stability in the new, (2) successful transition is generally achieved when approached intentionally and with an understanding of the associated challenges, and (3) transition is more likely to succeed when a support system is in place to aid in overcoming challenges and adjusting to the new (Turner, 2007).

Transitions, both welcome and unwelcome, have been identified as a source of stress for children and adolescents—and adults. Developing the attitudes and skills for successful transitioning at an early age is critical to continued health and well-being during periods of change. Framing the experience of transition and change (and life!), largely dependent upon our attitudes, helps students to understand that they control the processes, perceptions, and outcomes of their internal experiences and are victims or victors of their attitudes.

School counselors begin by helping students to normalize change, that is, to view change as a necessary characteristic of life. School counselors offer programming that identifies and helps students to develop competencies essential to successful transitions and continued growth, including support systems, self-care, stress management, decision making, problem solving, communication, and positive attitude.

School counseling programs and activities include transition programs for those students who are entering middle school and high school. Successful transitioning programs invite parent participation, identify social supports, highlight positive aspects of the new setting, underscore increased freedoms and choices associated with maturity, and address the following frequently identified fears of students entering secondary school (Akos, 2002):

- Bullying by older students
- New rules
- Forgetting locker combinations
- Switching classes
- Getting lost
- Not succeeding academically
- Increased responsibility
- Understanding class scheduling.

Transition programs also provide students with faculty, staff, and school information as well as a map of the school. This information helps students to identify who to go to and how to get there. New students are often reluctant to ask for help. For this reason, during the transition program, school counselors present the concept of asking for help as a positive and strength-building characteristic, reminding students that even the greatest of men recognize and confess that "no man is an island" (Donne, n.d.). School counselors collaborate with students to establish and coordinate peer-mentoring programs for transfer students. This is particularly helpful for students who are coming from culturally and linguistically different backgrounds.

School counselors encourage parents and teachers to look for maladaptive behaviors or behaviors that are not typical for the student (personal, emotional, social, and academic), which may be indicators of unsuccessful transitioning. School counselors work individually with students who are experiencing transition difficulties using a variety of counseling techniques and approaches, as well as family and peer support systems.

## *Dropout*

Dropping out of school is a national issue of growing concern. The most recent data from the National Center for Educational Statistics (2014) reports 6.5 percent dropout rates nationally among all races between the ages of 16 and 24. It is essential that school counselors continue to act as programming pit bulls to reclaim the graduation march for our nation's challenged students—pomp and circumstance for all!

---

### *ASCA's Position on Identification, Prevention, and Intervention of Behaviors that are Harmful and Place Students At Risk*

Professional school counselors work in a leadership role with student service professionals, administrators, faculty, school staff, community members, and parents/guardians to provide comprehensive school counseling programs. Such comprehensive programs identify and prevent behaviors that place students at risk of not completing school and/or harming self or others by promoting student resilience and success.

*Position statement adopted 1989–1990; revised 1993, 1999, 2004, 2011*

---

Understanding that which places students at risk for not completing school is the first step to developing creative programming to keep our students in school. Risk factors for dropping out of school are as diverse as the student body and become more salient predictors of dropout when found in combination. These risk factors, which can be indicators of dropout as early as elementary school, include: poor academic performance; negative attitude toward school; hostile school climate; low parental involvement; low student involvement; behavioral problems; poor teacher–student relationships; low socioeconomic status; educational levels of parents; and personal, social, and emotional issues (Dupere, Leventhal, Dion, Crosnoe, Archambault, & Janosz 2015; Parr & Bonitz, 2015).

Addressing these barriers to graduation requires programming that (1) supports student and parent involvement in the school, (2) enhances academic performance with supplemental knowledge and skill building, (3) promotes a more encouraging school climate, (4) links school to career and life after high school, (5) provides counseling services to mediate life's challenges, (6) mediates behavioral problems, (7) addresses the needs of students in financially challenged homes, and (8) focuses on early intervention. Programming to keep students in school requires collaboration within and outside of the school with a variety of stakeholders.

## School Violence and Bullying

Safe and prosocial school environments are essential to academic success and student safety. However, aggressive student interactions often permeate a school's culture and create hostile learning environments that stifle the academic productivity and student success and well-being (Schellenberg, 2000).

### ASCA's Position on Bullying, Harassment, and Violence Prevention

School counselors recognize the need for all students to attend school in a safe, orderly and caring environment. To promote this type of environment, comprehensive school counseling programs include anti-bullying/harassment and violence-prevention programs along with comprehensive conflict-resolution programs to foster a positive school climate.

*Position statement adopted 1994, 2000;*
*revised 2005, 2011*

School counselors seek to implement programs that foster a positive climate and optimal learning environment that respects diversity to promote peaceable schools. One of the most widely used programs for promoting peaceable schools and prosocial behavior is character education. *Character education* involves, first and foremost, modeling. Educators impact the character development of their students through their own attitudes, expectations, and behaviors. Character education involves shaping students' thoughts, emotions, and behaviors to reflect core values of caring citizenship, which may include characteristics such as responsibility, respect, courage, perseverance, fairness, trust, integrity, honesty, cooperation, empathy, and acceptance.

## *ASCA's Position on Character Education*

School counselors endorse and actively support character education programs and include them in the implementation of a comprehensive school counseling program. The school counselor also promotes the infusion of character education in the school curriculum by encouraging the participation of the entire school community.

*Position statement adopted 1998,*
*revised 2005, 2011, 2016*

Another approach that is often used in the schools is *conflict resolution*. ASCA calls for conflict resolution as a vital component of a comprehensive school counseling program. *Peer mediation*, a *peer-helping* program, is a form of conflict resolution that aids students in resolving interpersonal problems peacefully. Peer mediation provides students with a safe place in which to resolve interpersonal conflict peacefully while learning effective communication, conflict resolution, problem solving, appreciation for differences, and relationship building.

Research identifies a link between peer mediation programs and school-wide violence reduction. Development of students' knowledge and skills related to conflict resolution strategies and prosocial behaviors paves the way for increased academic performance (Bell, Coleman, Anderson, Whelan, & Wilder, 2000; Schellenberg, Parks-Savage, & Rehfuss, 2007).

*Bullying*, too, often unresponsive to peer mediation and conflict resolution, poses a threat to school safety and to the physical and emotional well-being of others. Let us not forget that bullies are victims unto themselves, requiring intervention that disrupts the self-destructive path and aids in charting a new course. School counselors work with teachers, administrators, and law enforcement officers to create programs that deliver strong anti-bullying messages using everyday examples of the paralyzing atrocities and life-destroying impacts of bullying on named children and adolescents. School counselors educate students regarding bullying and teach strategies for dealing with bullies, such as maintaining a confident demeanor; making eye contact; delivering strong, assertive, nonemotional communication to the bully; and confiding in a trusted adult.

## Internet Safety and Cyberbullying

Advances in technology have heightened the need for school counselors to educate students on issues related to Internet safety, *cyberbullying*, and the misuse of cell phones. Programming pertaining to Internet and cell phone use and safety should include Internet addictions, illegal download of music and clipart, stalking and luring, access to illicit drugs, inappropriate chat rooms, invasion of privacy, safeguarding personal information, identity theft, sexting (e.g., the texting/transmission of sexually explicit language/materials), the misuse of personal pictures and information, and school policies pertaining to cyberbullying during and outside of school (Huda et al., 2017).

ASCA recommends that school counselors provide educators and parents with guidelines for the appropriate use of technology by students, for example, keeping computers (with electronic filtering and monitoring programs installed) in a room that is clearly visible by responsible adults; strongly encouraging children and teens to discuss anything they have received that is confusing, uncomfortable, or frightening; and establishing rules for the use of available technologies. It is also critical that parents understand and relay to their children and adolescents the ethical and legal implications of electronic actions and words and the dangers of giving out personal information and photographs in an electronic environment that is often permanent and irreversible.

## ASCA's Position on Student Safety and the Use of Technology

School counselors encourage students to take advantage of the wealth of opportunities, information and resources available through the use of technology. However, because students are vulnerable to the risks that technology poses, school counselors, in collaboration with families, educators and law enforcement officials, alert students to these risks and encourage them to use technology responsibly.

*Position statement adopted 2000, 2006, 2012*

School counselors include cyberbullying as an essential topic when discussing Internet safety. Cyberbullying is a disturbing issue of grave concern with dire consequences. Cyberbullies often perceive themselves to be invisible, believing that their communications are anonymous and that they will not be caught or held responsible in cyberspace. Ensuring that students understand that all communications online can be tracked may have an immediate and lasting impact on the reduction of cyberbullying.

It is also important that students understand that cyberbullying is considered by law to be a criminal offense when it (1) involves repeated or

### WILL I GO TO JAIL?

Steven, a high school junior, comes to you very upset because he was angry with his best friend. He said that he sent a nude picture of his girlfriend to his best friend's cell phone because his friend did not believe that Steven's girlfriend would ever take her clothes off for him. His friend spread the picture around, and someone loaded it to Facebook, and his girlfriend's parents called the police. He said, "It isn't fair—she said I could take the picture, and I'm not the one who spread the picture around school or created the Facebook page." The student asks, "Will I go to jail"? If you were Steven's school counselor, how would you respond?

excessive harassment with or without threats, (2) encourages/suggests suicide, (3) threatens harm to a person or their property, (4) threatens to commit a crime, and/or (5) posts private information in a public forum (Willard, 2006). Actions that can be taken by students to defend against cyberbullies include blocking the sender, avoiding chat rooms where the attacks occur, saving and sharing communications with parents and law enforcement, and changing passwords/accounts. As with other types of bullying, students are encouraged to send a strong, assertive, nonemotional message to the bully along with the action to be taken if the messages continue.

## Substance Use, Abuse, Addiction

*Addiction* can be categorized as process addiction and substance addiction (Capuzzi & Stauffer, 2015). Process addiction refers to behavioral patterns, and addictions may include gambling, shopping, Internet, eating, working, sex, and more. Substance addiction refers to the ingestion of mood-altering substances such as alcohol and other drugs, including anabolic steroids, which is a growing concern in high school athletic circles.

There are many models, noted below, that attempt to explain the etiology of addiction (Capuzzi & Stauffer, 2015). Psychological models look to cognitive-behavioral, psychodynamic, personality, and learning models for explanations for addiction. Sociocultural models suggest that addiction is contextual and related to the social and cultural environment in which an individual interacts. The disease model holds the addiction as an incurable and progressive disease that one is powerless over, once contracted. Family models suggest that addiction is behaviorally based, with the family interactions and members reinforcing the addiction, either consciously or unconsciously. Biological models hold genetics and our brain's chemical reactions as creating predispositions to addiction. Finally, the moral model holds addiction as a matter of personal choice. As a society, we have now, for the most part, rejected the idea that addiction is the result of immorality. At the present time, our society and our public health system embraces a multi-causal model that considers the interaction of the individual, environment, and the substance or process.

School counselors do not treat addiction. In the school setting, the primary emphasis is on understanding addiction, identifying and referring students who may be suffering from addiction, and providing primary prevention, secondary prevention, and tertiary prevention programming described earlier in this chapter and illustrated below. School counselors develop primary prevention programs to prevent drug use. School counselors also coordinate existing nationally recognized campaigns such as Just Say No and Drug Abuse Resistance Education (DARE) programs within the schools. To date, there is no significant research to support the effectiveness of the Just Say No and DARE programs (Birkeland, Murphy-Graham, & Weiss, 2005).

Founded in 1983, the DARE program is the most widely used drug prevention program in our schools today. The DARE program's mission is to provide students with skills and education to live drug and violence free. The program is focused on abstinence from drug use and is generally delivered by law enforcement officers during the school day with a curriculum that is sequentially designed for grades K–12. The program now offers community-based programs as well to promote parent involvement and to provide after-school activities and support for families.

The Just Say No to drugs campaign was championed by then First Lady Nancy Reagan in the 1980s in response to the War on Drugs movement. This primary prevention program, grounded in the prevention efforts of the National Institutes of Health, enlists the support of other nationally recognized organizations such as the Girl Scouts of America and the Kiwanis Club. The program is intended to educate and inoculate students on the negative impact of drug use and to provide students with skills for resisting peer pressure and drug experimentation.

School counselors collaborate with local police officers, community agencies, and other school personnel (e.g., school nurses, coaches, and school psychologists) to implement a variety of primary prevention strategies aimed at promoting healthy and drug-free lives. Primary prevention may also include parent and teacher education aimed at recognizing the signs and symptoms of addiction and resources for treatment. In-home drug testing is fast becoming a commonly practiced strategy in the homes of our families, aiding parents in early identification of *substance use* and *substance abuse*.

School counselors also implement secondary prevention strategies that target students who may be at risk for substance use, abuse, and addiction. School counselors are in an ideal position to identify students who are already demonstrating negative attitudes and risky behaviors. Like in-home drug testing, in-school drug testing is a growing strategy in today's schools, resulting in early treatment for students who test positive. There are legal considerations, including parental consent, and schools will need community support before implementing drug-screening strategies. Secondary prevention programs may include small groups on topics related to living responsibly, health and *wellness*, the effects of drug consumption, healthy choices, and Internet addiction.

Recognizing the signs and symptoms of addiction is essential to tertiary prevention, which involves identifying students who are already ingesting chemical substances and are displaying behavior patterns associated with process addiction. Signs and symptoms of addiction include neglecting responsibilities, increased tolerance, preoccupation with the substance or behavior, engaging in risky behaviors such as stealing and driving under the influence, changes in levels of social interaction or a change of friends, abandonment of hobbies and activities that used to be enjoyable, mood swings, paranoia, irritability, interference with daily functioning (e.g., sleep, diet, hygiene), and a general change in what was considered typical behavior for the individual.

## THE BEST FOOTBALL PLAYERS

You are the high school counselor at Crossroads High School. The physical education (PE) teacher has asked you to meet with a group of six male students on the football team because he overheard them chatting about giving anabolic steroids a try, to build muscles and be the best football players on the team. The PE teacher said he already spoke to the parents of the students, who are in agreement with the students meeting with the school counselor. How should you proceed, and is this an example of primary, secondary, or tertiary prevention?

Once identified, school counselors work with parents and community agencies to secure appropriate counseling services for the student and family. Some schools now have student assistance counselors, discussed in Chapter 1, who collaborate with community agencies to help students with substance abuse and other addictive behaviors.

## *Divorce*

Divorce is a growing trend in our society. Over one million children and adolescents are affected by parental divorce each year in the United

States, where the divorce rate is the highest in the world (Cohen & Weitzman, 2016).

Generally speaking, research suggests that children of divorce adjust well if divorce is accompanied by amiable parental interactions, quality parenting, and reassurance of continued contact after separation and divorce and if the divorce does not substantially impact lifestyle (e.g., finances, discipline, transitions). Other characteristics that are linked to positive adjustment after divorce include level of resiliency and preexisting personal assets (discussed in greater detail in the "Strengths-Based Counseling" section of this chapter). Age and gender, too, are associated with the level of adjustment for children of divorce; however, the link is largely contextual.

On the other hand, compared with children and adolescents from intact healthy functioning families, children of divorce often demonstrate a variety of issues (Cohen & Weitzman, 2016; Schaan & Vogele, 2016). These issues include:

- Sadness and depression
- Anxiety and fear
- Rejection
- Anger
- Insecurity
- Drug and alcohol use
- Misbehavior
- Feelings of grief and loss
- Poor academic performance
- Interpersonal problems
- School dropout.

The issues listed above can last well into adulthood. School counselors help children and adolescents to adjust to divorce with a variety of interventions that build protective factors and resilience and allow students to express and work through emotions, share experiences, resolve self-blame, and accept divorce. Small group counseling for children of divorce provides mutual support and allows students to normalize divorce (Corey, 2015). Also, encouraging students to engage in positive school and community activities and build relationships with trusted adults outside of the home helps to build protective factors. School counselors assist parents by providing community resources, including family counseling services, and the research noted above depicts the factors that have been associated with positive adjustment for children of divorce.

## *Parenting Style*

Parenting is not instinctual but requires specific knowledge and skills to raise a well-adjusted adult and contributing member of society. Parenting style has a profound impact on child and adolescent development.

The four widely recognized parenting styles with which school counselors are knowledgeable are authoritative (collaborative, respectful, reasonable consequences), authoritarian (strict, demanding, harsh punishment), permissive (lenient, indulgent), and uninvolved (detached, neglectful). The authoritative parenting style has been found to be the most beneficial to the child, resulting in a well-adjusted, confident, self-controlled, and academically successful child. Inconsistency, ignoring, and intimidation associated with the permissive, uninvolved, and authoritarian parenting styles, respectively, have been linked to the development of emotional, social, psychological, behavioral, and academic problems (Rothrauff, Cooney, & Shin An, 2009).

School counselors provide parental consulting and parenting workshops identifying different parenting styles and the impact of each on child development. Additionally, they help parents to realize that each sibling is an individual and so what works for one may not work for another. Also, they help parents to realize that a child's performance is not an indicator of self-worth and that mistakes are a part of learning and misbehavior as part of childhood, and they prepare the parent for the realities of parenthood. Parenting is a job—likely the most difficult and high-stress job on the planet.

# Career Development

Another of the three broad developmental domains of a CDSCP and ASCA's *Mindsets and Behaviors for Student Success* (2014) is *career development*. School counselors create activities that are career specific and developmentally appropriate.

There are three fundamental differences in career development at each level of K–12 education: career awareness, career exploration, and career planning. At the elementary level, school counselors promote career awareness. *Career awareness* activities might include exposing students to diverse occupations through career day/week guided activities. These activities might include speakers from a variety of occupations, displays of books in the library dedicated to diverse occupations, dressing like a favorite occupation, and mystery career games whereby students guess the occupation based on a description. Any activity that supports the student's curiosity and develops their sense of self and the world of work is appropriate at the elementary level.

*Career exploration* is the focus at the middle school level, while *career planning*, also referred to as career orientation or career preparation, is the focus at the high school level. Secondary school counselors engage students in career development activities that typically combine counseling, education, and the administration and interpretation of *career development inventories* (e.g., interests, skills, work values). This comprehensive approach to career development at the secondary level emphasizes the importance of going beyond trait and factor theory to understand the whole person and explore the many internal and external variables that influence a student's career decision making.

Delivering effective career development programs in the schools necessitates that the school counselors apply *career counseling* and *career development* theories and strategies; stay abreast of relevant legislation, research, trends, and resources; identify and administer interest, values, and skills inventories, and other career-related assessments; and understand the influences on career development.

## Influences on Career Decision Making

Helping students to identify personally satisfying career paths requires the application of career development theory, techniques, sound counseling practices, and information. School counselors blend career counseling, assessment, and career education to aid students in (1) understanding and preparing for transition into the world of work, (2) selecting a career path that will be meaningful and satisfying, and (3) ultimately becoming productive members of society.

School counselors engage in career counseling with a sound understanding of the diverse influences on career choice. School counselors aid students in understanding these influences to make informed decisions about their future. Career choice influences include, but are not limited to, family of origin, access to career information, socialization (beliefs and values), personality (including multiple intelligences, discussed in Chapter 6), parent's employment and educational status, early work experiences, economy, socioeconomic status, gender, ethnicity, and development level of functioning.

Research indicates that children begin to limit their career aspirations as early as first grade based on gender, ethnicity, race, and social class (Porfeli, Hartung, & Vondracek, 2008). For example, let us consider the impact of socialization on career choice with regard to gender. Traditionally, women have been guided toward occupations such as teacher, cosmetologist, and nurse, while males have been encouraged to pursue careers such as doctor, mechanic, and scientist.

For this reason, school counselors are now developing programs that educate students with regard to these historical trends, who may not realize how early social interactions have influenced their career decision making. As a result, males are beginning to pursue careers in nursing, accounting, and other occupations that have historically been occupied by females. Females are beginning to pursue careers in science and math and in occupations that have traditionally been dominated by males. There is now a growing trend toward promoting *nontraditional occupations* at every level of education.

In addition to promoting nontraditional career paths, school counselors promote a variety of postsecondary career paths. Our society has come to realize that college is not for everyone and that because a student does not want to attend college it does not mean that the student will not have a successful and fully satisfying career. Students' career choices may take them on a journey down one of five paths after high school: apprenticeship, college (2 or 4 years), technical/trade school, employment, or military service. Well, there is always couch-warming and channel surfing—oh, how parents will rejoice!

## *Career Development Theory and Career Counseling*

School counselors apply career development theory to help students make sense of their experiences and how those experiences influence career decision making. Career counseling grounded in sound theoretical principles offers education, insight, and alternatives during the process of career planning. Like counseling theories, there is a multitude of career development and career counseling theories, models, and approaches. This section highlights the major theories, theorists, and key constructs. Figure 2.1 is provided to promote the learning and recall of this material.

In general, there are two camps to consider when conceptualizing career development theories (Savickas, 2000): objectivist and constructivist. The objectivist school of thought may also be referred to as the traditional ideology, the positivistic approach, or the established theoretical view, depending on the company of career theorists you are keeping. The objectivist ideology, as the name implies, is an objective and measurable construct that matches individuals to occupations based on personality and occupational work environment. The constructivist school of thought, also known in certain circles as the emerging postmodern ideology, views career development as an ever-changing, contextual, and dynamic process that is driven by personal perceptions, interactions, and experiences. Figure 2.1 places the variety of career development theories in the respective categories to aid you in the cognitive organization of the many career theories.

*Objectivist Ideology*

The objectivist school of thought began with Frank Parsons. Parsons (1909), who became known as the father of vocational guidance, developed the trait and factor theory, which matches individual traits (e.g., aptitudes, interests, and abilities) to job factors. The trait and factor theory has dominated the field of career development since its inception some one hundred years ago.

John Holland's (1966, 1985) typology is an example of a trait and factor approach that is still widely used today. Holland's constructs include six broad occupational environments. RIASEC is the acronym used to represent Holland's workplace environments and points on his well-known hexagon. Holland theorizes that individual personalities can be matched to workplace environments for a "good occupational fit." For example, "R" represents the "Realistic" environment, which is the more physically demanding jobs working with tools, machines, automobiles, or animals. Realistic personality types are those who enjoy working with their hands and interacting with things versus people. "I" represents "Investigative" environments, requiring scientific and mathematical problem solving. Investigative personalities enjoy solving puzzles and researching for solutions. "A" or "Artistic" work environments prize creativity and match to personalities that enjoy free expression often inherent in occupations associated with music, art, theater, and writing.

**Career Development Theories: Objectivist and Constructivist Schools of Thought**

| Objectivist Ideology (Traditional) | Constructivist Ideology (Emerging Models) |
|---|---|
| Traits and work environment match<br>Administers assessment instruments<br>Objective reasoning/measurement are key | Socially constructed, dynamic, ever-changing<br>Individuals' interactions and experiences<br>Subjective intention and perspectives in context |

**\*Frank Parsons: Trait and Factor**
Match individual traits with job factors
Focus on 3-step process
Understanding self, diverse occupational
characteristics, and relationship of the two

**\*\*David Tiedeman: Career Construction**
Career choice based on evolving ego/self-
development – total cognitive development and
process of decision making
Focus on differentiation (evaluating self and self in
the world) and integration (find congruence in world
of work); parallels Erikson's stages of development

**John Holland: Typology**
Individuals express self through career
Focus on assigning individuals and work
environments into 6 categories

**Larry Cochran: Narrative**
Individual "tells story" about past and present
career experiences and related interactions;
counselor assists in creating future career story
Focus on phases, episodes, plots:
making meaning out of narrative; enacting the role;
and crystalizing a decision

**Donald Super: Life Span Life Space**
Career choice is an expression of self-concept
and changes across lifespan
Focus on 5 major life stages; career maturity;
career determinants; role of self-concept

**Mark Savickas: Narrative**
Individual "tells story" about past and present
career experiences and related interactions;
counselor assists in creating future career story
Focus on four areas:
vocational personality (uses Holland's typology);
developmental tasks (uses Super's life stages);
adaptability; life themes (mattering)

**Linda Gottfredson: Self-Creation**
Career choice based on social-psychological self,
created by heredity/biological factors
Focus on self-concept, cognitive maps,
circumscription and compromise

**Duane Brown: Values-Based**
Work values influence occupational choice
Focus on the importance of cultural values
and differences

**Anne Roe: Personality Development**
Career choice based on psychological needs
derived from parent–child relationships
Focus on relating six attitudes of parent–child
interactions to specific occupational groups

**Susan Phillips Developmental-Relational**
Career choice based on relationships with
important others – family, friends, teachers
Focus on two themes:
actions of others and self-directedness

**John Krumboltz: Social Learning**
Career choice based on cumulative interactions
and experiences with people and environment
Focus on behavior and cognitions; teaching
career decision-making techniques

*\*Parsons is considered father of vocational guidance*
*\*\*Tiedeman is considered the author/engineer of the first postmodern career theory*

**Figure 2.1  Career development theories: objectivist and constructivist schools
of thought.**

"S" represents the "Social" work environment that involves interaction with other individuals. Social environments often appeal to those who wish to help and provide human services to others, which may include teaching, counseling, and medical professions. "E" encompasses the "Enterprising" work environments that attract those who wish to lead, persuade, sell, and gain positions that provide a level of power. Enterprising individuals are drawn to politics, real estate, business, insurance, and the stock market. "C" is the "Conventional" work environment, which is often office positions. Individuals who enjoy organizing and performing tasks related to accounting, clerical, and record keeping are good fits for the conventional work setting. It is important to note that no one work environment fits one specific type, but involves a combination of types. Therefore, no one personality type fits squarely into one work environment. Instead, an individual's personality may be well-suited to multiple occupational environments. Holland created a career interest inventory known as the *self-directed search* (SDS) for this purpose (Holland, 1974). The SDS is discussed later in this chapter in the section titled "Assessment Instruments and Career Information Delivery Systems."

Donald Super's (1949, 1970, 1980) work in career development may be the most extensive of all the career development theorists, particularly pertaining to the career development of children and adolescents. Major constructs defining Super's lifespan–life space approach include life stages, career maturity, life-career rainbow, self-concept, and the archway of career determinants. Super's model of career development in children contends that, driven by curiosity, children explore the environment and interact with others, thereby maturing and developing self-control and time perspectives that lead to planful career decision making and implementation of self-concept. Super provides school counselors with a sound theoretical foundation from which to plan and implement developmentally appropriate career activities.

Linda Gottfredson (1981), too, emphasized self-concept in her theory of career development, which focused on childhood and adolescence. Gottfredson's theory of self-creation through interactions with the environment underscores the role of prestige, gender, and cognitive development in career decision making. Other theoretical constructs include circumscription (i.e., eliminating alternatives perceived as inappropriate due to societal expectations, prestige, gender) and compromise (i.e., giving up desired alternatives for those that are more accessible). Gottfredson's views magnify the need for school counselors to address historical trends in career development programming and to explore with students what might be perceived as self-imposed and obstacles to desired careers.

### I WANT TO BE A NURSE

You are the elementary school counselor delivering a career awareness classroom guidance lesson to first graders. You are holding up pictures of an array of people dressed in attire that depicts specific occupations. You hold up a card of a male who is dressed in a nursing uniform, and the class begins to guess the occupation. Some of the students shout out "doctor." You say, "Well, it could be that this person is a doctor, but the card said that he is a 'nurse.'" One of the male students says quietly, "I wanted to be a nurse, but my father said that I could not be a nurse because that was a job for girls." According to Gottfredson's theory, is this an example of compromise or circumscription?

Anne Roe (1957) provides school counselors with a career development theory that is grounded in personality development. Roe suggests that there are six parent attitudes toward, or away from, their children that impact a child's personality development. As such, Roe contends that a child's career choice is based on psychological needs derived from these early interactions. School counselors can help students to identify how early interactions with parents may have impacted their career development.

Broadening Roe's parent–child interactions, Susan Phillips postulates that career choices are grounded in interactions with all important others (Phillips, Christopher-Sisk, & Gravino, 2001). Phillips created categories of relational responding, suggesting that others impact our career choices either by inviting themselves into our career decision making (i.e., actions of others) or our inviting others into our career decision making (i.e., self-directedness). It is important to help students identify the strengths and weaknesses of career decision-making influences.

In this section, we have covered the key career theories from the objectivist school of thought. The theories that follow are grounded in the ideologies of the constructivist school of thought.

*Constructivist Ideology*

David Tiedeman (1961) has been credited for engineering the constructivist ideologies, earning himself the title of author, or engineer, of the first postmodern career theory. Tiedeman broke away from traditionalist thought, declaring that career decision making is far more personal and subjective because it is created from an individual's unique perceptions and *worldview*. Tiedeman's theory holds career decision making as an evolving process across developmental stages that parallel those of Erikson. Tiedeman's major constructs included differentiation (i.e., evaluating self and self in the world) and integration (i.e., finding congruence in the world of work). School counselors use Tiedeman's developmental perspectives and theory of the evolving ego, or self, to encourage students at specific developmental stages to consider how this unique self would fit into a variety of occupations.

Larry Cochran (1997), following Tiedeman's theory of the evolving self, provides school counselors with a constructivist approach that allows students to tell their story about career and related interactions. Together, the school counselor and student create a future career story that is a more ideal career narrative, which Cochran refers to as crystalizing a decision. Major theoretical constructs include phases, episodes, plots, narratives, characters, and enacting a role.

Mark Savickas (1997, 2000) also supports the narrative approach in career counseling, believing that clients construct their own career in unique, subjective, and complex ways. He departs a bit from Cochran in his integration of objectivist theories such as Super's life stages and Holland's typology. Savickas focuses on four areas in his theory of career development: vocational personality, developmental tasks, adaptability, and life themes. Savickas integrates Holland's typology in vocational personality and Super's life stages in his developmental tasks. Mattering is a key construct of Savickas' life themes, that is, Savickas explores life themes to determine that which matters to an individual. Mattering, according to Savickas, brings purpose and meaning to work, while adaptability melds the vocational self with an occupational role.

Duane Brown (2015) presents a theory that focuses on the impact of contextual variables on career decision making, satisfaction, and success. Brown's contextual variables include values, gender, family, socioeconomic status, and discrimination. Key constructs are Brown's values-based theoretical propositions.

John Krumboltz (1994) presents a career theory that is grounded in social learning theory. Krumboltz contends that career decisions are made based on an interaction of genetic endowment, learning experiences, environment (e.g., conditions and events), and task approach skills. School counselors who conceptualize career development using Krumboltz's theory will likely use traditional behavioral interventions in career counseling, such as role playing, simulation, reinforcement, and role modeling.

### TED'S FUTURE

You are a high school counselor meeting with Ted, who is uncertain about his career path. During your session you are focused on teaching Ted career decision-making strategies. Which of the career development theories discussed in this section are you implementing?

## *Career and College Transitions*

Although career development and college preparation has remained a primary function of the school counselor since the guidance movement, there has been a resurgence in popularity and support over the past two decades. Many school systems are hiring school counselors to specifically serve as career counselors at the high school level with an emphasis on preparing today's students for tomorrow's world of work.

Primary legislation pertaining to the school-to-work movement includes *Goals 2000 (1994): Educate America Act, National Skills Standards Act*, and the *School-to-Work Opportunities Act of 1994*. This legislation, simply stated, promotes the development of occupational standards and an integration of vocational and educational competencies so that students will be well prepared to enter and be successful in our multifaceted and technologically advanced workforce.

School counselors are creative in meeting school-to-work initiatives using a variety of strategies to integrate occupational information and college readiness activities using classroom guidance, small groups, and individual counseling/planning. Activities at the elementary level designed to introduce students to the world of work and college may include career day/week, videos, activity sheets, books, skits, fieldtrips, and tutoring at local colleges. Activities at the secondary level designed to assist students in exploring and planning for college and career include job shadowing and internships; college and career fairs; collaboration with college access professionals; financial aid workshops; scholarship application process and resources; athletic eligibility; college entrance exams, dates, and procedures; college essay writing; mock interviewing; college tour fieldtrips; and panel presentations by former high school students sharing career and college success stories.

---

## ASCA's Position on College Access Professionals

School counselors play a critical role in preparing all students for life-long learning and success in a global environment. To ensure students have opportunity to reach their full potential, school counselors collaborate with community-based organizations, including college access organizations and college access professionals, within the framework of a comprehensive school counseling program.

*Position statement adopted 2016*

---

Many high school counselors partner with community colleges to offer students the opportunity to take the American College Testing (ACT)-sponsored WorkKeys assessments. Students who pass the three WorkKeys assessments (i.e., applied mathematics, locating information, and reading for information) earn the national Career Readiness Certificate. The certification is gaining recognition as a viable screening, hiring, and promotion tool among prospective employers.

Students can now earn industry certifications in many high schools. Industry certifications are generally attached to specific elective courses. For example, students taking culinary arts may be eligible to take the National Occupational Competency Testing Institute (NOCTI) assessment, leading to certification in commercial foods. Students taking marketing classes may be eligible to take the National Retail Foundation (NRF) assessments, leading to certifications in customer service and sales. Industry certifications are also available in a variety of software packages and linked to business and technical education courses (see Chapter 8).

School counselors make students aware of WorkKeys and industry certifications during course scheduling. School counselors often go to the classrooms to promote the benefits of these voluntary certifications, which may include course credit and additional diploma seals. Certifications also demonstrate a commitment on the part of the student toward a specific occupation and earnestness about postsecondary employment and/or education.

School counselors adhere to the professional competencies and ethical issues involved in providing career counseling services to minors. School counselors are well advised to become familiar with the *Multicultural Career Counseling Minimal Competencies* (National Career Development Association [NCDA], 2009) provided by the NCDA, a division of ACA, as well as the ASCA Model's (2014) student competencies for the career development domain.

Section A.4.a. of the ASCA *Ethical Standards for School Counselors* (ASCA, 2016a) emphasizes the responsibilities of school counselors to work with all students to develop personalized academic and career goals that will lead to postsecondary opportunities of their choice. This may necessitate "collaboration with administrators, teachers, staff and decision makers to create a culture of postsecondary readiness." School counselors remain mindful during these collaborative communications of issues related to confidentiality and compliance with FERPA.

## ASCA's Position on Postsecondary Student Recruitment

School counselors encourage and promote positive and equitable reception of career and postsecondary educational institution recruiters into the school setting. These recruiters may include individuals from organizations such as but not limited to:

■ apprenticeship programs
■ athletic programs
■ branches of the military

- career and technical education institutions
- colleges and universities

*Position statement adopted 2004; revised 2009, 2015*

---

Most states have adopted requirements pertaining to the formal creation of an academic and career plan. The plan, generally, begins in middle school and is updated annually through the senior year of high school. The plan identifies the courses, specialized programs, and steps needed for the student to attain their desired career and postsecondary education and training.

---

## ASCA's Position on Academic and College/Career Planning

School counselors recognize that each student possesses unique interests, abilities and goals, which will lead to various future opportunities. Collaborating with students, families, educational staff and the community, the school counselor works to ensure all students develop an academic and career plan reflecting their interests, abilities and goals and includes rigorous, relevant coursework and experiences appropriate for the student.

*Position statement adopted 1994;*
*revised 2000, 2006, 2012, 2013*

---

Transitioning from school to work or to any of the other postsecondary career options presents unique challenges for young adults. In addition to the general transitioning support noted earlier in this chapter, school counselors can help students to make successful transitions to work and college by offering programming on topics such as workplace skills, job market trends, resume and cover letter writing, interviewing, application completion, networking, securing mentors, managing time and money, and balancing social and academic/work life.

## Assessment Instruments and Career Information Delivery Systems

School counselors will often begin the career development process with career-related inventories that assess students' interests, work values, and skills. Information gleaned from these assessments aids in the career planning process, providing both the counselor and student with valuable information from which to identify possible career paths and establish career goals. Like other student appraisal instruments, however, school counselors do not rely on the results of career assessment alone to guide students' career planning, because such instruments do not provide a comprehensive conceptualization of individual complexities. Additionally, some of these instruments lack cultural validity, that is, not all appraisal instruments consider worldviews that differ from the dominant culture.

The three most commonly used career inventories in the schools are the *SDS*, the *SII*, and the *KOIS*. All three inventories are based on John Holland's theory of typology and yield Holland codes. The SDS (Self-Directed Search; Holland, 1974) helps students to identify preferences for specific activities, matching personality type with six workplace environments using the three-letter Holland code. Information about the SDS is available at www.self-directed-search.com. The SII (Strong Interest Inventory; Strong & Campbell, 1974) provides information about careers that match students' codes and is available at www.cpp.com/products/strong/index.asp. The KOIS (Kuder, 1964) suggests occupations and college majors based on students' interest patterns. Information about the KOIS is available at www.kuder.com.

It is not necessary to memorize all the different types of assessment instruments and tests. It is important, however, for the purpose of school counseling exams, to know the difference between career assessments, personality assessments, intelligence tests, aptitude tests, and other types of assessments, inventories, and tests, as well as situations in which you might administer a particular type of assessment over another. Assessments are discussed in greater detail in Chapter 4.

Career development instruments are often included in career information delivery systems (CIDS), also referred to as *computer-assisted career guidance systems* (CACGS), to aid students in career planning. This Internet-based career development tool is available 24/7 to help students plan postsecondary careers and education.

There are many CIDS available for school counselor and student use. Some of the most widely used systems in school counseling include Choices Explorer, Choices Planner, SIGI Plus, DISCOVER, Bridges' Paws in Jobland, and Career Trek. In brief, Bridges' Paws in Jobland is used with elementary school students. Career Trek is primarily used for grades four through middle school. Choices Explorer is generally used with middle school students. Choices Planner is appropriate for career planning at the high school level. DISCOVER is used at both the middle and high school levels, and SIGI Plus is often used for college-bound juniors and seniors, students in 2- and 4-year colleges, and adult populations.

There is often some overlap with regard to the developmental level within which these systems are used. For example, although DISCOVER is often used at the middle school level, it may also be used by some school counselors at the high school level. For this reason, selection of one particular system over another is often a matter of school counselor and student preference.

Nationally recognized resources include the *Occupational Outlook Handbook* (OOH) and *Occupational Information Network* (O*NET). The OOH provides information about the job market and specific information about hundreds of occupations. O*NET is a national, interactive database that allows you to explore and search hundreds of occupations and to participate in assessment instruments to aid in career decision making.

Card sorts, too, are an informal and fun way to gain insight into possible occupational choices and can be used with students of all ages. School counselors provide students with a stack of cards. Each card identifies a specific occupation. The student begins placing cards in categories such as (1) "I might consider," (2) "I would not consider," and (3) "I am not sure if I would consider." Once the student sorts the stack of cards, the school counselor explores the student's reasons for the selections (e.g., education, training, characteristics of the job, salary).

## Academic Development

The final of the three broad developmental domains of a CDSCP and ASCA's *Mindsets and Behaviors for Student Success* (2014) is *academic development*. The domain of academic development has evolved over the past decade. Efforts to change the direction of school counseling have placed considerable emphasis on academic-focused practices in school counseling.

Topics related to academic development during the elementary school years emphasize paying attention, focusing, following directions, listening, completing classwork and homework, organization, goal setting, study and test-taking skills, and test anxiety. School counselors at the secondary level generally focus on goal setting, time management, study skills, test-taking skills, test anxiety, identifying learning styles, course selection, college admission success, post-high school athletic programs, financial aid for college, college testing requirements, and identification of academic programs at the postsecondary level. Academic development is covered in greater detail in Chapter 6.

# Delivery

School counselors take a balanced approach to service delivery that provides both direct and indirect student services to meet the immediate needs of students. The school counseling core curriculum, responsive services, and individual student planning make up the direct services delivery system. Indirect service delivery includes referrals, consultation, and collaboration, which are covered in Chapter 7.

## *School Counseling Core Curriculum*

The school counseling core curriculum includes both group activities —not to be confused with group counseling—and classroom guidance. Group activities as part of the core school counseling curriculum is also preventative in nature and may include peer helping programs, transitioning programs, and any number of group activities offered to the student body to aid in heading potential problematic issues off at the pass.

Classroom guidance is composed of structured, written lessons on specific topics that address student knowledge, skills, and attitudes using differentiated instructional strategies as discussed in Chapter 6. Classroom guidance is the mainstay of school counseling, deeply rooted in the teaching profession during the vocational guidance movement. Although classroom guidance is effective at all grade levels, an extensive review of school counseling interventions found classroom guidance to be more effective than individual and group counseling at the middle and high school levels (Whiston et al., 2011).

Classroom guidance lessons may be implemented to cover a single topic in one lesson or in multiple lessons as a unit over a specified period of time. At times, classroom guidance is conducted at the request of the classroom teacher to supplement specific course material and/or to address pressing sensitive issues or issues that have surfaced unique to the needs of their classroom and interfering with classroom instruction.

Classroom guidance lessons may be 20–90 minutes, depending on the developmental level of the students. Kindergarten and first grade lessons are likely to be about 20–25 minutes to accommodate the shorter attention spans of young children. Classroom guidance lessons for the upper elementary level students and middle school students (i.e., grades three–eight) are generally 30 minutes to an hour. Classroom guidance for high school students can take an entire class period, even 90-minute block schedules, as long as the teacher's schedule permits.

## Responsive Services

Responsive services are direct student services delivered by way of individual counseling, small group counseling, and/or crisis response. Responsive services meet students' pressing developmental or situational needs, including crises situations whereby school counseling aid students in working through emergency and/or disaster situations. Students in need of responsive services are generally self-identified or identified by way of a referral from a concerned teacher, parent or guardian, and/or school administrator.

Although research is limited on the effectiveness of responsive services, to date, interventions considered to be responsive services have been effective (Whiston et al., 2011). Method of responsive service delivery will depend on the number of students in need of intervention and the nature and scope of the expressed difficulty or crisis situation. School counselors determine the best method of program delivery on a case-by-case basis, which involves assessing the student's current functioning, the nature of the presenting issue (include assessing severity, frequency, and immediacy), and the student's desired level of privacy.

Responsive services are short-term. "Short-term" should be emphasized because school counseling alone is not in the best interest of children and adolescents experiencing severe, persistent, and progressive issues. Additionally, to provide ongoing counseling sessions with students whose issues cannot be sufficiently addressed within the scope of school counseling and within the expertise of the school counselor is in violation of professional ethical guidelines (see Chapter 1). School counselors can best meet the specific personal, social, and emotional needs of students meeting such criteria, using a collaborative model that involves referral services.

School counselors engage in individual counseling with students who are generally experiencing some kind of difficulty (e.g., family, peer relations, bullying, depression, chronic illness, pregnancy, abuse, truancy, substance abuse, crisis) that requires clinical intervention, information, community agency referral, problem solving, and/or decision making.

Individual counseling in the schools requires that the school counselor draw upon the counseling theories and techniques noted earlier in this section. School counselors understand the importance of establishing and maintaining effective counseling relationships throughout the counseling process, from goal setting to termination.

Group counseling is considered both educational and therapeutic. Psychoeducational groups are most widely used in the schools and are time limited, imparting information and offering opportunities for self-development. For example, psychoeducational groups in the school may include study skills, social skills, test-taking strategies, conflict resolution, organization, time management, problem solving, and anger management. Psychoeducational groups are also used to respond to the needs of students in crisis and/or experiencing difficult life situations such as the deployment of a military family member, death, adoption, divorce, and family transitions (e.g., leaving for college, moving, remarriage, and blending families).

## *ASCA's Position on Group Counseling*

Group counseling is vital in the delivery of the ASCA National Model to students as part of an effective comprehensive school counseling program supported by school administration and school districts.

*Position statement adopted 1989; revised 1993, 2002, 2008; reviewed 1999, 2008, 2014*

One of the most significant concerns with group work is that, despite the school counselor's vigilance in protecting the psychological and physical well-being of group participants during member interactions within the group, confidentiality cannot be guaranteed due to the nature of group work. For this reason, school counselors are just as vigilant in ensuring that parents and students understand the limits of confidentiality in group counseling.

Group counseling unites students with shared issues; promotes supportive relationships, healthy personal development, team problem solving, and cooperative behaviors; and provides opportunities for building communication, knowledge, and coping skills. The group experience may also enhance students' ability to empathize with others, to more fully understand the behavior of others, and to develop insight into themselves and into the unique and common aspects of their problems. For example, *dyadic counseling*, a form of group counseling that is popular in the schools, involves pairing two children in a relationship that revolves around play. In dyadic counseling, these children are paired based on opposing interpersonal orientations and guided by the school counselor toward more developmentally mature social interactions.

The Association for Specialists in Group Work (ASGW), a division of the ACA, as well as ASCA, promotes the value of group work in the school

---

**TEST-TAKING AND STUDY SKILLS**

You are a middle school counselor creating a school counseling intervention that targets special education students in eighth grade who are performing below average in mathematics. After careful data analysis, you have identified 20 students. You are creating small groups to work with these students on test-taking and study skills while also crosswalking the school counseling standards with mathematics standards as a part of the structured small group curriculum. Your intervention is considered to be

a. Small group method
b. Responsive services
c. a and b
d. None of the above

setting at the elementary, middle, and high school levels. The Council for Accreditation of Counseling and Related Education Programs (CACREP) and ASCA underscore the need for school counselors to develop professional competencies in group work. Section A.7.h. of the ASCA *Ethical Standards for School Counselors* (ASCA, 2016a) emphasizes this as well, calling for school counselors to "practice within their competence level and develop professional competence through training and supervision" in group work.

The process of group counseling coordination and facilitation for school counselors may look like this: (1) selecting/screening group members, (2) defining the group's purpose based on student need, (3) securing parent, teacher, and student permissions, (4) identifying meeting space, (5) determining length and number and days and times of meetings, (6) developing group activities, (7) facilitating group movement through the four stages of the process (i.e., initial stage, transition stage, working stage, and termination), (8) evaluating the effectiveness of the group intervention, and (9) providing for group follow-up. While planning small groups, the school counselor also considers whether or not the group will be an *open group* (i.e., new members are accepted after the group facilitation process in underway) or a *closed group* (i.e., new members are not accepted after the initial group meeting).

When screening, group members look for appropriate fit and aligned goals in relation to the group's purpose and focus. School counselors may elect to create small groups that are homogeneous (i.e., members share a variety of common characteristics), heterogeneous (i.e., diverse membership), or a combination of the two.

An example of a homogeneous group would be a self-esteem group for sixth-grade African American male students with similar backgrounds, experiencing low self-esteem. An example of a heterogeneous group would be a study skills group for grade three–six students, who may or may not be experiencing study skills issues, who represent a mix of race, gender, age, backgrounds, ethnicity—a microcosm of society. An example of group members that may be both heterogeneous and homogeneous is a social skills group at the elementary level may be homogeneous in that all members are having some issues with social skills and that they are all in third grade. However, the group may be heterogeneous in that the group is cross-cultural and includes both male and female students.

The number of group sessions and the length of the group sessions generally vary by school, often dependent upon teacher and administrator support because students will miss class time to take part in counseling. ASCA recommends that groups be brief and solution-focused. Generally speaking, small groups in the school setting meet once or twice a week for a total of four to eight sessions. Groups are typically 30 minutes in length for students at the elementary level and 40–60 minutes for students at the secondary level.

In addition to individual counseling and small group counseling, school counselors provide *crisis* management as part of responsive services. School counselors prepare for the unexpected, defining and documenting their roles during student, family, and school-wide crisis situations. School counselors provide information and conduct workshops for faculty addressing appropriate responses and intervention during a human crisis (e.g., accidental death, suicide and homicide, terrorism) and natural disaster (e.g., hurricane, earthquake, tornado).

## ASCA's Position on Crisis/Critical Incident Response in the Schools

School counselors recognize the impact a safe, orderly and caring environment has on student achievement and social/ emotional development. To promote this type of environment, comprehensive school counseling programs promote the inclusion of anti-bullying/harassment and violence-prevention programs, schoolwide positive behavior interventions and support, along with comprehensive conflict-resolution programs to foster a positive school climate.

*Position statement adopted 2000; revised 2007, 2016*

School divisions generally have established crisis-management plans mandated by state/local policy that clearly define the chain of command, school personnel roles, collaboration with community services (e.g., fire, police, medical), media and community responding guidelines, and follow-up procedures. Schools also have crisis-management teams that involve the school counselor. The school counselor provides guidance to the committee with regard to meeting the psychological and emotional needs of students, faculty, and parents during a crisis.

In times of crisis, school counselors occupy an important role that includes leadership, collaboration, and advocacy. School counselors' response to crisis can be summarized in three significant, systematic steps: (1) assess students' level of risk, (2) stabilize the situation with counseling intervention, and (3) follow-up to assess well-being and determine the need for further intervention (Kerr, 2016).

When evaluating level of risk, school counselors quickly assess for further threat (physical or psychological) and identify immediate security methods and coping mechanisms. During the process of crisis counseling, school counselors establish a trusting and positive therapeutic relationship in what is often a very limited amount of time. Using basic attending skills (e.g., active listening, *paraphrasing, summarizing*), school counselors foster a safe climate that invites students to identify and express emotions and thoughts and make sense of the traumatic experience. School counselors aid students in identifying copying strategies by exploring past coping successes and promising support systems. The very nature of crisis, and unexpected tragic event, calls for diligence on the part of the school counselor to identify students and members of the school community who may be grieving, traumatized, and experiencing suicide ideation. Suicide assessment is discussed in Chapter 4.

## ASCA's Position on Trauma Informed Practices

School counselors understand the impact adverse childhood experiences have on students' academic achievement and social/emotional development. School counselors strive to identify, support and promote the success of students who have experienced trauma through the implementation of a comprehensive, data-driven school counseling program.

*Position statement adopted 2016*

When working with grieving children and adolescents, it is important to understand (1) the child's developmental level, (2) the child's level of maturity, (3) the family's values, perceptions, and rituals related to death and burial, and (4) the factors surrounding the death (sudden, anticipated, relationship). School counselors also look for behaviors that are out of the ordinary and impact on academic, social, and emotional functioning. It is also important to be familiar with the stages of grieving (i.e., denial/isolation, anger, bargaining, depression, acceptance) to identify the difference between the normal grieving process and possible post-traumatic stress (Kubler-Ross & Kessler, 2014).

Often, parents consult with the school counselor about whether or not to allow their child to participate in a funeral. After fully explaining to a child what a funeral entails, allowing the child to attend based on his or her level of maturity and desire to attend provides the child with an understanding of a customary practice and the opportunity to grieve, say goodbye, and experience closure.

Post-crisis follow-up and the provision of resources are critical because stress reactions are not always immediate (Kerr, 2016). Follow-up is recommended at intervals (e.g., 1 month, 4 months, crisis anniversaries). Follow-up after a crisis will help to identify those students who are experiencing symptoms of post-traumatic stress, prolonged grief-loss reactions, and/or unresolved issues that require more intense counseling services.

## KYLEIGH'S MOTHER

Kyleigh, a second grader, is meeting with the school counselor due to the death of her mother, which occurred during a natural catastrophe 1 week ago. Kyleigh has been uncharacteristically quiet since the tragedy. What might be your primary focus during this first session with Kyleigh?

a. Reassuring Kyleigh that everything will be okay
b. Assisting Kyleigh in identifying and expressing her feelings appropriately
c. Sharing your own experience with death
d. Having Kyleigh recall the experience

## *Individual Student Planning*

Individual student planning entails the coordination of activities designed to aid students in establishing unique personal, academic, and career goals. Relating learning to students' career aspirations and providing students with opportunities for success and involvement in courses perceived as interesting have been linked to enhanced academic motivation, discussed in Chapter 1. Additionally, individual planning teaches students problem-solving skills that transfer to real life into adulthood (Whiston et al., 2011).

Individual student planning activities may be delivered on an individual basis or in a small group setting and may include immediate, short-term, and long-term planning. Individual student planning topics may include postsecondary educational and career planning, transitioning from school to postsecondary training/employment, test review and score interpretation, career-related assessment, success strategies, action plan development, promotion/retention, course selection, financial aid, and college/job application. During individual student planning, school counselors often discuss the student's performance progress by examining the average of all their grades, referred to as the student's grade point average (GPA). The importance of GPA in relation to college entrance and scholarships is also discussed.

# Theories and Techniques for the School Setting

There are hundreds of counseling and psychotherapy theories, models, and approaches (Wedding & Corsini, 2013). The theoretical approach(es) a school counselor elects to use will depend on the topic and goals of counseling, student characteristics (e.g., culture, developmental level), and the comfort level of the school counselor with a specific approach.

School counselors are well advised to consider the principle of reductionism when considering the complexities of a student's case, that is, the child is but one part of an intricate system of multiple interacting parts. Systems theory necessitates that school counselors consider students in the context of their relationship to other family members, because each part (individual) influences the whole (family). When there is evidence of a family dysfunction, school counselors strongly encourage parents to consider counseling by a licensed marriage and family therapist.

Deemed critical to the personal, social, and cognitive development of a healthy child, incorporating play therapy techniques into counseling services is another consideration for school counselors (Santrock, 2014). Play therapy may be directive, nondirective, or a combination of approaches. Play therapy has been associated with enhanced social skills, communication, attention, self-control, and self-esteem, as well as reduced levels of *aggression*, depression, anxiety, and *antisocial* and delinquent behaviors. Play therapy has also helped many children and adolescents to work through emotional, personal, and interpersonal issues associated with trauma (e.g., grief, abuse, disaster) and family issues (e.g., divorce, adoption, deployment). Play therapy also enhances cognitive and psychosocial functioning in students with disabilities and is used as a diagnostic tool to appraise psychosocial functioning (Kottman & Meany-Walen, 2015).

During play therapy, the school counselor systematically applies one or more of the theoretical approaches covered in this chapter. Toys are used and often represented in categories such as nurturing, aggressive, scary, expressive, and pretend. Some of the toys may fit into several categories, which are listed in the following paragraphs (Kottman & Meany-Walen, 2015). Nurturing toys help students to express and act out relationships and past, present, or future events. School counselors are careful to include dolls that represent different cultures for exploring differences and similarities. Nurturing toys may include the following:

- Dolls or people puppets (some with anatomical parts and removable clothing)
- Child-size furniture (e.g., kitchen sink, stove, refrigerator)
- Kitchenware (e.g., plates, pots, pans, cups)
- Doll clothing
- Blankets
- Stuffed animals.

Aggressive toys help children and adolescents to express feelings of anger appropriately or symbolically. School counselors often elect not to include aggressive toys in their office, preferring to avoid conveying a message that violence of any kind is acceptable. Aggressive toys may include:

- Punching bag
- Rubber mallet

■ Soft boxing gloves
■ Foam bats.

Scary toys help children and adolescents to express fear; to symbolically represent abusive, frightening, or past traumatic situations; and to practice ways in which they can keep themselves safe. Scary toys may include:

■ Plastic insects
■ Rubber snake
■ Plastic dinosaur, shark, rat, alligator
■ A variety of puppets and stuffed toys representative of scary animals (e.g., lion, gorilla, bear, wolf, tiger).

Toys that allow children to pretend, or fantasize, promote behavioral and emotional expression, communication, role exploration, and the reenactment of past and present life events. Students use these toys for metaphorical expression of ideas and experiences. These toys may include:

■ Clothing
■ Jewelry
■ Telephones and computers
■ Puppets and puppet stage
■ Blocks
■ Masks
■ Kits (e.g., doctor, geologist)
■ Hats
■ Magic wands
■ Fantasy creatures (e.g., unicorn, leprechaun, witch, troll, fairy princess)
■ Superheroes (e.g., Superman, Spider-Man, Batman)
■ Villains (e.g., Joker, Riddler, Dr. Doom).

Expressive toys help students to communicate difficult emotions through actions and symbols while finding the appropriate vocabulary for verbal expression of emotions. Expressive toys also help students gain a greater understanding of themselves, their environment, and the self in relation to others. Use of expressive toys with children has been linked to enhanced problem solving, self-confidence, creativity, self-control, and emotional and cognitive expression. Expressive toys include:

- Games
- Musical instruments
- Paint
- Play dough
- Blocks
- Books
- Sand and water trays
- Stuffed animals
- Beads
- Construction paper, tape, scissors, pencils, glue sticks, markers
- Yarn.

## PLAY THERAPY

Yasmin is an 8-year-old female student whose grandfather died suddenly last week. Yasmin's teacher reports that Yasmin is very quiet and withdrawn. Also, her classwork is not completed, which is not typical for Yasmin. The parent and teacher have asked the school counselor to meet with Yasmin. What toys might be particularly helpful to Yasmin at this time?

a. Scary
b. Nurturing
c. Expressive
d. Aggressive
e. Pretend

The sections that follow will cover nine of the most widely used theories and associated techniques for counseling children and adolescents in the schools. For ease of learning and recall, each theory will be summarized in a chart that includes the following: theorist and philosophy, therapeutic relationship, key concepts and techniques, and multicultural responsiveness. The following theories are covered in this section:

- Adlerian
- Behavioral
- Cognitive behavioral

- Gestalt
- Person-centered (also called Rogerian and humanistic)
- Rational emotive behavior therapy (REBT)
- Reality
- Solution-focused brief counseling (SFBC)
- Strengths-based.

## Adlerian

Developed by Alfred Adler (1925), Adlerian counseling, also referred to as individual psychology, is defined by its encouraging, goal-driven approaches that focus on immediate behavioral change (Table 2.1). School counselors with Adlerian orientations often rely on play therapy methods to induce communication, interaction, and problem solving while acting out appropriate responding and behavioral expectations (e.g., differentiating good behavior from bad behavior).

**Table 2.1 Adlerian Counseling**

| Theorist and philosophy | Alfred Adler's theoretical philosophy holds internalized feelings of inferiority/inadequacy and resulting frustration and discouragement as the source of difficulties and misbehavior. The underlying belief is that social interest/inherent human desire for success drives behavior. Counseling is directive. |
| --- | --- |
| Therapeutic relationship | School counselor is supporter, encourager, facilitator. |
| Key concepts/ techniques | Self-awareness is encouraged. Using structured questions, confrontation, and *play therapy*, students share perceptions of their lives, family history, and social interactions. Students identify unconstructive behaviors by catching oneself and more constructive alternatives. Together, goals are established toward creating a desired lifestyle that gives students a sense of equality. *Inferiority complex* (an advanced sense of inability and inequality in meeting life's demands) is a concept born out of Adler's work. |
| Multicultural responsiveness | Focus on individuality is not compatible with some cultures; individualized approach is culturally sensitive and accommodates the student's frame of reference/worldview; focus on the holistic approach and social responsibility is compatible with some cultures; focus on shared goal setting is culturally sensitive. |

## *Behavioral*

B. F. Skinner (1971) developed behavioral counseling. The defining characteristics of behavioral counseling (see Table 2.2) involve identifying behavioral influences and helping students to eliminate problematic behavior and learn more functional behaviors. School counselors who practice from a behavioral orientation view behavior as learned and therefore focus on teaching new behaviors.

Three approaches are generally associated with behavioral theory. The first, *stimulus–response*, which applies to involuntary behaviors illustrated by the classical experiments with Pavlov's dog, is not covered in this study guide. The stimulus–response method is rarely, if ever, applied in the school setting because educators are more concerned with voluntary behaviors. The other two approaches, *operant conditioning* and *social-cognitive*, are covered in this study guide and are often used by school counselors to bring about behavioral change.

**Table 2.2 Behavioral Counseling**

| Theorist and philosophy | B. F. Skinner's philosophy holds environmental factors responsible for creating dysfunctional behaviors. Behavior is learned; therefore, behaviors can be unlearned and modified. Counseling is directive. |
|---|---|
| Therapeutic relationship | Counselor is teacher, collaborator, advisor, facilitator, and reinforcer. |
| Key concepts/ techniques | Operant conditioning using a behavior modification technique that involves introducing a *stimulus* (activating event), applying (positive) or withdrawing (negative) a reinforcer or punisher to elicit a desire or undesired *consequence* that changes behavior (extinguishes undesired/promotes desired), particularly when using schedules of reinforcement (repeated over time). Other techniques used toward collaboratively established goals include *behavioral rehearsal* (practicing desired behavior), *assertiveness training* (reducing anxiety in appropriate emotional expression), and *contingency* or *behavioral contracts* (identifies target behavior and rewards/ punishments involved). |
| Multicultural responsiveness | Focus on behavior versus feelings is compatible with many cultures; focus on shared goal setting is culturally sensitive; focus on collaboration is empowering for many cultures; the definition of "appropriate" behavior may differ across cultures; passivity is revered in some cultures. |

Operant conditioning, more recently referred to as applied *behavioral analysis*, applies punishment or reward to specific behaviors to reduce or eliminate undesirable behaviors and to promote desirable behaviors. Operant conditioning is exemplified when the school counselor applies intrinsic and extrinsic rewards in an attempt to modify behavior. Chapter 1 describes the process of *behavior modification* using operant conditioning and the use of intrinsic and extrinsic rewards in greater detail.

The social-cognitive approach is grounded in the concept of *modeling*, that is, that students learn new behaviors by observing the behaviors of others. Observational learning is a powerful phenomenon that has a lasting impact on a student's behavior. School counselors apply the social-cognitive approach in peer-helping programs, mentor programs, and by exposing students to prominent current and historical figures and community participants during career week.

---

**LEARNING TO RESOLVE CONFLICT**

During a small group session, an elementary school counselor introduces the students to a conflict resolution strategy and names several historical figures who used conflict resolution to deflect war and improve lives. Members of the group take turns role-playing the strategy. This is referred to in behavioral counseling as

a. Teaching new behavior
b. Rehearsal
c. Social cognitive learning
d. All of the above

---

## Cognitive Behavioral

Aaron Beck (1979) developed cognitive behavioral counseling, also referred to as cognitive behavioral theory/therapy (CBT). Beck has been referred to in cerebral circles as the father of cognitive therapy. Beck developed a banquet of self-report measures related to the assessment of thoughts and feelings associated with depression, hopelessness, anxiety, and suicide. The defining characteristics of cognitive behavioral counseling (see Table 2.3) involve viewing counseling as learning and emphasizing the role of

**Table 2.3 Cognitive Behavioral Counseling**

| Theorist and philosophy | Aaron Beck's philosophy holds that one's thoughts determine one's feelings and behaviors. Dysfunction is a result of faulty cognitions. Directive approach to counseling. |
|---|---|
| Therapeutic relationship | Counselor is teacher and collaborator. |
| Key concepts/ techniques | *Cognitive restructuring* (replacing maladaptive thoughts with more functional thoughts) is a core technique in this psychoeducational model that is direct, goal-driven, and structured. Other techniques include identifying faulty thinking that leads to self-defeating behaviors; using *reframing* (alternative perceptions), cognitive modeling (self-talk), *Socratic dialogue* (how questioning); and *thought stopping* (yelling STOP or visualizing a STOP sign when the target thought surfaces) to change thought patterns. *Stress inoculation* (teaching cognitive and physical skills for heading off future stress and identifying automatic thoughts—triggers), *guided imagery* (mental picture—past, present, or future), and problem solving (step-by-step process) aid in reducing stress, relieving anxiety, and gaining alternative perceptions of events and direction. Homework is often assigned as a strategy to change and practice new thought processes and behaviors. |
| Multicultural responsiveness | Focus on thinking versus feelings is compatible with many cultures; focus on teaching and learning is better suited to cultures that hold a negative view of mental health counseling; challenging belief systems may not be compatible with some cultures. |

cognitions and internal dialogue (i.e., thinking) in bringing about emotional and behavioral responses (i.e., doing). In other words, our emotions and behaviors are slave to our thoughts. School counselors used this structured and time-sensitive approach to teach and practice new skills and behaviors, problem-solving approaches, and to promote self-control.

## *Gestalt*

Gestalt theory, developed by Fritz Perls (1969), focuses on here-and-now processes (i.e., thinking, perceiving, feeling, acting) of the whole (Table 2.4). The whole is considered more than the sum of its parts but

**Table 2.4 Gestalt Counseling**

| Theorist and philosophy | Fritz Perls' philosophy holds that disturbance may be due to any number of issues such as overintellectualizing (i.e., out of touch with emotions); unresolved or unfinished business; loss of contact with environment or overinvolved in the environment and loss of contact with self; pulled in too many directions; conflict between what we want to do and what we feel we should do. |
|---|---|
| Therapeutic relationship | The therapeutic relationship is considered critical to successful outcomes; counselor is caring, warm, accepting, and nonjudgmental. |
| Key concepts/ techniques | Counselor helps students to resolve current life problems; to meet needs to achieve homeostasis; to become more self-aware; to develop holistically (mind, body, emotions, sensations); and to identify, clarify, and take responsibility for behaviors using direct experiencing with techniques such as *psychodrama* (enacting conflicts), *empty chair* (enacting dialogues), *I Take Responsibility* (student completes sentences pertaining to an issue with "I take responsibility for it"), and *confrontation* (counselor challenges student's actions or words). |
| Multicultural responsiveness | Working within students' values and acceptance of uniqueness and diverse worldviews; appreciates cultural differences; focus on holistic development is incompatible with some cultures. |

the unification of those parts as observed by the relationship between those parts. School counselors help students to identify what they are doing and how they can change while gaining insight and learning to appreciate of self.

School counselors may rely on gestalt theory to assist students in crisis and to help students get in touch with their emotions through self-exploration and in-the-moment experiencing. School counselors might use gestalt techniques to aid students in resolving past problems so that they might move toward the future, to meet needs as they arise in order to regain a sense of balance, and to recognize that the future is impacted by our choices in the present.

## *Person-Centered*

Carl Rogers (1961, 1969) developed person-centered counseling, also referred to as humanistic and Rogerian counseling. The defining

**Table 2.5  Person-Centered (Humanistic) Counseling**

| Theorist and philosophy | Carl Rogers' philosophy holds that disturbance is due to incongruence between the real and ideal self. Nondirective approach to counseling. |
|---|---|
| Therapeutic relationship | Therapeutic relationship is considered essential to effective outcomes; counselor is nurturing, warm, and genuine and exhibits unconditional positive regard for the client. |
| Key concepts/ techniques | Counselor promotes self-exploration in a safe climate with *active listening*, reflecting feelings, *paraphrasing*, and clarifying so that client recognizes barriers to performance and growth and identifies new aspects of self. |
| Multicultural responsiveness | Working within students' values appreciates cultural differences; focus on feelings may not be compatible with some cultures; some cultural populations desire more activity. |

characteristics of person-centered counseling (see Table 2.5) involve viewing the student as having the capacity for growth and self-direction, as well as the potential to understand and resolve life problems.

School counselors may apply person-centered counseling to help students gain a greater understanding of self and daily experiences and work through brief, situational stress and anxiety. School counselors rely on the person-centered approach to establish positive, nurturing counselor–student relationships that allow for the incorporation of more directive counseling techniques and approaches.

## *Rational Emotive Behavior Therapy*

Ellis and Dryden (1997) developed rational emotive behavior therapy (REBT), born out of cognitive behavioral theory. The defining characteristics of REBT (see Table 2.6) involve encouraging clients to confront and gather evidence to dispute irrational beliefs and faulty assumptions that are believed to result in negative emotional and behavioral consequences.

School counselors use REBT to promote change and choice by helping students to better understand their thought processes and the relationship between those processes and emotional and behavioral responding. School counselors seek to ultimately empower students to apply REBT in daily living for self-regulation of emotions and behaviors.

**Table 2.6 Rational Emotive Behavior Therapy**

| Theorist and philosophy | Albert Ellis' cognitive-behavioral theoretical philosophy holds that faulty/irrational thinking is the cause of dysfunction. Directive approach to counseling. |
| --- | --- |
| Therapeutic relationship | Collaborative. |
| Key concepts/ techniques | Use the A–B–C Model to debunk irrational thinking. The process involves identifying the activating event and the faulty belief about the event that contributes to the consequence, or self-defeating behavior. Counselors challenge faulty assumptions using questioning and identify alternatives to change internal dialogues and previously held beliefs, and, consequently, emotional and behavioral responses. |
| Multicultural responsiveness | Working within the student's values appreciates cultural differences. |

**MEAN GIRLS**

Elijah comes to you, the elementary school counselor, very upset. He said that a group of girls on the playground were teasing him, so he is never going to talk to girls again because girls are so mean. Which counseling approach might best describe Elijah's thoughts in this case, and how might the school counselor apply this approach to help Elijah?

## Reality Counseling

William Glasser (1998) developed reality therapy, also referred to as *control* or *choice* theory, to promote effective decision making and responsible living. The defining characteristics of reality counseling (see Table 2.7) involve helping students to identify inappropriate decisions and honestly evaluate and take responsibility for their current self-defeating behaviors. As Shakespeare proclaimed—*to thine own self be true!*

School counselors may find reality counseling helpful for students who have a pattern of making poor choices, exhibiting an external locus of control, and lacking realistic goals. School counselors use choice theory to

**Table 2.7 Reality Counseling**

| Theorist and philosophy | William Glasser's theoretical philosophy holds unmet needs due to unproductive/ineffective behaviors as the source of dysfunction and that all behavior is an attempt to control the environment to meet our needs. Directive approach to counseling. |
|---|---|
| Therapeutic relationship | Facilitator. |
| Key concepts/ techniques | Focusing on responsibility, choice, and doing, the counselor asks the student: (1) *What do you want?* (2) *What are you doing to get what you want?* (3) *Is it working?* Counselor challenges current behaviors and encourages students to self-evaluate and judge quality of their behaviors toward getting what they want. Together, a workable plan is established to change unproductive behaviors to more productive behaviors that guide future direction and meet needs/desires. |
| Multicultural responsiveness | Focus on students' evaluation of self within their own cultural frame of reference prizes diversity and accommodates differing worldviews; focus on personal responsibility for change does not account for external factors of discrimination and racism; individualized approach is culturally sensitive. |

help students to understand that they are in control of their lives and possess the ability to change, grow, and achieve, using self-evaluation and relevant planning (Gilchrist-Banks, 2009).

## *Solution-Focused Brief Counseling*

Solution-focused brief counseling (SFBC), introduced by Steve de Shazer (1985), is a growing and promising approach particularly suited to school counseling because of its brief nature. SFBC has been vigorously inducted into the not-so-secret society of positive psychology discussed in the next section. The defining characteristics of solution-focused brief counseling (see Table 2.8) involve focusing on solutions versus problems based on what the student is already doing that works, nurturing internal assets, and involving important others (e.g., teachers, parents).

In addition to brevity, SFBC is particularly useful with children and adolescents because of its focus on developmental stages, social support,

**Table 2.8 Solution-Focused Brief Counseling**

| | |
|---|---|
| Theorist and philosophy | Steve de Shazer's solution-focused brief counseling focuses on a student's strengths and abilities rather than weaknesses and inabilities and on solutions rather than problems. Time-limited, directive approach to counseling. |
| Therapeutic relationship | Collaborative. |
| Key concepts/ techniques | Students' inner and external resources with attention to developmental level are accessed. The counselor identifies what has worked for the student in the past and focuses on goals. Techniques may include the *miracle question* (If magic happened and the problem was gone, what would be different?), *exceptions* (Identify times where the problem is not present—what does it look like?), *scaling* (On a scale of 1–10, with 10 being the hardest day and 1 being after the miracle, where would you be right now?), *mindmapping* (e.g., identify what you did that made you successful in the past), *reframing* (viewing problems in more positive terms), and *assigning behavioral tasks* (e.g., doing more of the exceptions). |
| Multicultural responsiveness | Compatible with some cultures that prefer time-limited, practical applications; viewing the student as the expert and working within the student's frame of reference are culturally sensitive and accommodate differing worldviews; using developmentally appropriate, flexible interventions congruent to students' culture is culturally responsive. |

appropriate use of humor, and active techniques. School counselors identify developmental struggles and help students to identify internal and external resources to create realistic solutions germane to the developmental stage.

## Strengths-Based Counseling

*Strengths-based counseling*, an emerging positive psychology pioneered by Martin Seligman, accesses inherent strengths to identify the student's resources and supports for addressing the problem. The strengths-based approach underscores the value of protective factors in combating *risk factors* and enhancing resilience, embracing the philosophy that treatment is not just about fixing what is broken, but nurturing what is best within ourselves (Seligman, 2004). Defining characteristics of strengths-based counseling (see Table 2.9) involves identifying current and past successes to address future challenges.

Unlike many theories focused on deficit reduction, school counselors use strengths-based counseling to build on students' unique assets to empower, strengthen, instill hope, and strengthen resilience. The Search Institute (2007) has developed lists of developmental assets for early childhood, middle childhood, and adolescence. These lists are available at www.search-institute.org/developmental-assets/lists. Each list depicts 40 developmental assets considered to be building blocks for healthy development, which include eight categories:

1. Support
2. Empowerment
3. Boundaries and expectations
4. Constructive use of time
5. Commitment to learning
6. Positive values
7. Social competencies
8. Positive identity.

**Table 2.9 Strengths-Based Counseling**

| Theorist and philosophy | Strengths-based counseling is a therapeutic approach that is grounded in the belief that personal strengths enable individuals to achieve, change, and grow. Counseling is directive. |
|---|---|
| Therapeutic relationship | Collaborative; counselors are guides. |
| Key concepts/ techniques | Accesses students' unique, inherent strengths and builds upon those strengths to empower, promote change, and encourage self-help. This is often found in what has generally been identified as a weakness. For example, being very talkative and opinionated is viewed, instead, as having great passion, conviction, and being communicative. |
| Multicultural responsiveness | Working within the client's values; appreciates cultural differences; focusing on inner strengths, assets, and resources is compatible with many cultures. |

In turn, developmental assets will aid in preventing and mediating problems and promote change. School counselors may find strengths-based counseling particularly helpful for students with low self-esteem, marginal academic performance, and a lack of self-confidence and motivation.

---

### THE MEANING OF LIFE

Kafi is a middle school student whom you meet for issues associated with low motivation and poor self-esteem. During today's session, Kafi remarks, "My life just has no meaning . . . who am I . . . what can I do about anything anyway . . . what kind of future could I possibly have?" Which category of the developmental assets likely needs to be the focus of this counseling session?

# Chapter 2: Case Conceptualization Responses

# Comprehensive School Counseling Programs

*The Parents Do Not Trust Me*
The school counselor explains to the teacher that parent involvement at the elementary level is far greater than at the high school level and that due to their child's developmental level parents tend to be much more protective and engaged in the elementary school child's school years.

## Social/Emotional Development

### *Internet Safety and Cyberbullying*

*Will I Go to Jail?*
Steven's school counselor cannot comment on what the law may or may not do in his case. The school can educate Steven, by letting him know that what he did is considered "sexting" and that sexting is against the law, with some state prosecutors charging teens with felonies, including child pornography. It is important that Steven explores his actions, assumes responsibility for his actions, and considers the consequences of his actions on others.

### *Substance Use, Abuse, Addiction*

*The Best Football Players*
Although the PE teacher has touched base with the parents, the school counselor, too, will want informed consent from the parents due to the sensitive nature of the topic and the limited confidentiality of a counseling group as a matter of best practices. Meeting with the students to determine their motivation toward group participation is critical as well. Participating in the group to merely satisfy the coach is not sufficient. If the students are motivated and give assent to counseling, they should be given signed consent forms for parental approval to participate in counseling related to this topic. The group would be considered secondary prevention because the students are currently at risk for engaging in the behavior.

# Career Development

## *Career Development Theory and Career Counseling*

*I Want to Be a Nurse*
According to Gottfredson, this is an example of circumscription. The first-grade student is ruling out nursing because his father has signified the occupation as socially unacceptable based on gender.

*Ted's Future*
You are applying Krumboltz's social learning theory, which focused on actions and cognitions and teaching career decision-making techniques.

# Delivery

## *Responsive Services*

*Test-Taking and Study Skills*
The correct response is "c." This is both a small group (i.e., method of delivery) and a responsive service (i.e., responding to the immediate needs of students).

*Kyleigh's Mother*
The correct response is "b." Children of Kyleigh's age may experience difficulty labeling and expressing the emotions they are experiencing as a result of the death of a loved one. School counselors can help Kyleigh to identify, label, and express what she is feeling. As counselors, we do not tell clients "everything will be okay" (response option "a"). Everything may not be okay.

# Theories and Techniques for the School Setting

*Play Therapy*
The correct response is "c." Yasmin would likely benefit from expressive toys that will allow her to work through a variety of emotions. The school counselor can explore metaphorical and symbolical expressions of

emotions that may be associated with grief, helping Yasmin to identify emotions and work through difficult emotions.

## Behavioral

*Learning to Resolve Conflict*
The correct response is "d." All the possible responses in this scenario are examples of behavioral counseling. *Behavioral rehearsal* involves teaching new behaviors (i.e., conflict resolution) and having students practice those behaviors in some fashion (i.e., role play). Introducing historical figures as models of a specific behavior is a social-cognitive learning approach used in behavioral counseling.

## Rational-Emotive Behavior Therapy

*Mean Girls*
Albert Ellis might describe Elijah's thoughts as irrational. Elijah is overgeneralizing the behavior of girls based on the behavior of a few select girls in one situation. Debunking Elijah's irrational thoughts using the A–B–C model of REBT might be helpful for Elijah.

## Strengths-Based Counseling

*The Meaning of Life*
The school counselor should focus on the developmental assets category of "positive identity," empowering Kafi and encouraging her to be an explorer of her world and all the possibilities.

# Chapter 2: Simulation

# High School Career Development

## Brief Case Description

You are a high school counselor creating a career development classroom guidance unit to target ninth-grade students. Your lesson objectives include (1) increasing student knowledge of self in relation to career, (2) enhancing knowledge of resources available for career exploration and decision making, and (3) creating a career and academic plan.

## Section A: High School Career Development

What information about the ninth-grade student population would be helpful to know when developing your curriculum?

(Select as many as you consider indicated in this section.)

| | |
|---|---|
| _____A—1. | Gender |
| _____A—2. | Attendance |
| _____A—3. | Developmental level of functioning |
| _____A—4. | Retentions |
| _____A—5. | Ethnicity |
| _____A—6. | Discipline |
| _____A—7. | Grades |
| _____A—8. | Course selections |

## Section B: High School Career Development

Which Internet-based career information system might you consider most appropriate to introduce to ninth-grade students in your classroom guidance lesson?

(Select ONLY ONE in this section.)

| _____B—1. | WISC |
| --- | --- |
| _____B—2. | Choices Planner |
| _____B—3. | MBTI |
| _____B—4. | SDS |
| _____B—5. | Stanford-Binet |

## Section C: High School Career Development

You want to include an activity in your career development program curriculum that will aid students in developing an understanding of how they come to make career decisions over time, including developmental interests and self-control. Which career theorist's model or approach would be the most useful in helping you to develop your activity?

(Select ONLY ONE in this section.)

| _____C—1. | Parsons |
| --- | --- |
| _____C—2. | Super |
| _____C—3. | Krumboltz |
| _____C—4. | Savickas |
| _____C—5. | Holland |
| _____C—6. | Gottfredson |

## Section D: High School Career Development

When delivering culturally sensitive career development programs to a diverse student population, school counselors consider the following influences on career choice.

(Select as many as you consider indicated in this section.)

| _____D—1. | Allocentrism |
| _____D—2. | Social relationships |
| _____D—3. | Availability of occupation information |
| _____D—4. | Beliefs and values |
| _____D—5. | Favorite meal |
| _____D—6. | Gender |
| _____D—7. | Personal appearance |
| _____D—8. | Job factors |
| _____D—9. | Socioeconomic status |
| _____D—10. | Developmental level of functioning |

## *Section E: High School Career Development*

What other strategies might be introduced in your curriculum to aid students in exploring diverse careers?

(Select as many as you consider indicated in this section.)

| _____E—1. | Resume and cover letter writing |
| _____E—2. | Community service |
| _____E—3. | Job shadowing |
| _____E—4. | Developing a career portfolio |
| _____E—5. | Informational interviewing |
| _____E—6. | Creating a career and academic plan |
| _____E—7. | Obtaining a part-time/summer job |

## Section F: High School Career Development

Which interest inventory might you consider including in your curriculum to aid students in understanding self and the work environments for which they may be best suited?
(Select ONLY ONE in this section.)

| | |
|---|---|
| _____F—1. | SDS |
| _____F—2. | Connors Scale |
| _____F—3. | ASVAB |
| _____F—4. | Career beliefs inventory |
| _____F—5. | WISC |
| _____F—6. | Vineland |

## Section G: High School Career Development

Once your unit is implemented, your principal, who emphasizes accountability and outcomes, would like to know how effective you were in meeting lesson objectives aimed at enhancing student development and career readiness. What information would you provide?
(Select as many as you consider indicated in this section.)

| | |
|---|---|
| _____G—1. | The number of students who participated in the lessons |
| _____G—2. | Pre-/post-measure of knowledge of career resources |
| _____G—3. | Pre-/post-measure of student attendance and participation |
| _____G—4. | Feedback from students about the lesson's usefulness |
| _____G—5. | The number of students who completed a career and academic plan |
| _____G—6. | Pre-/post-measure of students' knowledge of self related to career |
| _____G—7. | Measure of academic performance pre- and post-lesson implementation |

# Chapter 2: Simulation Answers

# High School Career Development

## Brief Case Description

You are a high school counselor creating a career development classroom guidance unit to target ninth-grade students. Your lesson objectives include (1) increasing student knowledge of self in relation to career, (2) enhancing knowledge of resources available for career exploration and decision making, and (3) creating a career and academic plan.

## Section A: High School Career Development

What information about the ninth-grade student population would be helpful to know when developing your curriculum?

(Select as many as you consider indicated in this section.)

| A—1. | Gender |
|---|---|
| | Yes |
| | Gender is applicable when considering the promotion of nontraditional occupations and the enhancement of student knowledge of self in relation to career. It is also critical that school counselors understand and provide information to students related to gender and the world of work (e.g., gender-role stereotyping, gender segregation, bias in occupational information). Such information enhances student knowledge for career decision making and understanding self in relation to career, two of the objectives identified for this classroom guidance lesson. |
| A—2. | Attendance |
| | No |
| | Attendance is not a factor for consideration because it has no bearing on the objectives identified for this classroom guidance lesson. |
| A—3. | Developmental level of functioning |
| | Yes |
| | Students' levels of social and cognitive functioning is important to consider when creating and delivering a developmentally appropriate educational curriculum. Otherwise, students may not be capable of grasping the material presented, and the school counselor is unable to meet the objectives of the lesson. |

| A—4. | Retentions<br>No<br>Knowing which students have been retained or the number of students with retentions is not a factor for consideration because it has no bearing on the objectives identified for this classroom guidance lesson. |
|---|---|
| A—5. | Ethnicity<br>Yes<br>Ethnicity is a consideration when creating any curriculum that is sensitive to the needs of a diverse population. It is important for school counselors to understand how ethnicity impacts career decision making and critical that school counselors provide students with information related to culturally diverse individuals and the world of work (e.g., stereotyping, discrimination, affirmative action, bias in occupational information). Such information enhances student knowledge for career decision making and understanding self in relation to career, two of the objectives identified for this classroom guidance lesson. |
| A—6. | Discipline<br>No<br>Discipline is not a factor for consideration because it has no bearing on the objectives identified for this classroom guidance lesson. |
| A—7. | Grades<br>No<br>Grades are not a factor for consideration because they have no bearing on the objectives identified for this classroom guidance lesson. |
| A—8. | Course selections<br>No<br>Although students will be identifying courses and programs as part of the curriculum for this classroom guidance lesson (e.g., creating a career and academic plan), knowing students' current course selections is not a factor for consideration because it has no bearing on the objectives identified for this classroom guidance lesson. |

## Section B: High School Career Development

Which Internet-based career information system might you consider most appropriate to introduce to ninth-grade students in your classroom guidance lesson?

(Select ONLY ONE in this section.)

| B—1. | WISC<br>No<br>The WISC is often used in schools for diagnostic testing to assess level of intelligence. |
|---|---|
| B—2. | Choices Planner<br>Yes<br>Choices Planner is a comprehensive career information system for career planning at the high school level and the single best selection for this item. |
| B—3. | MBTI<br>No<br>The MBTI, although sometimes used in career counseling, is considered a personality test. |
| B—4. | SDS<br>No<br>The SDS is a career interest inventory. |
| B—5. | Stanford-Binet<br>No<br>The Stanford-Binet is an intelligence test often used in the schools for diagnostic testing. |

## Section C: High School Career Development

You want to include an activity in your career development program curriculum that will aid students in developing an understanding of how others influence career decision making. Which career theory, model, or approach would be the most useful in helping you to develop your activity?
 (Select ONLY ONE in this section.)

| C—1. | Cochran's narrative career counseling theory<br>No<br>This theory focuses on a person's narrated story based on perceived interactions with the world. Although the story may include important others in the individual's life, the instructions stated to select "only one" and this is not the most relevant response among the choices provided. |
|---|---|
| C—2. | Super's lifespan theory<br>Yes<br>This model demonstrates how childhood career development evolves. |

| C—3. | Krumboltz's social learning theory<br>No<br>Social learning theory emphasizes the role of behavior and cognitions in career decision making. Important others may have served as role models or important reinforcers of behavior. However, relationship is not the single most applicable construct for this theory or response for this item. |
|---|---|
| C—4. | Savickas' career construction approach<br>No<br>Seeks to identify meaningful life themes and one's adaptation to the environment and unique situations. |
| C—5. | Cognitive information-processing approach<br>No<br>Emphasizes how one's thoughts influence career development. |
| C—6. | Gottfredson's theory of circumscription and compromise<br>No<br>Focus is on developmental processes in career decision making. |

## Section D: High School Career Development

When delivering culturally sensitive career development programs to a diverse student population, school counselors consider the following influences on career choice.

(Select as many as you consider indicated in this section.)

| D—1. | Allocentrism<br>Yes<br>It is important to understand the way the student views career selection. |
|---|---|
| D—2. | Social relationships<br>Yes<br>Career choice is influenced by important others in the student's life. |
| D—3. | Availability of occupation information<br>Yes<br>Students from low-socioeconomic environments do not have the same access to career information and career development tools. |

| D—4. | Beliefs and values<br>Yes<br>Understanding how one's general and work-related beliefs and values impact occupational choices is critical to aiding individuals in making decisions that result in satisfying careers. |
|---|---|
| D—5. | Favorite meal<br>No<br>This would not be relevant to career decision making. |
| D—6. | Gender<br>Yes<br>Gender influences career selection. Encouraging students to consider nontraditional careers is a growing trend in today's schools. |
| D—7. | Personal appearance<br>No<br>A student's appearance does not impact career decision making. However, it is important to consider that how students feel about themselves (e.g., appearance, intelligence) may impact career decision making. |
| D—8. | Job factors<br>Yes<br>Job factors (e.g., salary, environment, physical ability, education, and training) influence career decision making. |
| D—9. | Socioeconomic status<br>Yes<br>Students may rule out particular careers (ruling in others) based on socioeconomic status. Also, students from low socioeconomic backgrounds may not be knowledgeable of all the different career opportunities due to limited career resources and information. |
| D—10. | Developmental level of functioning<br>Yes<br>A student's ability to perform the occupation of choice must be considered. |

## Section E: High School Career Development

What other strategies might be introduced in your curriculum to aid students in exploring diverse careers?

(Select as many as you consider indicated in this section.)

| E—1. | Resume and cover letter writing<br>No<br>Resumes and cover letters are important tools for applying for colleges, jobs, military, apprenticeships, and technical schools. However, students will not find these tools useful for exploring diverse careers. |
| --- | --- |
| E—2. | Community service<br>Yes<br>Community service is a valuable way for students to learn about different occupations while also providing a valuable service to the community. |
| E—3. | Job shadowing<br>Yes<br>Job shadowing allows students to observe, first-hand, the characteristics of specific occupations from which to further development career interests. |
| E—4. | Developing a career portfolio<br>No<br>Career portfolios are important tools for enhancing application to colleges, jobs, military, apprenticeships, and technical schools. However, students will not find this tool useful for exploring diverse careers. |
| E—5. | Informational interviewing<br>Yes<br>Informational interviewing provides students with relevant and real-world information about specific occupations. Informational interviews allow students an opportunity to ask valuable questions that might not be asked in a job interview for fear of revealing a lack of knowledge to a prospective employer. |
| E—6. | Creating a career and academic plan<br>No<br>Creating a career and academic plan is an objective of the career development program. However, it is not a strategy that will aid students in exploring diverse careers. It will aid students in identifying future course selections and programs based on identified careers of interest. |

| E—7. | Obtaining a part-time/summer job<br>Yes<br>Part-time and summer jobs are excellent ways for students to explore a variety of occupations and work environments. |
| --- | --- |

## *Section F: High School Career Development*

Which interest inventory might you consider including in your curriculum to aid students in understanding self and the work environments for which they may be best suited?

(Select ONLY ONE in this section.)

| F—1. | SDS<br>Yes<br>Holland's SDS assigns individuals and work environments into six categories using a three-letter code. |
| --- | --- |
| F—2. | Connors Scale<br>No<br>The Connors Scale is an instrument used to assess for ADHD. |
| F—3. | ASVAB<br>No<br>The ASVAB, often used to identify areas of strength, can drive career decision making, but it does not yield information about self and the work environment. |
| F—4. | Career beliefs inventory<br>No<br>Krumboltz's career beliefs inventory identifies problematic self-perceptions and worldviews. |
| F—5. | WISC<br>No<br>The WISC is often used in schools for diagnostic testing to assess level of intelligence. |
| F—6. | Vineland<br>No<br>The Vineland measures levels of personal and social functioning and is considered to be a personality test. |

## Section G: High School Career Development

Once your unit is implemented, your principal, who emphasizes accountability and outcomes, would like to know how effective you were in meeting lesson objectives aimed at enhancing student development and career readiness. What information would you provide?

(Select as many as you consider indicated in this section.)

| | |
|---|---|
| G—1. | The number of students who participated in the lessons<br><br>No<br><br>The number of participants does not indicate the lesson's effectiveness in meeting the identified objectives for this career development program. |
| G—2. | Pre-/post-measure of knowledge of career resources<br><br>Yes<br><br>Pre- and post-lesson assessments of knowledge gains related to career resources measure one of the lesson's objectives (i.e., enhancing knowledge of resources available for career exploration and decision making) and would be valuable information to submit to your principal in a results report. |
| G—3. | Pre-/post-measure of student attendance and participation<br><br>No<br><br>Student attendance and participation does not indicate the lesson's effectiveness in meeting identified objectives for this career development program. |
| G—4. | Feedback from students about the lesson's usefulness<br><br>No<br><br>Feedback from students pertaining to their perceived value of the lesson is useful information for program improvement and/or continuance. However, it is not useful information to submit to your principal, who is requesting outcome data related to meeting the program's objectives. |
| G—5. | The number of students who completed a career and academic plan<br><br>Yes<br><br>Creating a career and academic plan is an objective of the program. For this reason, providing your principal with the number of students who created a plan is appropriate to his or her request. In this situation, it would be appropriate to provide the number of participants as well, because participation provides a point for comparison (i.e., number of participants and number of participants who completed a career and academic plan). |

| G—6. | Pre-/post-measure of students' knowledge of self related to career |
|---|---|
| | Yes |
| | Increasing student knowledge of self in relation to career is an objective of the program. For this reason, providing your principal with this outcome data is appropriate to his or her request. |
| G—7. | Measure of academic performance pre- and post-lesson implementation |
| | No |
| | Enhanced academic performance is not an objective of this program. |

# Chapter 2: Guided Reflection

Describe in your own words a comprehensive school counseling program.

Explain the significance of social/emotional development in school counseling.

The following are critical issues/incidents associated with the social/emotional development of students in the school setting. Define each critical incident and identify related constructs and its significance to school counseling.

Transitioning

Crisis management

Dropout

School violence and bullying

Internet safety and cyberbullying

Substance use, abuse, addiction

Divorce

Parenting style

The following are critical issues/incidents associated with the career development of students in the school setting. Define each critical incident and identify related constructs and their significance to school counseling.

Influences on career decision making

Career development theory and career counseling

Career and college transitions

Assessment instruments and career information delivery systems

Describe, compare, and provide examples as needed for clarification for each of the following methods of service delivery used by school counselors.

School counseling core curriculum

Group activities

Classroom guidance

Responsive services

Group counseling

Individual counseling

Individual student planning

The following are the most widely used counseling theories in the school setting. For each theory, identify the theorist and associated techniques and constructs, and summarize the theory. Last, provide one example for each theory of a situation in which the theory might be selected over another and why.

Adlerian

Behavioral

Cognitive behavioral

Gestalt

Person-centered

Rational emotive behavior therapy (REBT)

Reality

Solution-focused brief counseling (SFBC)

Strengths-based

# Chapter 3

# Diversity and Advocacy

Never in the history of school counseling have our student populations been more lusciously diverse than they are at the present time. Multilingual, multiethnic, and multicultural students are expected to become the majority by the close of the next decade (Holcomb-McCoy, 2004). In order to continue to practice effectively, professionally, and ethically, school counselors must be culturally competent with a sound commitment to understanding how unique student characteristics impact learning and educational experiences.

School counselors advocate for the acceptance, respect, and fair and equal treatment of all people (ASCA, 2012b). The Tucson shootings and the youth camp massacre in Norway are recent reminders of the international scope and magnitude of the need for a call to arms of the people to advocate for one another—in our homelands and across oceans.

## ASCA's Position on Transgender/Gender Non-Conforming Youth

School counselors recognize all students have the right to be treated equally and fairly with dignity and respect as unique individuals, free from discrimination, harassment and bullying based on their real or perceived gender identity and gender expression. School counselors work to safeguard the well-being of transgender and gender-nonconforming youth.

*Adopted 2016*

School counselors actively challenge oppressive conditions, teach social responsibility, promote climates of acceptance and safety, and seek to remove barriers to success for all individuals. Advocacy is driven by the school counselor's compassion for others and conviction to promoting social justice. *Social justice* is an ideological approach to the professional and ethical practice of professional school counseling. Section B.3.i. of the ASCA *Ethical Standards for School Counselors* (ASCA, 2016a) states that school counselors "monitor and expand personal multicultural and social justice advocacy awareness, knowledge and skills to be an effective culturally competent school counselor."

## ASCA's Position on LGBTQ Youth

School counselor promote equal opportunity and respect for all individuals regardless of sexual orientation, gender identity or gender expression. School counselors recognize the school experience can be significantly more difficult for students with marginalized identities. School counselors work to eliminate barriers impeding LGBTQ student development and achievement.

*Adopted 1995, Revised 2000, 2005,*
*2007, 2013, 2014, 2016*

Six key elements have been identified as key to implementing a social justice approach in school counseling. The following six Cs of school counseling encompass the life-force of social justice (Holcomb-McCoy, 2007):

- Counseling and intervention planning
- Consultation
- Connecting schools, families, and communities
- Collecting and utilizing data
- Challenging bias
- Coordinating student services and support.

The ASCA *Ethical Standards for School Counselors* (ASCA, 2016a) reiterates school counselors' responsibility to serve as "advocates, leaders, collaborators and consultants who create systemic change by providing equitable educational access and success by connecting their school counseling programs to the district's mission and improvement plans."

The ACA adopted the *Advocacy Competencies* (Lewis, Arnold, House, & Toporek, 2003), which aid school counselors in better understanding our roles associated with advocacy and how advocacy competencies apply vis-à-vis school counseling. Table 3.1 provides a brief overview of the advocacy competencies for each of the six domains. For a detailed listing of the competencies for each domain, go to the ACA website at www.counseling.org.

School counselors are the rock stars of advocacy, belting out the lyrics of equity and access for quality curriculum and educational and career resources for all. Data and evaluation are the instruments used to identify and remove obstacles to student success and to challenge oppressive policies and practices. Emphasis is placed on social justice, empowerment, and equality, creating opportunities to promote students' strengths and academic, career, and *personal–social development*. School counselors apply systems-focused practices and leadership while collaborating and consulting with important others both within and outside of the school on behalf of students and families.

Barriers to academic success are identified by disaggregating data from a variety of sources by race, ethnicity, special needs, gender, and teacher. ASCA (2016b, 2012, 2010), Erford (2014), and Schellenberg (2013, 2008) provide a list of whole-school data elements, which have been embellished to provide you with a comprehensive listing of school-wide data sources that when examined can identify access, attainment, and achievement gaps (see Table 3.2).

## Table 3.1 Advocacy Competencies

| | |
|---|---|
| Community collaboration | Their ongoing work with people gives counselors a unique awareness of recurring themes. Counselors are often among the first to become aware of specific difficulties in the environment. |
| | Advocacy-oriented counselors often choose to respond to such challenges by alerting existing organizations that are already working for change and that might have an interest in the issue at hand. |
| | In these situations, the counselor's primary role is as an ally. Counselors can also be helpful to organizations by making available to them our particular skills: interpersonal relations, communications, training, and research. |
| Systems advocacy | When counselors identify systemic factors that act as barriers to their students' or clients' development, they often wish that they could change the environment and prevent some of the problems that they see every day. |
| | Regardless of the specific target of change, the processes for altering the status quo have common qualities. Change is a process that requires vision, persistence, leadership, collaboration, systems analysis, and strong data. In many situations, a counselor is the right person to take leadership. |
| Public information | Across settings, specialties, and theoretical perspectives, professional counselors share knowledge of human development and expertise in communication. |
| | These qualities make it possible for advocacy-oriented counselors to awaken the general public to macrosystemic issues regarding human dignity. |
| Social/political advocacy | Counselors regularly act as change agents in the systems that affect their own students and clients most directly. This experience often leads toward the recognition that some of the concerns they have addressed affected people in a much larger arena. |
| | When this happens, counselors use their skills to carry out social/political advocacy. |

*Source*: Adapted from Lewis, J., Arnold, M., House, R., & Toporek, R. (2003). *Advocacy competencies*. Retrieved March 7, 2011, from www.counseling.org/resources.

**Table 3.2 School-Wide Data for Gap Identification**

| Access (or Opportunity) | Enrollment patterns and participation in: |
|---|---|
| | • AP, IB, honors, college preparation, and enrichment classes |
| | • Special education programs |
| | • 504 plans |
| | • Gifted and talented programs |
| | • Student Council |
| | • Governor's School |
| | • ESL/ELL learner classes/programs |
| Attainment | • Attendance |
| | • Dropout rates and graduation rates |
| | • Promotion and retention rates |
| | • Homework completion rates |
| | • Course completion and pass rates |
| | • Nontraditional program tracks (GED, Job Corps) |
| | • In-school and out-of-school suspensions and expulsion rates |
| | • Study abroad |
| | • Parent participation rates |
| | • GED attainment rates |
| | • College/postsecondary acceptance patterns |
| | • College application completion |
| | • FAFSA completion |
| | • Scholarship submissions |
| | • Participation in Individual Planning with the School |
| | • Counselor |
| | • Rates of participation in interest inventories, career development activities, college entrance testing, industry certifications, learning style inventories, academic portfolios development |
| Achievement | • Grade point averages |
| | • Scores on classroom assignments end-of-course tests |
| | • Scores on standardized achievement tests |
| | • Scores on homework assignments |
| | • Scores on aptitude tests |
| | • Course grades in all subjects |

# Equity and Access

As the rock stars for advocacy, school counselors promote the equity and access tour, ensuring quality curriculum and educational resources for all. School counselors use data and evaluation to identify and remove obstacles to student success, challenging oppressive policies and practices and emphasizing social justice, empowerment, and equality. Systems-focused practices and leadership are also paramount to equity and access, collaborating and consulting with important others both within and outside of the school on behalf of students and families.

## ASCA's Position on Equity for All Students

School counselors recognize and distinguish individual and group differences and strive to value all students and groups equally. School counselors advocate for the equitable treatment of all students in school and in the community.

*Position statement adopted 2006, 2012*

Equity and access begins with compassion and an appreciation of diversity (e.g., socioeconomic background, family and community, culture, gender, ethnicity, levels of intelligence and functioning). School counselors understand that issues related to diversity impact learning and academic achievement as well as students' personal, social, emotional, and career development. The goal is to create encouraging and safe learning environments perfumed with social consciousness and compassion for all regardless of race, culture, gender, sexuality, religion, family and community, levels of intelligence and functioning, and socioeconomic standing or status.

## ASCA's Position on Gender Equity

School counselors are committed to creating an emotionally, intellectually and physically safe environment for all students and to use inclusive language and positive modeling of gender equity, facilitating and promoting the development of each individual by removing bias and stereotypes for all students in school.

*Adopted 1983; revised 1993, 1999, 2002, 2008, 2014*

Diversity has many faces. It has been defined as the array of cultures and subcultures that characterize attitudes, values, beliefs, rituals, norms, symbols, conventions, customs, ideologies, and behaviors (Sue & Sue, 2015). School counselors spread the aroma of respect and value for diverse individuals and groups, seeking to eliminate hostility and inappropriate language. Inclusive language, too, is modeled to foster a nonjudgmental environment where diversity is embraced and celebrated.

## ASCA's Position on Cultural Diversity

School counselors demonstrate cultural responsiveness by collaborating with stakeholders to create a school and community climate that embraces cultural diversity and helps to promote the academic, career and social/emotional success for all students.

*Position statement adopted 1988;*
*revised 1993, 1999, 2004, 2009, 2015*

Resolving identified inequities may involve reviewing and making suggestions for more inclusive classrooms, curriculum, instructional strategies, textbooks, classroom management approaches, and spearheading changes to local and state policy. Challenging the system in this manner may result in resistance and disequilibrium, necessitating that the school counselors aid the system in working through difficult changes and rediscovering new balance.

National legislation, enacted under the Rehabilitation Act of 1973, also referred to as Section 504, and the IDEA, ensures that all students receive

**HELP ME TO REACH MY POTENTIAL**

Jameel, a 10th-grade student, comes to you, his new school counselor, to discuss college opportunities. You notice that Jameel's classes are not rigorous and may limit his college options, while his GPA is consistent with a high-functioning student. Upon further investigation, you notice that students from low socioeconomic backgrounds and ethnically diverse students are underrepresented in rigorous courses. This is an example of:

a. Access gap
b. Attainment gap
c. Achievement gap
d. None of the above.

*free appropriate public education* (FAPE). Additionally, students who are limited English proficient (LEP) or use ESL are entitled to specialized instructional and testing accommodations. Students with special needs are guaranteed access to general and specialized educational aids and services to meet their individualized learning needs.

## ASCA's Position on Students with Disabilities/Special Needs

School counselors encourage and support the academic, career and social/emotional development of all students through comprehensive school counseling programs. School counselors are committed to helping all students realize their potential and meet or exceed academic standards with consideration for both the strengths and challenges resulting from disabilities and other special needs.

*Position statement adopted 1999;*
*revised 2004, 2010*

School counselors ensure that instructional strategies include accommodations for students with special needs (i.e., students with an IEP, 504 plan, *medical plan*, and/or LEP students). Accommodations may include alternative testing programs; extended time on classwork, homework, and tests; the use of translators and bilingual or multilingual instruction; resources in a variety of languages, large print, or Braille; reduced assignments and homework; special seating arrangements; and specialized equipment.

The promotion, retention, and placement of students are monitored by the school counselor by participating on committees (e.g., child study, student assistance, early intervention, RTI) that review individual student needs and provide specialized instruction to meet those needs. School counselors create programs and classroom guidance lessons and facilitate small groups designed to close gaps identified through data sources, observation, and established research.

---

## ASCA's Position on Retention, Social Promotion, and Age-Appropriate Placement

School counselors are best prepared through master's- and doctoral-level programs that align with the philosophy and vision of the ASCA National Model (2012), the ASCA School Counselor Competencies (2012), The ASCA Mindsets & Behaviors for Student Success (2015) and the ASCA Ethical Standards for School Counselors (2010). These programs emphasize training in the implementation of a comprehensive school counseling program promoting leadership, advocacy, collaboration and systemic change to enhance student achievement and success.

*Position statement adopted 2006; revised 2012*

---

Equity and access for all students also applies to those students who are advanced functioning. Students who are more advanced cognitively need to be intellectually challenged. Advanced functioning students benefit from participation in gifted and talented programs such as Governor's School and/or advanced placement and summer enrichment classes, discussed in Chapter 6.

When school counselors hear "gifted student," our antennas begin to flail and hum in readiness to pick up on any frequency of distress, because cognitively advanced students are often the suffer-in-silence type. Gifted students may experience a host of social, emotional, and behavioral difficulties unique to the characteristics of giftedness calling for both preventive and responsive services that take into consideration the academic pressures, intellectual excitabilities, and heavy commitments that may lead to stress, depression, and career uncertainty (Elijah, 2011).

## ASCA's Position on Gifted and Talented Student Programs

The school counselor delivers a comprehensive school counseling program as an integral component of the school's efforts to meet the academic and developmental needs of all students. Gifted and talented students have unique and diverse needs that are addressed by school counselors within the scope of the comprehensive school counseling program and in collaboration with other educators and stakeholders.

*Position statement adopted 1988; revised 1993, 1999, 2001, 2007, 2013*

Low socioeconomic status (SES) poses unique challenges for schools, families, and communities. Low SES can have a negative impact on family structures, housing, individual identity, self-esteem, health, and access to educational and career resources. School counselors act as advocates for social change, social responsibility, and social justice in the school and community, providing students from low SES and impoverished backgrounds with much-needed consideration to ensure equity and access to programming and services. Advocating for equity and access necessitates active participation, action, and unity. Toward this end, school counselors coordinate and engage in community efforts to combat poverty, empower, support, and give a voice to diverse student populations and the family system.

Confronting barriers to academic achievement and student wellness may also involve helping parents and students to identify and access resources, communicate needs, and advocate for themselves. School counselors can take the lead in establishing strategies that will help to remove some of the more common barriers to parents' participation in school activities, such as

- Brainstorming ways to welcome parent participation
- Providing child care during school meetings and events
- Arranging school bus transportation to school events
- Developing needs assessments
- Coordinating car pools
- Providing information regarding bus transportation
- Offering multiple times for program presentations including weekends.

Admittedly, during my years as a practicing school counselor, the fierce growl of my inner bear would emerge in the face of injustice. Hey, it happens. Plus, most of the snarls were equivalent to a quake of no more than a 2.0 in seismic energy on the Richter scale. So, with about 8,000 quakes of this size each day across the nation, at times, the growl was barely noticeable. When the bear is riled, we simply (and sometimes not so simply) keep the expletives to ourselves as if performing a soliloquy, ask for strength from our Creator, and stay mindful that the inner bear, too, works responsibly, professionally, and ethically with others to effect change. That is, we show our teeth, but we are careful not to bite anybody!

Section B.2.s. of the ASCA *Ethical Standards for School Counselors* (ASCA, 2016a) reminds us that when working in situations or faced with policies that do not reflect the ethics of the profession, school counselors collaborate with others, working "responsibly through the correct channels to try and remedy work conditions that do not reflect the ethics of the profession." School counselors labor under the philosophy that it really does *take a village*—and sometimes a bear.

**FAPE**

You are a school counselor and member of the child study team at your school. During today's meeting, a parent became quite upset and roared, "I am going to seek legal advisement . . . you are denying my child a free and appropriate education." The parent is likely referring to which legislation:

    a. IDEA
    b. ADA
    c. FERPA
    d. McKinney-Vento Act

# Multicultural Competence

School counselors understand how students' self-perceptions and worldviews (e.g., conceptualization of the world) are shaped by culture and cultural experiences. As such, culturally sensitive responsive services and competent *multicultural counseling* are used to clarify feelings, promote self-understanding and self-esteem, and develop the personal, social, and emotional well-being of students from all cultures and backgrounds.

To promote equitable practices, school counselors are culturally competent and seek to improve the cultural competence of others with whom they interact. CACREP (2012) defines multicultural as "the diversity of racial, ethnic, and cultural heritage; socioeconomic status; age; gender; sexual orientation; and religious and spiritual beliefs, as well as physical, emotional, and mental abilities" (p. 141).

Section A.1.f. of the ASCA *Ethical Standards for School Counselors* (ASCA, 2016a) emphasizes that school counselors "exercise great care to avoid imposing personal beliefs or values rooted in one's religion, culture, or ethnicity." Toward this end, school counselors should become familiar with the Multicultural Counseling Competencies and Standards developed by the AMCD, a branch of the ACA. The Multicultural Counseling Competencies and Standards are available at www.amcdaca.org.

School counselors who wish to gain a greater understanding of the knowledge and skills areas needed to provide culturally competent counseling should refer to the *School Counselor Multicultural*

*Competence Checklist* (Holcomb-McCoy, 2004). The checklist is also helpful in heightening self-awareness of current levels of cultural competence and assessing the school's policies, procedures, and programs for cultural competence. As noted above, Section B.3.i. of the ASCA *Ethical Standards for School Counselors* (ASCA, 2016a) underscores the importance of the school counselor's self-knowledge and an understanding of oppression and the development of racial identity and worldviews as key to multicultural competence.

Reducing and, moreover, eliminating issues associated with *encapsulation* and developing the ability to provide students from diverse backgrounds with the optimal environment for success call for a keen sense of one's cultural self (dominant and minority cultures) and the affirmation of nondominant cultures, which involves

- Awareness of one's own assumptions, racial biases, and attitudes
- Awareness of the environmental forces that have impacted minority students
- Understanding the importance of worldviews and the similarities and differences between the school counselor and the culturally different student and how those characteristics impact counseling process
- Understanding differences in language, terminology, and communication styles
- Possessing an empathetic attitude
- Possessing a knowledge of a variety of counseling theories and techniques and their strengths and weaknesses with diverse cultures
- Possessing a knowledge of racial identity development
- Learning a variety of languages
- Participating in multicultural development workshops
- Staying abreast of current literature on topics related to counseling the culturally different
- Participating in cultural immersion experiences.

School counselors realize that racial identity development is a multifaceted process, and are careful not to conceptualize students within a universal grouping based on culture or subculture. In other words, they avoid stereotyping. Individuality is multifaceted and influenced by numerous personal and environmental factors. Models of racial identity development affirm varying levels of enculturation among members of a particular race or culture. That is, on the basis of social and cultural influences, some students feel a stronger identification with their culture than others, which, in turn, impacts acculturation, which is the individual's personal struggle to adapt to a new and unfamiliar culture (Matsumoto & Juang, 2016).

School counselors are aware that students who enter a school where the dominant culture is different from their own will experience varying levels of adjustment based on the strength of their enculturation. The internal process of acculturation is influenced by assimilation, a process external to the individual and determined by the dominant culture's acceptance of the individual from a new and unfamiliar culture (Matsumoto & Juang, 2016), which can be negatively impacted by encapsulation.

## THE FISH MARKET

Kwame, a new student from Ghana, is sitting in his new American fifth-grade elementary school class. While the teacher is teaching the mathematics lesson, she notices that Kwame appears confused and asks him if he understands what she is teaching. He responds that he does not understand and that this is really different from the way he learns in his country. He goes on to say that he learned math by selling fish. The class laughs, and the teacher, taking Kwame's remark as a personal affront, tells him that math instruction is not the time to be joking around. The teacher's response is an example of:

a. Assimilation
b. Acculturation
c. Encapsulation
d. Enculturation

Recognizing that culture impacts a student's thoughts, beliefs, view of self, problem-solving and decision-making processes, orientation to time, and verbal and nonverbal communications—their very being—school counselors are students and teachers of multiculturalism. In addition to becoming culturally competent, school counselors teach cultural sensitivity to teachers and to students using systemic approaches such as classroom guidance lessons, school-wide presentations, transitioning programs, and small groups. The following topics are recommended when teaching others to be sensitive to those from culturally diverse backgrounds (Erford, 2014):

- Affirming differences
- Using accurate multicultural terminology
- Exploring one's own biases
- Learning about ethnic and racial identity models
- Understanding diverse worldviews
- Challenging oppression
- Understanding the dangers of stereotyping
- Exploring racial, ethnic, and cultural histories.

Affirming cultural diversity within and outside of the school setting aids students of the nondominant culture in developing a strong racial identity. A strong racial identity is a protective factor that promotes resilience. The importance of resilience and additional ways that school counselors can build resilience in children and adolescents is discussed in Chapter 2.

---

### LOOK AT ME WHEN I AM TALKING TO YOU

Maya, an Asian high school student, comes to you, her alphabet counselor, because the student assistance counselor is out with the flu. She discusses an important family issue with you, hoping to make some critical decisions related to the issue. When the student assistance counselor returns, you let her know about your brief session with Maya. The student assistance counselor immediately knows who you are referring to and says that she, too, met with Maya once for about 10 minutes, and adds, "Did you notice how little eye contact she makes with you—it's a cultural thing." The alphabet counselor replies, "I did not notice." The student assistance counselor is making a generalization based on Maya's culture, which is considered

    a. Acculturation
    b. Encapsulation
    c. Assimilation
    d. Stereotyping

## *Spirituality*

Spirituality has been a taboo topic in the public school system as a result of the separation of church and state. However, heightened emphasis on the importance of spirituality in the ethical and culturally competent practice of counseling is opening the school doors for the return of spirituality as a topic crucial to holistic student development.

Spiritual development is a critical aspect of human development, a cultural agent, and a natural component for exploration in the counseling process that significantly impacts the student's worldview and the counseling relationship (Kimbel & Schellenberg, 2014). How can you study Naples, Italy, and disregard the pizza pie?

Kimbel and Schellenberg (2014) created School Counselor Spiritual and Religious Competencies to aid school counselors in integrating spirituality and religion into counseling services in K–12 schools in a manner that is ethical, legal, and culturally sensitive. Those competencies were published by ASCA in their journal, *Professional School Counseling*, and featured in their magazine, *ASCA School Counselor*, underscoring the importance and appropriateness of spiritual development as part of a comprehensive school counseling program.

As noted earlier, ASCA *Ethical Standards for School Counselors* (ASCA, 2016a) call for the respect of individual and family values, beliefs and cultural background cautioning against imposing personal values on students or their families. Uncertain as to how to address the sensitive topic of spirituality in a manner that would be considered by parents, students, and administrators to be ethical, professional, and legal, school counselors have elected to avoid the topic.

Like the path to multicultural competence, becoming a school counselor competent in addressing matters of spirituality begins with identifying personal biases with regard to spiritual and religious beliefs and traditions and a commitment to learning more about the spiritual and religious practices of others. Socrates, a Greek thinker and architect of Western philosophies, is viewed by some as a martyr for moral virtue. Socrates emphasized the importance of not being blind to our own (and others') deep-seated beliefs and presuppositions. Like Socrates, school counselors are heartened to live by the truism "To know thyself," seeking a path for ourselves and our students in what Italians refer to as living *la dolce vita*, or the good life.

Helping students to gain insight into their worldviews and working within the worldviews of students necessitates cultural diplomacy. That is, having a dialogue about how religious or spiritual beliefs, as well as tradition, lifestyle, ideas, beliefs, and values, may impact the student's personal–social, academic, and career decisions. For example, it is virtually impossible to understand Indians apart from their religion because it is so deeply ingrained in everyday personal and public living.

Allow teaching versus preaching to be the guiding philosophy (Wolf, 2004). That is, objectively educate students about spirituality and religion by (1) being descriptive and unbiased in the information presented, (2) teaching respect and appreciation of diversity, and (3) introducing literature or current events that involve spirituality, religion, personal beliefs, and values for class or group discussion. Discussing issues related to spirituality is both constitutional and ethical in accordance with the First Amendment of the Constitution and the ASCA *Code of Ethics*, respectively (Wolf, 2004). Just as Michelle Obama has the right to bare arms, school counselors have the right to remove the sleeves that cover critical areas of human development in our efforts to provide culturally competent counseling services.

Maintaining objectivity in school counseling activities related to spirituality and religion begins with an understanding of the differences between spirituality and religion. Religion is more of an organized practice that involves specific beliefs. Religion generally involves worship by groups

---

### AN INTERNATIONAL BROUHAHA

Michelle Obama's reaching out to shake the hand of the conservative Indonesian government official has been viewed as a culturally insensitive gesture grounded in a lack of knowledge pertaining to the Indonesian culture. This would also demonstrate the profound impact of the following religious beliefs in shaping the cultural customs and identity of many Indonesian people:

a. Muslim
b. Christian
c. Protestant
d. None of the above

of individuals in a ritualized fashion and in a brick-and-mortar establishment such as a church. Spirituality is broad, unstructured, and focused on the individual's essence of being in relation to nature and the universe and may include religion. Fundamental principles of spirituality include hope, meaning in life, and compassion.

In addition to teaching, school counselors might also consider participating in student-initiated spiritual and religious events such as the annual See You at the Pole prayer meeting. Section 9524 of the Elementary and Secondary Education Act (ESEA) constitutionally protects prayer in public schools (United States Department of Education, 2003). School counselors who explore issues of spirituality with students are engaging in both ethically responsible and culturally sensitive counseling practices.

# Chapter 3: Case Conceptualization Responses

## Equity and Access

*Help Me to Reach My Potential*
The correct response is "a." Jameel has not been given access to rigorous coursework despite his ability to succeed in advanced placement classes. School counselors consider the student's ability and aptitude based on past academic performance and take future career and college desires into consideration when determining core and elective course placements.

*FAPE*
The parent is referencing the language used in the IDEA, which ensures that students receive a FAPE.

## Multicultural Competence

*The Fish Market*
The correct response is "c." The teacher's response is demonstrative of encapsulation and a lack of cultural sensitivity. The teacher is encapsulated in the Western culture whereby mathematics is taught in a formal educational institution and classroom. In Ghana, many children learn math in the community, through the elderly, and in trades such as marketing fish.

*Look at Me When I Am Talking to You*
The correct response is "d." The student assistance counselor is stereotyping. Generally speaking, the Asian culture views direct eye contact with elders and with those in authority as rude and confrontational. Maya's lack of eye contact could be related to culture and her way of showing the school counselor respect. However, it may not be related to culture; the alphabet counselor did not notice a lack of eye contact when speaking with Maya. Consequently, some secondary schools divide school counselor load by alphabet, and those school counselors are often referred to as the alphabet counselor. Other schools may assign students to school counselors by grade level, in which case the school counselor is often referred to as the grade level counselor.

## *Spirituality*

### *An International Brouhaha*

The correct response is "a." Many, if not most, of the people of Indonesia practice the Muslim faith. This real-world case drives home the importance of spirituality and religion in shaping the practices and worldview of individuals, which must not be ignored in counseling and in the specialty of school counseling as well as in the teachings in our schools. Whether we are of the majority or minority population of a Western or non-Western culture, we need to learn about (or, in this case, be advised on) the cultures with whom we are interacting to develop positive relations.

# Chapter 3: Simulation

# The Newbie

## Brief Case Description

You are a newly practicing elementary school counselor developing your first classroom guidance lesson for fifth graders.

## Section A: The Newbie

One of the teachers informs you that the principal requires that special education students be pulled out of class to be with resource teachers for academic tutoring during the school counselor's classroom guidance lessons. The teacher said the principal announced this practice during a faculty meeting a few years ago, as a way to provide special education students with extra academic support and improve test scores. What is your response?

(Select ONLY ONE in this section.)

| | |
|---|---|
| _____A—1. | Comply with the principal's requirements and develop the curriculum for the general education student population at that grade level. |
| _____A—2. | Go to the principal and explain how this practice is not equitable and limits access to important programming for special education students. |
| _____A—3. | Strongly encourage the teacher to keep special education students in the class during classroom guidance. |
| _____A—4. | Talk to the special education teachers to ensure classroom guidance by the school counselor is a part of the students' IEP so that students are included in the lessons. |

## Section B: The Newbie

Now that the classroom guidance lesson will be delivered to both general education and special needs students, which of the following applies?
(Select as many as you consider indicated in this section.)

| | |
|---|---|
| _____B—1. | Curriculum should be developed based on the grade level of the student regardless of special needs status to ensure access to rigorous, age-appropriate curriculum. |
| _____B—2. | Curriculum should be modified to meet the special needs of each student in the classroom. |
| _____B—3. | Because it is impossible to meet the special needs of all students, develop a curriculum that meets the needs of the majority. |
| _____B—4. | Make every effort to ensure special needs students sit grouped together so that you can better monitor their understanding of the lesson's content. |
| _____B—5. | Teachers need to inform school counselors of the needs of the special education students in their class because school counselors are not privy to this information. |

## Section C: The Newbie

One of the teachers who is receiving your classroom guidance lesson informs you that one of her students, Sabrina, will not be a part of the classroom guidance lesson because she is an ESL student and her translator is out on the day of the lesson. Your response is:
(Select ONLY ONE in this section.)

| | |
|---|---|
| _____C—1. | All students need to be present for the lesson, so you will reschedule the lesson. |
| _____C—2. | You will meet with Sabrina and her translator individually on another day to deliver the content of the lesson. |
| _____C—3. | Have Sabrina participate in the lesson without her translator to ensure equity and access to all programming. |

| _____C—4. | Identify others in the building who can translate for Sabrina and see if someone can translate on the day of the lesson while also talking to the principal about getting a substitute. |
|---|---|
| _____C—5. | Tape the classroom guidance lesson so that Sabrina and her translator can watch it together when the translator returns. |

## Section D: The Newbie

During the classroom guidance lesson, a female student sitting by herself answers a question you posed. You notice that the student has an olive complexion, is very soft-spoken, and has an accent. Her response is uncommon, so you let her know that her response is interesting and offers a unique perspective. Another female student blurts out in a sarcastic tone, "Yeah, you mean a weird perspective," and she and the girl next to her laugh along with the rest of the class. How would you respond?

(Select as many as you consider indicated in this section.)

| _____D—1. | Continue the lesson, careful not to give the girls an audience. |
|---|---|
| _____D—2. | Stop the lesson and have the two girls removed from the class. |
| _____D—3. | Reassure the student that the response she gave was appropriate and worthwhile. |
| _____D—4. | Tell the girls that those comments are unacceptable and mean-spirited, redirecting the lesson to one of diversity appreciation, respect, and the power of words. |
| _____D—5. | Continue the lesson, and ask to see the two girls after class. |
| _____D—6. | Tell the girls that those comments are unacceptable and mean-spirited and then continue the planned lesson. |
| _____D—7. | Come back the following week to teach a lesson on appreciation of diversity. |

## Section E: The Newbie

The day after the lesson, the student comes to you to thank you and lets you know that the girls have been nicer to her. She begins to share some family and personal issues that are bothering her. As a culturally sensitive counselor, how might you proceed?

(Select ONLY ONE in this section.)

| | |
|---|---|
| _____E—1. | Let the student know that you are not familiar with her culture, express your interest in learning about her culture, and ask her to educate you. |
| _____E—2. | Sensitive not to make the student uncomfortable about her culture, just listen and reflect her feelings. |
| _____E—3. | Ask her to identify her culture and to come back later, so you can find out more about her culture before she returns. |
| _____E—4. | Let the student know that you are not familiar with her culture, so she should talk to her parents about her concerns to ensure cultural sensitivity. |
| _____E—5. | Let her know that you are not familiar with her culture, and share with her how the dominant culture handles those types of issues. |
| _____E—6. | Let her know that you are unfamiliar with her culture, but offer your thoughts and beliefs on the issues. |

# Chapter 3: Simulation Answers

# The Newbie

## *Brief Case Description*

You are a newly practicing elementary school counselor developing your first classroom guidance lesson for fifth graders.

## *Section A: The Newbie*

One of the teachers informs you that the principal requires that special education students be pulled out of the class to be with resource teachers for academic tutoring during the school counselor's classroom guidance lessons. The teacher said the principal announced this practice during a faculty meeting a few years ago, as a way to provide special education students with extra academic support and improve test scores. What is your response?

  (Select ONLY ONE in this section.)

| | |
|---|---|
| A—1. | Comply with the principal's requirements and develop the curriculum for the general education student population at that grade level. <br><br> No <br><br> School counselors advocate for equity and access in educational programming. |
| A—2. | Go to the principal and explain how this practice is not equitable and limits access to important programming for special education students. <br><br> Yes <br><br> School counselors advocate for equity and access in educational programming. |
| A—3. | Strongly encourage the teacher to keep special education students in the class during classroom guidance. <br><br> No <br><br> This puts the teacher in the position of disobeying the principal's directives. |
| A—4. | Talk to the special education teachers to ensure classroom guidance by the school counselor is a part of the students' IEP so that students are included in the lessons. <br><br> No <br><br> Access to general education programming for special education students does not need to be in their IEP. It is the right of all students to participate in this programming. |

## Section B: The Newbie

Now that the classroom guidance lesson will be delivered to both general education and special needs students, which of the following applies?
(Select as many as you consider indicated in this section.)

| | |
|---|---|
| B—1. | Curriculum should be developed based on the grade level of the student regardless of special needs status to ensure access to rigorous, age-appropriate curriculum. <br><br> No <br><br> The school counselor needs to consider the special accommodations of special needs students in the classes for which they are conducting classroom guidance lessons. |
| B—2. | Curriculum should be modified to meet the special needs of each student in the classroom. <br><br> Yes <br><br> Like teachers, school counselors must follow students IEPs, 504 plans, and the accommodations afforded to those students whose primary language is not English. Also, there may be students in the class who are under a temporary medical plan (e.g., broken finger). |
| B—3. | Because it is impossible to meet the special needs of all students, develop a curriculum that meets the needs of the majority. <br><br> No <br><br> School counselors create curriculum to meet the needs of all students to whom the curriculum is being implemented. |
| B—4. | Make every effort to ensure special needs students sit grouped together so that you can better monitor their understanding of the lesson's content. <br><br> No <br><br> School counselors and teachers do not segregate students based on ability, disability, gender, ethnicity, and so on. |
| B—5. | Teachers need to inform school counselors of the needs of the special education students in their classes because school counselors are not privy to this information. <br><br> No <br><br> School counselors may ask teachers to identify special needs students so that they can pull those students' IEPs, 504 plans, or ESL plans for compliance. Many school counselors have access to the special needs status of students in every classroom via student information systems. |

## Section C: The Newbie

One of the teachers, who is receiving your classroom guidance lesson, informs you that one of her students, Sabrina, will not be a part of the classroom guidance lesson because she is an ESL student and her translator is out on the day of the lesson. Your response is:

(Select ONLY ONE in this section.)

| | |
|---|---|
| C—1. | All students need to be present for the lesson, so you will reschedule the lesson.<br>No<br>All students cannot always be present for every classroom guidance lesson. |
| C—2. | You will meet with Sabrina and her translator individually on another day to deliver the content of the lesson.<br>No<br>School counselors do not meet with students individually to make up a classroom guidance lessons missed. The swollen counselor-to-student ratio makes it virtually impossible to provide this service to students unless mandated by student IEP and 504 plan or is a part of Sabrina's LEP services plan. |
| C—3. | Have Sabrina participate in the lesson without her translator to ensure equity and access to all programming.<br>No<br>It is not equity and access to have Sabrina participate without the accommodations she needs to comprehend the material presented. |
| C—4. | Identify others in the building who can translate for Sabrina and see if someone can translate on the day of the lesson while also talking to the principal about getting a substitute.<br>Yes<br>Advocating on behalf of the student for her rightful accommodations in order to access programming is an important function of the school counselor. |
| C—5. | Tape the classroom guidance lesson so that Sabrina and her translator can watch it together when the translator returns.<br>No<br>Viewing the lesson as a spectator is not the same as interacting with other students and being a part of the lesson. However, in the event that a translator is not made available to Sabrina, then this would be an alternative to her missing the lesson entirely. |

## Section D: The Newbie

During the classroom guidance lesson, a female student sitting by herself answers a question you posed. You notice that the student has an olive complexion, is very soft-spoken, and has an accent. Her response is uncommon, so you let her know that her response is interesting and offers a unique perspective. Another female student blurts out in a sarcastic tone, "Yeah, you mean a weird perspective," and she and the girl next to her laugh along with the rest of the class. How would you respond?

(Select as many as you consider indicated in this section.)

| | |
|---|---|
| D—1. | Continue the lesson, careful not to give the girls an audience.<br>No<br>This is bully behavior and needs to be addressed. |
| D—2. | Stop the lesson and have the two girls removed from the class.<br>No<br>This action would not teach the girls appropriate behavior. |
| D—3. | Reassure the student that the response she gave was appropriate and worthwhile.<br>Yes<br>This is appropriate in addition to intervention in the moment. |
| D—4. | Tell the girls that those comments are unacceptable and mean-spirited, redirecting the lesson to one of diversity appreciation, respect, and the power of words.<br>Yes<br>Use this as an immediate opportunity (a teachable moment) to demonstrate a zero tolerance for bullying and to promote a climate of compassion and acceptance. |
| D—5. | Continue the lesson, and ask to see the two girls after class.<br>No<br>This is a teachable moment for all, and counselors address behavior but not as disciplinarian. |
| D—6. | Tell the girls that those comments are unacceptable and mean-spirited and then continue the planned lesson.<br>No<br>Chances are, the girls already know that what they are saying and doing is bullying. Continuing with your lesson as planned after pointing out the obvious will not eliminate the problem or appeal to the support of the group or to the human compassion of the "mean" girls. |

| D—7. | Come back the following week to teach a lesson on appreciation of diversity. |
|------|------------------------------------------------------------------------------|
|      | No |
|      | The teachable moment will have passed. School counselors are flexible. |
|      | You may be able to cover your intended lesson as well as the unexpected lesson. |

## Section E: The Newbie

The day after the lesson, the student comes to you to thank you and lets you know that the girls have been nicer to her. She begins to share some family and personal issues that are bothering her. As a culturally sensitive counselor, how might you proceed?

(Select ONLY ONE in this section.)

| E—1. | Let the student know that you are not familiar with her culture, express your interest in learning about her culture, and ask her to educate you. |
|------|------------------------------------------------------------------------------|
|      | Yes |
|      | This is the culturally sensitive response. The student will recognize that you want to help and appreciate your honesty. |
| E—2. | Sensitive not to make the student uncomfortable about her culture, just listen and reflect her feelings. |
|      | No |
|      | This will only take you so far, and you risk the student misinterpreting your lack of knowledge about her culture as not being genuine, or worse. |
| E—3. | Ask her to identify her culture and to come back later, so you can find out more about her culture before she returns. |
|      | No |
|      | The student is asking for assistance now, and it may have taken much courage to come to you on her own. Now is the moment. |
| E—4. | Let the student know that you are not familiar with her culture, so she should talk to her parents about her concerns to ensure cultural sensitivity. |
|      | No |
|      | The student came to you, not her parents. She may not want her parents to know because what she is experiencing is contrary to deeply held cultural beliefs. |

| E—5. | Let her know that you are not familiar with her culture, and share with her how the dominant culture handles those types of issues.<br><br>No<br><br>You are espousing your personal beliefs onto your client. This is against our code of ethics. |
|------|---|
| E—6. | Let her know that you are unfamiliar with her culture, but offer your thoughts and beliefs on the issues.<br><br>No<br><br>You are espousing your personal beliefs onto your client. This is against our code of ethics. |

# Chapter 3: Guided Reflection

Define diversity, and describe its importance in school counseling.

Define advocacy, and describe its importance and function in school counseling.

Examine the concept of equity and access, and explain the construct and the function of the school counselor toward achieving equity and access.

Compare and contrast access, attainment, and achievement gaps. Give one example of each and a corresponding strategy to address the gap based on your example.

Describe what it means to be a multicultural-competent school counselor.

Recommend approaches a school counselor can use to appropriately address spirituality in the public school setting.

# Chapter 4

# Assessment

The legacy of student *appraisal* is rooted in the vocational guidance movement whereby school counselors used standardized tests to assess student knowledge, skills, abilities, and aptitudes in order to make the most advantageous occupational choices. The movement gained popularity and school counselors began coordinating and administering assessments to make school placement decisions and to monitor student achievement. *Assessment* in educational practices has a long history. In this educational climate of accountability and results-based outcomes, a secure shelf life is certain—death and taxes.

As such, the colossal influx of broadened assessment demands left school counselors feeling our way, as though in the midst of a blinding sandstorm of assessment requirements in the Taklamakan Desert—you know—the one that legend says you can enter but you can never leave. As usual, the cavalry, that is ASCA, brought camels and guides! Consequently, the nostalgia for our assessment roots may not find its way out of that desert.

Recognizing the rapidly growing demands of assessment assigned to the duties of school counselors, ASCA, in collaboration with the Association for Assessment in Counseling (1998), now the Association for Assessment in Counseling and Education (AACE), a division of ACA, identified the following nine Competencies in Assessment and Evaluation for School Counselors:

1. Selecting appropriate assessment strategies
2. Identifying, accessing, and evaluating the most commonly used assessment instruments

3. Administering and scoring assessments
4. Interpreting and reporting assessment results
5. Using assessment results for decision making
6. Interpreting and presenting statistical information about assessment results
7. Evaluating school counseling practices and programs
8. Developing assessments (e.g., surveys, questionnaires) to meet local needs
9. Observing professional and ethical standards related to assessment.

## Student Appraisal

School counselors use data from individual student appraisals to identify and target prevention and intervention strategies. While engaging in student appraisal, school counselors carefully consider the use of both formal and informal assessments and appropriate procedures for assessment administration in a variety of situations with diverse populations (e.g., language proficiency, special needs). A combination of both formal and informal approaches are recommended as best practices for school counselors for assessing individual needs and academic and counseling progress. Together, informal and formal assessments ensnare all the senses and sensibilities, capturing the whole essence of the individual.

School counselors are vigilant in evaluating assessments for cultural bias (no one assessment instrument is entirely bias-free), applying basic principles for scoring assessments, interpreting the results, and relaying assessment outcomes to students, parents, and important others. Section A.13. of the ASCA *Ethical Standards for School Counselors* (ASCA, 2016a) dedicates an entire section to evaluation, assessment, and interpretation. Read it, learn it, live by it. Table 4.1 describes specific measurements concepts with which school counselors need to be familiar in order to adequately interpret assessment outcomes: measures of central tendency, norms, rank, percentile rank, grade/age equivalents, standard deviation, standard scores, raw scores, derived scores, criterion-referenced scores, correlation, reliability, validity, and norm-referenced assessments.

Often shared responsibilities with the school psychologist, school social worker, educational diagnostician, and teachers, formal and informal assessments are useful tools that provide a deeper understanding of

## Table 4.1 Measurement Concepts

| |
|---|
| *Correlations* are the degree to which two measures/constructs are related (e.g., the examination between a class of students' test scores in mathematics and their level of self-esteem). |
| *Criterion-referenced assessments* are those that compare an individual's score with a pre-established standard. |
| *Derived scores* are scores that are drawn from raw scores by comparing the raw score with those of a norm group; sometimes referred to as norm-referenced scores. |
| *Grade/age equivalents* are a type of developmental score that compares an individual student's raw score with that of others of a certain grade/age level. |
| *Measures of central tendency*, known as *mean, median,* and *mode,* are representative of averages. The mean is the mathematical average of a set of scores; the median is the middle score below which, and above which, half of the scores of a set of scores will fall; the mode is the score that appears the most frequently in a set of scores. |
| *Norm-referenced assessments* are those that compare an individual's score with that of a norm group. |
| *Norms* are representative of a distribution of scores obtained through the administration of an instrument to a standardized sample against which all other scores are assessed. |
| *Percentile rank* is the percentage of scores that are at or below a named score. |
| *Rank* is the relative position, standing, or degree of a specific grouping, often used at the secondary and postsecondary levels of education to describe a student's standing in relation to others based on GPA. |
| *Raw scores* are original scores that have not yet been converted into a meaningful score. |
| *Reliability* refers to the consistency with which an instrument measures that which it purports to measure (i.e., does the instrument yield the same or similar results at each administration for the same individual?). |
| *Standard deviation* is a measure of variability in a given set of data. |
| *Standard scores* represent the distance between a given score and the mean and are used in norm-referenced (see *norms* above) assessments to compare a student's performance with that of his or her peers. |
| *Validity* refers to the extent to which an instrument measures that which it purports to measure (i.e., can meaningful inferences be made based on the instrument's results?). |

students' issues in relation to their personal, social, environmental, developmental, and cultural worlds. Assessments are used to:

- Identify student strengths and challenges.
- Develop targeted interventions.
- Provide optimal learning environments.
- Provide important information to parents, students, and school personnel.

In some school divisions, formal assessment is conducted by school psychologists, school social workers, and educational diagnosticians.

---

**JENNIFER'S SCORE**

Jennifer is a high school student who obtained a raw score of 73 on her mathematics exam. Her score was compared with that of a norm group in order to obtain a derived score. Jennifer must have taken:

a. A nonstandardized assessment
b. A norm-referenced assessment
c. A criterion-referenced assessment
d. An informal assessment

---

## Formal Assessment

Standardized tests, or assessments, are objective, often norm-referenced (e.g., compare scores against an average), generally quantitative in nature, and ensure consistency in content, administration, scoring, and interpretation. Standardized tests are frequently referred to as formal assessments.

It is essential that school counselors are able to identify a variety of formal assessments based on type or purpose. There are generally five categories: achievement, aptitude, intelligence, interests, and personality. The assessments most often used in the schools within each category are summarized in Table 4.2. School counselors become familiar with the validity, reliability, limitations, bias, and characteristics of the assessments they plan to administer. While committing this information about each individual assessment is not necessary, it is important to understand the appropriate uses of each category of assessment in a given situation with a specific population and possess the ability to identify specific assessments and the category to which they belong.

School counselors are aware of the options available to students with special needs (e.g., Braille print, large print, tape-recorded tests). Also, students whose primary language is not English may need bilingual test administration, test administration by a translator or interpreter, and/or a version of the test written in the students' primary language.

The most well-known and controversial formal assessments are the academic achievement tests. These tests are designed to measure a

### Table 4.2 Summary of Key Assessments Used in Schools

| Assessment Category | Assessments |
|---|---|
| *Achievement* evaluates general knowledge/ performance in a variety of subject areas. | Woodcock–Johnson Test of Achievement (Woodcock–Johnson) <br> PIAT <br> Stanford Achievement Test Series ACT—college entrance |
| *Aptitude* evaluates potential or ability to learn, assessing a variety of specific areas. | ASVAB <br> GATB <br> Kaufman Assessment Battery for Children <br> PSAT—practice for SAT <br> SAT—college entrance |
| *Intelligence* evaluates general cognitive ability. | WISC <br> WAIS <br> Stanford–Binet Intelligence Scales (Stanford–Binet) |
| *Interests* identify preferences for specific activities, matching personality type with six workplace environments. | SDS <br> SII <br> KOIS |
| *Personality* identifies attitudinal, emotional, interpersonal, and motivational characteristics. | Vineland Adaptive Behavior Scales (Vineland) <br> MBTI |

student's knowledge of subject content based on core academic standards up to the date of test administration. Achievement tests vary by name across states but are often referred to as *high stakes testing*. They are high stakes because, in most states, students cannot graduate without passing scores on these tests, and school and teacher performance is often measured by student performance on these tests.

While serving as an elementary school counselor, I coordinated school-wide standardized achievement testing for 8 years—SOL in Virginia. Over the years, I became consumed with admiration and respect for classroom teachers who, instead of kicking and screaming, gazed fearlessly into the eyes of achievement tests as Ahab into the eyes of the massive Moby Dick.

In addition to academic standards-driven achievement tests, other achievement tests, often used in the schools to assess students in kindergarten to grade 12 for gifted or special education, include the Woodcock–Johnson Test of Achievement (Woodcock–Johnson) and the PIAT. The Woodcock–Johnson and the PIAT reveal present levels of performance compared with that of peers and identify students' academic areas of strengths and weaknesses.

The Stanford Achievement Test Series is often used in the schools as a measure of achievement from kindergarten to grade 12. It is a general test of knowledge in a variety of subjects including math, English, science, and writing for each grade level. The test yields national percentile bands that illustrate how a student scores in relation to others students at that grade level.

---

### MY STUDENT MAY HAVE A DISABILITY

A third-grade teacher comes to you, the elementary school counselor and child study chair, to arrange for a child study meeting because she suspects that one of her students may have a learning disability, based on low academic functioning in math and writing. Which of the following would be useful in assessing the student?

 a. Peabody
 b. Standardized grade-level tests in math and writing
 c. Classroom and homework assignments
 d. All of the above

The ACT is one of the most widely used achievement tests taken by high school students to satisfy college entrance requirements. Total composite scores for all core subject areas covered (English, math, reading, science) by the test range from 1 to 36. The ACT writing test is optional.

Aptitude assessments are designed to evaluate an individual's potential or ability to learn. They measure a variety of specific areas such as art, music, mechanical, verbal, spatial, reasoning, critical reading, writing, and coding. Aptitude tests are primarily used in schools for the purpose of career decision making, special education screening, and entrance into the military. The most widely used aptitude tests in the schools are the ASVAB, the GATB, and the Kaufman Assessment Battery for Children. The ASVAB and GATB assessments are intended for students at the high school level. The Kaufman is used for children ages 3–18.

The SAT is the most widely used college entrance test and is often used with the ACT test to assess academic readiness for college. The test yields scores in three subject areas (critical reading, writing, and mathematics), with 800 being the highest possible score for each section for a total score of 2,400. The average score is 1,500. The SAT is most often taken during the spring of the junior year of high school and again in the fall of the senior year of high school. Many students take the PSAT as a practice test to the SAT during the ninth- and 10th-grade years, although some students take it during the fall of their junior year of high school. The PSAT is also used to make scholarship awards.

Intelligence assessments are used in the schools to determine a student's general cognitive ability. Intelligence tests yield a single *intelligence quotient* (IQ) score. The majority of individuals have an IQ score between 85 and 115, with 100 being the average. IQ scores above 115 are considered to depict superior intelligence, whereas IQ scores below 85 indicate borderline deficiency, with a score of 70 or less signifying retardation. IQ scores are often used to determine student placement in gifted and special education programs and aid educators in identifying a variety of cognitive challenges.

The most widely used intelligence tests in the schools are the WISC, ages 6–16, and the WAIS, ages 16–19. Individuals who are 16 can take either the WAIS or the WISC. Each assessment yields a verbal IQ, performance IQ, and full IQ (total cognitive development) score with a standard deviation of 15 and a 95 percent confidence level. Also widely used in schools is the Stanford–Binet Intelligence Scales (Stanford–Binet). The assessment can be administered on individuals ages 2 to 90 and yields

### THE COLLEGE DREAM

The mother of Carolyn, one of your 11th-grade high school students, is in your office expressing concern about Carolyn's ability to be successful in college. She shares that they do not have the money to pay for Carolyn's college just for Carolyn to "flunk out." She said that Carolyn told her that she does not qualify for any scholarships that are listed in the scholarship binder at school. You notice in the student information system that Carolyn has a GPA of 3.9 and is not showing any scores for college entrance testing. You ask the parent if Carolyn has taken any college entrance assessments as of yet. The parent said no because those, too, are expensive and she just is not sure about the whole college thing. The parent begins to cry, stating that it is just she and Carolyn, and the only income is her disability check. She said she feels lost because neither she nor anybody else in her family has ever gone to college. What other information might you want to find out in this case? How would you help this parent and Carolyn?

a verbal IQ, a nonverbal IQ, and a full-scale IQ with a standard deviation of 15 and a 95 percent confidence level.

Interest assessments, often referred to as interest inventories, discussed in Chapter 2, are primarily used for career development purposes. Generally, results obtained from interest inventories are derived by comparing student responses with those of individuals who have been successful in specific occupations or by comparing student responses with those of their peers. The most widely used interest inventories in the schools include the SDS, the SII, and the KOIS.

Standardized personality assessments provide information about a student's attitudinal, emotional, interpersonal, and motivational characteristics. Personality assessment may be used for (1) gaining insight into students' thoughts and behaviors, (2) placement into specialized programs (e.g., gifted, special education), and (3) career decision making. The most widely used personality assessments in the schools include the Vineland Adaptive Behavior Scales (Vineland), which measures levels of personal and social functioning, and the MBTI, which identifies patterns of behavior and preferences for relating to ideas, others, and the environment.

**MEETING ANDRE'S NEEDS**

Andre is a third-grade student whose misbehavior at school has become increasingly persistent. Andre has been consistently achieving academically at higher grade levels than third grade in all subject areas. Andre scored 5.3 (grade equivalent score) on his mathematics achievement test. How would you interpret this score for Andre's parents? What programs might you want to recommend that would help to further develop Andre's academic knowledge and skills and ensure that Andre remains challenged with a rigorous program to meet his special needs? How might you address Andre's misbehavior at this time?

## Informal Assessment

Nonstandardized assessments are subjective, are not norm-referenced, are generally qualitative in nature, and may be variable in their content, process, administration, scoring, and interpretation procedures. Nonstandardized tests are often referred to as informal assessments.

School counselors are careful to consider context, developmental level, and students' cultures and worldviews when using both formal and informal assessments. School counselors are also keenly alert to the subjective nature of informal assessment, exercising caution during implementation and interpretation. Additionally, school counselors do not rely on any single assessment but use a variety of informal assessments when appraising student functioning, which may include:

- Records review
- Observation
- Case study
- Role play
- Checklists
- Storytelling and story completion
- Student self-assessment and self-monitoring
- Portfolio
- Work samples and writings
- Consultation with teachers, parents, and other school personnel.

Informal interviews are often used by school counselors in the initial counseling sessions and as a means for assessing student progress on a continuous basis. In addition to fully exploring the issues that brought the student to counseling, school counselors may find helpful information when exploring the student's attitude, emotionality, thought processes, academic progress, school attendance and experiences, and relationships with family and home, school, and virtual friends.

Clinicians from outside the school system will often request a release of student records and call upon teachers, school nurses, and school counselors to collaborate and consult with regard to student functioning in order to assist in diagnosing disorders such as ADHD. A widely used informal student appraisal instrument for this purpose is the Connors Scale, which is also referred to as the Connors Test and the Connors Checklist. The Connors Scale is completed by educators and others who work closely with the student, documenting observations to aid clinicians in making a diagnosis. The Connors Scale is generally associated with assessment related to the diagnosis of ADHD.

**Table 4.3  BASIC ID**

| |
|---|
| (B)ehavior<br>Fine and gross motor skills and activities. |
| (A)ffect<br>Observed or client self-reported emotions. |
| (S)ensation<br>Sensory experiencing: taste (gustatory), touch (kinesthetic), sight (visual), smell (olfactory), hearing (auditory). |
| (I)magery<br>Mental pictures that have an impact on the client. |
| (C)ognition<br>Client thoughts and beliefs. |
| (I)nterpersonal relationships<br>Observed or self-reported interactions with others. |
| (D)rugs/diet<br>Biochemical and/or nutritional impact on the client. |

**Table 4.4 SOAP Notes**

| |
|---|
| (S)ubjective observations<br>Counselor perceptions of client thoughts, attitudes, emotions, and dispositions during sessions and the client's self-reported experiencing/observations (e.g., hopelessness, depression, client perceptions, anger). |
| (O)bjective observations<br>Directly observed behaviors and emotional experiencing during the counseling sessions (e.g., crying, posture, hygiene, orientation to time/place, physical appearance). |
| (A)ssessment<br>Appraisal based on counselor's general impressions of the client's psychological, social, and emotional functioning. |
| (P)lan<br>Treatment strategies to mediate presenting client concerns, which may include individual, small group counseling, and/or family counseling and a variety of theoretical approaches and counseling techniques. The plan might also include referral and further information gathering strategies. |

A commonly used method for informal student appraisals was developed by Lazarus (1976) and referred to as the BASIC ID approach (see Table 4.3). The acronym represents seven interdependent categories, or modalities (behavior, affect, sensation, imagery, cognition, interpersonal relationships, and drugs/diet), that aid school counselors in organizing case notes, identifying the individual's preferred modalities, clarifying problems, creating counseling interventions, and assessing the effectiveness of interventions and the progress of treatment.

SOAP notes (Cameron & Turtle-Song, 2002), too, are used by school counselors to organize case notes and develop case conceptualizations. Table 4.4 describes the characteristics of each of the four components of SOAP notes: (1) subjective observations, (2) objective observations, (3) assessment, and (4) plan.

# Life-Saving Assessment

Assessing the needs of individual students is important to identifying levels of academic performance as well as barriers to academic performance.

Identification and removal of barriers that impede a student's ability to be successful in school and in life is a goal of the school counseling program. There are times when appropriate individual student appraisal can save the life of a child. Children and adolescents live at the maximum pace of wide open. School counselor must go Mach 2 with our hair on fire, just to keep up (a pilfered line from *Top Gun*). At this speed, things can get very real, very fast.

When conducting student appraisals, school counselors look for the signs and symptoms associated with physical, verbal, and emotional child abuse and neglect, violence, substance abuse, depression, eating disorders, and attention deficit disorder in children and adolescents. Changes in behavioral, emotional, and attitudinal patterns are often clues alerting school counselors to the possibility of problematic issues in the student's life. One or more changes, unexplained by developmental stages, and the frequency, duration, and magnitude of behaviors noted as follows, should be explored (Morrison, 2016):

- Periods of disinterest
- Flat affect
- Interpersonal conflicts
- Sense of worthlessness or guilt
- Passivity
- Agitation or irritability
- Significant weight loss or weight gain
- Fatigue
- Changes in sleeping patterns (e.g., hardly sleeping, wanting to stay in bed)
- Trouble concentrating and following directions
- Inattentive
- Decline in academic performance
- Excessive absences
- Frequent/unexplained injuries
- Flinching
- Withdrawn
- Unattended medical conditions
- Emotionality
- Does not care to (or want to) go home.

## *Child Abuse and Neglect*

Conversations with parents and observations of parent–child interactions may expose additional signs of possible child abuse or neglect, or other problems related to family functioning. The following signs portrayed by a parent or guardian may signal child abuse or neglect (Child Welfare Information Gateway, 2013):

- Showing little concern for the child
- Indifference toward the child
- Apathy or depression
- Abusing alcohol or other drugs
- Irrational or bizarre behavior
- Being secretive or isolated
- Being overly protective, severely limiting child's contact, especially with opposite gender
- Being jealous or controlling
- Denying the existence of, or blaming the child for, problems at home or school
- Asking the teacher to use harsh punishment on the child for misbehavior
- Viewing the child as entirely bad, burdensome, or worthless
- Demanding a level of physical or academic performance that the child cannot achieve
- Looking primarily to the child for care, attention, and satisfaction of emotional needs
- Parent and child rarely touch or look at each other
- Parent and child view their relationship as entirely negative
- Parent and child state that they do not like each other.

There are also additional signs that warrant further exploration into possible sexual abuse. Students who are being sexually abused may exhibit one or more of the following as well as any of the signs and symptoms noted above (Bauman, 2008; Child Welfare Information Gateway, 2013):

- Nightmares
- Bed wetting
- Difficulty sitting or walking
- Sophisticated sexual knowledge or bizarre sexual behaviors

---

**AYMEE'S BASIC ID**

Aymee is a middle school student who is seeing you, her school counselor, because of social issues that she is experiencing in school. You are assessing Aymee's progress and determine interventions using BASIC ID, which is considered to be which type of assessment?

a. Standardized
b. Objective
c. Formal
d. Informal

---

- High-risk behaviors
- Running away
- Early pregnancy
- Change in appetite
- Refusal to change for gym class
- Thoughts of suicide
- Substance abuse
- Frequent medical conditions
- Anxiety/stress
- Depression
- Interpersonal relationship difficulties.

School counselors are mandated reporters of suspected child abuse and neglect, discussed in Chapter 1. Additional information on violence prevention and child abuse and neglect, along with mandated reporting requirements and Child Abuse and Neglect Training Modules, are available at www.dss.virginia.gov/family/cps/mandated_reporters/cwse5691/story.html.

## Substance Abuse

Substance abuse, too, often involves specific signs and symptoms. For example, children and adolescents who are using or abusing substances may exhibit one or more of the following behaviors (Capuzzi & Stauffer, 2015):

- Withdrawal from responsibility
- Increased secretiveness
- Wearing sunglasses inappropriately
- Wearing long sleeves in hot weather
- Stealing money
- Having associations with known substance abusers
- Taking risks
- Avoiding family members
- Talking excessively about drug/alcohol use
- Getting into legal trouble.

Duration, frequency, and intensity are important factors to consider when making student appraisals along with information shared during counseling sessions. When in doubt, consult, consult, consult, and err on the side of student safety. That is, make the call to the parent, legal system, or child protective services, as deemed appropriate. School counselors balance students' rights to privacy and confidentiality with duty to warn and duty to protect while also considering parental rights in the cases of minors, discussed in Chapter 1.

During assessment, school counselors may find that a recent death of an important other, a family transition, and/or a crisis situation have occurred in the student's life that accounts for observed changes. In such cases, school counselors explore the student's thoughts and emotions for possible *suicide ideation* because risk factors for child and adolescent suicide include recent losses or other events perceived as distressing by the student (McWhirter & McWhirter, 2012).

## Self-Harm

Intervening in cases where students are presenting self-injurious behaviors and/or suicide ideation is critical. Assessment is warranted when a student is experiencing an intense affective disturbance (e.g., rage, guilt, hopelessness, fear, depression, abandonment, anxiety), particularly when the precipitating event/issue is vague. Assessing for suicide is also warranted when a student is engaging in self-mutilating behaviors and/or is having thoughts of suicide, writing about suicide, has made comments about wanting to die, or has implied that others would be better off as a result of his or her death. Risk factors for suicidality in children and adolescents include (McWhirter & McWhirter, 2012):

- Negative family and/or peer interactions
- Loneliness/isolation
- Impulsivity
- Low tolerance for frustration
- Poor self-esteem
- Lack of problem-solving skills
- Faulty cognitions/negative beliefs
- Substance use
- A tendency toward risk-taking reactions to distress.

Once the school counselor feels confident that *suicide assessment* is needed, ask the student plainly, "Are you having thoughts about committing suicide now, or recently?" Depending on the developmental level of the child, the question may need to be, "Are you thinking about hurting yourself on purpose?" or "Are you thinking about killing yourself?" School counselors should assess for a plan and a means for following through on the plan. However, as noted above, err on the side of caution—above all else protect the child or adolescent; in this case, from the self.

While safeguarding the student until the parent or CPS arrives (see Chapter 1), school counselors should consider creating a no-suicide contract with the student, which can be verbal (with a handshake) or written (a document with a signature), affirming that the student will not harm himself or herself intentionally. Additionally, school counselors can help students by:

- Establishing a positive relationship (the crux of counseling)
- Assisting the student in identifying support systems and internal strengths to build protective factors
- Exploring and validating emotions
- Identifying problems; teaching and engaging the student in problem-solving strategies.

School counselors provide teachers and staff with suicide awareness training as part of a comprehensive approach to preventing student suicide. Elements of the training include recognizing the suicide risk factors noted previously and identifying behavioral and verbal warning signs and steps for intervention.

Behavioral warning signs may include giving possessions away, declining academic performance, a change in social interactions, and an increase in school absences. Verbal warning signs may also be present to include statements such as "life has no meaning," "nobody would miss me," and "my life is meaningless." Steps for intervention may include a formal written policy that outlines the process for referring students who may be at risk of suicide to the school counselor.

There are mixed views among school administrators and school counselors with regard to screening students for suicide ideation and implementing student programs aimed at suicide prevention education. Those who are against the screenings and prevention education believe that these strategies draw attention to suicide and may result in increased suicide attempts. Those who are in favor of these strategies believe that education will reduce the incidence of suicide. Because of this confluence of conflicting views, school counselors work closely with school administrators when planning suicide prevention programming.

Students at risk of suicide need mental health counseling and possibly hospitalization. Some schools will not allow students to return to school until parents or guardians have secured such counseling, because students experiencing this level of emotional disturbance are deemed harmful to themselves and possibly others.

### THE DIVORCE OF GEOFFREY'S PARENTS

Geoffrey, a 13-year-old student, expressed to you, his middle school counselor, that he is angry because of his parents' recent divorce. This was the second time Geoffrey came to you, but this time he seemed much more unkempt and upset. His hair was disheveled and his clothes were dirty. During this second session, Geoffrey sat slumped over with his hands clinched and began to cry, saying that his mother must now work so he never sees her, and his dad does not care enough to even visit on the days he has visitation. Geoffrey said that sometimes he just feels numb and other times he is so angry he could explode. He went on to say that he feels all alone and just wants to quit school because he does not understand the point of it all. Use SOAP notes to conceptualize this case.

Self-mutilation (e.g., cutting, burning, interfering with wound healing, biting, scratching) has been identified as a reaction and coping mechanism associated with feelings of depression, anger, frustration, and hopelessness and resulting in feelings of guilt, shame, and regret (Moyer & Nelson, 2007). Research has identified the importance of allowing students engaging in self-mutilating behaviors the opportunity to talk about the experiences—"to be heard" (p. 47) and to ask questions in a nonjudgmental environment.

Self-mutilation is viewed by the school counselor as an imminent risk and treated in the same fashion as suicide ideation with regard to involving parents or child protective services and providing referral resources. Some students try to convince school counselors that their self-mutilating behaviors are self-decoration. Avoid succumbing to deception by staying abreast of current developments in these areas of high-risk behavior. Training oneself, as well as teachers, parents, and administrators, in understanding the difference between self-mutilation and self-decoration is critical. In the end, when in doubt, err on the side of protecting the student from him- or herself.

Symptoms consistent with *anorexia* and *bulimia* are also viewed by the school counselor as imminent risk and should be brought to the attention of parents or child protective services. School counselors will also have resources ready to share as part of their ever-evolving resource listing for parents. The growing number of adolescents with eating disorders is alarming, calling for systemic prevention efforts on topics related to body image and the all too real natural consequences of eating disorders and anabolic steroid use.

To promote a continued trusting relationship with students for whom you must break confidentiality, remind the student of your legal and ethical responsibility to protect. You will have covered the limits of confidentiality earlier in the session or in your initial session with the student.

## Assessment and Diagnosis

School counselors are careful not to offer diagnoses. Even those school counselors who hold advanced licensure and national credentialing are discouraged from diagnosing students' mental health issues in the school setting. Clinical diagnosis is more often than not considered to be outside the scope of the practice of school counseling. Instead, when deeper issues are presented that are outside of the expertise of the school counselor or the scope of school counseling practices, school counselors strongly encourage parents and guardians to seek the assistance of a mental health counselor, psychologist, psychiatrist, physician, or family therapist.

Instead of a diagnosis, school counselors may wish to share observations as being "consistent with symptoms that are associated with_____" and provide parents with a list of counseling resources that address a broad range of services (e.g., family counseling, parenting education, mental health counseling, counseling for victims of abuse or sexual abuse, substance abuse counseling, support groups for children and parents, crisis–suicide intervention centers and numbers).

## Needs Assessment

Unlike formal and informal individual student assessments, needs assessments are generally used to systematically identify the needs of broader populations (e.g., student body, teachers, parents, community agencies) and subpopulations (e.g., special education students, fifth-grade teachers, parents of gifted students, mental health agencies). Information obtained from needs assessments aids school counselors in designing or redesigning programs for targeted populations and topics and continuous program improvement.

Needs assessment may be conducted using existing data or by gathering data in the form of participant perceptions from the target population using a needs assessment technique or instrument. Needs may be assessed using a selection of data or a selection of participants from the population to be served. An exhaustive list of existing data sources are provided in Chapter 5. When using existing data sources to assess need, school counselors look for patterns and inconsistencies. Assessing needs based on participant perceptions is not generally considered standardized but can take a more formal tone versus an informal tone. They may be written (e.g., survey, questionnaire) or oral (e.g., interview) and conducted in person, on the telephone, via the Internet, or by mail.

When assessing needs based on participant perception, the school counselor might also elect to use focus groups, community forums, and/or key informants. School counselors who elect to use focus groups select several individuals representative of the population to be served—like apple picking. Collectively, in a structured or semistructured format, differing needs are discussed and together the group prioritizes needs. If you picked any bad apples, this is where you will find out. Community forums have merit in that any stakeholder wishing to be involved may participate. School counselors announce the community forum meeting and the topic of discussion, and those interested participate in much the same fashion as the focus group. Key informants are selected by the school counselor based on their vast knowledge of the target population but may not necessarily be a member of the population. Key informants are generally surveyed individually or in small groups.

Needs assessments that seek participant perceptions may include any number of questions deemed important by the school counselor. The following sampling of questions would be considered appropriate for assessing the needs of upper elementary school students, adults, and students at the high school level:

■ What school counseling services do you find helpful?
■ What additional school counseling services would you find helpful?
■ What are the strengths of the school counseling program?
■ What suggestions do you have for possible improvements to the school counseling program?

Needs assessments for children may be read aloud with interpretations dependent upon developmental level. Needs assessments that make use of the check system are ideal for children and special needs populations. The following is a sample that illustrates how students would simply place a check in the box beside the topic(s) of interest:

■ Dealing with bullies
■ Making and keeping friends
■ Dealing with anger
■ Getting along with others
■ Making good choices
■ Doing more chores (tossed it in to see if you are still listening).

**DR. DATARULES**

Dr. Datarules, your school principal, has asked you, the school counselor, to provide him with data other than what is already available to him (e.g., school report cards, standardized testing results, classroom assessment results) that identifies instructional strategies that are both enjoyed by students and effective in producing higher levels of academic achievement. You decide to administer a needs assessment. Who would be the target of your assessment?

## Translating Needs: Developing Program Goals and Objectives

Once the school counselor has identified stakeholder needs, those needs are converted to goals that are supported by measurable objectives. For example, a goal based on need might be to manage school-wide conflict. The goal, as written here, does not lend itself to measurement. ASCA (2016b, 2012a) recommends creating SMART (**S**pecific, **M**easurable, **A**ttainable, **R**esults-oriented, **T**ime-bound) goals for the school counseling program. The following is an example of a SMART goal based on examination of the school's annual discipline report, which confirmed the highest number of incidences were in the category of "threaten, intimidate and/or physical contact with another student" (ASCA, 2016b, p. 45):

■ By May 20, 2017, the number of discipline referrals involving "threaten, intimidate and/or physical contact with another student" will decrease by 20 percent from 62 (previous school year) to 50 (current school year).

Based on a program's SMART goal, which was based on need, school counselors develop programming to turn goals into reality. One program toward this goal might be problem-solving. An objective toward this goal might be: "upon completion of the problem solving classroom guidance lesson, students will be able to identify four problem-solving strategies." We conclude, then, that there must be at least four problem-solving strategies covered in the curriculum content—aren't we brainiacs! Curriculum development is discussed in Chapter 6.

ASCA provides school counselors with three broad developmental domains (academic, career, and social/emotional) from which flow 35 Mindsets and Behaviors for Student Success standards. School counselors are encouraged to identify one or two specific Mindsets and Behaviors relevant to the program goal. The standard can then be operationalized (i.e., made more specific and measurable) by selecting a grade-level competency from the Mindsets and Behaviors database located at www.schoolcounselor.org/mindsetsandbehaviors, or school counselors are encouraged to write their own competency (i.e., specific, measurable objective) based on their unique school population/need and crosswalk with academic standards (ASCA, 2016b). Table 4.5 describes a method for creating measurable objects using a (W)ho, (H)ow, (W)hat process.

**Table 4.5  Who? How? What? of Objectives**

| |
| --- |
| (W) *Who* are the participants receiving the program/intervention?<br>    *Who* examples:<br>        "Students will"<br>        "Teachers will"<br>        "Parents will" |
| (H) *How* will we know the behavior is achieved?<br>    *How* examples:<br>        "Students will identify"<br>        "Parents will be able to"<br>        "Teachers will develop" |
| (W) *What* is the desired behavior?<br>    *What* examples:<br>        "Students will identify five study skills strategies"<br>        "Parents will be able to define ADHD"<br>        "Teachers will develop five auditory teaching strategies" |

**CAN THIS BE MEASURED?**

You are a school counselor facilitating a small group on the topic of anger management. The goal of the group is to learn how to express anger in a healthy way. This is a fine goal, to be sure; however, it is not measurable as it is. Which of the following would be a possible measurable objective to support this worthy group goal?

    a. Students will learn healthy ways to express anger.
    b. Students will express anger in ways that are not hurtful to others.
    c. Students will complete an anger management worksheet.
    d. Students will identify three anger management strategies.

# Chapter 4: Case Conceptualization Responses

# Student Appraisal

*Jennifer's Score*
The correct response is "b." Jennifer took a norm-referenced assessment, which is a standardized, formal assessment.

## Formal Assessment

*My Student May Have a Disability*
The correct response is "d." School counselors advocate for student appraisal that draws from multiple sources of both formal and informal assessments to promote practices that reduce premature or inaccurate diagnoses of learning disabilities.

*The College Dream*
Carolyn's GPA would indicate that she is academically successful. For this reason, the school counselor may wish to inquire as to why the parent believes her daughter will "flunk out" of college. It is important for the parent to know that the SAT is an aptitude test as well as a college entrance exam, which aids in predicting Carolyn's future performance as a college student. Also, providing the parent with an SAT fee waiver may help with the financial burden. Finally, walking the parent through the steps needed to complete and submit the Free Application for Federal Student Aid, or providing her with a contact that will assist her, is crucial to guiding the parent of a first-generation college student. This parent could also use some college preparation and financial aid information. Finally, considering the family's financial challenges and Carolyn's GPA, there may be scholarships available, so offering to assist Carolyn with the scholarship search and identifying colleges of interest is critical to helping Carolyn to realize the college dream. It would also be prudent to explore Carolyn's thoughts regarding attending college.

*Meeting Andre's Needs*
Andre's grade equivalent score on the mathematics test indicates that he has performed at the level of an average fifth-grade student, 3 months into the school year. Andre's persistent achievement in all subject areas

indicates the need for a more rigorous or advanced curriculum to keep him motivated toward academics. The school counselor may want to recommend Andre for accelerated learning and enrichment programs such as the school's gifted and talented program and the Governor's School, as well as summer enrichment experiences. The school counselor may want to reassess Andre's need for intervention pertaining to his misbehavior until he has engaged in these extracurricular activities. Andre's misbehavior may be due to boredom or frustration with the nondescript pace of the on-grade-level curriculum.

## Informal Assessment

*Aymee's BASIC ID*
The correct response is "d." BASIC ID is a comprehensive, nonstandardized, informal, and subjective assessment method that identifies students' specific strengths and needs, which allows the school counselor to tailor counseling to meet those needs.

*The Divorce of Geoffrey's Parents*
(S)ubjective observations
Anger (self-report), helplessness/depression (counselor observed).
(O)bjectives observations
Poor hygiene, sitting slumped over, hands clinched, crying.
(A)ssessment
Geoffrey appears to be somewhat depressed and anxious as a result of his parents' divorce. He also appears to be experiencing a sense of hopelessness about the future based on his statement that he wants to quit school because he does not understand the point of it.
(P)lan
The school counselor might provide Geoffrey with anger management techniques and combat possible depression with cognitive behavioral strategies. The school counselor might also offer strengths-based counseling to build resiliency and identify internal and external resources. Person-centered counseling, too, will allow Geoffrey the opportunity to express his emotions and gain insight into his emotional experiencing. Geoffrey would likely benefit from the support of a small group with other students whose parents are divorcing or already divorced. It would also be prudent to suggest parent involvement with Geoffrey.

## *Needs Assessment*

*Dr. Datarules*

Creating a needs assessment(s) that could be administered to both teachers and students would be warranted in this case. Teachers are in the best position to identify instructional strategies that work; students are in the best position to identify instructional strategies that are enjoyable. You can use a comparative analysis to provide Dr. Datarules with data that identify instructional strategies that are both effective and enjoyed by students.

## *Translating Needs: Developing Program Goals and Objectives*

*Can This Be Measured?*

The correct response is "d." This option will demonstrate that the student has learned strategies for expressing anger in a healthy way, which is the goal of the group. The objective is also written using the (W)ho, (H)ow, (W)hat for creating measurable program objectives. Options "a" and "b" cannot be measured as written, reading more like goals than objectives. Option "c" is an activity that will take place to support the goal, but completing the worksheet does not demonstrate that the student has learned healthy ways to express anger. This option does not provide the "what" of the desired behavior (i.e., healthy ways to express anger) to be accomplished.

# Chapter 4: Simulation

# Student Appraisal

## *Brief Case Description*

Timmy, a fifth-grade male, has been referred to the Child Study Team by his teacher because of both behavioral concerns and academic performance. You are the school counselor and chair of the Child Study Team. Based on the information presented in the meeting, the team decides testing is needed. The school counselor explains to Timmy's mother, who is present at the meeting, that the team will administer a series of assessments that will include assessing personality, achievement, aptitude, intelligence, and adaptive and social functioning.

## *Section A: Student Appraisal*

The parent inquires as to how personality tests will get to the root of Timmy's behavior. The school counselor responds that understanding Timmy's personality is important to helping the team to more fully understand Timmy's behavior, because the assessment reveals the following information:

(Select as many as you consider indicated in this section.)

| | |
|---|---|
| _____ A—1. | Emotional functioning |
| _____ A—2. | Level of knowledge |
| _____ A—3. | Motivation |
| _____ A—4. | Social functioning |
| _____ A—5. | Skills |
| _____ A—6. | Attitude |
| _____ A—7. | Abilities |
| _____ A—8. | Level of achievement |

## Section B: Student Appraisal

The parent asks the school counselor to identify the personality assessment that will be administered to her son. The school counselor identifies the following standardized personality test for the school setting at the elementary level:

(Select ONLY ONE in this section.)

| _____ B—1. | SII |
|---|---|
| _____ B—2. | KOIS |
| _____ B—3. | SAT |
| _____ B—4. | Vineland |
| _____ B—5. | ACT |

## Section C: Student Appraisal

The parent also asks which achievement test will be used. The school counselor replies, identifying the following standardized achievement test:

(Select ONLY ONE in this section.)

| _____ C—1. | MBTI |
|---|---|
| _____ C—2. | Woodcock–Johnson |
| _____ C—3. | Vineland |
| _____ C—4. | Stanford–Binet |
| _____ C—5. | SDS |
| _____ C—6. | ASVAB |
| _____ C—7. | SAT |

## Section D: Student Appraisal

The parent requests that the team also includes an aptitude test because she is worried about her son's potential for learning. The school counselor identifies the following standardized aptitude test appropriate for Timmy's age:

(Select ONLY ONE in this section.)

| | | |
|---|---|---|
| _____ D—1. | ACT |
| _____ D—2. | Kaufman Assessment Battery for Children |
| _____ D—3. | Vineland |
| _____ D—4. | Woodcock–Johnson |
| _____ D—5. | WISC |
| _____ D—6. | GATB |

## Section E: Student Appraisal

The team decides that meeting with the school counselor individually would also be beneficial. The school counselor gathers information using the following nonstandardized approaches to better understand Timmy and his situation:

(Select as many as you consider indicated in this section.)

| | | |
|---|---|---|
| _____ E—1. | Observation |
| _____ E—2. | WISC |
| _____ E—3. | Portfolio |
| _____ E—4. | ACT |
| _____ E—5. | Counseling notes |
| _____ E—6. | Consulting with teachers |
| _____ E—7. | School records |
| _____ E—8. | SAT |
| _____ E—9. | GATB |

## Section F: Student Appraisal

After four sessions, the school counselor becomes concerned about Timmy's increasingly flat affect, sense of worthlessness, excessive absences, inability to focus, lack of personal hygiene, and frequent injuries. The school counselor cannot get Timmy to communicate. The school counselor calls a meeting with Timmy and his mother. When his mother arrives, she is agitated and expresses what a terrible inconvenience this is, reiterating that she was just here a month ago. During the meeting, the school counselor identifies the following behaviors, coupled with the information she already has, as indicators of child abuse or neglect:

(Select as many as you consider indicated in this section.)

| | |
|---|---|
| _____ F—1. | Mother smells of alcohol |
| _____ F—2. | Mother asks school counselor to be sensitive to her son |
| _____ F—3. | Mother and son rarely make eye contact |
| _____ F—4. | Mother is apathetic |
| _____ F—5. | Mother allows son to control the conversation |
| _____ F—6. | Mother is indifferent toward son |
| _____ F—7. | Mother and son appear secretive |
| _____ F—8. | Frequent touch between mother and son |
| _____ F—9. | Son flinches when mother turns in his direction |

## Section G: Student Appraisal

After the meeting, the school counselor suspects that Timmy is being neglected and abused. The school counselor should take the following course of action:

(Select ONLY ONE in this section.)

| | |
|---|---|
| _____ G—1. | Contact local police |
| _____ G—2. | Contact Timmy's dad |
| _____ G—3. | Contact the emergency contact on Timmy's health card |
| _____ G—4. | Contact CPS |
| _____ G—5. | Ask the principal for appropriate course of action |
| _____ G—6. | Inform the mother of her suspicions, and say if it continues she will report her |

# Chapter 4: Simulation Answers

# Student Appraisal

## *Brief Case Description*

Timmy, a fifth-grade male, has been referred to the Child Study Team by his teacher because of both behavioral concerns and academic performance. You are the school counselor and chair of the Child Study Team. Based on the information presented in the meeting, the team decides testing is needed. The school counselor explains to Timmy's mother, who is present at the meeting, that the team will administer a series of assessments that will include assessing personality, achievement, aptitude, intelligence, and adaptive and social functioning.

## *Section A: Student Appraisal*

The parent inquires as to how personality tests will get to the root of Timmy's behavior. The school counselor responds that understanding Timmy's personality is important to helping the team to more fully understand Timmy's behavior because the assessment reveals the following information:

(Select as many as you consider indicated in this section.)

| A—1. | Emotional functioning<br>Yes<br>The personality assessment provides this information. |
|---|---|
| A—2. | Level of knowledge<br>No<br>The personality assessment does not provide this information. Tests of achievement and intelligence tests measure knowledge. |
| A—3. | Motivation<br>Yes<br>The personality assessment provides this information. |
| A—4. | Social functioning<br>Yes<br>The personality assessment provides this information. |

| A—5. | Skills<br>No<br>The personality assessment does not provide this information. Aptitude tests measure skills. |
|------|------------------------------------------------------------------------------------------------------------------|
| A—6. | Attitude<br>Yes<br>The personality assessment provides this information. |
| A—7. | Abilities<br>No<br>The personality assessment does not provide this information. Aptitude tests measure abilities. |
| A—8. | Level of achievement<br>No<br>The personality assessment does not provide this information. Achievement is measured using achievement tests such as the Stanford series. |

## Section B: Student Appraisal

The parent asks the school counselor to identify the personality assessment that will be administered to her son. The school counselor identifies the following standardized personality test for the school setting at the elementary level:

(Select ONLY ONE in this section.)

| B—1. | SII<br>No<br>The SII measures career interest. |
|------|-------------------------------------------------|
| B—2. | KOIS<br>No<br>The KOIS is used for career exploration and planning. |
| B—3. | SAT<br>No<br>The SAT is an aptitude test. |

| B—4. | Vineland<br><br>Yes<br><br>The Vineland measures levels of personal and social functioning and is considered to be a personality test. |
|---|---|
| B—5. | ACT<br><br>No<br><br>The ACT is a test of achievement. |

## Section C: Student Appraisal

The parent also asks which achievement test will be used. The school counselor replies identifying the following standardized achievement test:
(Select ONLY ONE in this section.)

| C—1. | MBTI<br><br>No<br><br>The MBTI is a personality test. |
|---|---|
| C—2. | Woodcock–Johnson<br><br>Yes<br><br>The Woodcock–Johnson is a test of achievement. |
| C—3. | Vineland<br><br>No<br><br>The Vineland is considered a personality test/test of adaptive behavior. |
| C—4. | Stanford–Binet<br><br>No<br><br>The Stanford–Binet is a test of intelligence. |
| C—5. | SDS<br><br>No<br><br>The SDS is a career interest inventory. |
| C—6. | ASVAB<br><br>No<br><br>The ASVAB is an aptitude test. |
| C—7. | SAT<br><br>No<br><br>The SAT is an aptitude test. |

## Section D: Student Appraisal

The parent requests that the team also includes an aptitude test because she is worried about her son's abilities and potential for learning. The school counselor identifies the following standardized aptitude test appropriate for Timmy's age:

(Select ONLY ONE in this section.)

| D—1. | ACT<br>No<br>The ACT is an achievement test. |
|---|---|
| D—2. | Kaufman Assessment Battery for Children<br>Yes<br>The Kaufman Assessment Battery for Children is an aptitude test often used in schools for ages 3–18. |
| D—3. | Vineland<br>No<br>The Vineland is considered a personality test/test of adaptive behavior. |
| D—4. | Woodcock–Johnson<br>No<br>The Woodcock–Johnson is a test of achievement. |
| D—5. | WISC<br>No<br>The WISC is often used in schools for diagnostic testing to assess level of intelligence. |
| D—6. | GATB<br>No<br>The GATB is an aptitude test, but it is intended for students in grades nine and higher. |

## Section E: Student Appraisal

The team decides that meeting with the school counselor individually would also be beneficial. The school counselor gathers information using the following nonstandardized approaches to better understand Timmy and his situation:

(Select as many as you consider indicated in this section.)

| E—1. | Observation<br>Yes<br>School counselors gain valuable information by observing students and their interactions with peers and adults in the classroom, on the playground, at lunch, and so on. |
|---|---|
| E—2. | WISC<br>No<br>This is a standardized test for intelligence. |
| E—3. | Portfolio<br>Yes<br>Portfolios provide a chronicle of information about a student's interests, strengths, and challenges. |
| E—4. | ACT<br>No<br>This is a standardized measure of achievement. |
| E—5. | Counseling notes<br>Yes<br>School counselor case notes provide a means by which to follow a student's progress from initial session to final session. |
| E—6. | Consulting with teachers<br>Yes<br>Consultation with other school personnel is a valuable means by which to learn more about a student by someone who may know the student better and/or in a different capacity. |
| E—7. | School records<br>Yes<br>A thorough review of the student's cumulative record provides the school counselor with insight into the student's health, personal–social, academic, and possibly psychological, social, and emotional functioning. |

| E—8. | SAT<br>No<br>The SAT is a standardized measure of aptitude. |
|------|----------------------------------------------------------------|
| E—9. | GATB<br>No<br>The GATB is a standardized aptitude measure. |

## Section F: Student Appraisal

After four sessions, the school counselor becomes concerned about Timmy's increasingly flat affect, sense of worthlessness, excessive absences, inability to focus, lack of personal hygiene, and frequent injuries. The school counselor cannot get Timmy to communicate. The school counselor calls a meeting with Timmy and his mother. When his mother arrives, she is agitated and expresses what a terrible inconvenience this is, reiterating that she was just here a month ago. During the meeting, the school counselor identifies the following behaviors, coupled with the information she already has, as indicators of child abuse/neglect:

(Select as many as you consider indicated in this section.)

| F—1. | Mother smells of alcohol<br>Yes<br>Alone this would not be an indicator. However, coupled with other indicators this is considered. |
|------|--------------------------------------------------------------------------------------------------------------------------------------|
| F—2. | Mother asks school counselor to be sensitive to her son<br>No<br>Generally, abusive parents will encourage the school counselor to use stern punishment. |
| F—3. | Mother and son rarely make eye contact<br>Yes<br>Alone this would not be an indicator. However, coupled with other indicators this is considered. |
| F—4. | Mother is apathetic<br>Yes<br>Alone this would not be an indicator. However, coupled with other indicators this is considered. |

| F—5. | Mother allows son to control the conversation<br>No<br>Generally, the abusive parent will control the conversation. |
|------|------------------------------------------------------------|
| F—6. | Mother is indifferent toward son<br>Yes<br>Alone this would not be an indicator. However, coupled with other indicators this is considered. |
| F—7. | Mother and son appear secretive<br>Yes<br>Alone this would not be an indicator. However, coupled with other indicators this is considered. |
| F—8. | Frequent touch between mother and son<br>No<br>Generally, the abusive parent will not openly display intimacy.<br>Frequent touching and inappropriate or questionable touching could be an indicator of sexual abuse. All to be considered in context and in relation to other signs. |
| F—9. | Son flinches when mother turns in his direction<br>Yes<br>This behavior may be associated with physical and sexual abuse. |

## Section G: Student Appraisal

After the meeting, the school counselor suspects that Timmy is being neglected and abused. The school counselor should take the following course of action:

(Select ONLY ONE in this section.)

| G—1. | Contact local police<br>No<br>The local police may refer the child to CPS, or make contact with CPS themselves. |
|------|------------------------------------------------------------|
| G—2. | Contact Timmy's dad<br>No<br>The school counselor cannot be sure that Timmy's dad is not involved or will protect Timmy. |

| G—3. | Contact the emergency contact on Timmy's health card<br>No<br>School counselors have a legal responsibility to report suspected child abuse to appropriate authorities (i.e., CPS). |
|---|---|
| G—4. | Contact CPS<br>Yes<br>This is the professional, ethical, and legal course of action. |
| G—5. | Ask the principal for appropriate course of action<br>No<br>Principals depend upon school counselors to know the appropriate and legal course of action in these situations. Principals generally like to know when calls are made to CPS, because social workers often visit the child at the school and go through the front office. |
| G—6. | Inform the mother of her suspicions, and say if it continues she will report her<br>No<br>This could anger the parent, who, if she is abusive, may take it out on Timmy. Instead of protecting Timmy, you may have placed him in harm's way. The responsible, ethical, and legal course of action is to report suspected child abuse to CPS. |

# Chapter 4: Guided Reflection

Compare individual and program assessment. Then, describe the differences between assessing individual needs (or student appraisal) and assessing program needs.

Discuss the importance of assessment (both individual and program) in identifying needs and creating a needs-driven school counseling program.

Compare and contrast formal and informal assessments. Give examples of each.

After examining the construct, summarize (rewrite in your own words) what is meant by life-saving assessment. Then, discuss the importance of assessment in the following critical incidents:

Child abuse and neglect

Substance abuse

Self-harm

Describe how the school counselor generally engages in assessment in the school setting.

Describe how the school counselor generally engages in diagnosis in the school setting.

Explain what a needs assessment is, and create one item that might be on a needs assessment for each of the following developmental levels: (1) elementary students, (2) middle school students, and (3) parents.

Compare goals and objectives. What are the differences? Give an example of a goal. Then, create one supporting objective for that goal.

*Chapter 5*

# Research and Evaluation

School counselors make use of research and engage in research, particularly program evaluation, to create a cycle of research consumption and production. The importance of accountable practices cannot be overstated. The fundamental fact is, a tried-and-true school counseling intervention can forever change the direction of a student's life.

Research and program evaluation are the school counselor's bread and butter. Data gleaned from the analysis of research and program evaluation are essential in order to

- Identify practices that contribute to academic success and the personal–social and career development of students.
- Develop empirically supported curriculum.
- Engage in professional advocacy.
- Provide reliable consultation services.
- Make programming decisions.
- Enhance accountability.
- Shape policy in the schools and at the local, state, and federal levels.
- Inform and sustain the profession.

## Research

School counselors are savvy consumers of professional literature and research. Unlike the scratchings of graffiti and murmurs of idle gossip, research communicates factual information. Information shared through published research identifies evidence-based techniques, models, and approaches, identifying what works and with whom, that is, best practices.

Best practices are the compass for school counselor prevention and intervention programs, techniques, and methods of service delivery. Best practices are easily located but require that school counselors know their way around professional peer-reviewed education and counseling journals. The application of best practices requires the ability to identify and critically evaluate important components of relevant studies such as (1) theoretical orientation, (2) target population, (3) intervention used, (4) method of data collection and analysis, and (5) results.

School counselors plan curriculum targeting students' needs as indicated by an analysis of data derived from needs assessment and/or existing school sources. During program planning, school counselors determine ways in which they will measure the program's effectiveness in meeting the stated goals and objective(s), discussed later in this chapter. In this regard, school counselors are creating and delivering research-supported curriculum that is both data driven and data producing.

ACA has a list of counseling-related peer-reviewed journals on their website at www.counselor.com. There are two primary professional school counseling journals available that identify innovative methods and research for promoting effective practices in school counseling. *Professional School Counseling* (PSC) is the American School Counselor Association (ASCA's) award-winning, peer-reviewed journal published five times a year and free of charge to ASCA members. PSC is available in print or online. The peer-reviewed *Journal of School Counseling* (JSC), sponsored by the College of Education, Health, and Human Development at Montana State University, is an online journal dedicated to the practice of school counseling (www.jsc.montana.edu/index.html).

The National Technology Institute for School Counselors at www.tech counselor.org houses research-supported information and resources.

*ASCA Scene* at www.schoolcounselor.org/SCENE is loaded with research-supported programs and interventions. *Cultivating Performance* at www.thenewschoolcounselor.com introduces culturally sensitive research-supported crosswalking strategies to close the achievement gap and enhance total student development. *Cultivating Performance* also introduces interactive action plan (SCOPE) and results report (School Counseling Operational Report of Effectiveness, or SCORE) templates that walk school counselors through programming from conception to evaluation. SCOPE is illustrated in Chapter 6, and SCORE is illustrated later in this chapter in the section titled "Documenting Outcomes with Results Reports."

---

**DROPOUT PREVENTION**

A high school counselor designed a program using attendance and graduation reports to identify specific populations of students, who for a variety of reasons are not coming to school. He designed a program to meet the needs of these students with the goal of reducing truancy and school dropout rates and improving school attendance. The school counselor just evaluated the program to find that the program has been effective in meeting the established goals. Which of the following would best describe the practices used by this school counselor?

   a. Data-producing program
   b. Data-driven and data-producing program
   c. Research-based programming
   d. None of the above

---

## Center for School Counseling Outcome Research and Evaluation

The Center for School Counseling Outcome Research and Evaluation (CSCORE) was established by a diverse group of counselor educators to aid school counselors in identifying school counseling practices that result in positive student outcomes. CSCORE provides international leadership that focuses on research-supported systemic programming and evaluation to support families and communities and students to achieve academically. To access CSCORE, go to www.umass.edu/schoolcounseling.

## School Counseling Analysis, Leadership, and Evaluation

ASCA established the School Counseling Analysis, Leadership, and Evaluation (SCALE) Research Center to aid school counselors in identifying best practices that demonstrate how a comprehensive school counseling program is connected to student success. The SCALE Research Center helps to connect school counselors with counselor educators for collaborative research design, implementation, evaluation, and publication. The center also provides school counselors with professional development opportunities grounded in accountable research-supported programming and practices, as well as training related to data collection and analysis. To access the SCALE Research Center, go to http://scale.schoolcounselor.org.

## Program Evaluation

Section B.2.n. of the ASCA *Ethical Standards for School Counselors* (ASCA, 2016a) states that school counselors "adhere to educational/psychological research practices, confidentiality, safeguards, security practices and school district policies when conducting research." Program evaluation is the most widely used method of research in the schools, providing school counselors with information about what works, demonstrating *evidence* over *effort*—and answering the pressing question: "How are students different as a result of the school counseling program?" Program evaluation keeps us out of the shadows and in the sunlight.

School counselors are called to systematically collect and analyze data in order to improve programming and to demonstrate program effectiveness by measuring the outcomes of school counseling practices (ASCA, 2016b, 2013, 2012a). Effective practices sustain and strengthen the school counseling profession. For these reasons, there is a resounding call to school counselors from school counseling and educational leaders to engage in program evaluation as a primary and critical area of *action research* (Erford, 2014). Program evaluation is also the ethical responsibility of school counselors. Section A.3.e. of the ASCA *Ethical Standards for School Counselors* (ASCA, 2016a) calls for school counselors to "collect process, perception and outcome data and analyze the data to determine the progress and effectiveness of the school counseling program."

Just as research-supported practices necessitate that school counselors become savvy consumers of research, demonstrating results-based practices and accountability to stakeholders requires that school counselors become efficient producers of research. As an essential competency, legislative mandate, and ethical responsibility, it is important that program evaluation becomes an integral component of the school counseling program's research, review, and feedback structure.

Historically, service logs have been used to document time on task and illustrate the numerous and diverse duties and levels of responsibilities of the school counselor. For example, service logs include how often or how much time school counselors spend doing the following:

■ Community and parent contacts
■ Teacher and colleague consulting and collaboration
■ Referrals to outside agencies
■ Committee meetings
■ Individual counseling
■ Small group counseling
■ Classroom guidance
■ Program coordination.

Although services delivered has its value in identifying *what* it is that school counselors do from day to day, it is inadequate in an outcome-driven educational environment. As the axiom goes, "We are drowning in information, but starved for knowledge." Ongoing evaluation satisfies that hunger by collecting and analyzing data that increases knowledge. That is, program evaluation demonstrates outcomes pertaining to the effectiveness and/or successful implementation of services in measurable terms.

**TROY**

You are a seasoned elementary school counselor mentoring Troy, your itinerant, first-year elementary school counselor. Troy wants to demonstrate the helpfulness of the small group intervention he created because it has become so popular and many students are asking to be a part of future groups. He asks you what method he should use to demonstrate how the groups have helped students. You reply

a. Program evaluation to demonstrate effectiveness in meeting objectives
b. Service logs to demonstrate how many students have been seen and how many groups have been conducted
c. Both a and b
d. None of the above

Data collected through program evaluation demonstrates how school counselors are contributing to positive student outcomes. Stakeholders review data collected through program evaluation to assess the value of the school counseling programs in meeting student needs and the needs of the collective. School administrators use these data to justify resource allocations and the existence of school counseling programs and to demonstrate accountability, which is permeating every molecule of the school counseling profession. Program evaluation may very well be the lifeline for school counseling programs hovering on the brink of extinction. Program evaluation does not equal accountability but precedes it as a means by which to demonstrate credible professional practices. Accountability also includes data-driven practices and prevention and intervention programming that are supported by standards and research.

---

**ACCOUNTABILITY**

Principal Sorretusay requires that all the high school counselors in her building implement programs that demonstrate accountability. One of the school counselors conducted a program evaluation on the current transitioning program being used for incoming freshmen. The principal said she was pleased, but that she was sorry to say that this was not enough. Principal Sorretusay commented that she believed that school counselors should be evaluating their programs on an ongoing basis as a matter of professional practice. What is the assumption, or misconception, on the part of the school counselor in this case?

---

## Outcome and Process Evaluations

Program evaluations that measure outcome, that is, the effectiveness of the program in achieving intended goals and objectives, are important in establishing a causal link between school counseling programs and student change. *Outcome evaluations*, sometimes referred to as summative evaluations or quantitative evaluations, seek to answer a significant question: "Did it work?"

**PRINCIPAL SHOME**

Your principal, Dr. Shome, is not convinced that interrupting a teacher's instructional time with classroom guidance lessons is beneficial. He has come to you requesting data that shows "how" your school counseling classroom guidance lessons are making a positive difference in the lives of students. Which of the following types of program evaluation methods would be most useful in responding to your principal's request?

a. Results of a student and teacher survey assessing their perceptions of a classroom guidance lesson.
b. Results of a forced-choice, pre-/post-classroom guidance lesson measure created from lesson content.
c. Results of a pre-classroom guidance lesson measure that asks students what they hope to learn from the lesson, and a post-lesson measure that asks students what they learned from the lesson.
d. A post-classroom guidance measure that asks students to describe what they liked about the lesson and their suggestions for how the program may have made more of a positive difference for them.

Program evaluations can also measure process. *Process evaluations* assess program functioning, strengths, weaknesses, and the extent to which the program meets the expectations of and serves the target population. Process evaluations, also known as formative evaluations and qualitative evaluations, are useful for program decision making and program improvement. Process evaluations seek to answer questions such as: "How did it work?" "How or with what population did it work best?" "Is the program proceeding as planned?"

Although the call from educational and school counseling leaders is focused on outcome measures, the importance of process measures cannot be underestimated. For example, should results of a program evaluation demonstrate less than positive outcomes, process evaluation may provide school counselors with information for program changes that may improve future outcomes. Additionally, even when outcome measures are positive, additional program data (i.e., process and perception data) might provide information that can be used to strengthen program outcomes, uncover further needs and unexpected benefits of the program, and/or identify additional target populations.

---

**OUTCOME OR PROCESS?**

You are the middle school counselor at Sunflower Middle School in Pratt, Kansas. You have been facilitating a peer mediation program for the past 2 years, and you want to determine whether or not the program is meeting the established goals and gain information that will identify areas of strengths and weaknesses for improving the program. What type of evaluation would be the most useful?

    a. Process evaluation
    b. Outcome and process evaluations
    c. Outcome evaluation
    d. None of the above

---

## Proximal and Distal Evaluations

Proximal evaluation measures student characteristics immediately before and after the program or intervention. The administration of proximal evaluations allows school counselors to establish correlations and, in some cases, depending upon the strength of the research design, a causal link between school counseling interventions and outcomes.

Distal measures do not generally take place immediately following the program or intervention, but it is possible depending upon research design. Distal evaluation outcomes alone do not definitively link school counseling programming to student change because of the great number of factors (i.e., extraneous variables) that impact student development over time (i.e., between phases of evaluation).

There has been some debate over the significance of proximal (immediate) versus distal (over time) program evaluation in linking school counseling program activities to what students know and can do as a result of the intervention or program. However, since measuring the effectiveness of school counseling programs is the professional *zeitgeist*, then proximal outcome evaluation takes priority. Proximal evaluation methods, then, are primarily used to establish correlation, if not causality, whereas distal evaluations are often used as a means of cross-validation to further support, or call into question, proximal evaluation outcomes.

---

**DARE TO SAY NO**

A middle school counselor created a classroom guidance unit that involves two visits to the health and PE classrooms over a period of 2 weeks to cover a drug and alcohol prevention program to supplement the DARE and Just Say No programs at their school. During the first visit, the school counselor administered two questionnaires developed from the content of the curriculum. One of the questionnaires included items that would be covered during this first lesson; the other questionnaire included content that would be covered in the entire 2-day program. On the second visit, the school counselor administered a questionnaire that included items that would be covered during this second lesson. One week following the unit, the school counselor returned to the classrooms to administer a questionnaire that was identical to the one administered during the first lesson, which included content that would be covered in the entire 2-day program. This is an example of the following type of program evaluation:

    a. Proximal
    b. Distal
    c. Outcome
    b. Proximal and distal

---

## Methodology

Program evaluation is a type of field-based outcome study, or applied research. There are many other types of outcome research designs that could be used to measure any number of research questions. In fact, an infinite number of possibilities exist. Table 5.1 lists the three most

**Table 5.1 Frequently Used Outcome Research Methodologies**

| |
| --- |
| *Non-experimental (or Pre-experimental)* |
| Pretest–posttest (one group only) |
| Case study (examination of one individual or group) |
| *Quasi-experimental* |
| Pre-test–post-test (two or more groups) |
| Non-equivalent control group (use of a control group and a pre-/post-measure to understand similarities and differences of groups prior to intervention). |
| Time series design (no control group; one sample with multiple measures on three or more occasions) |
| *True experimental* |
| Randomized pre-test/post-test with control group |
| Randomized post-test only with control group |

commonly used designs (i.e., non-experimental, quasi-experimental, and true experimental) by school counselors when conducting outcome research in the school setting (Erford, 2014).

There are basic differences in the three designs. The true experimental design uses random sampling and control groups; the quasi-experimental design shares similar characteristics of the true experimental design but does not use random assignment. The quasi-experimental design involves multiple groups or multiple measures. Non-experimental designs are generally one-time surveys and single observations. The true experimental design is the strongest for assessing cause and effect, with non-experimental designs having the least value for determining cause and effect between the intervention and the outcome.

Non-experimental and quasi-experimental designs do not allow school counselors to absolutely conclude that observed changes were due to their intervention. Nonetheless, these designs are invaluable in the educational setting where true experiments are extremely difficult because of vast uncontrollable variables and the ethical concerns of randomly assigning children and adolescents to treatment conditions and control groups. In

**IS PEER HELPING—HELPING?**

A school counselor conducts a program evaluation that assesses the impact of a peer-helping program in five classrooms over a 4-week period of time. This methodology is considered to be

a. True experimental design
b. Non-experimental design
c. Quasi-experimental design
d. All of the above

the educational setting, the non-experimental and quasi-experimental pre-/post-program evaluation is the most widely used research design.

Program evaluations that use triangulation (i.e., the incorporation of multiple sources of data), in addition to both proximal and distal measures, strengthen confidence in observed changes. Figure 5.1 is an example of such a design, illustrating the evaluation questions, data sources, and methods of data analysis of a comprehensive and collaborative peer mediation program evaluation conducted by a school counselor in collaboration with counselor educators (Schellenberg et al., 2007).

# Role of Data

While presenting in particular circles, just my mentioning the word *data* elicits a stomach-knotting panic response that is transparent on anguish-stricken faces. It is as though I just tried to pickpocket their superhero powers. My compassion runs deep on this issue, and I find myself wanting to say it in the most sincere way that I can muster: "Relax Superman, it is not kryptonite." If you relate to this remark, as I once did—yes, I admit it—then the time is now to square with data. Because the thing is, as the tide of accountability rises, so too does the demand for data. Best practices necessitate that school counselors use data to create needs-driven programs and to assess the effectiveness of school counseling programs and practices.

The study of data is a powerful process that reveals not only stakeholder needs but inequities and barriers to academic achievement and other

**Evaluation Question, Data Sources, Methods of Data Analysis**
**(Quasi-experimental Design)**

*(Reducing Levels of Elementary School Violence with Peer Mediation)*
Schellenberg, Parks-Savage, & Rehfuss, 2007

---

Do peer mediation sessions result in the successful resolution of student conflict?

Data Source: peer mediation session records over one academic year

Data Analysis: Percentages

---

Do the number of school-wide out-of-school suspensions decrease with the implementation of the Peace Pal program?

Data Source: out-of-school suspension data over a 5-year period

Data Analysis: Frequencies and percentages

---

Do disputing students who participate in peer mediation sessions view the sessions as valuable?

Data Source: peer mediation session records over one academic year

Data Analysis: Percentages

---

Do Peer mediators perceive the Peace Pal program as valuable?

Data Source: process questions 5 years post-program

Data Analysis: Percentages and qualitative

---

**Figure 5.1 Evaluation question, data sources, methods of data analysis (quasi-experimental design).**

*Source*: Adapted from Schellenberg, R., Parks-Savage, A., & Rehfuss, M. (2007). *Professional School Counseling, 10*, 475–481.

information essential to targeted, goal-focused programming and continuous improvement. Data, data, everywhere! The effective management of data is essential to organizing critical information about the past and the present while guiding the future of the school counseling program. Table 5.2 lists data skills considered essential to effectively managing data in the school counseling program (Erford, 2014; ASCA, 2012a, 2013; Schellenberg, 2008).

**Table 5.2 Essential Data Skills for School Counselors**

- Ability to identify existing data sources within and outside of the school.
- Ability to collect process, perception, and outcome data related to individuals, groups, and programs.
- Ability to disaggregate data and identify inequities and barriers to student success.
- Ability to analyze and interpret data to identify and prioritize needs and develop appropriate programming.
- Ability to establish baselines and create measurable goals and action plans based on data.
- Ability to assess counseling progress and evaluate programs to determine effectiveness of practices.
- Ability to use data to create a continuous cycle of program improvement.
- Ability to create results reports from program outcome data.

Developing data skills; thus, your competency in working with data is not difficult once you make data your friend. To increase your data competency, review school data reports and report cards over time to observe trends, changes, and gaps and collect and examine pre- and post-test data from school counseling curriculum lessons and group counseling (Kaffenberger & Young, 2013).

ASCA calls for school counselors to collect three types of data: (1) process data, (2) perception data, and (3) outcome data when evaluating programs/services (ASCA, 2012a, 2016b). Process data is simply the number of students, number of sessions/lessons, length of sessions/lessons, and how/when the counseling service(s) is delivered. Perception data measures what participants think they know, believe, or can do, and/or attitudes, knowledge, and skills attained by participants, using self-report measures before (pre-test) and after (post-test) the counseling service. Outcome data supports the need for a particular counseling service, primarily classroom guidance lessons or group counseling, and is used to demonstrate the impact of the counseling service with objective/standardized data.

School counselors can visit the state department of education website and/or school and school division websites for detailed local data that depict the unique needs of the population they serve. School counselors who make use of the robust sources of outcome data on hand in their schools have a foundation for accountable program construction. As discussed earlier, it is prudent to capture data from multiple sources in order to clearly identify needs and level of needs, and to strengthen confidence in observed changes demarcated by outcome data. The following list includes a few possible outcome data sources for needs identification and program evaluation generally available to school counselors within the school in which they practice:

■ Attendance rates
■ Career assessments
■ Classroom performance data
■ College acceptance rates
■ Course enrollment
■ Demographic data
■ Discipline records
■ Dropout rates
■ Expulsion records
■ General Equivalency Diploma track records
■ Gifted education placement records
■ Grade point average
■ Grade reports
■ Graduation rates
■ Program placement
■ Promotion and retention rates
■ Scholarship records
■ Special education placement records
■ Standardized assessment data
■ Suspensions (in school)
■ Suspensions (out of school).

## Documenting Outcomes with Results Reports

School counselors share the outcomes of program evaluations in order to inform the profession and to demonstrate program effectiveness. Inquiring minds want to know *how* we make a difference in the lives of students. *Results reports* are the medium used to accomplish this communication. Results reports document program effectiveness in meeting stated goals and objectives.

Student change and the level of change as a result of the application of school counseling program interventions and strategies are demonstrated on the results report. For example, the report may indicate that the students' test scores improved as a consequence of participation in small group counseling on the topic of test-taking strategies. The immediate and long-term impact of the outcome and the implications for the school counseling program are also included. Results reports include a minimum of the following components (ASCA, 2012a):

■ Grade level of participants
■ Content/curriculum (sometimes listed in accompanying action plan)
■ Process data (number of lessons or sessions and number of participants)
■ Knowledge gains (or other short-term perception data)
■ Impact on behavior, attendance, achievement (or other long-term results)
■ Implications for the school counseling program.

Figure 5.2 illustrates *SCORE* (Schellenberg, 2008). SCORE illustrates the outcomes of a responsive, crosswalking intervention that is culturally sensitive and aimed at closing the achievement gap (Schellenberg & Grothaus, 2009).

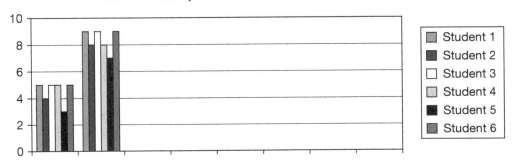

**Figure 5.2 SCORE.**

*Source*: From Schellenberg, R. (2013). *A New Era in School Counseling*. Lanham, MD: Rowman Littlefield Education. Reprinted with permission.

# Chapter 5: Case Conceptualization Responses

## Research

*Dropout Prevention*

The correct response is "b." The school counselor is demonstrating school counseling practices that are both data driven (i.e., he or she reviewed data to identify and create a program based on student need) and data producing (i.e., he or she evaluated the program to obtain data that supports the effectiveness of the program).

## Program Evaluation

*Troy*

The correct response is "a." Troy wants to demonstrate how his small group has helped students. Service logs will only show the number of times the group has been facilitated. Demand for the group does not mean that it is effective. Student may just really like Troy, the group experience, or getting out of class. Troy needs to conduct program evaluation to determine the outcome of his efforts.

*Accountability*

The assumption, or misconception, on the part of the school counselor is his or her belief that program evaluation equals accountability. Program evaluation is a component of accountability, but accountable school counseling programs also include needs assessment based on collected or existing data and programming and interventions that are grounded in research and standards. School counselors use action plans and results reports to document and share accountable practices with stakeholders.

### *Outcome and Process Evaluations*

*Principal Shome*

The correct response is "b." Dr. Shome is asking for *outcome* data. By administering a forced-choice (e.g., multiple choice, true–false) pre-lesson measure and post-lesson measure created from lesson content and lesson objectives, you can objectively measure your lesson outcome. Because you are administering the measure immediately before and immediately following the lesson (proximal evaluation), you can claim with some certainty that change is due to your intervention.

*Outcome or Process?*
The correct response is "b." Both outcome and process evaluations would be most useful based on your purposes for evaluation. Outcome evaluation will provide you with what is needed to determine effectiveness toward meeting program goals. To determine whether or not the program is being implemented as planned and to determine which components are responsible for the program's success or lack of success, process evaluation is needed.

# Proximal and Distal Evaluations

*DARE to Say No*
The correct response is "d." This is an example of both proximal (immediate) and distal (over time) evaluations.

## *Methodology*

*Is Peer Helping—Helping?*
The correct response is "c." This is an example of a quasi-experimental design because the methodology of the evaluation examines multiple groups as well as multiple measures.

# Chapter 5: Simulation

# Program Evaluation

## *Brief Case Description*

You are the school counselor at an elementary school. The principal wants to ensure that you are implementing a data- and needs-driven, comprehensive school counseling program. As such, she has requested that you present her with a 5-year plan for meeting the needs of stakeholders and evaluating the school counseling program.

## *Section A: Program Evaluation*

What strategies would you include in your plan to ensure that the school counseling program is appropriately evaluated?

(Select as many as you consider indicated in this section.)

| | |
|---|---|
| _____A—1. | Pre-program surveys |
| _____A—2. | Student names for interview by the principal |
| _____A—3. | Needs assessment |
| _____A—4. | Post-program surveys |
| _____A—5. | Teacher names for interview by the principal |
| _____A—6. | Teacher program perception surveys |
| _____A—7. | Parent reports to the principal |
| _____A—8. | Student program perception surveys |
| _____A—9. | Community member names for interview by the principal |
| _____A—10. | Statistical testing of pre-/post-data |
| _____A—11. | Committee meeting involvement |
| _____A—12. | Website development |

## Section B: Program Evaluation

The principal likes the strategies you have designed to include in your 5-year plan for accountable school counseling practices. She is uncertain as to how you would objectively measure each classroom guidance lesson and small group activity to ensure that you are making a positive difference in the lives of the students. She is focused on data that will demonstrate how well you have met stated goals, objectives, and standards. Which of the following types of evaluation will yield this data?

(Select ONLY ONE in this section.)

| | |
|---|---|
| \_\_\_\_\_B—1. | Process evaluation using a pre- and post-measure |
| \_\_\_\_\_B—2. | Formative evaluation using a pre- and post-measure |
| \_\_\_\_\_B—3. | Outcome evaluation using a pre- and post-measure |
| \_\_\_\_\_B—4. | Pre- and post-questionnaire of participants' perceptions of the program |
| \_\_\_\_\_B—5. | Program review by teachers |

## Section C: Program Evaluation

In a recent faculty meeting, your principal stressed the importance of developing research-supported curriculum. You are about to develop a small group for second-grade students on social skills. What information do you need from the research to develop a research-supported curriculum?

(Select as many as you consider indicated in this section.)

| | |
|---|---|
| \_\_\_\_\_C—1. | Previous successful social skills programs |
| \_\_\_\_\_C—2. | Age-/grade-specific social skills activities |
| \_\_\_\_\_C—3. | Correlation between social skills and academic achievement |
| \_\_\_\_\_C—4. | Effectiveness of small group programs for enhancing social skills |
| \_\_\_\_\_C—5. | Definition of social skills |
| \_\_\_\_\_C—6. | Use of recognized interventions for social skills improvement |

## Section D: Program Evaluation

Which of the following resources would be most useful in providing research pertaining to school counseling and school counseling interventions?
(Select as many as you consider indicated in this section.)

| | |
|---|---|
| _____D—1. | *ASCA Scene* |
| _____D—2. | Wikipedia |
| _____D—3. | *Counseling Today* |
| _____D—4. | National Technology Institute for School Counseling |
| _____D—5. | Peer-reviewed journals |
| _____D—6. | Center for School Counseling Outcome Research |
| _____D—7. | Webster Dictionary Online |
| _____D—8. | NBCC Newsletter |
| _____D—9. | *PSC* |

## Section E: Program Evaluation

The data collected from your social skills group indicated that the group intervention was not effective in meeting the stated objectives. What type of program evaluation would have been useful to determine the program's strengths and weaknesses and provide information that could be used for program improvement?
(Select ONLY ONE in this section.)

| | |
|---|---|
| _____E—1. | Process evaluation |
| _____E—2. | Formative evaluation |
| _____E—3. | Outcome evaluation |
| _____E—4. | Program evaluation |
| _____E—5. | Student evaluation |

# Chapter 5: Simulation Answers

# Program Evaluation

## Brief Case Description

You are the school counselor at an elementary school. The principal wants to ensure that you are implementing a data- and needs-driven, comprehensive school counseling program. As such, she has requested that you present her with a 5-year plan for meeting the needs of stakeholders and evaluating the school counseling program.

## Section A: Program Evaluation

What strategies would you include in your plan to ensure that the school counseling program is appropriately evaluated?

    (Select as many as you consider indicated in this section.)

| A—1. | Pre-program surveys<br>Yes<br>Pre-program measures provide school counselors with a baseline for assessing change. |
|---|---|
| A—2. | Student names for interview by the principal<br>No<br>Principals do not have time to interview students about their perceptions of the effectiveness of the school counseling program. Also, principals are generally more interested in data that identifies the outcome of school counseling practices. |
| A—3. | Needs assessment<br>Yes<br>Needs assessments are a time-honored means for collecting data from stakeholders for needs-driven program decision making. |
| A—4. | Post-program surveys<br>Yes<br>Post-program assessment provides program outcome data. School counselors combine pre- and post-program measures to assess academic and behavioral change. |

| A—5. | Teacher names for interview by the principal |
| | No |
| | Principals do not have time to interview teachers about their perceptions of the effectiveness of the school counseling program. Also, principals are generally more interested in data that identifies the outcome of school counseling practices. |
| A—6. | Teacher program perception surveys |
| | Yes |
| | Although program outcome data is necessary in today's educational climate that asks how school counselors are making a difference in the lives of students, process data from perception surveys depicts how the school counseling program is viewed by others and may identify areas of strength and weakness for program improvement. |
| A—7. | Parent reports to the principal |
| | No |
| | Principals do not have time to read parent reports or receive visits from parents of all the students regarding the school counseling program. |
| A—8. | Student program perception surveys |
| | Yes |
| | Program outcome data is critical to answering the important question "How do school counselors make a difference in the lives of students?"; however, process data from perception surveys are helpful in identifying areas of strength and weakness for program improvement. |
| A—9. | Community member names for interview by the principal |
| | No |
| | Principals do not have time to interview community members about the effectiveness of the school counseling program. |
| A—10. | Statistical testing of pre-/post-data |
| | Yes |
| | Statistical tests of program data are useful in understanding if changes related to program implementation are significant, which can be documented in results reports to school administrators and stakeholders. |
| A—11. | Committee meeting involvement |
| | No |
| | Although school counselors are encouraged to participate in committees and collaborate with others within and outside of the school, membership does not offer insight into the effectiveness of the school counseling program. |

| A—12. | Website development <br><br> No <br><br> School counselors are encouraged to have a presence on the Web. However, having a website does not offer insight into program effectiveness. |
|---|---|

## Section B: Program Evaluation

The principal likes the strategies you have designed to include in your 5-year plan for accountable school counseling practices. She is uncertain as to how you would objectively measure each classroom guidance lesson and small group activity to ensure that you are making a positive difference in the lives of the students. She is focused on data that will demonstrate how well you have met stated goals, objectives, and standards. Which of the following types of evaluation will yield this data?

(Select ONLY ONE in this section.)

| B—1. | Process evaluation using a pre- and post-measure <br><br> No <br><br> Process evaluation yields formative information that identifies program strengths and weakness. |
|---|---|
| B—2. | Formative evaluation using a pre- and post-measure <br><br> No <br><br> Formative evaluation, also referred to as process evaluation, provides information about program strengths and weaknesses. |
| B—3. | Outcome evaluation using a pre- and post-measure <br><br> Yes <br><br> Outcome evaluation yields objective data that demonstrate the effectiveness of the program in meeting stated goals and objectives. |
| B—4. | Pre- and post-questionnaire of participants' perceptions of the program <br><br> No <br><br> Perceptions will not objectively measure program effectiveness. The principal is requesting objective outcome data. |
| B—5. | Program review by teachers <br><br> No <br><br> Teacher reviews will yield perception data, which will not objectively measure program effectiveness. |

## Section C: Program Evaluation

In a recent faculty meeting, your principal stressed the importance of developing research-supported curriculum. You are about to develop a small group for second-grade students on social skills. What information do you need from the research to develop a research-supported curriculum?

   (Select as many as you consider indicated in this section.)

| | |
|---|---|
| C—1. | Previous successful social skills programs<br>Yes<br>Understanding what social skills interventions have worked in the past is helpful to present planning. |
| C—2. | Age-/grade-specific social skills activities<br>Yes<br>Understanding what social skills interventions have worked in the past for a particular age group is helpful when considering the application of those interventions to the age group of the target population. |
| C—3. | Correlation between social skills and academic achievement<br>Yes<br>A brief statement in a school counseling action plan about how social skills connect to academic achievement demonstrates how your intervention relates to academic achievement. |
| C—4. | Effectiveness of small group programs for enhancing social skills<br>Yes<br>The school counselor wants to demonstrate with research that small group interventions are effective methods of delivery for social skills development. |
| C—5. | Definition of social skills<br>No<br>Defining social skills does not contribute to a research-supported curriculum. |
| C—6. | Use of recognized interventions for social skills improvement<br>No<br>"Recognized" interventions may not be research-supported interventions. |

## Section D: Program Evaluation

Which of the following resources would be most useful in providing research pertaining to school counseling and school counseling interventions?

(Select as many as you consider indicated in this section.)

| | |
|---|---|
| D—1. | *ASCA Scene*<br><br>Yes<br><br>The *ASCA Scene* provides school counselor with an abundance of resources, which may include research and research-supported interventions. |
| D—2. | Wikipedia<br><br>No<br><br>Wikipedia is a fine resource, but it is not considered scholarly. |
| D—3. | *Counseling Today*<br><br>No<br><br>*Counseling Today*, ACA's magazine, is not considered scholarly and does not generally include research. |
| D—4. | National Technology Institute for School Counseling<br><br>Yes<br><br>School counselors can access this resource for research on a variety of school counseling-related topics. |
| D—5. | Peer-reviewed journals<br><br>Yes<br><br>Peer-reviewed journals are considered the best source for scholarly research. |
| D—6. | Center for School Counseling Outcome Research<br><br>Yes<br><br>School counselors access this resource for school counseling-related research. |
| D—7. | Webster Dictionary Online<br><br>No<br><br>This is a fine resource but does not include scholarly research articles. |
| D—8. | NBCC Newsletter<br><br>No<br><br>The NBCC newsletter provides a wealth of information to members pertaining to the professional of counseling. However, it does not include scholarly research articles. |

| D—9. | PSC<br>Yes<br>This is ASCA's peer-reviewed journal, which contains the most relevant scholarly research for the profession of school counseling. |
|------|------|

## Section E: Program Evaluation

The data collected from your social skills group indicated that the group intervention was not effective in meeting the stated objectives. What type of program evaluation would have been useful to determine the program's strengths and weaknesses and provide information that could be used for program improvement?

(Select ONLY ONE in this section.)

| E—1. | Process evaluation<br>Yes<br>Process evaluation provides data about the strengths and weaknesses of a program. |
|------|------|
| E—2. | Summative evaluation<br>No<br>Summative evaluation, also referred to as outcome evaluation, provides objective data about the effectiveness of the intervention in meeting stated goals and objectives. |
| E—3. | Outcome evaluation<br>No<br>Provides data related to program effectiveness. |
| E—4. | Program evaluation<br>No<br>May be process or outcome, and the school counselor is seeking process data. |
| E—5. | Student evaluation<br>No<br>Identifies who is participating in the evaluation instead of the type of evaluation. |

# Chapter 5: Guided Reflection

Examine and compare the concepts of research and evaluation. Then, define each in a way that illustrates the differences.

Design a blurb to market the Center for School Counseling Outcome Research and Evaluation.

Design a blurb to market the School Counseling Analysis, Leadership, and Evaluation Research Center.

Define program evaluation, and describe its importance to school counselors and its connections to accountability.

Compare outcome and process evaluations and describe each to include how they are different.

Compare proximal and distal evaluations and describe each to include how they are different.

Examine the construct of methodology, and describe how the construct relates to program evaluation and research.

Discuss the role of data in school counseling.

What are results reports and why are they needed in school counseling?

Identify the essential components of a results report.

# Chapter 6

# Academic Development

Academic development, one of the three developmental domains of a comprehensive school counseling program, gained considerable ground when it became the focus of new vision school counseling. New vision school counseling shifted the paradigm from individual- and mental health-focused practices to systems- and academic-focused practices. The shift to an academic focus recognizes the school counselor's professional identity of counselor and its importance in maintaining an intact sense of our chief function and specialization: counseling. However, the academic focus of the new vision does call upon our dual role of educator to aid in aligning the school counseling program with the fundamental mission of schools: academic achievement.

Like a well-played game of chess, we are strategically planning our moves and positioning ourselves to check the king and seize academic success for all. Hand in hand with teachers and administrators, school counselors assist in identifying systemic areas of academic deficits and specific low-achieving student populations. Programming is tailored to target those academic needs while simultaneously meeting the personal, social, and career development needs of all students. School counselors deliver services aimed at enhancing knowledge of testing programs, developing test-taking skills, reducing testing anxiety, teaching study methods, and identifying sources for test preparation and tutoring.

---

### ASCA's Position on Test Preparation Programs

School counselors assist students in preparing for standardized tests by promoting opportunities designed to increase knowledge and improve test-taking skills. School counselors help students and their families become knowledgeable about test preparation programs and assist them as they decide which programs best meet their needs.

*Position statement adopted 1989;*
*revised 1993, 1999, 2001, 2006, 2012*

---

School counselors apply their knowledge of human development, behavior and learning theories, and principles of motivation to enhance student academic achievement and attitudes toward school. Believing in the capacity of all students to obtain high levels of academic achievement, school counselors help to prepare students for meaningful futures in a global economy and technologically advanced world. In the words of Journey's timeless, sleep-deprived classic that took the midnight train to the number one digital track of all time—"Don't Stop Believin'."

## Curriculum Development

Chapters 4 and 5 discussed how school counselors identify stakeholder needs, turn those needs into measurable objectives, and identify methods for evaluating the effectiveness of the program. This chapter focuses on creating research-supported curriculum that directly aligns with the objectives. For example, if the goal is to improve student test scores, a measurable objective supporting this goal is "Students will identify five strategies for overcoming test-taking anxiety." The curriculum will include research-supported content and activities specific to achieving this objective. That is, the content will, in some fashion, introduce five research-supported strategies for reducing test-taking anxiety.

Let us consider the concept of self-esteem. Negative self-esteem has had a long and prosperous career in invading minds, hearts, and souls with self-destructive rubbish, making the self our best friend or our worst enemy. The benefits of positive self-esteem are as widely recognized as the entertaining GEICO gecko for offering an insurance policy that kicks in when life serves up spontaneous catastrophe.

## SCHOOL CLIMATE

The school counselor, Fernando, is creating a video program to enhance the school's social climate, identified as an area of need on the recently completed needs assessment. One of the program's measurable objectives is "Students will identify and apply three strategies for improving social skills." What would the video program content need to include?

Relying on research, school counselors reveal the link between self-esteem and personal, social, career, and academic development. The school counselor will particularly underscore the relationship between academic success and self-esteem to demonstrate a clear alignment with the academic mission of schools. Once this link is established, research-supported interventions that have been successful in building a positive self-esteem are identified. The following questions help to guide school counselors toward this end:

■ Does a correlation exist between self-esteem and academic performance?
■ What does the research say about the academic proficiency of students who have negative self-esteem versus those who have positive self-esteem?
■ Is poor self-esteem considered a barrier to academic achievement? If so, would it be logical to conclude that programs that enhance self-esteem remove a barrier to academic achievement?
■ Which counseling and instructional interventions have been used in the past with positive outcomes?
■ With what populations were the counseling and instructional interventions successful?

**Table 6.1 Overview of Gardner's Multiple Intelligences and School Counseling Strategies**

| Intelligence | Description | Counseling Strategies |
|---|---|---|
| Linguistic | Reliance on spoken and written words; individuals generally adept in reading, writing, and speaking. | Narrative counseling, storytelling, journaling, letter writing, sentence completion, bibliotherapy. |
| Logical–mathematical | Reliance on reasoning, numbers, and logic; individuals generally adept in scientific thinking, investigation, and making complex calculations. | Genograms, games, strategic planning, objectifying, outlining, exploring, topic-specific crossword or wordsearch activities. |
| Musical | Reliance on rhythmic sounds, pitch, and tones; individuals generally adept in singing, playing musical instruments, and composing music. | Creating lyrics to music, moving to music, musical motivation (e.g., during homework, classwork); musical meditation (e.g., meditation that involves soothing tunes). |
| Spatial | Reliance on the mind's eye; individuals generally adept in design, puzzles, navigation. | Cognitive mapping, visualization/imagery, pretend. |
| Bodily kinesthetic | Reliance on touch and movement; individuals generally adept in dance and sports. | Role-playing, psychodrama, exercise, yoga, dance, interactive games/play. |
| Naturalistic | Reliance on nurturing and that which is associated with nature; individuals generally adept at classifying organisms and understanding of the natural environment. | Outdoor activities, discussions and observations related to natural consequences and human nature. |
| Interpersonal | Reliance on interactions with others; individuals generally adept at identifying the needs of others and working cooperatively with others. | Role play, group counseling, collaborative work/play. |
| Intrapersonal | Reliance on introspection, intuition, and self-reflection; individuals generally adept in understanding self and self-control. | Questioning, journaling, studying, meditation, self-play, quiet time. |

*Source*: Adapted from Gardner, H., & Moran, S. (2006). *Educational Psychologist, 41*(4), 227–232.

When developing curriculum, school counselors are sensitive to the diverse learning styles of their target population, as discussed in Chapter 1. School counselors are also mindful of the theory of *multiple intelligences* when seeking to create lessons and group sessions that are geared toward holistic student development.

Howard Gardner (1983) proposed the theory of multiple intelligences, contending that human cognition is made up of eight independent, yet interactive, intelligences across a variety of disciplines. Gardner defines intelligence as "biopsychological potential to process information that can be activated in a cultural setting to solve problems or create products that are of value in a culture" (Gardner & Moran, 2006, p. 1). The eight intelligences (i.e., linguistic, logical–mathematical, musical, spatial, bodily kinesthetic, naturalistic, interpersonal, and intrapersonal) along with possible counseling strategies for students with a propensity toward a particular intelligence are summarized in Table 6.1.

The interactive nature of multiple intelligences offers insight into the workings of the human mind. Whether intriguing or deeply disturbing, this information is nothing less than invaluable in developing and delivering curriculum that nurtures the diverse intelligences for optimal cognitive and affective learning experiences. Also noted in Chapter 2, identifying students' propensities toward specific intelligences provides information useful in career decision making.

## Response-to-Intervention

*Response-to-intervention* (RTI) is an early intervention process used to help struggling students to improve behavior, achieve academically, and stay in school. RTI is a responsive service driven by data. School counselors can reduce self-punishing data-seeking behaviors by making use of the sizeable variety of data sources already available in the schools when seeking to identify populations in need of RTI. Chapter 5 provides a selection of flavors to satisfy your intellectual preference.

The understanding that some students need more intense or individualized instruction in order to be successful learners is the core belief of RTI. Struggling students are identified and screened so that individualized services can be designed to meet their unique, multifaceted, and sometimes complex needs. Interventions are put into

**WHITNEY'S BEHAVIOR**

A school counselor has been working with Whitney, a middle school student, for several months. Whitney is having many behavioral problems. The school counselor began working with Whitney when she was referred to the school's early intervention team. The intervention plan was not successful in creating behavioral change. The school counselor continued to consult and collaborate with the school psychologist and school social worker but the strategies designed to help Whitney continued to be unsuccessful. The school counselor is now strongly encouraging Whitney's parents to seek outside mental health counseling services and has provided the family with a resource list from which to select an individual and family counselor. When considering ASCA's tiers of the RTI process, which tier represents the current role of the school counseling in helping Whitney?

  a. Tier two
  b. Tier three
  c. Tier one
  d. None of the above

place, and students are monitored to ensure progress toward established goals.

Multidisciplinary RTI teams of professional educators are established in each school as part of a multitiered system of supports (MTSS) and/or a student support team (SST) (ASCA, 2016b). The RTI team consists of a special blend of expertise (e.g., school counselor, school psychologist, teacher, school social worker, reading specialist). The union of disciplines allows for a deeper conceptualization of student needs and a holistic and integrated perspective from which to identify promising interventions and tools. RTI services may be delivered by select professionals within and outside of the school based on student needs.

School counselors use a multitier approach to aligning the comprehensive school counseling program with the RTI process. Educational and behavioral data are examined to monitor student progress. Table 6.2 demonstrates this alignment (ASCA Position Statements, 2017).

**Table 6.2 Response-to-Intervention in a Comprehensive School Counseling Program**

| RTI Tiers and Processes | ASCA National Model Systems and Related Components |
| --- | --- |
| Tier one:<br>Universal core instructional interventions: all students, preventative, and proactive | Foundation: Standards and competencies<br>Delivery: Classroom guidance and individual student planning<br>Management: Action plans<br>Accountability: Results reports |
| Tier two:<br>Supplemental/strategic interventions: students at some risk | Foundation: Standards and competencies<br>Delivery: Responsive services (i.e., individual counseling, individual student planning, small group advising/counseling and consultation)<br>Management: Closing the achievement gap action plans<br>Accountability: Closing the achievement gap results reports |
| Tier three:<br>Intensive, individual interventions: students at high risk | Foundation: Standards and competencies<br>Delivery: Responsive services (i.e., individual student counseling, small group counseling, consultation, and referral)<br>Management: Closing the achievement gap action plans<br>Accountability: Closing the achievement gap results reports |

*Source*: Adapted from American School Counselor Association (2012a).

RTI services are as unique as the students, varying in type, intensity, and duration. RTI services are based on student needs and established educational, career, and personal–social goals. A sampling of services may include

- Dropout prevention
- Decision making
- Behavioral support
- Referral
- Counseling
- Career planning
- Assessment
- Goal setting
- Parenting skills
- Transitioning.

# Closing the Achievement Gap

The school counselor's role in academic development includes assisting in meeting the mandates of No Child Left Behind (NCLB) (United States Department of Education, 2001). NCLB is considered by many to be the most significant and controversial of educational reform legislation in our nation's history. The primary goal of NCLB was to ensure that all students obtained proficiency in mathematics and language arts by 2013–14.

All in all, educators agreed with NCLB legislation. However, there were some who viewed NCLB as an encounter with the Ebola virus and others who would have prefered to contract the Ebola virus. Disenchantment with NCLB did not appear to be grounded in its philosophies and goals, but in the tough realities of its implementation based on limited human and material resources. Driven to do what is best for children, educators nevertheless gave it their all and hammered out results with minimal provisions.

The TSCI and ASCA support the primary objectives of NCLB. These objectives include closing the achievement gap, demonstrating accountability, and providing students with a safe and positive learning environment. Under NCLB, schools must establish time lines for closing achievement gaps and tracking student progress toward meeting standards, ensuring adequate yearly progress (AYP) toward academic proficiency. Closing achievement, attainment, and opportunity gaps are also considered to be the school counselor's ethical responsibility, as discussed in Chapter 3.

Achievement gaps exist between males and females and between students from underprivileged backgrounds and those from more affluent backgrounds. Achievement gaps have also been identified between students whose native languages differ and between students of differing ability levels. Achievement gaps vary from school to school and state to state. The most consistently documented achievement gap is based on national data. These data indicate an achievement gap between races, namely Caucasian students and African Americans, Latinos, and Native Americans.

Efforts to close the achievement gap are the impetus behind the call for school counselors to engage in practices that more clearly focus on academic achievement. Historically, school counselors have viewed their function as indirectly increasing academic achievement. School counselors have done this by removing physical, personal, social, emotional, behavioral, and environmental obstacles to learning. School counselors have also contributed to academic achievement by teaching strategies that help students to master the skills needed for academic success and self-directed learning (e.g., test taking, studying, note taking, time management, goal setting). Communications with school administrators, however, tend to depict the belief that school counselors should take a more direct role in helping students to achieve academically (Shoffner & Williamson, 2000).

## Crosswalking Curriculum

ASCA encourages school counselors to develop programs that demonstrate a direct impact on academic achievement and more overt alignment with the mission of schools. Leaders in education and school counseling agree that implementation of standards-based programs that align school counseling programs with academic achievement missions are best practices for school counselors. Crosswalking is encouraged by ASCA as an integral and academic-focused component of a comprehensive school counseling program. In case you did not notice, this makes crosswalking our new best friend.

Standards blending is a promising crosswalking approach that demonstrates a more direct alignment and impact on academic achievement. Research on standards blending (Schellenberg, 2007, 2008; Schellenberg & Grothaus, 2009, 2011) has resulted in increased academic achievement in language arts and mathematics as well as achievement in the personal–social and career development domains. Standards blending has also been identified as a culturally sensitive, RTI strategy for closing the achievement gap, discussed later in this chapter.

Crosswalking approaches directly and overtly align school counseling programs with academic achievement missions. School counselors methodically identify and merge specific core academic standards with school counseling standards. This integrated approach aids students in connecting curriculum to real life and across disciplines. School counselors give special consideration to crosswalking the school counseling standards with language arts and mathematics standards to aid schools in meeting the overarching goal of NCLB. Also, reading, writing, and arithmetic are considered the building blocks of a sound educational foundation.

As a primary and anchored appendage to a comprehensive developmental school counseling program, crosswalking strategies help to establish academic-focused practices that make use of school counselors' skills as both educators and counselors. So, pull in those bewildered and unsuspecting jaywalkers who may otherwise collide with the driving force of school administrators who only give way for those who are crosswalking.

---

**NEW VISION SCHOOL COUNSELING**

You are the elementary school counselor practicing from the new vision's academic-focused paradigm. You create a small group for fourth-grade African American male students who are having issues related to poor self-esteem. In talking with the teachers of these students, you find that the students are also performing below grade level in mathematics. On the basis of information from teachers and a review of the students' standardized test scores, you create a small group that addresses the students personal–social needs (i.e., self-esteem) as well as their academic needs (i.e., mathematics). Your small-group program is an example of:

 a. A systems-focused approach
 b. A closing-the-achievement-gap strategy
 c. A crosswalking approach
 d. All of the above

---

## Action Plans/Lesson Plans

Action plans and lesson plans are used by school counselors as part of the management system. These plans aid school counselors in effectively delivering curriculum that addresses the needs of students. School counselors create action plans and lesson plans to demonstrate how desired results are to be achieved.

Action plans are used within three areas: (1) school counseling curriculum, (2) small groups, and (3) closing the achievement gap

(ASCA, 2012a). ASCA recommends the follow components in an action plan:

■ Goal(s)
■ Developmental domain and Mindsets and Behaviors for Student Success
■ Description of activities
■ Title of curriculum
■ Completion timeline
■ Name(s) of person responsible for delivery
■ Method for evaluation (process, perception, outcome data)
■ Anticipated outcome in terms of measurable objectives.

Lesson plans are specific to the delivery of classroom guidance lessons. ASCA recommends the following components in a lesson plan:

■ Mindsets and Behaviors for Student Success
■ Learning objectives
■ Materials
■ Procedure
■ Plan for evaluation
■ Follow-up.

Figure 6.1 illustrates a combination action plan and lesson plan that meets the ASCA recommended components of each using the School Counseling Operational Plan for Effectiveness (SCOPE) (Schellenberg, 2008). SCOPE illustrates needs-based programming with measurable objectives, research-supported curriculum, and a crosswalking approach (e.g., standards blending) that is culturally sensitive, responsive, and aimed at closing the achievement gap.

## Instructional Strategies and Classroom Management

School counselors draw upon training in counseling, school counseling, and education to create effective instructional and classroom management strategies. There are times when school counselors must make split-second decisions in Chicago winds while holding on to our hats, or royal fascinators for you Kate Middleton fans. Predetermined, reliable classroom

**SCOPE**
**School Counseling Operational Plan for Effectiveness**

---

**School Counselor(s):** *Schellenberg*          **Others:** *None*

**Action Plan/Lesson Plan Date :** *2017*          **Title:** *The Me I Wanna Be*

☐ Small Group          ☒ **School Counseling Curriculum**          ☐ **Individual Student Planning**

**Need/Purpose:** *Low self-esteem and low academic achievement in Language Arts and Mathematics*

☐ **Closing Achievement Gap Strategy**          **Data Used to Identify Gap Population:** *Teacher referral; Test Scores*

**Target Population:**          **Students in Grade(s):** *3*          **Other:**          **Number of Participants:** *6*
**Describe:** *Six African-American males*

**Goal(s)-Objective(s)**
*Group Goal: To enhance self-esteem and academic achievement (LA & Mathematics) for all group members.*
*Session 1 Objectives: Enhance the ability to identify the characteristics of biographies and autobiographies.*
                    *Develop an understanding of the importance of positive peer relationships.*
*Session 2 Objectives: Enhance the ability to gather, evaluate, synthesize data and communicate findings.*
                    *Develop an understanding of self in relation to others.*
*Session 3 Objectives: Develop a greater understanding of mathematical inverse operations.*
                    *Gain an understanding of goal setting and attaining.*
*Session 4 Objectives: Develop a greater understanding of fractions as parts of a whole.*
                    *Understand the purpose of and demonstrate the use of positive self-talk.*

**School Counseling Standards: Mindsets & Behaviors**

☒ Academic *M 3*
☒ Social/Emotional *B-SS 1; B SS 2*
☒ Career *M 6*

**Core Academic/Other Standards**

☒ Mathematics *NM-NUM.3-5.1.3; NM-NUM.3-5.2.3; NM-PROB.PK-12.2; NM-PROB.CONN.PK-12.1*
☐ Language Arts *NLA.4; NLA.12; NLA.1; NLA.7*
☐ Science
☐ Social Studies
☐ Other

Plan for Evaluation: ☒ **Process**          ☒ **Perception**          ☒ **Outcome**          ☒ **Proximal**          ☒ **Distal**
**Data Sources:** *Pre- and post-test; academic test scores*

**Curriculum**
**Number of lessons/sessions:** *4, 30 minutes each*          **Timeline:** *Once a week X 4*   **Date Implemented:** *Jan 2017*

**Content**
*School counselors may wish to include standards specific to their state here.*
*Research-Supported Group Activities:*

*Session 1 (You and Me):*
*Literature and research underscores the importance of having a sense of affiliation and friendship during the elementary school years in developing a sense of belonging and positive self-esteem (Dalgas-Pelish, 2006; Leary, Schreindorfer, & Haupt, 1995; Roberts, 2002; Schellenberg, 2000).*
*Activities: Students are introduced to the counselor, fellow students, topic, and group process. Group rules are discussed. Students pretend to be reporters interviewing an important person--as we all are! In pairs, students ask each other three questions that they would like to know about the other. A list of questions are provided for students if desired. Students note the question asked and response received. Characteristics of biographies and autobiographies are described. Individually, students write a biography of the student interviewed. Papers are shared and the importance of friendship and positive relationships with others is discussed.*

---

## Figure 6.1 SCOPE.

*Source:* From Schellenberg, R. (2013). *A New Era in School Counseling.* Lanham, MD: Rowman Littlefield Education. Reprinted with permission.

*Session 2 (We are the Same, We are Different):*
*The self-belief that one does not meet societal norms or have a sense of individual identity contributes to a low sense of competence (Kagan & Snidman, 1991; Schellenberg, 2000). Relationship building activities help students to recognize their own sense of individualism and self in relation to others, fostering an environment of belonging, and creating a feeling of competence, which is linked to academic achievement and self-efficacy (Anderman & Leake, 2005).*
*Activities: Round-Robin check-in. In pairs, students spend 5-10 minutes talking to each other to gather information about how each are different and alike. Prior to the information gathering, students are given 2 minutes to think about the questions they would like to ask. After the information gathering, individually, students reflect on the information, synthesize it, comparing and contrasting self in relation to the other student, and share their findings. Students are encouraged to think about what they learned from their partner's biography in the previous group session.*

*Session 3 (Goals are not just for Football):*
*A sense of mission contributes to motivation and goal attainment (Ross & Broh, 2000; Youngs, 1992), which leads to a sense of competence (Anderman & Leake, 2005). The process of goal achievement requires individuals to identify limitations and problem solve, promoting a sense of autonomy and personal control (Wigfield & Eccles, 2000).*
*Activities: Round-Robin check-in. Goals (short- and long-term) are defined. Students are asked to select one of the three goals listed on the board to achieve during this session. The goals are: 1) say something nice to a group member, 2) say something nice to the school counselor, 3) ask someone for help during the lesson. A deck of cards, self-created or other, with a goal on one side and the steps to achieve the goal on the other. Students take turns reading the goal and asking fellow group members to identify possible steps to achieve the goal. The cards are manipulated by the school counselor to demonstrate the mathematical concept of inverse operations. Students identify by a show of hands who met their goals. Obstacles encountered? What each might do differently next time?*

*Session 4 (Thought Power)*
*Individuals who perceive self as competent and worthy behave in ways that create success and view self as successful (Ellis & Harper, 1997; Ross & Broh, 2000). Self-perception is altered by internal dialogue that creates our thoughts, and, in turn, our feelings and behaviors (Ellis & Harper).*
*Activities: Self-talk is defined, modeled, and demonstrated by students. The effects of positive vs. negative self-talk are discussed and examples are provided on 20 individual strips of paper (10 positive self-talk statements and 10 negative self-talk statements). The strips of paper are described as a whole and then manipulated to illustrate fractions. Students take turns manipulating the strips. Group closure.*

SCORE (completed after counseling services implemented; see Figure 5.2)

**SCORE**
**School Counseling Operational Report of Effectiveness**

**SCOPE Title:**                              Date Implemented:

**Number/Description of Participants:**

**Impact/Implications:**

**Follow-up Plan:**

**Pre-Post Data**
**Worksheet**

**Figure 6.1** *continued*

management strategies and instructional practices help us to avoid flying by the seat of our pants—or our proper toppers!

School counselors use differentiated instruction and provide teacher support in the use of differentiated instruction to meet the learning needs of diverse students. Differentiated instructional strategies are empirically supported as equitable and effective methods that result in positive student outcomes (Akos, Cockman, & Strickland, 2007). School counselors use differentiated instruction primarily in the delivery of classroom guidance lessons.

CACREP (2012) defines differentiated instruction as "matching curriculum materials, teacher, delivery style, classroom management strategies, and behavioral/learning expectations to the student's motivation and learning needs" (p. 140). The concept of differentiation is grounded in the belief that all students have diverse interests, readiness levels, and *learning profiles* that when addressed will maximize the student's capacity to learn. School counselors do not attend to every student's unique learning profile but seek to deliver classroom guidance lessons that accommodate various learning profiles by diversifying approaches and offering task and assessment choices (Akos et al., 2007). Indeed, variety is the spice of life—and learning.

Like instructional strategies, classroom management is a skill specialty practiced by school counselors and shared with teachers. While some students stroll through the school years with no greater ambition than to please the teacher, others seem to plow through school with no greater purpose than to make us nuts—a comforting theory I turn to in order to normalize the phenomenon. Of course I'm struck by the notion of what a brief metamorphosis to nut it would be for some of us. In all fairness to students, it is very likely the same for them!

Establishing understandable, unbiased, and realistic rules is crucial to effective classroom management. Established rules need to be clearly communicated along with the consequences for breaking the rules. Consequences need a little R-n-R—no, not that R-n-R. Consequences need to be reasonable and respectful. Also, both natural and logical consequences should be explained; that is, "If you grab another student's crayon, they may smack you" (natural consequence) and/or "If you grab another student's crayon, one minute will be taken off of your recess" (logical consequence). Finally, applying rules and consequences in a consistent manner is critical to continued behavioral management and for reducing behavioral back-sliding. If I can get away with texting even once during your lecture, I will likely try again.

In addition to rules and consequences, it is important to catch students engaging in desired behaviors and reinforce those behaviors. Chapter 1 discusses behavior modification and the use of both extrinsic and intrinsic motivation to shape student behavior.

Classroom management is more than managing student behavior. The arrangement of the classroom is critical to accomplishing targeted instructional goals. For example, some teachers and school counselors may prefer a formal tone to the classroom, and an environment that promotes individual work versus group work. In this case, desks or tables in the classroom might be physically arranged in a U-shape, V-shape, or lecture hall style. School counselors and teachers who desire a more relaxed tone and an environment that promotes cooperative learning may desire a physical arrangement that places the desks or tables in a square, circle, or small groupings.

Well-executed classroom management strategies help students to understand the power of good choices and to understand how our lives are the cumulative consequences of those choices. Additional areas to consider for effective classroom management include:

- Noise levels
- Resources
- Volunteers
- Breaks
- Bathroom visits
- Homework and classwork submission
- Procedures for visiting the school nurse or school counselor.

Classrooms do not need to resemble holding cells where the sound of the bell is the signal for escape with students firing off vows of freedom while fleeing with inmates. An effective system of classroom management maintains a student-friendly focus and air of nurturing—interrogation is optional and identified as Socratic dialogue.

# Specialty Programs

Specialty programs have multiple identities, such as alternative education programs, special education programs, nontraditional education programs, gifted education, and the list goes on. These programs may entail homeschooling, online learning, enrichment courses, and multilingual instruction. Specialty programs are geared toward any number of special needs student populations (e.g., students with IEPs, students with 504 plans, students with limited English proficiency, students who are at risk of dropping out of school, advanced functioning students).

Specialty programs are goal-focused to meet the special needs of a specific student or student population and generally involve more individualized instruction, alternative methods of instruction, smaller class sizes, and/or alternative learning environments. School counselors are diligent in maintaining current information, programs, policies, and legislation as it pertains to specialty programs, approaches, and activities.

## Homeschooling

Homeschooling is the education of a student by the parent or a tutor outside of the traditional public or private school setting. Homeschooling has grown in popularity in recent years for a variety of reasons. Some of the most common reasons noted by parents include issues associated with bullying, negative peer pressure, school violence, a desire to provide religious-based education, a lack of confidence in academic instruction, and/or as a matter of convenience.

Parents' homes are sovereign nations where instruction can be customized to the unique learning style and ability level of their child and around the family's schedule. Homeschooling also allows unlimited freedom to provide instruction in a manner that is consistent with family values and religious beliefs. The homeschooling environment is controlled by the parent, who takes on the responsibility for their child's education. The parent, too, provides opportunities for adequate social interaction to promote personal and social development.

Generally, children who are homeschooled tend to spend more time with parents, which can be a double-edged sword. This increased time together can result in a strengthening of family relationships or it can strain the ties that bond. School counselors understand the pros and cons of homeschooling and consider the unique personality and abilities of the child when discussing this as an educational program option. Sharing information and resources and speaking candidly about the realities of homeschooling help parents to make the best decisions for their children and family.

## The Virtual Classroom

Virtual classrooms offer online instruction outside of the school building, generally at the high school level. Not all schools offer online instruction; however, the forecast is favorable for continued growth. There are a variety of reasons that a student might wish to take classes in this manner. Some students have an illness that may hinder their ability to participate in daily classes at school, whereas others simply do not like the in-school experience. Still others may wish to take additional courses or advanced courses for college credit supplementing a full daily in-class schedule.

Virtual learning environments require a self-disciplined and self-motivated mind. Online courses are designed to be just as rigorous as those in the traditional school setting, and students will need to be self-motivated time managers. Students also need to possess the skills to manipulate the online environment with basic computer skills (e.g., word processing, e-mail, Internet), or more advanced computer skills, depending upon the educational management system used. While some students flourish in the online learning environment, others learn quickly that it is not the Utopia they had envisioned. Instead, they find themselves mourning the loss of the four classroom walls.

School counselors are becoming increasingly involved in the enrollment and coordination of virtual learning programs. For this reason, school counselors are called upon to understand the nature of online learning in relation to the characteristics of students who would most likely succeed in this unique and challenging environment.

## Programs for Students with Disabilities

Students with documented physical, emotional, social, and learning challenges require differentiated instructional strategies, often in a more structured environment with smaller class sizes or placement in *inclusion classrooms*. Special education students who have an IEP and students who have 504 plans are by law entitled to special accommodations to ensure their educational success and well-being (see Chapter 1).

The IEP of special education students experiencing behavior problems will include a behavior intervention plan (BIP). The IDEA also requires that the special education student's IEP include a comprehensive transition plan to prepare the student for life after high school. At the present time, transition plans are not required as a component of the 504 plan.

Educators seek to provide special needs students with accommodations that will promote success while doing so in the *least restrictive environment*. Therefore, many special needs students are placed in general education classrooms while also participating in resource classes to provide additional academic support.

IEPs and 504 plans are reviewed upon parent request and updated at least annually to assess progress toward goal attainment and appropriateness of accommodations as the student grows and matures. Accommodations vary by student need and can range from extended time on a test to a personal assistant throughout the school day. School counselors apply their knowledge of child development and learning theories to advocate for balanced accommodations, that is, they identify accommodations that provide the optimal level of assistance: not too little, not too much—just right.

**THE INCLUSION CLASSROOM**

Genita is an elementary school student who has an IEP. The parent visited the school to discover that Genita was in a regular classroom with about 20 other students. The parent went directly to the school counselor, who had been a part of the IEP meeting, and asked why her daughter was not in a special education classroom. The school counselor said that Genita was performing very well in the inclusion classroom and receiving the IEP accommodations needed to be successful, so there was no need for a more restrictive environment. Is the school counselor correct?

## ESL Programs

Students who are limited in their ability to speak English because English is not their native language are referred to as LEP students. ELL has also been used to identify students whose native language is not English. LEP students may qualify for *English as a second language* (ESL) services/programs. To identify learning needs, LEP students participate in a home language survey. If indicated, students will then be assessed in reading, writing, listening, and speaking to determine their level of English proficiency and thus identify their needs for specialized instruction and accommodation.

Like students with IEPs and 504 plans, LEP students receive special accommodations and services to promote academic success and total student development. The goal of the ESL program is to help LEP students to achieve English proficiency while accommodating their needs to promote academic success until such proficiency is attained. LEP students are monitored and routinely assessed using both formal and informal measures to determine their progress toward achieving English proficiency. Adjustments to instruction and accommodation are made accordingly.

The educational approach selected for assisting LEP students is at the discretion of the school division. Educational approaches are driven by best practices and the number of LEP students in the school as well as the level of English proficiency for the LEP population to be served. Some schools use: (1) immersion in the general classroom with interpreters, (2) ESL courses taught entirely by bilingual instructors, or (3) individual tutoring. Any combination of multiple approaches may be adopted to meet the needs of LEP students.

School counselors are familiar with the process for identifying and meeting the needs of LEP students. School counselors advocate for LEP student participation in all educational programs regardless of their level of English proficiency. School counselors also make every effort to ensure that LEP students receive the accommodations needed in order to participate in the variety of educational programs.

## Enrichment Programs

Students with exceptional abilities require differentiated instruction within a more rigorous and engaging curriculum that allows for higher-order cognitive skills and more complex problem solving. Meeting the advanced capacities of gifted students is essential to encouraging their full potential.

Enrichment programs begin as early as kindergarten. The names and types of programs offered vary from state to state, school division to school division, and even school to school. Some of the more common programs include the Governor's School for the Arts, Science and Technology Academy and the International Baccalaureate program. Honors and advanced placement courses are also designed to meet the exceptional needs of this special population.

Advanced functioning students are sometimes identified as those students in a class that are exhibiting social, emotional, and behavioral problems. With more neurons in the human brain than planets in our Milky Way galaxy, the voltage of billions of transmitting neurons alive in the minds of geniuses at any given time must be astronomical. With this kind of neuroactivity, our most brilliant prodigies could go supernovae. For this simpleton, that kind of inner-galactic energy is mind-boggling.

**I WANT TO BE A PERFORMANCE ARTIST**

Angela is a new school counselor at a large suburban high school. Yesterday, Angela met with Tamika, a 10th-grade student who has a GPA of 3.9 and had some questions regarding the PSAT. Tamika came into Angela's office very excited because she just got her first part in the community theatre. Tamika said, "I'm so happy—I want so badly to be a performance artist!" Which of these programs might be the most appropriate to discuss with Tamika at this time?

a. ESL program
b. Homeschooling
c. Virtual classroom
d. Governor's School

We can understand, then, why classroom observations often explain the behavioral mishaps of gifted children and adolescents. Advanced functioning students tend to experience boredom with the general education curriculum, viewing it as mundane. Finishing tasks more quickly than peers, gifted students seek ways to occupy an overactive mind until the transition to a new subject. During this time, the gifted child may engage in activities that disrupt class. School counselors collaborate with teachers and students to find creative ways to fill this time with activities that stimulate and challenge the student's intellect and creativity.

The academically high functioning and asynchronous development of gifted students may also manifest itself as affective disturbances such as feelings of loneliness, anxiety, and depression, as well as social isolation and poor relational skills (Elijah, 2011). However, because of their independent and self-sufficient nature, the need to maintain a perfectionist image, and/or the belief that they may disappoint important others, gifted students often do not ask for help. Chapter 3 discusses the personal, social, and emotional issues unique to the advanced cognitive functioning of the gifted child.

## GED Programs

Keeping students in school is our goal as educators and as a society. Despite all attempts at intervention, the school setting and structured school day are a struggle for some students. For this reason, school counselors provide students who are at risk of dropping out of school with alternative educational program options. Some programs lead to a high school diploma, while others result in obtaining a GED (general equivalency diploma).

GED-track programs vary in eligibility requirements from state to state but generally require that students are at risk of dropping out of school and are at least 16 years old. Students generally take an official GED practice test with an established minimum score criteria for entrance in to the GED-track program. GED-track programs through the public schools can take weeks to years to complete, although it is generally about 1 month to 12 months depending upon the program. Some programs offer a track to the high school diploma or the GED, such as Job Corps. Job Corps is a nationally recognized, highly structured program directed by the Department of Labor that provides at-risk teens, beginning at age 16, with residential housing, allowances, and vocational training. Completion of the Job Corps program generally takes 8 months to 2 years.

School counselors are resource agents. Knowledge of a single resource can make the difference between a student dropping out of school or gaining an education, securing a satisfying career, and becoming a contributing member of society.

---

### I WANT MY HIGH SCHOOL DIPLOMA

Reginald is a high school junior who has failed 11th grade twice. He told you, his high school counselor, that he hates school and just does not know what to do. He said his mom is about to move in with her mom, and he does not know what is going to happen to him because there is not enough room for him and his sisters and brothers at his grandmother's house. His mother suggested that he get his GED and get a job. Reginald said he thinks he will just quit school but that he really wanted a diploma and a career. Which of the following programs may meet Reginald's needs at this time?

    a. Governor's School
    b. Virtual classroom
    c. Job Corps
    d. GED track

# Chapter 6: Case Conceptualization Responses

# Curriculum Development

*School Climate*
Fernando's video program content would need to introduce students to at least three strategies for improving social skills and demonstrate the application of those strategies.

# Response-to-Intervention

*Whitney's Behavior*
The correct response is "b." The level at which Whitney's academic and behavioral performance has declined places her at high risk, requiring that the school counselor work at the tier three level to help Whitney to be successful. At the tier three level, students are provided with intense individualized attention and referred for additional school or community services. In Whitney's case, in-school supports and referrals have not been successful, calling for more intense support from outside of the school.

# Crosswalking Curriculum

*New Vision School Counseling*
The correct response is "d." The new vision for school counseling is both systems- and academic-focused. Small-group methods for services delivery are systems-focused. And, you are creating and implementing a crosswalking approach because of your integration of both core academic and school counseling standards. Your small group is considered as closing-the-achievement-gap strategy because you have included members of the gap (i.e., African Americans) in your group membership.

# Specialty Programs

## *Programs for Students with Disabilities*

*The Inclusion Classroom*
Yes, the school counselor is advising the parent correctly. By law, special education students are to be in the least restrictive environment with supports as listed in the student's IEP.

## *Enrichment Programs*

*I Want to Be a Performance Artist*
The correct response is "d." Tamika has the academic performance and a passion for the performing arts that makes her a prime candidate for the Governor's School for the Arts enrichment program.

## *GED-Track Programs*

*I Want My High School Diploma*
The correct response is "c." The GED track, although an option for Reginald, is not the best response choice. Reginald has been clear that he really wants his high school diploma. Job Corps offers students the opportunity to earn either a GED or a high school diploma. Reginald also wants a career. Job Corps teaches a variety of occupational skills, and, upon earning his high school diploma, Reginald can go to college. Finally, Job Corps can offer Reginald a structured living environment, providing him with a place to live, which is a concern for him at the current time.

# Chapter 6: Simulation

# Academic Success

## Brief Case Description

You are a high school counselor, and a career and technical education teacher requests a classroom guidance lesson on career readiness. Practicing from an academic-focused paradigm, you seek to crosswalk your school counseling curriculum with academic standards.

## Section A: Academic Success

What resources/information do you need in order to fully develop your curriculum that will promote universal academic achievement?
   (Select as many as you consider indicated in this section.)

| | |
|---|---|
| _____A—1. | Percentage of non-Caucasian students in class |
| _____A—2. | Standardized tests data |
| _____A—3. | Mathematics standards |
| _____A—4. | Grade level of students in the class |
| _____A—5. | Number of special needs students in the class |
| _____A—6. | Language arts standards |
| _____A—7. | Special education labels of students in class |
| _____A—8. | Accommodations for special needs students in the class |

## Section B: Academic Success

The pre-/post-lesson evaluation data reveal low scores on both the school counseling and academic domains for five students, who are not special needs students. The teacher shares that there have also been some behavioral issues with these students. Based on the lesson outcome data

and the teacher's comments, which of the following would be the best
course of action at this time?

(Select ONLY ONE in this section.)

| | |
|---|---|
| _____B—1. | Refer students to peer tutoring |
| _____B—2. | Design an RTI |
| _____B—3. | Call a parent conference |
| _____B—4. | Ask the teacher to provide individual tutoring |
| _____B—5. | Refer students for child study |
| _____B—6. | Refer students to a 504 committee |

## Section C: Academic Success

During a session, one of the students tells you that he is going to drop out
of school. The student just turned 17 and is still in the 10th grade. He says
that he hates coming to school because his classmates are so immature.
He says he hates studying and doing homework. In an effort to prevent
this student from dropping out of school, which course of action would be
best at this time?

(Select as many as you consider indicated in this section.)

| | |
|---|---|
| _____C—1. | Refer the student to the peer tutoring program |
| _____C—2. | Suggest he wait until he is 18 and then he can drop out |
| _____C—3. | Share information about the GED track |
| _____C—4. | Encourage the student to talk to his parents about his plan to drop out of school |
| _____C—5. | Share information about Job Corps |
| _____C—6. | Give him the official GED practice test during the session |

## Section D: Academic Success

The student returns to you the next day and says that his parents got so mad because you talked to him about alternative education programs. Tears in his eyes, the student says, "I'm already almost 2 years behind, and I'm failing math and English now . . . I'm just going to quit school . . . I don't care what my parents say." What is your best course of action at this time?

(Select ONLY ONE in this section.)

| | |
|---|---|
| _____D—1. | Help the student to secure a tutor |
| _____D—2. | Set up a meeting with the parents and student |
| _____D—3. | Refer the student for peer tutoring |
| _____D—4. | Request that the principal contact the student's parents |
| _____D—5. | Request that the school counseling director contact the student's parents |
| _____D—6. | Encourage the student to talk to his parents again |

## Section E: Academic Success

Before the meeting with the student's parents, the student tells you that the only alternative he would consider to dropping out of school is the GED track. He agrees to discuss this openly and calmly with his parents. During a meeting with the student and his parents, the school counselor focuses on the following:

(Select ONLY ONE in this section.)

| | |
|---|---|
| _____E—1. | A plan for staying in school |
| _____E—2. | Pros and cons of the GED track |
| _____E—3. | Other alternative education programs available |
| _____E—4. | The parents' unrealistic expectations of their son |
| _____E—5. | Apologizing for sharing alternative education program information with their son without their knowledge |

# Chapter 6: Simulation Answers

# Academic Success

## *Brief Case Description*

You are a high school counselor, and a career and technical education teacher requests a classroom guidance lesson on career readiness. Practicing from an academic-focused paradigm, you seek to crosswalk your school counseling curriculum with academic standards.

## *Section A: Academic Success*

What resources/information do you need in order to fully develop your curriculum that will promote universal academic achievement?
    (Select as many as you consider indicated in this section.)

| A—1. | Percentage of non-Caucasian students in class<br>No<br>This is not needed to develop your academic-focused curriculum. |
|---|---|
| A—2. | Standardized tests data<br>Yes<br>Standardized test scores may help you to understand the area of greatest academic need and high school grade levels to customize your curriculum. |
| A—3. | Mathematics standards<br>Yes<br>Core academic standards are needed for crosswalking. |
| A—4. | Grade level of students in the class<br>Yes<br>Your curriculum needs to be developmentally appropriate. |
| A—5. | Number of special needs students in the class<br>No<br>The number of special needs students in the class is not needed to develop your curriculum. |

| A—6. | Language arts standards<br>Yes<br>Core academic standards are needed for crosswalking. |
|---|---|
| A—7. | Special education labels of students in class<br>No<br>The labels of special needs students in the class are not needed to develop your curriculum. Classroom accommodations and testing accommodations (if pre-/post-testing) are needed. |
| A—8. | Accommodations for special needs students in the class<br>Yes<br>Although school counselors often develop curriculum based on grade level and modify the curriculum to the special needs of students during or prior to delivery, it is helpful to know what types of instructional accommodations are needed when developing your curriculum. |

## Section B: Academic Success

The pre-/post-lesson evaluation data reveal low scores on both the school counseling and academic domains for five students, who are not special needs students. The teacher shares that there have also been some behavioral issues with these students. Based on the lesson outcome data and the teacher's comments, which of the following would be the best course of action at this time?

(Select ONLY ONE in this section.)

| B—1. | Refer students to peer tutoring<br>No<br>More needs to be known about these students first, and the only concern is not academic. |
|---|---|
| B—2. | Design an RTI<br>Yes<br>RTI is early intervention aimed at exploring the issues related to students' academic and behavioral problems and mediating those issues with individualized strategies designed by a multidisciplinary team. |
| B—3. | Call a parent conference<br>No<br>The student needs academic and behavioral intervention; therefore, more than a parent conference is warranted. The parent will be contacted once a plan of action is determined. |

| B—4. | Ask the teacher to provide individual tutoring<br><br>No<br><br>It is not the teacher's responsibility to provide outside tutoring, and academics are not the only issue. |
|---|---|
| B—5. | Refer students for child study<br><br>No<br><br>There is not enough information at this time to refer the students to child study. |
| B—6. | Refer students to a 504 committee<br><br>No<br><br>There is not enough information at this time to refer the students to a 504 team. |

## Section C: Academic Success

During a session, one of the students tells you that he is going to drop out of school. The student just turned 17 and is still in the 10th grade. He says that he hates coming to school because his classmates are so immature. He says he hates studying and doing homework. In an effort to prevent this student from dropping out of school, which course of action would be best at this time?

(Select as many as you consider indicated in this section.)

| C—1. | Refer the student to the peer tutoring program<br><br>No<br><br>Peer tutoring is for additional assistance with specific course material, not an intervention for students who express a desire to drop out of school. |
|---|---|
| C—2. | Suggest he wait until he is 18 and then he can drop out<br><br>No<br><br>Although students may be eligible to drop out of school as an adult once the student becomes 18, school counselors strive to keep students in school. |
| C—3. | Share information about the GED track<br><br>Yes<br><br>School counselors have been identified as resource brokers. As such, the school counselor should provide the student with information about alternative education programs that will result in a diploma or GED rather than risk the student dropping out of school. |

| C—4. | Encourage the student to talk to his parents about his plan to drop out of school<br><br>Yes<br><br>School counselors encourage parent–student communication and empower students to talk to parents about important decisions in their life. |
|---|---|
| C—5. | Share information about Job Corps<br><br>Yes<br><br>As a resource broker, the school counselor should provide the student with information about Job Corps, an alternative education program that will result in a diploma or GED, rather than risking the student dropping out of school. |
| C—6. | Give him the official GED practice test during the session<br><br>No<br><br>Unless the student is an emancipated minor, parent permission is required to test the student. Also, parents need to know that their teen is planning to go the GED track versus general education. |

## Section D: Academic Success

The student returns to you the next day and says that his parents got so mad because you talked to him about alternative education programs. Tears in his eyes, the student says, "I'm already almost 2 years behind, and I'm failing math and English now . . . I'm just going to quit school . . . I don't care what my parents say." What is your best course of action at this time?

(Select ONLY ONE in this section.)

| D—1. | Help the student to secure a tutor<br><br>No<br><br>The student wants to drop out of school; tutoring is not indicated at this time. |
|---|---|
| D—2. | Set up a meeting with the parents and student<br><br>Yes<br><br>The school counselor is a student and family advocate and collaborator. It is time for the family to come together to discuss all options. Discuss this option with the student. |

| D—3. | Refer the student for peer tutoring<br>No<br>Tutoring is not indicated at this time. |
|------|------|
| D—4. | Request that the principal contact the student's parents<br>No<br>The principal looks to you, the school counselor, to make parent contacts and apply consultation, collaboration, advocacy, and leadership skills. |
| D—5. | Request that the school counseling director contact the student's parents<br>No<br>Parent contact, even in times of adversity, is the function of a school counselor. |
| D—6. | Encourage the student to talk to his parents again<br>No<br>The student has tried to communicate with his parents. You do not want the student to drop out. Provide the student (and family) with support and discuss with the student a family conference at school. |

## Section E: Academic Success

Before the meeting with the student's parents, the student tells you that the only alternative he would consider to dropping out of school is the GED track. He agrees to discuss this openly and calmly with his parents. During a meeting with the student and his parents, the school counselor focuses on the following:

   (Select ONLY ONE in this section.)

| E—1. | A plan for staying in school<br>No<br>This is not the purpose of the meeting as agreed upon by you and the student. |
|------|------|
| E—2. | Pros and cons of the GED track<br>Yes<br>Helping the family to understand what how the GED track works and what it means to their son's future is crucial. |

| E—3. | Other alternative education programs available<br>No<br>This is not the purpose of the meeting as agreed upon by you and the student. |
|------|------|
| E—4. | The parents' unrealistic expectations of their son<br>No<br>Unrealistic or not, school counselors respect parents' beliefs and understand that parents want the best for their children. |
| E—5. | Apologizing for sharing alternative education program information with their son without their knowledge<br>No<br>The school counselor acted appropriately, providing the student with alternatives to dropping out of high school. |

# Chapter 6: Guided Reflection

Explain the process of curriculum development, as if your audience know absolutely nothing about it.

Define RTI, and create one example to illustrate an RTI strategy.

Define achievement gap. Name the populations of students that have been identified as part of the national achievement gap.

Discuss ways that the school counselor can identify achievement gaps in the school.

Design one activity that illustrates the integration (or crosswalking) of mathematics with one of the three school counseling developmental domains and the Mindsets and Behaviors for Student Success.

What are action plans and why are they needed in school counseling?

Action plans are used within what three areas?

Identify essential components of an action plan.

Identify essential components of a lesson plan.

Define and describe the importance of instructional strategies and classroom management, and when they would most likely be used in school counseling.

Describe and identify key components of the following specialty programs offered in schools:

Homeschooling

The virtual classroom

Programs for students with disabilities

ESL programs

Enrichment programs

GED programs

## Chapter 7

# Collaboration, Consultation, and Referral

School counselors broaden and strengthen their ability to provide a time-efficient and cost-effective comprehensive school counseling program using indirect student services such as collaboration, consultation, and referral. School counselors engage in consultation and collaboration on a daily basis, involved in activities such as staff development, parenting workshops, parent–teacher conferences, committee membership, and program development.

For example, school counselors may collaborate/consult with teachers to develop classroom guidance lessons that blend academic standards with the ASCA (2014) *Mindsets and Behaviors*. School counselors may collaborate/consult with the school nurse to develop a school-wide primary prevention program to address teen pregnancy and positive body image. The school counselor might work with school administrators and teachers to create a program to improve school climate. School counselors may collaborate/consult with school administrators and teachers to design system-wide programs that use a combination of primary, secondary, and tertiary prevention interventions to help close the achievement gap, reduce dropout rates, improve attendance, promote positive attitudes toward school, and reinforce instruction using crosswalking strategies discussed in Chapter 6.

One of a school counselor's most valuable resources for helping students are students. There is much research to support the positive outcomes of peer-to-peer helping programs (Whiston et al., 2011), which are also encouraged by ASCA (2012a). Section A.8. of the ASCA *Ethical*

**APRIL'S IEP**

You are a middle school counselor who just participated in an IEP meeting for April, one of the middle school students at your school. The individuals present at the meeting included the principal, special education teacher, one general education teacher, and the parents. You collaborated with these individuals to identify strategies to include in the student's IEP. Participating in the IEP meeting in this manner is an example of providing what type of services to April?

a. Direct
b. Indirect
c. Both a and b
d. None of the above

*Standards for School Counselors* (ASCA, 2016a) addresses peer-to-peer programs to ensure that student welfare is safeguarded by emphasizing the importance of proper training and supervision of peer helpers by school counselors.

## ASCA's Position on Peer-Support Programs

ASCA believes the effectiveness of school counseling programs is enhanced by the informed implementation of a peer support program, which can provide increased outreach and expansion of services.

*Position statement adopted 1978;*
*revised 1984, 1993, 1999, 2002, 2008, 2015*

Peer-to-peer programs might also include transition/orientation programs, whereby a more senior student serves as an escort and friend to new individual students and groups of students (i.e., elementary students transitioning to middle school and middle school students transitioning to high school) to promote a successful transition. Another type of peer-helping program would include peer tutoring, whereby a student who is adept in a particular subject coaches a student who is struggling in that subject.

While delivering consulting and collaborative services, school counselors are mindful of the culturally diverse populations being served. As discussed in Chapter 3, culture impacts our thought processes and the manner in which a given situation or problem is perceived. Thus, cultural sensitivity during the consultation and collaboration process is crucial to establishing shared goals and achieving desired outcomes. The culturally sensitive school counselor is able to identify prejudicial attitudes and stereotyping that permeates and poisons the consultation and collaboration process. School counselors mediate those obstacles to promote effective consultation and collaboration outcomes.

School counselors are aware of the professional hierarchy that exists in the schools, as well as the educational and political forces involved at the school and community levels. This understanding of the unique associations between parents, teachers, school administrators, and important others sets the stage for team decisions and winning results.

Organized forces for engaging consultation and collaboration include the school counseling advisory council and the school leadership team. While school administrators generally establish school leadership teams, school counselors establish advisory councils as an important component of a comprehensive school counseling program (discussed in Chapter 8).

School leadership teams are responsible for analyzing academic data and establishing school-wide goals and objectives. Participation in the school leadership team is invaluable to gaining a greater understanding of the subsystems operating within the school, as well as areas of strength and challenge related to the school's unique student population and climate. Membership of the school leadership team also allows school counselors to have a voice on important issues impacting the students and community we serve.

# Collaboration

Collaboration involves a partnership between two or more individuals sharing areas of expertise, decision-making power, and responsibility for outcomes (Dougherty, 2013). School counselors generally collaborate with parents, teachers, administrators, and community members, focusing on a unified goal that is grounded in improving student performance and well-being.

Why collaboration? Strange though it may seem, we can look to nature for that answer. I am not saying that we need to be tree-huggers, although I find that concept appealing. What I am saying is that animals have collaborative instincts that guide their behavior in the most productive ways. Take ants, for example, which our airlines have studied to fashion more effective passenger seating processes. Singularly, ants have little or no ability to make an impact (other than annoying *Homo sapiens*), but altogether ants accomplish amazing feats in the most simplistic of ways with no leadership. Each ant is born with specific traits and applies their expertise as needed to ensure the survival of the species.

Also, consider the flight patterns of geese, which have been adopted by our nation's fighter pilots. By flying in a V-formation, geese conserve energy and maximize coordination and communication while attending to the well-being of each member. Using collaborative efforts, school counselors, like geese, harness the amplified power, energy, intellect, resources, and spirit by engaging the collective. Now, if we only had wings, we could really soar!

Collaboration, a fundamental concept, creates an intense life force through the interdependent nature and the shared resources and expertise of each member. It is this interdependence and sharing of specialties that distinguishes collaborative consultation discussed in the consultation section of this chapter.

Establishing a collaborative cohesive relationship with important individuals in a student's life requires teambuilding. Teambuilding strategies may include (Dougherty, 2013):

- Conflict resolution
- Mediation
- Empowerment
- Cross-cultural training
- Analysis of member interaction
- Facilitation
- Coordination
- Problem solving
- Brainstorming
- Encouragement
- Negotiation.

Collaborative partnerships heighten the likelihood of identifying creative solutions to problems or services for the client system that might otherwise go unrecognized by any one individual. Figure 7.1 illustrates the collaboration process. The big arrows indicate the primary structure of the collaboration process (Dougherty, 2013), while the small arrows indicate interactions that may take place in collaborative situations in the schools between either the collaborator and the client system at a given time for assessing needs, clarifying information, or asking questions.

Partnerships with other professionals in the school allow school counselors to provide optimal services to all students and to better identify and tackle obscured obstacles to student performance. School counselors build collaborative, internal multidisciplinary teams that may include the school nurse, school psychologist, school social worker, *educational diagnostician*, principal, teachers, and other school personnel.

As a member of the collaborative team, a special education teacher may share knowledge and skills related to the developmental needs of students with a variety of disorders and the unique educational approaches and tools available to assist these students. The educational diagnostician may share knowledge of educational assessment and diagnostic approaches to identify students who need more intense services in the school setting. The school nurse is able to provide important medical information regarding specific conditions and treatments.

In-house teams might also include collaboration with students. Peer-helping programs, discussed in Chapter 2, are instrumental in a variety of ways (e.g., mediation, tutoring, speakers, aids, mentors). Student office aids provide helpful services while gaining valuable interpersonal and professional skills. Students also gain a sense of empowerment and confidence by assisting school counselors and other adults in the school. Students, too, are generally more in tune with the needs of other students

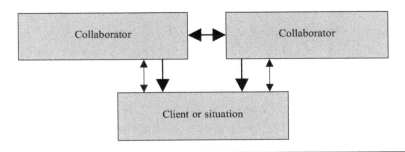

**Figure 7.1 The process of collaboration.**

and the school community, making them an invaluable extension to the comprehensive school counseling program.

School counselors also invest time and energy creating external teams with shared goals, responsibilities, and outcomes. The time is well spent. Partnering with parents and members of the community builds the foundation upon which universal student success can be achieved and systemic change can be realized.

## ASCA's Position on School–Family–Community Partnerships

School counselors have an essential and unique role in promoting, facilitating and advocating for collaboration with parents/guardians and community stakeholders. These collaborations are an important aspect of implementing equitable, data-driven, comprehensive school counseling programs promoting all students' successful academic, career and social/ emotional development.

*Position statement adopted 2010; revised 2016*

Collaboration with parents and community members multiplies the players and broadens the playing field. These partnerships may result in more funding and additional materials. Collaboration also helps school counselors to meet demanding student case loads and systemic programming needs.

Research has identified parent workshops as highly effective interventions in the schools. Parent education has been linked to heightened involvement in the schools and improved parent–child relations (Wright & Stegelin, 2002). Collaborating to provide parent workshops on a diverse number of topics supports the entire school community.

Collaborating to provide professional development opportunities for teachers, who can apply that knowledge to students with whom they spend much time, provides systems support for the school counseling program. Offering topics to teachers such as identifying signs of suicide ideation and homicide ideation, abuse/neglect, cutting, and eating disorders aids in meeting desired outcomes of the comprehensive school counseling program.

## PROFESSIONAL DEVELOPMENT

A high school counselor is planning to implement a teacher workshop during staff development day on the topic of bullying. The principal has announced that the workshop is mandatory, due to the high incidence of bullying in the school. The teachers are complaining that they should not be required to attend a workshop when they are not experiencing any problems with bullying in their classrooms and when it is not related to teaching and learning, but the "job of the school counselor." The school counselor asks the principal if she can speak during the next faculty meeting to let the teachers know a bit more about the bullying workshop that will be presented during staff development. The school counselor shares with the teachers the hidden aspects of victims of bullying, and how it is often the "silent killer" that only teachers can detect given the substantial amount of time they spend with the students in their classes and in light of the special relationship teachers have with their students. The school counselor goes on to say that the workshop will offer some ways to identify and intervene on behalf of these students and involve the school counselor so that teachers can get back to the important task of teaching. Which leadership strategy is the school counselor using with the teachers?

a. Role modeling
b. Overcoming resistance
c. Empowering
d. All of the above

The school counselor interacts interdependently and collaboratively within the varied systems with which students interact to influence each part in order to bring about systemic change. In this regard, we are systems hackers. The systems perspective acknowledges that important others with whom the student interacts have a tremendous influence on the student's career and academic development and personal, social, physical, and emotional well-being. Understanding the profound impact of the interactions that influence an individual is paramount to understanding the individual. These powerful interactions transcend the family system, as the student and family interact with school personnel, all of whom interact with the community.

The importance of collaborative relationships within and outside of the school is most apparent during times of crisis. Collaboration during crisis response and post-crisis response heightens the school counselor's ability to coordinate integrated, multidisciplinary services in an efficient, unified, and timely manner. School counselors are instrumental in serving as community and school liaisons, creating and coordinating effective crisis response plans using the force of the collaborative. Use the force, new vision school counselors.

---

**TEAMBUILDING**

You are a school counselor collaborating with parents to establish a parent resource center at your school. Two of the parents are having a significant disagreement, which is interfering with progress. You are engaging your conflict resolution skills by providing mediation services to these parents with the hope that they will be able to negotiate a resolve. Conflict resolution, mediation, and negotiation are teambuilding skills that are helpful during the process of collaboration. Other teambuilding skills identified as helpful in the collaboration process are:

    a. Brainstorming
    b. Empowerment
    c. Cross-cultural training
    d. All of the above

---

# Consultation

Collaborative approaches to consultation are the most widely used method of consultation in the schools. The collaborative approach to consultation broadens the traditional process to include the expertise of the consultee.

That is, the consultee is recognized for his or her expertise on the clients and the system and shares this expertise in a partnership with the consultant. Together, they define the problem; establish goals; and create, implement, and evaluate a plan of action (Erford, 2014).

Consultation involves three parties: consultant, consultee, and a client or situation to be addressed (Dougherty, 2013). Consultation differs from collaboration in that the consultant (e.g., school counselor) shares a specific area of expertise and directs the consultation process, while responsibility for the outcome rests with the consultee (e.g., teacher, school administrator, or parent). The goal of consultation is to indirectly improve the client or situation by empowering and directly developing the knowledge, skills, and abilities of the consultee.

The triadic (i.e., consultant > consultee > client or situation) nature of the consultation process is illustrated in Figure 7.2. The large arrows indicate the primary structure of the consulting process (Dougherty, 2013), and the small arrows indicate interactions that may take place in some consulting situations in the schools between the consultant or the consultee and the client system at a given time for assessing needs, clarifying information, or asking questions.

In addition to understanding the structure of consulting relationships, school counselors understand the importance of the consultation process. The consultation process is flexible and generally involves four unique stages that can interact and overlap with consultants often moving backward and forward through stages and phases (Dougherty, 2013).

Stage one is known as the entry stage, which involves physically and psychologically entering the system and establishing a rapport with all involved. During the entry stage the school counselor identifies desired outcomes, explores needs, and negotiates a contract. Stage two, the diagnosis stage, involves four interconnected phases. During the diagnosis

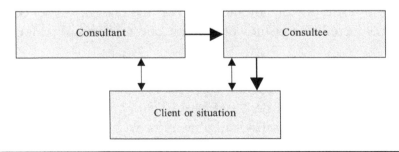

**Figure 7.2 The process of consultation.**

stage the school counselor gathers information and data, analyzes and defines the problem, establishes goals, and identifies possible interventions. Stage three is the intervention stage. This stage involves selecting and implementing an intervention and developing, implementing, and evaluating a plan.

Stage four, the disengagement stage, is the final stage of consulting. During the disengagement stage, the consultation process is evaluated, the consultant's involvement is reduced, and relationships are terminated while creating a plan for postconsultation (i.e., maintaining achieved goals).

---

### STAGES AND PHASES

You are a school counselor engaging in the consultation process. You have identified and clarified the problem and established goals for consultation. While working on creating a plan, you decide to tweak a couple of your interventions while continuing to move forward with plan development. What stage(s) and phase(s) of consultation are you in?

---

Providing consultation services to enhance the knowledge and skills of important others in a student's personal and academic life allows the school counselor to make a significant difference in student outcomes. School counselors are in the ideal position to offer consulting services in the schools because of their knowledge of the school's unique culture and student needs.

Parents and teachers are often the first to recognize the needs of students as a result of daily interactions. For this reason, school counselors are often contacted to consult with parents and teachers regarding student cases.

School administrators, too, refer students who have been brought to their attention because of truancy, suspensions, discipline, and other issues that might otherwise go undetected by the school counselor. Providing consulting services to the school administrator with regard to specific student cases establishes a caring environment that is student-centered and takes into account the circumstances of each individual student.

School counselors are sensitive to the needs of culturally diverse consultees and client systems when applying models of consultation. Models of consultation are generally ethnocentric; therefore, school counselors adjust consultation models and services to accommodate individual worldviews and bridge cultural differences.

## When to Consult and When to Collaborate?

The school counselor's decision to engage in either consultation or collaboration is often a matter of comfort level with a particular approach. Both approaches have resulted in positive outcomes in the school setting with a wide variety of client issues and situations. In addition to preference, the school counselor considers the contextual nature of the issue, desired goals, and the knowledge, skills, and abilities of those who may be involved or who may need to be involved in the helping process.

### THE STALEMATE

The school counseling advisory team that you established is holding its third meeting to discuss the progress of the bully prevention program that the team began working on 2 months ago. At this time sub-teams of individuals were established with specific tasks. You find out that the program has not made much progress, because the two advisory team members who were to develop a draft of the program goals and objectives have been unable to reach agreement. One of the team members is an Asian male, who owns a local restaurant and volunteered to be a part of the advisory team to give back to the community and students who support his business. He wants to see a more collaborative program reflected in the goals and objectives. The other member is a Caucasian female who is a stay-at-home parent of one of the students in the elementary school. She said she wants a systems focus, but she believes that the extent of collaboration that the other member is suggesting is not going to be efficient. How would you approach this issue? Are there unique worldviews to consider based on cultural differences? Would collaboration or consultation be the best way to go?

# Referrals

School counselors do not practice outside of their scope of expertise or outside of the scope of school counseling practices (see Chapter 1). So, in addition to consultation and collaboration, referrals are used as an indirect student service to support the comprehensive school counseling program. The use of referral enables the school counselor to fully meet the holistic needs of students, who may require more assistance than a school counselor can provide within the scope of practice and/or within the school setting. Referrals may also provide school counselors with the opportunity to collaborate/consult with important others on behalf of students and families.

Referrals may cover any of the three broad developmental domains. School counselors may refer students within or outside the school for tutoring services to aid in academic development. School counselors may refer students for additional career support. For example, students interested in joining the military may be referred to a recruiter for a specific military branch. School counselors may refer students to outside counselors for social, emotional, and mental health issues not limited to suicide ideation, substance abuse, eating disorders, abuse, violence, and depression. School counselors may strongly encourage parents to seek family counseling, providing parents with a list of potential counseling agencies.

# Chapter 7: Case Conceptualization Responses

## Collaboration and Consultation

*April's IEP*
The correct response is "b." You are providing indirect services to April through direct services to those who are working directly with April. As the teachers and parents implement strategies that you helped to put into place for April, you are assisting April, albeit in an indirect manner.

## Collaboration

*Professional Development*
The correct response is "b." The teachers are displaying resistance to the idea of mandatory training on a topic that they perceive as unrelated to teaching. The school counselor, in a nonconfrontational manner, helps teachers to understand how the topic of bullying is connected to the role of teacher and the importance of that role.

*Teambuilding*
The correct response is "d." All of the strategies listed have been identified as helpful in the collaboration process.

## Consultation

*Stages and Phases*
You are currently in the implementation stage of the consultation process. Because you are working toward creating the plan while also working on the interventions, you are moving back and forth between phases I and II on the implementation stage.

## When to Consult and When to Collaborate?

*The Stalemate*
A combination of both consultation and collaboration may be the best course of action at this time. Taking into consideration the unique and

possibly opposing worldviews of these two members (Eastern and Western cultural philosophies), while listening to and validating their thoughts pertaining to the direction for the program, will promote a trusting and safe climate for sharing ideas. Having these two members begin by sharing their ideas allows the school counselor to observe their interactions and identify commonalities upon which to encourage their positive relations. Also, invite the other team members to engage in positive communications about the program's direction and empower the entire team to begin the program planning process by establishing a primary goal(s) for the program and knocking around some measurable objectives. This would also be a good time to make use of teambuilding strategies (e.g., mediation, problem solving, and negotiation) and engage in collaborative consultation, that is, offering your ideas based on your training and experience in school counseling programming and student development as well as your knowledge of the school and student population. It is important to revisit the data that is driving the program in order to stay focused on meeting the needs of the students and school community and maintaining the shared focus.

# Chapter 7: Simulation

# Collaboration

## *Brief Case Description*

The principal of your high school asks you, the school counselor, to develop and deliver an Internet safety and cyberbullying program to the entire student body. Due to heightened incidences, time is critical and the expertise of others would be helpful in this endeavor. So, you collaborate with others within and outside of the school.

## *Section A: Collaboration*

Which of the following best describes your function in relation to other members of the team during the collaboration process?

(Select ONLY ONE in this section.)

| | |
|---|---|
| _____A—1. | Expert |
| _____A—2. | Equal |
| _____A—3. | Advisor |
| _____A—4. | Educator |
| _____A—5. | Coordinator |

## *Section B: Collaboration*

A teacher hears that you are developing an Internet safety program and comes to you about a student in her class, Kenji, whom she believes is a victim of cyberbullying, based on the student's behaviors. She is not sure how to approach the issue or what resources she can provide. When she brings up the subject, the student has little to say. What information should you obtain from the teacher before proceeding?

(Select as many as you consider indicated in this section.)

| _____B—1. | What behaviors indicate that the student is a victim of cyberbullying |
|---|---|
| _____B—2. | What friends say about the student's situation |
| _____B—3. | Frequency of behaviors |
| _____B—4. | Magnitude of behaviors and emotions |
| _____B—5. | Level of academic functioning |
| _____B—6. | The duration of specific behaviors |
| _____B—7. | Extracurricular activity involvement |
| _____B—8. | What the student has expressed |

## Section C: Collaboration

The teacher offers some insight into the situation, which depicts Kenji in considerable distress this morning in her class. You believe that giving the teacher resources may not be active enough in this situation. Kenji seems highly and negatively impacted by text messages he is receiving from an unidentified other. Which course of action would be most appropriate at this time?

(Select ONLY ONE in this section.)

| _____C—1. | Refer the case to peer mediation |
|---|---|
| _____C—2. | Involve the assistant principal |
| _____C—3. | Take away the cell phone |
| _____C—4. | Recommend an immediate school counseling session with Kenji |
| _____C—5. | Refer the student to the police |
| _____C—6. | Talk to the student's friends |
| _____C—7. | Recommend a school counseling session with Kenji during this teacher's block tomorrow after receiving parent permission |

## Section D: Collaboration

The teacher insists that you contact the parents because Kenji is Asian, and the parents need to be involved. The teacher says, "It is the Asian way." The culturally sensitive school counselor might respond in the following manner:

(Select as many as you consider indicated in this section.)

| _____D—1. | "You are correct, I will call the parents" |
|---|---|
| _____D—2. | "Yes, however, I would not want to stereotype Kenji based on his culture" |
| _____D—3. | "You are quite culturally diverse" |
| _____D—4. | "I appreciate your sharing; however, the Asian culture is also very respectful of parents, so Kenji may not wish to involve them at this point" |
| _____D—5. | "Kenji is a typical teen; we get too caught up in cultural differences" |
| _____D—6. | "Does Kenji have Asian friends we can talk to?" |

## Section E: Collaboration

After speaking with Kenji, you learn that he is a senior and 18 years old next month. Kenji is not distressed as a result of cyberbullying, but because he and his girlfriend of 3 years, who is not Asian and who is also a senior, are not accepted by his parents. They have been having some issues related to their families. As a culturally sensitive counselor, how would you help Kenji?

(Select as many as you consider indicated in this section.)

| _____E—1. | Advise Kenji to sit down and chat with his family |
|---|---|
| _____E—2. | Ask Kenji to let his parents know what is going on |
| _____E—3. | Suggest he finds quality time to sit down with his girlfriend because texting is not the best way to resolve their issues |

| _____E—4. | Call in Kenji's girlfriend and talk with both of them at the same time |
|---|---|
| _____E—5. | Encourage Kenji to understand the importance of family to his culture and take into consideration what his parents are advising |
| _____E—6. | Express your concern for him and invite him to share the issues and possible solutions he has considered |

# Chapter 7: Simulation Answers

# Collaboration

## Brief Case Description

The principal of your high school asks you, the school counselor, to develop and deliver an Internet safety and cyberbullying program to the entire student body. Time is critical, and the expertise of others would be helpful in this endeavor. So, you decide to collaborate with others within and outside of the school.

## Section A: Collaboration

Which of the following best describes your function in relation to other members of the team during the collaboration process?

(Select ONLY ONE in this section.)

| A—1. | Expert<br>No<br>Generally, this is the function taken on by the school counselor as a consultant. |
|---|---|
| A—2. | Equal<br>Yes<br>During the collaboration process, the school counselor works with others within and outside of the school as an equal member of the team, sharing knowledge as well as task and outcome responsibility. |
| A—3. | Advisor<br>No<br>Although the school counselor may offer advice during the collaboration process, this is not the distinguishing function of the school counselor during collaboration. |
| A—4. | Educator<br>No<br>The school counselor is certainly an educator during the process of collaboration; however, this is not the distinguishing function of the school counselor during collaboration. |
| A—5. | Coordinator<br>No<br>The school counselor may coordinate tasks and activities during collaboration; however, this is not the distinguishing function of the school counselor during collaboration. |

## Section B: Collaboration

A teacher hears that you are developing an Internet safety program and comes to you about a student in her class, Kenji, whom she believes is a victim of cyberbullying, based on the student's behaviors. She is not sure how to approach the issue or what resources she can provide. When she brings up the subject, the student has little to say. What information should you obtain from the teacher before proceeding?

(Select as many as you consider indicated in this section.)

| | |
|---|---|
| B—1. | What behaviors indicate that the student is a victim of cyberbullying<br>Yes<br>Clarifying "behaviors" that the teacher has specifically observed as "behaviors" is important to understanding Kenji's situation. |
| B—2. | What friends say about the student's situation<br>No<br>It is inappropriate for the teacher and school counselor to begin questioning the student's friends about Kenji's situation. |
| B—3. | Frequency of behaviors<br>Yes<br>Gaining a greater understanding of how often the observed behaviors occur is critical to behavioral assessment and timely intervention. |
| B—4. | Magnitude of behaviors and emotions<br>Yes<br>Gaining a greater understanding of the level of behavioral and emotional disturbances is vital to timely behavioral and emotional assessment and intervention. |
| B—5. | Level of academic functioning<br>No<br>There is no indication for assessing academic functioning at the present time. The teacher has not indicated concern in this area.<br>Should the issue persist, assessing its impact on academic functioning may be warranted. |
| B—6. | The duration of specific behaviors<br>Yes<br>Understanding how long behavioral and emotional disturbances have been present is useful in providing timely behavioral and emotional assessment and intervention. |

| B—7. | Extracurricular activity involvement<br><br>No<br><br>There is no indication for assessing extracurricular involvement at the present time. The teacher has not indicated concern in this area. Should the problematic behaviors persist or worsen, it may be useful to assess change in this area (e.g., the student's lack of interest in extracurricular activities that the student had considered enjoyable in the past). |
|---|---|
| B—8. | What the student has expressed<br><br>Yes<br><br>Understanding what the student has to say about the situations is critical. |

## Section C: Collaboration

The teacher offers some insight into the situation, which depicts Kenji in considerable distress this morning in her class. You believe that giving the teacher resources may not be active enough in this situation. Kenji seems highly and negatively impacted by text messages he is receiving from an unidentified other. Which course of action would be most appropriate at this time?

(Select ONLY ONE in this section.)

| C—1. | Refer the case to peer mediation<br><br>No<br><br>Peer mediation requires two identifiable others. More information is needed before considering mediation. |
|---|---|
| C—2. | Involve the assistant principal<br><br>No<br><br>At some point, this may become necessary, but this is not the best course of action at the present time. |
| C—3. | Take away the cell phone<br><br>No<br><br>Although texting should not be allowed during instructional time, this will not mediate Kenji's distress. |

| C—4. | Recommend an immediate school counseling session with Kenji<br><br>Yes<br><br>This is the best course of action at the present time. The teacher has observed that Kenji is in considerable distress and believes that it is linked to bullying. The school counselor needs to assess Kenji's emotionality and explore the situation. Bullying and cyberbullying have been linked to suicide and homicide. Immediate contact with the student is warranted. |
|---|---|
| C—5. | Refer the student to the police<br><br>No<br><br>This may become necessary. More information is needed. |
| C—6. | Talk to the student's friends<br><br>No<br><br>It is not appropriate to involve Kenji's friends at this point in this situation. |
| C—7. | Recommend a school counseling session with Kenji during this teacher's block tomorrow, after receiving parent permission.<br><br>No<br><br>The teacher has shared that Kenji presents with considerable distress today. The school counselor may be able to mediate Kenji's distress, and acting immediately could save lives. |

## Section D: Collaboration

The teacher insists that you contact the parents because Kenji is Asian, and the parents need to be involved. The teacher says, "It is the Asian way." The culturally sensitive school counselor might respond in the following manner:

   (Select as many as you consider indicated in this section)

| D—1. | "You are correct, I will call the parents"<br><br>No<br><br>Parent involvement is not indicated at the present time. Hearing what the student has to say first is the appropriate action at this time. |
|---|---|
| D—2. | "Yes, however, I would not want to stereotype Kenji based on his culture"<br><br>Yes<br><br>This statement is indicative of a culturally sensitive school counselor. |

| D—3. | "You are quite culturally diverse"<br>No<br>The school counselor would be reinforcing the teacher's stereotyping behavior. |
|---|---|
| D—4. | "I appreciate your sharing; however, the Asian culture is also very respectful of parents, so Kenji may not wish to involve them at this point"<br>Yes<br>This is the response of a culturally sensitive school counselor. |
| D—5. | "Kenji is a typical teen; we get too caught up in cultural differences"<br>No<br>Sensitivity to cultural, individual, and developmental differences is critical to effective counseling. |
| D—6. | "Does Kenji have Asian friends we can talk to?"<br>No<br>It is inappropriate to involve Kenji's friends in this situation at this time. |

## Section E: Collaboration

After speaking with Kenji, you learn that he is a senior and 18 years old next month. Kenji is not distressed as a result of cyberbullying, but because he and his girlfriend of 3 years, who is not Asian and who is also a senior, are not accepted by his parents. They have been having some issues related to the families. As a culturally sensitive counselor, how would you help Kenji?

(Select ONLY ONE in this section.)

| E—1. | Advise Kenji to sit down and chat with his family<br>No<br>Kenji is a young adult capable of making this decision. Exploring the level of family involvement Kenji would like to have and/or exploring possible support systems within and outside of the family is warranted. |
|---|---|
| E—2. | Ask Kenji to let his parents know what is going on<br>No<br>Kenji is a young adult capable of making this decision. Exploring the level of parent involvement Kenji would like to have and/or exploring possible support systems within and outside of the family is warranted. |

| E—3. | Suggest he finds quality time to sit down with his girlfriend because texting is not the best way to resolve their issues <br> No <br> The school counselor does not provide solutions to Kenji's issues but allows Kenji to explore and discover his own solutions. |
|------|---|
| E—4. | Call in Kenji's girlfriend and talk with both of them at the same time <br> No <br> It is not appropriate in this situation for the school counselor to pull Kenji's girlfriend out of class and away from instructional time to engage in personal counseling related to their relationship. |
| E—5. | Encourage Kenji to understand the importance of family to his culture and take into consideration what his parents are advising <br> No <br> Counselors do not espouse their own values onto the student, nor do counselors advise students with regard to the student's behavior in relation to the student's culture. Counselors work within the worldview of the student. |
| E—6. | Express your concern for him and invite him to share the issues and possible solutions he has considered <br> Yes <br> Empathizing and validating Kenji's concerns are warranted. Also, encouraging Kenji to explore the situation and solutions within his own worldview is appropriate. |

# Chapter 7: Guided Reflection

Compare collaboration and consultation. Then define both in a way that demonstrates the differences, including the nature of relationships.

Identify at least five teambuilding strategies deemed important in consultation and collaboration.

Describe the process of collaboration, and create two examples that illustrate when it would be appropriate to collaborate as a school counselor.

Explain the stages of consultation, identifying key activities at each stage. Create two examples that illustrate when it would be appropriate to engage in consultation as a school counselor.

What types of referrals might you make as a school counselor?

# Chapter 8

# Leadership

Both ASCA (2016b, 2012a) and CACREP (2016) underscore the role of leadership in the practice of school counseling. School counselors are leaders who can positively impact student learning outcomes and holistic student development.

School counselor leaders support the a comprehensive school counseling program (2012a) by: (1) developing vision and mission statements that align with that of the school, (2) using data to create equitable services for all students, (3) skillfully delivering direct and indirect services, (4) reflecting on the outcomes of services delivered in meeting the needs of all students, improving programming, and promoting systemic change, and (5) engaging in continuous self-improvement with professional development and continuous evaluation. ASCA (2012a) provides the following list of leadership characteristics and practices indicative of an effective school counselor leader capable of promoting change and implementing a successful comprehensive school counseling program:

- Visionary thinking
- Challenging inequities
- Shared decision making
- Collaborative processing
- Modeling excellence
- A courageous stance.

Practicing what we preach data was collected and disaggregated using the School Counselor Leadership Survey (Cashwell et al., 2013) in an effort to further identify leadership qualities that result in positive outcomes.

Survey results identify five characteristics and practices that are recommended for building school counselor leadership capacity:

- Resourceful problem solving
- Systemic collaboration
- Interpersonal influence
- Social justice advocacy
- Professional efficacy.

In addition to leadership characteristics and practices, leadership style is important. Erford (2014) names four styles of leadership found to be present in effective school counselors: (1) structural leadership, (2) human resources leadership, (3) political leadership, and (4) symbolic leadership. Structural leadership involves creating a plan for change and an approach for putting that plan into action. Human resources leadership is built upon the construct of empowerment. School counselors leading from this perspective seek to motivate and inspire students toward career and academic achievement and social/emotional well-being. Political leadership relies on the school counselor's ability to understand systems processes and effectively compromise and advocate using persuasive, convincing arguments with those in powerful positions. Lastly, symbolic leadership involves effectively communicating a vision of change/growth to all, including those in powerful positions. Clearly, a combination of leadership styles could be most helpful, enabling the school counselor leader to not only help students directly, but indirectly as well by winning the support of others both within and outside of the school.

Once we can look at leadership as an honor versus a responsibility, perhaps we can come to fully embrace our role as leader. Many of us lead every day and do not even realize that we are already leaders! John Quincy Adams summed it up nicely:

> If your actions inspire others to dream more, learn more, do more, and become more, you are a leader.

## Leadership and Learning

Collaborative leadership is essential to the effectiveness of school counseling programs, systemic change, and student learning and well-being. The collaborative concept of leadership is akin to the transformational leadership that positions the leader in an egalitarian role with power shared by other stakeholders. This view of leadership supports student learning and aids in meeting the mental health needs of students, aligning with contemporary school counseling practices that support a systems-focused comprehensive school counseling program (Capp, 2015). Still in the throes of leadership identity crises, we are making progress toward clearly establishing a profile for school counselor leadership (Mason, Ockerman, & Chen-Hayes, 2013; Ockerman, Patrikakou, & Hollenbeck, 2015). It will not be long now—but, I make no guarantees.

Triumphant school counseling programs, RTI strategies, student success, and systemic change have been linked to specific leadership skills and characteristics (Young, Dollarhide, & Baughman, 2015), supplementing those named by ASCA (2012a). These include:

- A clear vision (there's that *vision* word again—must be important)
- A realistic, goal-focused plan of action
- Clearly defined school counselor roles
- Ability to build a support system
- Ability to work through and grow from resistance
- A sense of responsibility for program effectiveness
- Ability to encourage, motivate, and empower others
- Actively seeking out supervision
- Willingness to continue to develop leadership skills
- Tackling tasks with determination.

School counselor leaders build strong foundations that clearly define *what* students will learn as a result of the program (ASCA, 2012a). School counselors accomplish this by attaching program activities to standards such as ASCA's *Mindsets and Behaviors* (ASCA, 2016b, 2014) and core academic standards. School counselors create mission statements that describe what the school counseling program does (ASCA, 2016b, 2012a). The school counseling program mission statement supports and aligns with the school's mission statement.

School counselor leaders also create vision statements that fully communicate the ultimate goals for students related to academic, career, and social/emotional development as outcomes of the school counseling program. Vision statements provide sufficient detail, but are not meant to be dissertations. Literary buffs may be tempted to create the next unabridged, complete, deluxe edition of John Dewey's works. I do not mean to blow the mood because, hey, I get it. The printed word is my ambrosia. Similar to the stirrings that consume my soul when I walk into a basilica, a euphoric virus invades my mind at the mere scent of books when I walk into a library. Lord knows, I stay in constant prayer that Kindle and Nook do not kill the printed text like "video killed the radio star." I suspect that my true birthplace was in the self-help stacks in a *biblioteca pubblica* in south-central Europe.

Okay, if I am not careful, we could be on that subject for the remainder of this chapter. The point is that the school counseling program vision statement is meant to be an inspiring futuristic description of optimistic outcomes for students that reflect mutually agreed-upon beliefs and worldviews of all stakeholders, specifically students—not too short, not too long. At times unearthing the appropriate optimistic words while writing a vision statement can be like locating a rental car in Bermuda. For this reason, ASCA offers guidance in writing superb mission and vision statements (ASCA, 2016b); however, you may still have to explore Bermuda by horse, taxi, bicycle, or carriage.

## VISION OR MISSION STATEMENT?

Is the following an example of an excerpt from a vision or mission statement?

"After participating in the school counseling program, all students of Overthetop Middle School use their strengths and talents to achieve desired goals."

School counselor leaders are excellent time managers. If school counselors do not plan their time, others will and historically have, resulting in inappropriate duties for the school counselor. ASCA provides school counselors with guidance regarding that which constitutes appropriate and inappropriate duties for the school counselor under the ASCA *National Model* (ASCA, 2012a). ASCA also offers recommendations for determining appropriate *time* allocations in each of the four methods of program delivery (see Table 8.1). In order to safeguard and balance the time needed to implement a school counseling program, school counselors create weekly, monthly, and yearly calendars. Creating and

**Table 8.1 Sample Distribution of Total School Counselor Time**

| Delivery System Component | Elementary School % of Time | Middle School % of Time | High School % of Time |
|---|---|---|---|
| Guidance Curriculum | 35%–45% | 25%–35% | 15%–25% |
| Individual Student Planning | 5%–10% | 15%–25% | 25%–35% |
| Responsive Services | 30%–40% | 30%–40% | 25%–35% |
| Systems Support | 10%–15% | 10%–15% | 15%–20% |

*Source*: Adapted from American School Counselor Association (2012a). *The ASCA national model: A framework for school counseling programs* (3rd ed.). Alexandria, VA: Author.

posting school counseling program calendars also informs stakeholders of scheduled activities.

An essential part of school counseling leadership is data management. School counseling programs are data driven. That is, school counselors make use of data to identify *why* a particular program, approach, or activity was selected for implementation and *how students are different as a result of the school counseling program* (ASCA, 2016b, 2013, 2012a). School

**DEMONSTRATING RESULTS**

You are a school counselor at Weecanduit High School. Your principal lets you know at the start of the school year that he wants you to be prepared to make a presentation during the spring open house demonstrating how the school counseling program has made a difference in the lives of the students at Weecanduit High School. How will you be able to demonstrate a results-driven program to stakeholders at the open house?

a. Share action plans
b. Highlight program evaluation outcomes
c. Review the management agreement
d. Emphasize the work of the advisory council

counselors achieve this by using program evaluation and documenting outcomes using results reports discussed in Chapter 5.

# School Counselor Use of Technology

The technological literacy of school counselors is becoming increasingly important in order to: (1) meet the demands of the information age, (2) enhance the learning environment, and (3) effectively manage and promote the school counseling program. Recognizing that counselors need to be leaders in the use of technology, ACES (2007) has identified 12 technology competencies that should be covered during master's level counselor education programs (see Table 8.2).

The use of technology may well be the mechanism that determines the level of success of school counseling programs and student learning outcomes. School counselors use technology to:

■ Deliver education and special education accommodations
■ Communicate with the masses
■ Share and disseminate information
■ Coordinate activities
■ Consult and collaborate
■ Advocate for students, families, and the profession
■ Broaden service delivery
■ Expedite tasks
■ Simplify data analysis and reporting
■ Fortify accountability efforts
■ Provide supervision and mentoring
■ Engage in video conferencing
■ Conduct research
■ Participate in professional development.

## *School Counseling Websites*

School counselors are encouraged to make use of technology to develop a presence on the Internet. Creating a departmental website or a personal website is a cost-effective and efficient way to provide information about the school counseling program to parents, students, and the community as recommended by ASCA. When advertising your website, remember your

## Table 8.2 ACES Technology Competencies

| | |
|---|---|
| 1. | Be able to use productivity software to develop Web pages, word processing documents (letters, reports), basic databases, spreadsheets, and other forms of documentation or materials applicable to practice. |
| 2. | Be able to use such audiovisual equipment as video recorders, audio recorders, projection equipment, video conferencing equipment, playback units, and other applications available through education and training experiences. |
| 3. | Be able to acquire, use, and develop multimedia software (i.e., PowerPoint/keynote presentations, animated graphics, digital audio, digital video) applicable to education, training, and practice. |
| 4. | Be able to use statistical software to organize and analyze data. |
| 5. | Be able to use computerized and/or Internet-based testing, diagnostic, and career decision-making programs with clients. |
| 6. | Be able to use e-mail. |
| 7. | Be able to help clients search for and evaluate various types of counseling-related information via the Internet, including information about careers, employment opportunities, educational and training opportunities, financial assistance/scholarships, treatment procedures, and social and personal information. |
| 8. | Be able to subscribe, participate in, and sign off on counseling-related listservs or other Internet-based professional communication applications. |
| 9. | Be able to access and use counseling-related research databases. |
| 10. | Be able to use the Internet to locate, evaluate, and use continuing education, professional development, and supervision options in counseling. |
| 11. | Be able to perform basic computer operation and maintenance tasks. |
| 12. | Be knowledgeable about legal, ethical, and efficacy issues associated with delivery of counseling services via the Internet. |

*Source*: Adapted from Association for Counselor Education and Supervision (2007). *ACES technology competencies for counselor education students.* Retrieved November 10, 2010 from http://files.acesonline.net/doc/2007_aces_ technology_competencies.pdf ethical mandate to identify ways that students and parents without Internet access can get this valuable information. Ideally, school counseling department websites communicate:

- Information about the comprehensive school counseling program
- Information related to the counseling process, including referral, signed consent, and confidentiality
- School counselor roles and functions
- Links to ASCA's ethical standards and professional competencies
- The school counselors' education, training, and credentials
- Information regarding professional associations
- Current trends and developments in the profession (the ASCA National Model, TSCI)
- Mission statements and program goals that clearly connect school counseling to the academic achievement mission of schools
- Program outcome data, including efforts to close the achievement gap
- Parent, student, teacher, and community resources
- Opportunities for school involvement.

Information and resources listed on school counseling websites can enhance student development and well-being and help to support healthy schools, homes, and communities. Some students are reluctant to ask for help and do not actively seek out support. It is the professional responsibility of school counselors to be creative in getting meaningful information to stakeholders for sound decision making, problem solving, and family support (Nelson, Tarabochia, & Koltz, 2015). Web-based information and resources might include information on:

- Crisis response information
- Support programs
- Parenting programs
- Tutoring contacts and test preparation
- Substance use/abuse
- Eating disorders
- Counseling services
- Problem solving, communication, and conflict resolution
- Self-mutilation
- Suicide and homicide ideation

- Financial aid and scholarships
- Summer programs and study abroad
- Special events
- Warning signs of troubled youth.

# Student Use of Technology

The school counselor's technological literacy and knowledge of human development intersect to provide students with developmentally appropriate technological interventions and training. Students must not leave high school without proficiency in the use of technology, which drives every aspect of our computerized world of work. Section A.14.a. of the ASCA *Ethical Standards for School Counselors* (ASCA, 2016a) calls for school counselors to

> demonstrate appropriate selection and use of technology and software applications to enhance students' academic, career and social/emotional development. Attention is given to the ethical and legal considerations of technological applications, including confidentiality concerns, security issues, and potential limitations and benefits and communication practices in electronic media.

**JEREMIAH'S CONCERN**

Jeremiah is a high school counselor who is quite versed in Web applications and website development. He created an outstanding website for the school counseling program. The website has all the information deemed important for school counseling websites. His director was pleased, since they no longer have to spend time, energy, and any of the budget to maintain the binders that housed summer and special programs, scholarships, study abroad, after-school jobs, and more. The director was pleased that now students and parents only need to look at the website. Jeremiah had an ethical concern about his school counseling director's response. What do you think it is?

Some of the more common information and networking technologies may include e-mail, Internet, blogs, electronic bulletin boards, text messaging, video conferencing, chat rooms, gaming devices, graphics software, websites, and SMART technologies. School counselors introduce these and other more sophisticated technologies and related terminology to enhance students' readiness for entry into today's workforce. ASCA provides an e-newsletter, *ASCA Aspects*, to association members in order to stay abreast of current technologies and tools on the Internet. School counselors incorporate information and networking technologies into all methods of service delivery.

Similar to industry certification assessments noted in Chapter 2 by NRF and NOCTI, students can earn industry certifications in specific software packages while attending high school to demonstrate advanced levels of competence in technology. Industry certification assessments such as Brainbench and Microsoft Office Specialist (MOS) are attached to numerous elective courses in business and technical education. Passing the course and assessment leads to certification in a variety of Adobe and Microsoft software packages. School counselors take the lead in ensuring that students gain information and opportunities to participate in industry certifications of interest.

School counselors lead the way in providing students, parents, and teachers with information pertaining to the safe use of technology. This is particularly critical in light of the increased prevalence of cyberbullying, seduction by Internet predators, and the misuse of cell phones. Chapter 2 discusses the school counselor's responsibility for providing students with education related to the potential threats posed when using technology.

## Systemic Change

School counselors are agents for systems change, identifying groups of students (versus a select few) who are not being successful and intervening to remove obstacles or provide support to promote success. Toward this end, school counselors not only engage in leadership, but in advocacy, collaboration, consultation, coordination, and referral as well. Serving as an agent for systemic change also necessitates an understanding of strategic planning and the principles of systems theory discussed in Chapter 2.

Schools are both systems and subsystems in a web of inter-connectedness that makes virtually everyone a stakeholder and client.

Systemic school counseling programs are those that encompass programming that is purposeful in its intentions to provide prevention and intervention to the entire student body and other stakeholders within and outside of the school. The ASCA *National Model* exemplifies such a systems-focused model. Only through systems-focused practices can the school counselor fully eliminate access, achievement, and attainment gaps.

## School, Family, and Community Partnerships

School administrators across the nation have made tremendous progress in promoting community and school relations, particularly through the American Association of School Administrators (AASA) Stand Up for Public Education call to action. School counselor leaders, too, are called upon to engage in action that removes the barriers that impede cooperative and productive partnerships with a child's most valuable educational resource—the parent.

It is strange to me that parents often remain an untapped resource in schools where human resources are generally limited. School counselors are encouraged to establish or tap into school-based parent–teacher–student resource centers (PTSRCs). PTSRCs provide information and resources that promote student development and family well-being. Who better than parent volunteers to oversee daily PTSRC operations? Parents, familiar with the community, are in an ideal position to coordinate requests for information and maintain the informational flow. Many parents want to get in the game but for a variety of reasons do not step up to the plate. Extend an invitation to parents and be specific about the position for which they are being recruited—with the bases loaded and the batter up, there is sure to be a home run!

In addition to parents, the level of success of the school counseling program is dependent upon the involvement and support of community businesses and agencies. These are your educational soulmates—individuals and agencies impacting or impacted by the schools. Many school systems have institutionalized the soulmate philosophy, adopting Partners-in-Education programs. These programs are often facilitated by school counselor leaders who link the school to specific local organizations and businesses. The organization unites with the school to support school improvement and student learning by providing invaluable human, financial, and consumable resources. Organizations (e.g., retail stores, banks, hospitals, fire stations, and restaurants) proudly display certificates of appreciation from the schools they support, which helps their business to prosper as parents and members of the community offer patronage in appreciation.

# Chapter 8: Case Conceptualization Responses

## Leadership and Learning

*Vision or Mission Statement?*
This statement is an example of an excerpt from a vision statement. This statement has a clear future orientation, describing what students will be/do after participating in the school counseling program.

*Demonstrating Results*
The correct response is "b." Program evaluation provides school counselors with program outcomes that demonstrate how the school counseling program is making a positive difference in the lives of students. Action plans and management agreements may depict what the school counselor is planning to implement and how the program or activity is to be evaluated, but these documents do not provide outcome data. Discussing the good work of the council is not the same as providing outcome data assessing the program's effectiveness.

## Student Use of Technology

*Jeremiah's Concern*
Section A.14.f. of the ASCA *Ethical Standards for School Counselors* (2016a) calls for school counselors to "advocate for equal access to technology for all students." Jeremiah is rightfully concerned that many of the students in his school will not get access to this important information because some do not have home computers and some with home computers do not have Internet access.

# Chapter 8: Simulation

# School Counselor Leader

## Brief Case Description

You are a middle school counselor whose principal has requested that you assist him in designing interview questions that may help him to hire a school counselor leader to replace one of your fellow school counselors who has decided to go back to school full-time to get his doctoral degree.

## Section A: School Counselor Leader

First, your principal asks you to identify a few leadership practices that are indicative of an effective school counselor.

(Select as many as you consider indicated in this section.)

| _____ A—1. | Models excellence |
|---|---|
| _____ A—2. | Engages in individual processing |
| _____ A—3. | Does not challenge inequitable processes that upset status quo |
| _____ A—4. | Challenges processes that are inequitable |
| _____ A—5. | Engages in shared decision making |
| _____ A—6. | Engages in visionary thinking |
| _____ A—7. | Creates clear mission statements that are distinct from the school's mission statement |

## Section B: School Counselor Leader

Your principal asks you to provide percentages based on the ASCA *National Model* that a middle school counselor should be spending in the various delivery system components. He understands the importance of the delivery system, as it makes up 80 percent or more of a school counselor's activities. This will aid him in assessing candidates' knowledge of the ASCA *National Model*.

(Select ONLY ONE in this section.)

| B—1. | Guidance Curriculum = 25%–35%<br>Individual Student Planning = 15%–25%<br>Responsive Services = 30%–40%<br>Systems Support = 10%–15% |
|---|---|
| B—2. | Guidance Curriculum = 15%–25%<br>Individual Student Planning = 10%–20%<br>Responsive Services = 40%–50%<br>Systems Support = 10%–15% |
| B—3. | Guidance Curriculum = 40%–50%<br>Individual Student Planning = 10%–20%<br>Responsive Services = 10%–15%<br>Systems Support = 20%–30% |
| B—4. | Guidance Curriculum = 10%–15%<br>Individual Student Planning = 15%–25%<br>Responsive Services = 30%–40%<br>Systems Support = 15%–25% |
| B—5. | Guidance Curriculum = 25%–35%<br>Individual Student Planning = 30%–40%<br>Responsive Services = 15%–25%<br>Systems Support = 10%–15% |

## Section C: School Counselor Leader

Your principal would like this new school counselor to develop a website for the school counseling program. What types of things should be communicated on the school counseling website?

(Select as many as you consider indicated in this section.)

| C—1. | Program outcome data |
|---|---|
| C—2. | Students' grades |
| C—3. | School counselor roles and functions |
| C—4. | Most promising teachers and their areas of expertise |
| C—5. | Parent, teacher, student, community resources |

## Section D: School Counselor Leader

The principal wants this new school counselor to serve primarily as the student assistance counselor, responding to the immediate needs of students. The two delivery methods critical to this position would include:
(Select ONLY ONE in this section.)

| | |
|---|---|
| D—1. | Individual counseling and individual student planning |
| D—2. | Small group counseling and core school counseling curriculum group activities |
| D—3. | Individual counseling and classroom guidance |
| D—4. | Individual counseling and small group counseling |
| D—5. | Group counseling and classroom guidance |

# Chapter 8: Simulation Answers

# School Counselor Leader

## *Brief Case Description*

You are a middle school counselor whose principal has requested that you assist him in designing interview questions that may help him to hire a school counselor leader to replace one of your fellow school counselors who has decided to go back to school full-time to get his doctoral degree.

## *Section A: School Counselor Leader*

First, your principal asks you to identify a few leadership practices that are indicative of an effective school counselor.

(Select as many as you consider indicated in this section.)

| _____ A—1. | Models excellence<br>Yes<br>School counselors model that which they teach/desire to develop in others. |
|---|---|
| _____ A—2. | Engages in individual processing<br>No<br>School counselors engage in collaborative processing. |
| _____ A—3. | Does not challenge inequitable processes that upset status quo<br>No<br>School counselors courageously challenge processes that are not equitable in a professional manner, understanding that it may upset the status quo. |
| _____ A—4. | Challenges processes that are inequitable<br>Yes |
| _____ A—5. | Engages in shared decision making<br>Yes<br>School counselors invite other stakeholders into the decision-making process. |

| _____ A—6. | Engages in visionary thinking<br>Yes<br>School counselors are visionaries, who fully articulate the school counseling program vision. |
|---|---|
| _____ A—7. | Creates clear mission statements that are distinct from the school's mission statement<br>No<br>School counselors create clear mission statements that are aligned and support the school's mission statement. |

## Section B: School Counselor Leader

Your principal asks you to provide percentages based on the ASCA *National Model* that a middle school counselor should be spending in the various delivery system components. He understands the importance of the delivery system, as it makes up 80 percent or more of a school counselor's activities. This will aid him in assessing candidates' knowledge of the ASCA *National Model*.

(Select ONLY ONE in this section.)

| B—1. | Guidance Curriculum = 25%–35%<br>Individual Student Planning = 15%–25%<br>Responsive Services = 30%–40%<br>Systems Support = 10%–15%<br>Yes |
|---|---|
| B—2. | Guidance Curriculum = 15%–25%<br>Individual Student Planning = 10%–20%<br>Responsive Services = 40%–50%<br>Systems Support = 10%–15%<br>No |
| B—3. | Guidance Curriculum = 40%–50%<br>Individual Student Planning = 10%–20%<br>Responsive Services = 10%–15%<br>Systems Support = 20%–30%<br>No |
| B—4. | Guidance Curriculum = 10%–15%<br>Individual Student Planning = 15%–25%<br>Responsive Services = 30%–40%<br>Systems Support = 15%–25%<br>No |

| B—5. | Guidance Curriculum = 25%–35% <br> Individual Student Planning = 30%–40% <br> Responsive Services = 15%–25% <br> Systems Support = 10%–15% <br> No |
|---|---|

## Section C: School Counselor Leader

Your principal would like this new school counselor to develop a website for the school counseling program. What types of things should be communicated on the school counseling website?

(Select as many as you consider indicated in this section.)

| C—1. | Program outcome data <br> Yes <br> Reporting program outcome data on the website allows stakeholders to review the effectiveness of the school counseling program. Include efforts to close the achievement gap as well. |
|---|---|
| C—2. | Students' grades <br> No <br> School counselors do not post students' grades to the website. |
| C—3. | School counselor roles and functions <br> Yes <br> It is important to demystify the school counseling process. Educating important others on the roles and functions of the school counseling, including training and credentials, helps to improve program understanding and supports your qualifications to work with students, parents, teachers, and the community. |
| C—4. | Most promising teachers and their areas of expertise <br> No <br> School counselors do not elevate one teacher over another and leave it to the teachers to create their own internal/external Web pages. |
| C—5. | Parent, teacher, student, community resources <br> Yes <br> School counselors are resource agents who provide information and referral resources on a variety of topics related to academic, career, and social/emotional development. As leaders, school counselors provide credible resources that aid stakeholders in sound decision making, problem solving, and family support. |

## *Section D: School Counselor Leader*

The principal wants this new school counselor to serve primarily as the student assistance counselor, responding to the immediate needs of students. The two delivery methods critical to this position would include: (Select ONLY ONE in this section.)

| D—1. | Individual counseling and individual student planning |
|---|---|
| | No |
| | Individual counseling is a responsive service that would be widely used by a counselor intending to meet the immediate needs of students and to intervene in crisis situations. Individual student planning is more preventative and used to aid students in development academic and career plans and life goals. |
| D—2. | Small group counseling and core school counseling curriculum group activities |
| | No |
| | Small group counseling is a responsive service that would be widely used by a counselor intending to meet the immediate needs of students and to intervene in crisis situations. Group activities are part of the core school counseling curriculum that is provided to all students as part of prevention vs. intervention. |
| D—3. | Individual counseling and classroom guidance |
| | No |
| | Individual counseling is a responsive service that would be widely used by a counselor intending to meet the immediate needs of students and to intervene in crisis situations. Classroom guidance is part of the core school counseling curriculum that is provided to all students as part of prevention vs. intervention. |
| D—4. | Individual counseling and small group counseling |
| | Yes |
| | Both individual counseling and small group counseling are responsive services that would be widely used by a counselor intending to meet the immediate needs of students and to intervene in crisis situations. |
| D—5. | Group counseling and classroom guidance |
| | No |
| | Group counseling is a responsive service that would be widely used by a counselor intending to meet the immediate needs of students and to intervene in crisis situations. Classroom guidance is part of the core school counseling curriculum that is provided to all students as part of prevention vs. intervention. |

# Chapter 8: Guided Reflection

Define leadership and describe its significance in school counseling.

Connect leadership in school counseling and learning.

Summarize how school counselors make use of technology to enhance professional practices and student learning. Create an example of an activity to illustrate: (1) a school counselor making use of technology to enhance professional practices; and (2) a school counselor making use of technology to improve student learning.

Identify the importance of professional school counseling websites and identify the recommended information for website inclusion.

Discuss the school counselor's responsibility with regard to the students' use of technology.

# Full-Length Practice Exam

## Scenario 1: College Readiness

### Brief Case Description

You are a high school counselor reviewing student surveys that were collected from 10th-and 11th-grade students, which indicate that 85 percent of the students in these grades plan to attend a 4-year college. However, an analysis of 10th- and 11th-grade academic performance records reveals that only 35 percent currently have the academic standing needed to get into college.

### Section A: College Readiness

What information would help you to identify that which may be contributing to this gap?

(Select as many as you consider indicated in this section.)

| | |
|---|---|
| _____A—1. | Access to enrichment activities |
| _____A—2. | Promotion and retention rates |
| _____A—3. | Hobbies |
| _____A—4. | Course enrollment patterns |
| _____A—5. | Time spent on the computer |
| _____A—6. | Standardized test scores |
| _____A—7. | Attendance rates |
| _____A—8. | College application completion |

| _____A—9. | Career assessment participation |
|---|---|
| _____A—10. | FAFSA completion |
| _____A—11. | Course completion rates |
| _____A—12. | Parent participation rates |

## Section B: College Readiness

What types of programming or strategies might you consider to help students to understand the connection between grades and getting into college and to close the gap between college goals and college readiness?
  (Select as many as you consider indicated in this section.)

| _____B—1. | Classroom guidance lessons on career planning |
|---|---|
| _____B—2. | Student participation in a small group on study skills |
| _____B—3. | College visitations/fieldtrips |
| _____B—4. | Individual academic advising |
| _____B—5. | SAT and ACT preparation program |
| _____B—6. | Peer-tutoring program |
| _____B—7. | Development of a career and academic plan |
| _____B—8. | Encourage participation in SCA |
| _____B—9. | Parent involvement programs |

## Section C: College Readiness

During your analysis of the school data, you find that there are high numbers of 10th-grade students failing the same required English class taught by the same teacher for the past 3 years. You point this out to your school counseling director, who says she has talked to the teacher several times about this, but the teacher just gets angry. What would be the best course of action at this time?
  (Select ONLY ONE in this section.)

| | |
|---|---|
| _____C—1. | Ask for a meeting with the teacher and principal |
| _____C—2. | Try to talk with the teacher again |
| _____C—3. | Bring this data to the attention of the principal |
| _____C—4. | Ask for a meeting with the teacher and school counseling director |
| _____C—5. | Do not fight this battle |
| _____C—6. | Encourage students to take a different English teacher during scheduling |

## Section D: College Readiness

Further data analysis reveals an alarming number of absences among the 10th- and 11th-grade student population. After talking to these grade-level teachers, you find that many students are performing poorly or failing classes due to excessive absences that result in missing homework and failing course tests, although they are passing the standardized tests. The majority of absences do not qualify for extenuating circumstances. What might you want to consider as possible courses of action to address this issue?

(Select as many as you consider indicated in this section.)

| | |
|---|---|
| _____D—1. | Phone calls to parents from the attendance office after a specified number of days |
| _____D—2. | Phone calls to parents from the teacher after a specified number of days |
| _____D—3. | Send letters home after a specified number of days |
| _____D—4. | Grade-level assemblies to stress the importance of attendance to academic success and college entrance |
| _____D—5. | Administer a needs assessment to the 10th- and 11th-grade students asking them to identify perceived obstacles to school attendance and to provide suggestions to improve attendance |
| _____D—6. | Develop harsher penalties for unexcused absences |
| _____D—7. | Strengthen attendance policy, by reducing the number of absences allowed each year |

## Section E: College Readiness

Further analysis reveals a pattern. Hundreds of students identify needs at home as the reason for missing so much school. Most of those reasons include after-school jobs to help parent(s) pay bills and staying home to take care of younger siblings while the parent works. You also find out that these students do not have materials at home to complete homework and study (e.g., calculators, paper, pencils, study space). These students do not have a home computer, printer, or Internet access in order to conduct required research and type papers. It is difficult, if not impossible, for these students to go to the library due to demands at home. Transportation is also an issue if they miss the bus. What can you, the school counselor, do to help these students?

(Select as many as you consider indicated in this section.)

| | |
|---|---|
| _____E—1. | Reduce homework for these students |
| _____E—2. | Sponsor school-wide drives for school supplies |
| _____E—3. | Work with community agencies to identify resources to help parents with child care and financial burdens |
| _____E—4. | Coordinate partnerships with local businesses to provide supplies |
| _____E—5. | Provide after-school homework assistance for these students |
| _____E—6. | Work with the principal to develop an academic enrichment class as a resource/elective class |
| _____E—7. | Give a list of student names needing school supplies to local media to "adopt a student" |
| _____E—8. | Do not require homework for these special needs students |
| _____E—9. | Apply for a grant to assist students in your school in "achieving the college dream" |

# Scenario 2: School Violence

## *Brief Case Description*

A teacher comes to you, the eighth-grade middle school counselor, because she has three male students in her science class who are entirely disengaged, quiet, and only hang out with each other. She saw them at lunch today sitting only with each other and not eating lunch. No other students were anywhere near them. The students dress in black most every day and routinely appear tired and unkempt. A student observed the teacher gazing at the three male students during lunch and said, "I hope someone is finally going to look more closely at those guys—they are so scary and make gestures when anyone gets near them while teachers are not looking."

## *Section A: School Violence*

What information might you want to gather about the students at this point in time?

   (Select as many as you consider indicated in this section.)

| | |
|---|---|
| _____A—1. | Current and past grades |
| _____A—2. | Attendance patterns |
| _____A—3. | Parents' knowledge of student behavior as reported by teachers |
| _____A—4. | After-school activities |
| _____A—5. | Information from other students |
| _____A—6. | Observations of these students by their other teachers |
| _____A—7. | Educational history from student records |
| _____A—8. | Time spent on the computer at home and school |
| _____A—9. | More information from the student who talked to the teacher about the three male students in the lunch room |
| _____A—10. | Disciplinary infractions |
| _____A—11. | Relationship with siblings and parents |

## Section B: School Violence

The information you gathered demonstrates a pattern of increasingly negative behavior by all three of the students despite school and parent intervention. One of the three students was expelled during middle school for threatening to kill a teacher. Based on the information you have gathered, you decide on the following course of action:

(Select ONLY ONE in this section.)

| _____B—1. | Request an intervention by the principal |
| --- | --- |
| _____B—2. | Request an intervention by the school's resource officer |
| _____B—3. | Meet with the students together |
| _____B—4. | Meet with the students individually |
| _____B—5. | Contact the students' parents for an urgent meeting |

## Section C: School Violence

The art teacher comes to you the next morning with a picture one of the three male students drew during art class. The picture appears to be one of the school cafeteria with all the doors closed. There are people lying face down on the floor and others that appear to be dead with blood on the floors and walls. There are three individuals on three sides of the cafeteria with guns pointed toward other individuals. The art teacher says the student tried to hide the picture and did not want to show it to her, but she demanded to see it. The art teacher had the student walk with her to the school counseling office, during which time he continued to reassure her that it was "just a picture and nothing more." Your concern is heightened because you know that this was the student who had threatened to kill his teacher during middle school. What is the best course of action at this time?

(Select ONLY ONE in this section.)

| | |
|---|---|
| _____C—1. | Involve the resource officer |
| _____C—2. | Involve the principal |
| _____C—3. | Talk to the student about the meaning of the picture |
| _____C—4. | Pull the other two students from class to discuss the picture |
| _____C—5. | Contact the student's parents |
| _____C—6. | Contact local police |
| _____C—7. | Contact Child Protective Services |

## Section D: School Violence

The following day, you call the home of the student, who has been suspended, to offer the parent counseling resources for her son. In conversation, the parent notes that she could give those to her son, who has just left with his two friends to come to the school to get some books he needs to complete some assignments while on the 3-day suspension. You confirm the names of his friends and let the parent know that suspended students are not allowed on school property during the suspension period, so you will be letting the principal know. Although the parent appears unalarmed, you check attendance on the other two students to find that they have been reported absent by the teachers. What action should you take at this point?
    (Select ONLY ONE in this section.)

| | |
|---|---|
| _____D—1. | No action required |
| _____D—2. | Call the parents of the other two students to report their absences |
| _____D—3. | Go directly to the truancy officer |
| _____D—4. | Notify the resources officer |
| _____D—5. | Go directly to the school principal to report this information |
| _____D—6. | Call the local police |

## Section E: School Violence

The resource officer sees two students letting the suspended student in the hall door that is locked. He recognizes the three students and sees a suspiciously bulky zipped jacket. He quickly notifies the principal via the two-way radio, who immediately calls a lockdown. The resource officer yells to the students while the lockdown is being called, but the students dart down the halls in separate directions. After some gunfire throughout the halls of the school, the police swarm the school, apprehend the three students, and secure the school. As the school counselor, what intervention would you consider after such an incident has occurred?

(Select ONLY ONE in this section.)

| | |
|---|---|
| _____E—1. | Begin meeting with small groups of students until you have met with all students school wide |
| _____E—2. | No action required at this time by the school counselor |
| _____E—3. | Just have teachers report any behavioral changes in students |
| _____E—4. | Visit all classes in the building to invite students to see the school counselor to talk about what they experienced |
| _____E—5. | Encourage students to resume their normal activities so as not to draw attention to the incident |

# Scenario 3: Esther

## Brief Case Description

You are an elementary school counselor. A parent refers her third-grade daughter to you. She says she does not have the money to pay for counseling right now and understands that you meet with students for a limited number of individual sessions. This year, Esther, her daughter, began picking her arms so badly that they bled. She took her daughter to the family physician, and he said it did not appear to be allergies or a rash but seemed to be more emotionally driven. When she asked Esther what was wrong, she said, "I don't know." The parent adds that Esther's grades have continued to be good, and the problem does not seem to be related to friendship issues, because Esther has positive relations with peers at home and at school.

## Section A: Esther

What information might be useful from the parent at this time?
    (Select as many as you consider indicated in this section.)

| | |
|---|---|
| _____A—1. | Frequency of behavior |
| _____A—2. | Student's diet |
| _____A—3. | Duration of behavior |
| _____A—4. | Medical history |
| _____A—5. | Onset of behavior |
| _____A—6. | Family events |
| _____A—7. | School events |
| _____A—8. | Student–family relations |
| _____A—9. | Mother's relationship with father |
| _____A—10. | Student's hobbies |
| _____A—11. | Living arrangements |
| _____A—12. | Time spent on the computer |

## Section B: Esther

You meet with Esther and notice that she is a small third grader and very shy. You ask a few open-ended questions related to friends and family, but Esther just gives a quick response that offers you no substantial insight. What approach might be the best to use with Esther at this time?

(Select ONLY ONE in this section.)

| | |
|---|---|
| _____B—1. | Strengths-based counseling |
| _____B—2. | Cognitive behavioral counseling |
| _____B—3. | Play therapy |
| _____B—4. | Gestalt |
| _____B—5. | REBT |

## Section C: Esther

During the second session, Esther enters the room and walks over to the toys, and selects a female doll and a plastic shark off your toy shelf. Esther sits on the mat on the floor and proceeds to have the shark eat the head off the female doll. What might be the most appropriate communication by you in order to gather needed information about this behavior?

(Select as many as you consider indicated in this section.)

| | |
|---|---|
| _____C—1. | Esther, you seem to be angry at that doll. |
| _____C—2. | Esther, do you like sharks? |
| _____C—3. | Esther, who is that doll? |
| _____C—4. | Esther, what is that shark doing? |
| _____C—5. | Esther, that is a mean shark, why did you choose to play with it? |
| _____C—6. | Esther, why are you angry? |
| _____C—7. | Esther, who is that shark? |

## Section D: Esther

During the third session, Esther expresses her anger toward her mother, stating, "Mom doesn't love me, all she cares about is my getting good grades." Which counseling approach might be the most useful at this time to help Esther confront this irrational thought?

    (Select ONLY ONE in this section.)

| | |
|---|---|
| _____D—1. | Reality |
| _____D—2. | Solution-focused |
| _____D—3. | Strengths-based |
| _____D—4. | Behavioral |
| _____D—5. | REBT |
| _____D—6. | Person-centered |

## Section E: Esther

As Esther enters your office for her fourth session, you notice that her arms are really picked and she is picking at her arms as she walks into your office. You ask her if she realizes that she is picking her arms. She says, "Yes." You ask her what she has been thinking about today. She says, "My test."
You realize that this morning third-grade students took an important standardized test. You asked, "What are you thinking about the test?" She responds, "I am so scared that I did not make an A, so Mom is going to take away my birthday party this summer." You ask, "Have you talked about this with your mother?" Esther says, "No, I'm afraid she will get mad and yell at me." What might be the best course of action at this time?

    (Select ONLY ONE in this section.)

| | |
|---|---|
| _____E—1. | Friendship group |
| _____E—2. | Self-esteem building |
| _____E—3. | Encourage and role-play communication with mother |
| _____E—4. | Strategies for reducing test-taking anxiety |
| _____E—5. | Study-skills group |
| _____E—6. | Encourage and role-play communication with teacher |

# Scenario 4: Early Intervention

## Brief Case Description

You are a middle school counselor. Your principal comes to you concerned about the disproportionately high number of students identified as special education and students with a 504 plan as compared with other schools in the district of similar size and population. He asks for suggestions that could reduce the number of students identified as special needs in your school while still providing students with the assistance that is needed to be successful. The principal also expresses his concern with the lack of referrals to the school-wide early intervention team, which you chair.

## Section A: Early Intervention

You provide the principal with the following suggestion:
  (Select ONLY ONE in this section.)

| | |
|---|---|
| _____A—1. | Require that teachers refer students to the early intervention team prior to referral to the 504 or child study teams, unless a parent objects |
| _____A—2. | Pay teachers for the time they spend in early intervention team meetings |
| _____A—3. | Require a minimum number of early intervention team meetings each academic year |
| _____A—4. | Require teachers and parents to refer students to the early intervention team prior to referral to a 504 or child study committee |
| _____A—5. | Require particular grade levels to go through the early intervention team prior to going through child study or the 504 team |

## Section B: Early Intervention

Joshua, a sixth-grade student, has been referred to the early intervention team for academic difficulties. His teacher expresses that he is well liked by other students and he is cooperative, and that she has not noticed any

other concerns apart from academic performance. What type of information or data would be important to acquire from the teacher and parents during the initial team meeting to assess Joshua's issues?
   (Select as many as you consider indicated in this section.)

| _____B—1. | Hobbies and interests |
|---|---|
| _____B—2. | Past and present social functioning |
| _____B—3. | Sleeping habits |
| _____B—4. | Medical information |
| _____B—5. | Behavioral records |
| _____B—6. | Family income |
| _____B—7. | Past and present academic performance |
| _____B—8. | Subjects with which the student is struggling |
| _____B—9. | Past and present emotional functioning |
| _____B—10. | Student's eating habits |
| _____B—11. | Environmental factors |

## Section C: Early Intervention

During the team meeting, an individualized intervention plan is established to target Joshua's areas of academic difficulty. After the early intervention team meeting, as the team's chair you would do the following:
   (Select ONLY ONE in this section.)

| _____C—1. | Distribute a copy of the intervention plan to all the members of the team, the student's teachers, the parents, and to the student's record |
|---|---|
| _____C—2. | Provide only the intervention team members and parents with a copy of the intervention plan |
| _____C—3. | Meet with the principal regarding the meeting outcome |
| _____C—4. | Ensure that the intervention plan does not become a part of the student's educational record |

## Section D: Early Intervention

Two weeks later, the team reconvenes at the request of the teacher, who reports that although Joshua's academics have improved slightly, Joshua is displaying behavioral issues such as agitation and bullying of other students, which is out of character for Joshua, according to his teacher. During the meeting, the parent shares that she and her husband are going through a divorce, which began just about the time that Joshua's academic performance declined. Based on this new information, Joshua's intervention plan was modified to include participation in a small group on divorce. The following permissions must be obtained:

(Select ONLY ONE in this section.)

| | |
|---|---|
| _____D—1. | Informed consent from the parents of all group members |
| _____D—2. | Because small groups are a primary method of school counseling program delivery, parental consent is assumed |
| _____D—3. | Informed consent of parents of all group members and participants |
| _____D—4. | Informed consent only from Joshua's parents because the activity is connected to an intervention plan |
| _____D—5. | No informed consent is required |

## Section E: Early Intervention

During your first group session, one of the most important issues you want to discuss with these adolescents relates to:

(Select ONLY ONE in this section.)

| | |
|---|---|
| _____E—1. | Goals |
| _____E—2. | Topic |
| _____E—3. | Member rights |
| _____E—4. | Confidentiality |
| _____E—5. | Informed consent |

| _____E—6. | Termination |
|---|---|
| _____E—7. | Process |
| _____E—8. | Emergency contact information |

## Section F: Early Intervention

During the third group session, one of the group members becomes very angry and says, "I never even got to tell the jerk what I thought of him before he left us." Which counseling techniques might be useful at this time to mediate the student's emotional distress and work through the issue presented?

(Select as many as you consider indicated in this section.)

| _____F—1. | Clarifying |
|---|---|
| _____F—2. | Empty chair |
| _____F—3. | Paraphrasing |
| _____F—4. | Relaxation techniques |
| _____F—5. | Guided imagery |
| _____F—6. | Stress inoculation |
| _____F—7. | Behavior contract |

## Scenario 5: Academic Achievement

### *Brief Case Description*

You are a school counselor at a large, pluralistic elementary school. Twenty percent of the student body is special education and ESL students. Nearly half of the student body receives free or reduced lunch. Your school did not make AYP last year, so everyone is academic-focused and implementing programs that will result in the immediate improvement of standardized test scores.

### *Section A: Academic Achievement*

What information do you need in order to begin planning strategies to improve academic achievement?
   (Select as many as you consider indicated in this section.)

| | |
|---|---|
| _____A—1. | Parent support |
| _____A—2. | Student interests |
| _____A—3. | Past successes |
| _____A—4. | School and community resources |
| _____A—5. | Target populations |
| _____A—6. | Students' favorite subjects |
| _____A—7. | Subject areas of weakness |
| _____A—8. | Subject areas of strength |

### *Section B: Academic Achievement*

Which data sources would provide useful information for creating classroom guidance lessons to target specific grade levels and subjects?
   (Select as many as you consider indicated in this section.)

| | |
|---|---|
| _____B—1. | Standardized test score reports |
| _____B—2. | School report card |

| _____B—3. | School-wide attendance patterns |
| _____B—4. | Individual disciplinary records |
| _____B—5. | Family structure |
| _____B—6. | Each student's academic record |

## Section C: Academic Achievement

Data analysis reveals grade three math and grade five English as areas of specific weakness, particularly among the special education and ESL populations and African American males. Which intervention would be most useful for providing responsive services for these struggling students?
(Select ONLY ONE in this section.)

| _____C—1. | Small group on study skills |
| _____C—2. | Classroom guidance lesson on study skills that crosswalks school counseling standards and core academic standards |
| _____C—3. | Small group on study skills that crosswalks school counseling standards and math and English standards |
| _____C—4. | Small group on test taking that crosswalks school counseling standards and core academic standards |
| _____C—5. | Classroom guidance lesson on test-taking skills that crosswalks school counseling standards and core academic standards |
| _____C—6. | Small group on test taking |

## Section D: Academic Achievement

While chatting with your school's test coordinator, you discover that many special education students have not been given special accommodations during standardized testing. When you voice your concern to the test coordinator, she says that as long as examiners and proctors are in short supply and because teachers are not always giving these students the accommodations during the school year, then she is not going to worry about it at testing time. What is the best course of action to take at this time?

(Select ONLY ONE in this section.)

| | |
|---|---|
| _____D—1. | Let the test coordinator know that you will be making the principal aware of these unlawful instructional and standardized testing practices |
| _____D—2. | Let the test coordinator know that you will be making the principal aware of these questionable instructional and standardized testing practices |
| _____D—3. | Let the test coordinator know that if this continues you will need to notify the principal |
| _____D—4. | Call a meeting of the teachers, test coordinator, and principal about these practices |
| _____D—5. | Voice your concerns to the test coordinator and trust her to correct the standardized testing practices |
| _____D—6. | Notify the school division's testing administrator about these questionable standardized testing practices |

## Section E: Academic Achievement

The actions of the teachers and test coordinator concern you, so you review some of the special education students' IEPs to find that several students were given special accommodations only on standardized tests, not on classroom tests. When you speak to one of the teachers of these students, he says that this was an IEP team decision that included the principal and that the decision was based on the lack of manpower during the school day. What is the best course of action to take at this time?

(Select as many as you consider indicated in this section.)

| | |
|---|---|
| _____E—1. | Talk to the principal about ways that these students can get the accommodations during the school day, not just on standardized testing days |
| _____E—2. | Contact the school division's test administrator |
| _____E—3. | Discuss with the principal your concern about setting the students up for failure on standardized testing days if they have not been pulled out of the class the entire year for testing |

| | |
|---|---|
| _____E—4. | Contact the State Department of Education |
| _____E—5. | Let the principal know that if he does not do something about this, then you are going to contact the Department of Education |
| _____E—6. | Contact your school division's supervisor of instructional practices so that he or she can talk to the principal about these practices |
| _____E—7. | Request to be a part of the IEP meetings, so that you can have a voice in the creation of students' IEPs |

## Scenario 6: Assessment

### *Brief Case Description*

You are a high school counselor. Terrance is a junior at the high school whose mother has requested that you pull his record and go over the grades and assessments with her so that she might better understand his academic status and level of functioning. She wants to know if he has the grades and intelligence to get into a 4-year college and to be successful in college. She says Terrance has identified seven colleges that offer majors in communication, which is his area of interest.

### *Section A: Assessment*

The first assessment you come to is the WAIS-II. You explain that Terrance has a verbal IQ score of 95 and a performance IQ score of 85, giving him a full-scale IQ of 90. Terrance's mother responds, "I don't know what that means." What information would you share with the student's mother?

(Select as many as you consider indicated in this section.)

| | |
|---|---|
| _____A—1. | Most individuals have an IQ score between 85 and 115 |
| _____A—2. | Because the assessment uses a 95 percent confidence level, Terrance's score could, at any given time, fall within 5 points in either direction |
| _____A—3. | Terrance's IQ score indicates genius |
| _____A—4. | Terrance has an average IQ |
| _____A—5. | Terrance has a very low IQ |
| _____A—6. | Terrance's IQ indicates mild retardation |

### *Section B: Assessment*

Terrance's mother also says that Terrance told her that he got a 34 on his ACT test. She begins to cry, stating that her son would "never get into college with such low scores on his college entrance exams." You look at Terrance's score report from ACT and see that, indeed, Terrance's score on the ACT was 34. What information would you share with this parent?

(Select as many as you consider indicated in this section.)

| \_\_\_\_\_B—1. | The average score of the ACT is 21 |
|---|---|
| \_\_\_\_\_B—2. | The average score on the ACT is 71 |
| \_\_\_\_\_B—3. | Because the high score is 75, Terrance did not do well |
| \_\_\_\_\_B—4. | ACT scores range from 1 to 36 |
| \_\_\_\_\_B—5. | ACT scores range from 25 to 75 |
| \_\_\_\_\_B—6. | Because the high score is 36, Terrance did very well |

## Section C: Assessment

As you go through Terrance's record you notice that there are no SAT scores. His mother says that he is not taking the SAT because he took the ACT. What advice would you give to the parent at this point?

(Select ONLY ONE in this section.)

| \_\_\_\_\_C—1. | The ACT is all he needs |
|---|---|
| \_\_\_\_\_C—2. | The SAT is the most widely used college entrance exam in the country although many colleges accept either the ACT or SAT |
| \_\_\_\_\_C—3. | The ACT measures the same thing as the SAT |
| \_\_\_\_\_C—4. | The SAT is not used very often for college entrance; however, it is a good measure of achievement |
| \_\_\_\_\_C—5. | The SAT is the only assessment that should be taken for college entrance |

## Section D: Assessment

Terrance's mother says that she is still a bit concerned about Terrance's choice of major. She worries that it will not be a good match. She adds that she knows Terrance is interested in communication, but she is not sure about his skills and abilities or that the work environment would fit his personality. The school counselor suggests that the career counselor administer the following career interest inventory:

(Select ONLY ONE in this section.)

| | |
|---|---|
| _____D—1. | ASVAB |
| _____D—2. | Kaufman |
| _____D—3. | SDS |
| _____D—4. | Super's model of career development |
| _____D—5. | WAIS |
| _____D—6. | Vineland |

## Section E: Assessment

Terrance's mother thanks you for your time and asks, "What do we need to do next, because it is the spring of Terrance's junior year?" The following information would be useful for the parent at this time:

(Select as many as you consider indicated in this section.)

| | |
|---|---|
| _____E—1. | FAFSA deadlines |
| _____E—2. | SAT information and deadlines |
| _____E—3. | ACT information and deadlines |
| _____E—4. | PSAT information and deadlines |
| _____E—5. | College fair dates |
| _____E—6. | GED Official Practice Test information and deadlines |
| _____E—7. | Scholarship websites |
| _____E—8. | Financial aid website |

# Scenario 7: Julianna

## *Brief Case Description*

Julianna is a fifth-grade African American student diagnosed with ADHD, and you are the elementary school counselor at her school. The teacher and parent report that Julianna consistently presents as hyperactive, restless, argumentative, and impulsive. Julianna's mother reports that the medication Julianna is taking does not appear to be working because Julianna continues to experience academic, social, and behavioral issues. Julianna's mother is a single parent and admits that she does not have much time to spend with Julianna and her other two children to help with their studies because she works two jobs. A 504 committee meeting was just held, and Julianna qualified for a 504 plan due to the academic and social impact related to Julianna's ADHD.

## *Section A: Julianna*

During the 504 meeting, you identified the following strategies and approaches to help Julianna and her family:

(Select as many as you consider indicated in this section.)

| | |
|---|---|
| _____A—1. | Homeschooling |
| _____A—2. | Social skills development |
| _____A—3. | Reduced television time |
| _____A—4. | Parenting skills training |
| _____A—5. | Family counseling |
| _____A—6. | Reduced computer time |
| _____A—7. | Change in diet |
| _____A—8. | Increased time spent with friends |
| _____A—9. | Counseling |
| _____A—10. | Reduced length of academic work |
| _____A—11. | Increased length of academic work |
| _____A—12. | Providing choices (academic and home tasks) |

## Section B: Julianna

Julianna's mother asks about what other things she can do at home to improve Julianna's behavior and increase cooperation. In addition to organization and maintaining a consistent schedule, you name the following:

(Select as many as you consider indicated in this section.)

| | |
|---|---|
| _____B—1. | Positive reinforcement |
| _____B—2. | Loss of privileges |
| _____B—3. | Allow more computer time |
| _____B—4. | Negotiated rewards |
| _____B—5. | Contracts |
| _____B—6. | Resist setting goals |
| _____B—7. | Mild consequences |
| _____B—8. | Give specific behavioral feedback |

## Section C: Julianna

What counseling theory might be most useful when working with Julianna?
(Select ONLY ONE in this section)

| | |
|---|---|
| _____C—1. | Gestalt counseling |
| _____C—2. | Behavioral counseling |
| _____C—3. | Reality counseling |
| _____C—4. | Person-centered counseling |
| _____C—5. | Adlerian counseling |
| _____C—6. | Cognitive behavioral counseling |

## Section D: Julianna

Several months into the 504 plan, the teacher and parent report that Julianna's behavioral and peer relations problems have increased, and her academic performance has declined. Julianna is now having full-blown temper tantrums at home, at school, and in the community. She is disobedient and blames others for her actions. The school counselor strongly encourages the following actions to help Julianna and her family:
   (Select as many as you consider indicated in this section.)

| _____D—1. | Referral to child study for possible testing and special education services |
|---|---|
| _____D—2. | Homeschooling |
| _____D—3. | Participation in Governor's School |
| _____D—4. | Medical examination by the child's physician |
| _____D—5. | Less time with peers |
| _____D—6. | Appointment with a child psychiatrist |
| _____D—7. | More time with peers |
| _____D—8. | Family counseling |
| _____D—9. | Resources related to helping children with disruptive behavior issues/disorders |

## Section E: Julianna

Julianna's mother returns to you a few weeks later and says that the psychiatrist has diagnosed Julianna with oppositional defiance disorder and recommended ongoing individual counseling for Julianna and the family. She asks if you would be Julianna's counselor over the next couple of years. Your response is:
   (Select ONLY ONE in this section.)

| _____E—1. | Of course |
|---|---|
| _____E—2. | I would like to, as I have enjoyed working with Julianna very much. However, I just do not have time as the only school counselor in the building |
| _____E—3. | Julianna's needs are beyond the scope of school counseling, but I have a list of counseling resources, which may be helpful in identifying a counselor |
| _____E—4. | I would not be able to do this during the school day, as it is beyond the scope of school counseling. However, I can provide counseling services to Julianna outside of school hours at your home or mine for a minimal charge |
| _____E—5. | Oppositional defiance disorder is not really my area of expertise, but I will work with Julianna because she and I already have a positive relationship |

# Practice Exam Answers

## Scenario 1 Answers: College Readiness

### Brief Case Description

You are a high school counselor reviewing student surveys that were collected from 10th-and 11th-grade students, which indicate that 85 percent of the students in these grades plan to attend a 4-year college. However, an analysis of 10th- and 11th-grade academic performance records reveals that only 35 percent currently have the academic standing needed to get into college.

### Section A: College Readiness

What information would help you to identify that which may be contributing to this gap?

(Select as many as you consider indicated in this section.)

| | |
|---|---|
| A—1. | Access to enrichment activities<br>Yes<br>Struggling students need access to enrichment activities to improve performance. |
| A—2. | Promotion and retention rates<br>Yes<br>This information will help school counselors to identify which populations of students are being successful in meeting their college goals and which are not. |

| A—3. | Hobbies<br>No<br>Hobbies will not provide useful information for identifying reasons for the gap. |
|---|---|
| A—4. | Course enrollment patterns<br>Yes<br>This information is helpful in providing insight into low GPAs. |
| A—5. | Time spent on the computer<br>No<br>This information would not be helpful in identifying that which is contributing to the gap in this scenario. |
| A—6. | Standardized test scores<br>Yes<br>Scores on these assessments will help to identify areas of struggle for targeted intervention. |
| A—7. | Attendance rates<br>Yes<br>Poor attendance can be a factor in low GPAs. |
| A—8. | College application completion<br>No<br>This information will not be helpful in identifying what may be contributing to the gap, which is related to academic performance prior to college application. |
| A—9. | Career assessment participation<br>Yes<br>Students who connect learning to real life and career aspirations are more likely to achieve at higher levels and experience higher levels of academic motivation. |
| A—10. | FAFSA completion<br>No<br>This information will not be helpful in identifying what may be contributing to the gap, which is related to academic performance prior to FAFSA and college application completion. |
| A—11. | Course completion rates<br>Yes<br>If students are not being successful in the courses in which they enroll, this needs to be identified and mediated. These data may also reveal specific classes in which masses of students are not being successful, indicating a problem with the course structure, content, and/or instructor. |

| A—12. | Parent participation rates<br><br>Yes<br><br>Students whose parents are involved in their education generally experience higher levels of academic achievement. |
|---|---|

## Section B: College Readiness

What types of programming might you consider to help students to understand the connection between grades and getting into college and to close the gap between college goals and college readiness?

(Select as many as you consider indicated in this section.)

| B—1. | Classroom guidance lessons on career planning<br><br>Yes<br><br>Connecting academic performance to college entrance and career goal attainment has been linked to heightened academic achievement. |
|---|---|
| B—2. | Student participation in a small group on study skills<br><br>Yes<br><br>Study skills have been linked to improved academic achievement. |
| B—3. | College visitations/fieldtrips<br><br>Yes<br><br>Campus tours help to motivate students toward college attendance and provide them with the opportunity to further understand the importance of high school grades and college admission. |
| B—4. | Individual academic advising<br><br>Yes<br><br>Individual academic advising is a primary delivery method used by school counselors. |
| B—5. | SAT and ACT preparation program<br><br>No<br><br>This strategy will not be a helpful strategy for closing the gap that exists between students' school performance and college entrance (e.g., high school GPA and required GPA for college entrance). |
| B—6. | Peer-tutoring program<br><br>Yes<br><br>Peer tutoring may be helpful for some of the population of 10th- and 11th-grade students that are struggling due to a specially challenging subject matter. |

| B—7. | Development of a career and academic plan<br>Yes<br>Students benefit from a plan of action that lays out exactly what courses and types of training are needed to meet postsecondary goals. |
|---|---|
| B—8. | Encourage participation in SCA<br>No<br>Participation in SCA would not necessarily be helpful in mediating the academic gap indicated in this scenario. |
| B—9. | Parent involvement programs<br>Yes<br>Parent involvement has been linked to higher levels of academic achievement. |

## Section C: College Readiness

During your analysis of the school data, you find that there are high numbers of 10th-grade students failing the same required English class taught by the same teacher for the past 3 years. You point this out to your school counseling director, who says she has talked to the teacher several times about this, but the teacher just gets angry. What would be the best course of action at this time?

(Select ONLY ONE in this section.)

| C—1. | Ask for a meeting with the teacher and the principal<br>No<br>This may result in the teacher feeling "cornered." |
|---|---|
| C—2. | Try to talk with the teacher again<br>No<br>Because your director already tried on multiple occasions, all indications are that the teacher will not heed your concern either. Meanwhile, more students continue to experience closed college doors. |
| C—3. | Bring this data to the attention of the principal<br>Yes<br>The principal will be able to address this with the teacher individually, allowing the teacher a private forum in which to communicate. These actions are indicative of student advocacy—a critical role for school counselors. |

| C—4. | Ask for a meeting with the teacher and the school counseling director<br>No<br>The teacher has already dismissed the concerns of your director. A meeting with you and the director may result in the teacher feeling "ganged up" on. |
|------|---|
| C—5. | Do not fight this battle<br>No<br>This is a battle worth fighting. Addressing issues of equity in access, attainment, and achievement for students is a critical aspect of the role of the school counselor in systems support, leadership, and advocacy. |
| C—6. | Encourage students to take a different English teacher during scheduling<br>No<br>This will not resolve the issue as some students will still have to take the required course with this teacher once other English classes reach capacity. |

## Section D: College Readiness

Further data analysis reveals an alarming number of absences among the 10th- and 11th-grade student population. After talking to these grade-level teachers, you find that many students are performing poorly or failing classes due to excessive absences that result in missing homework and failing course tests, although they are passing the standardized tests. The majority of absences do not qualify for extenuating circumstances. What might you want to consider as possible courses of action to address this issue?

(Select as many as you consider indicated in this section.)

| D—1. | Phone calls to parents from the attendance office after a specified number of days<br>Yes<br>Tracking student attendance and keeping parents informed is critical to helping to keep students in school. |
|------|---|
| D—2. | Phone calls to parents from the teacher after a specified number of days<br>Yes<br>Tracking student attendance and keeping parents informed is critical to helping to keep students in school. This also gives the teacher a chance to share the impact of attendance issues on the students' performance with the parents. |

| D—3. | Send letters home after a specified number of days<br>No<br>This is not cost-effective, and there is no way to be sure that parents will receive the letters. |
|------|---------------------------------------------------------------------------------------------------------------------------------------------------------------|
| D—4. | Grade-level assemblies to stress the importance of attendance to academic success and college entrance<br>Yes<br>Assemblies offer a systems-focused approach to informing the masses. |
| D—5. | Administer a needs assessment to the 10th- and 11th-grade students asking them to identify perceived obstacles to school attendance and to provide suggestions to improve attendance<br>Yes<br>If you want to know why masses of students are not attending school—ask them! |
| D—6. | Develop harsher penalties for unexcused absences<br>No<br>The penalty is already harsh—students are not performing academically and not meeting their postsecondary goal to get into college. |
| D—7. | Strengthen attendance policy by reducing the number of absences allowed each year<br>No<br>Because students cannot meet the attendance expectations as they are now, this action will likely result in increased numbers of students out of compliance with the attendance policy. |

## Section E: College Readiness

Further analysis reveals a pattern. Hundreds of students identify needs at home as the reason for missing so much school. Most of those reasons include after-school jobs to help parent(s) pay bills and staying home to take care of younger siblings while the parent works. You also find out that these students do not have materials at home to complete homework and study (e.g., calculators, paper, pencils, study space). These students do not have a home computer, printer, or Internet access in order to conduct required research and type papers. It is difficult, if not impossible, for these students to go to the library due to demands at home. Transportation is also an issue if they miss the bus. What can you, the school counselor, do to help these students?

(Select as many as you consider indicated in this section.)

| E—1. | Reduce homework for these students<br><br>No<br><br>Rigorous standards still need to be maintained, and without a special need (e.g., ESL, 504, IEP), students do not receive special accommodations. |
|---|---|
| E—2. | Sponsor school-wide drives for school supplies<br><br>Yes<br><br>Collaborating with student groups to donate school supplies is helpful. |
| E—3. | Work with community agencies to identify resources to help parents with child care and financial burdens<br><br>Yes<br><br>Parents appreciate this support and may not have the time or resources to identify the assistance needed. |
| E—4. | Coordinate partnerships with local businesses to provide supplies<br><br>Yes<br><br>Generally, businesses are responsive to the needs of the schools in their communities and understand the interdependent nature of the system. |
| E—5. | Provide after-school homework assistance for these students<br><br>No<br><br>These students have identified transportation and after-school jobs and caring for younger siblings as barriers. This might work for some, if transportation was also provided, and you find significant interest. Further information would be needed before implementing this strategy. |
| E—6. | Work with the principal to develop an academic enrichment class as a resource/elective course<br><br>Yes<br><br>This course could prove to be more valuable than some elective courses in helping students to prepare for postsecondary opportunities, particularly for this school's student population. |
| E—7. | Give a list of student names needing school supplies to local media to "adopt a student"<br><br>No<br><br>It would not be appropriate to distribute students' names in this manner. There are other more anonymous ways to meet these students' needs. |

| E—8. | Do not require homework for these special needs students<br><br>No<br><br>Rigorous standards still need to be maintained, and without a special need (e.g., ESL, 504, IEP), students do not receive special accommodations. |
|---|---|
| E—9. | Apply for a grant to assist students in your school in "achieving the college dream"<br><br>Yes<br><br>There are many education grants available for the asking; you have the data to support your need, and your grant could include many items (e.g., transportation, supplies, equipment, child care). |

# Scenario 2 Answers: School Violence

## *Brief Case Description*

A teacher comes to you, the eighth-grade middle school counselor, because she has three male students in her science class who are entirely disengaged, quiet, and only hang out with each other. She saw them at lunch today sitting only with each other and not eating lunch. No other students were anywhere near them. The students dress in black most every day and routinely appear tired and unkempt. A student observed the teacher gazing at the three male students during lunch and said, "I hope someone is finally going to look more closely at those guys—they are so scary and make gestures when anyone gets near them while teachers are not looking."

## *Section A: School Violence*

What information might you want to gather about the students at this point in time?
   (Select as many as you consider indicated in this section.)

| A—1. | Current and past grades |
|---|---|
| | Yes |
| | It is important to look for educational impact to understand how students' behavior may be affecting other areas of life or vice versa. |
| A—2. | Attendance patterns |
| | Yes |
| | It is important to look for impact on daily functioning to understand how students' behavior may be affecting other areas of life or vice versa. |
| A—3. | Parents' knowledge of student behavior as reported by teachers |
| | Yes |
| | Understanding how involved parents are in the students' lives and their level of support provides the school counselor with insight, resources, and direction. |
| A—4. | After-school activities |
| | No |
| | Although this may become important at a later time, this information at this time would not be useful. |

| A—5. | Information from other students<br><br>No<br><br>Perhaps in a time of crisis it may become necessary to elicit information about the three students from peers, but it is not warranted or appropriate at this time. |
|------|------|
| A—6. | Observations of these students by their other teachers<br><br>Yes<br><br>It is important for the school counselor to explore how these students interact with other teachers and in diverse classroom settings in order to establish patterns of behaviors and to understand the frequency and magnitude of behaviors. |
| A—7. | Educational history from student records<br><br>Yes<br><br>It is important for the school counselor to explore the students' history of academic performance and behavior in order to establish patterns of behaviors and to understand the frequency, magnitude, and onset of behaviors. |
| A—8. | Time spent on the computer at home and school<br><br>No<br><br>Although time spent on the computer would not be useful at this time, what the students are doing on the home computer (school computers are generally monitored) may be useful (e.g., violent video games, disturbing communications in chat rooms and blogs, disturbing Facebook pages). |
| A—9. | More information from the student who talked to the teacher about the three male students in the lunchroom<br><br>No<br><br>Perhaps in a time of crisis it may become necessary to elicit information about the three students from peers, but it is not warranted or appropriate at this time. |
| A—10. | Disciplinary infractions<br><br>Yes<br><br>A history of disciplinary actions aids the school counselor in identifying patterns, frequency, and magnitude of behaviors in order to adequately assess level, immediacy, and type of intervention needed. |
| A—11. | Relationship with siblings and parents<br><br>No<br><br>This information may be important at a later time, but it is not useful at this particular time. |

## Section B: School Violence

The information you gathered demonstrates a pattern of increasingly negative behavior by all three of the students despite school and parent intervention. One of the three students was expelled during middle school for threatening to kill a teacher. Based on the information you have gathered, you decide on the following course of action:

(Select ONLY ONE in this section.)

| B—1. | Request an intervention by the principal |
|---|---|
| | No |
| | The principal understands that some students may have a history of disciplinary infractions by the time they get to high school. The principal looks to the school counselor to mediate behavioral issues with counseling interventions. |
| B—2. | Request an intervention by the school's resource officer |
| | No |
| | The resource officer is a valuable resource; however, there is no action for the officer to take at this time. |
| B—3. | Meet with the students together |
| | No |
| | Together, the students will not likely openly communicate. |
| B—4. | Meet with the students individually |
| | Yes |
| | This is the most appropriate course of action to take at this time. Individually, the students may openly communicate, and you can explore each student's unique situation/issues. |
| B—5. | Contact the students' parents for an urgent meeting |
| | No |
| | At the present time there is no indication of urgency, and the academic history records parental awareness of each disciplinary incident to date. |

## Section C: School Violence

The art teacher comes to you the next morning with a picture one of the three male students drew during art class. The picture appears to be one of the school cafeteria with all the doors closed. There are people lying face down on the floor and others that appear to be dead with blood on the floors and walls. There are three individuals on three sides of the cafeteria with guns pointed toward other individuals. The art teacher says the student tried to hide the picture and did not want to show it to her, but she demanded to see it. The art teacher had the student walk with her to the school counseling office, during which time he continued to reassure her that it was "just a picture and nothing more." Your concern is heightened because you know that this was the student who had threatened to kill his teacher during middle school. What is the best course of action at this time?

(Select ONLY ONE in this section.)

| | | |
|---|---|---|
| C—1. | Involve the resource officer<br><br>No<br><br>The artwork should be viewed as an illustration of threat to others, particularly when coupled with the student's past disciplinary infractions and present behavioral concerns reported by the teacher. For this reason, the threat must be brought to the attention of the building head. | |
| C—2. | Involve the principal<br><br>Yes<br><br>This student's actions in context with other behavioral issues call for immediate action and must be taken seriously despite his contention that it is "just a picture and nothing more." | |
| C—3. | Talk to the student about the meaning of the picture<br><br>No<br><br>This is a matter of school-wide safety that will likely result in disciplinary actions, which should be handled by the principal/assistant principals. | |
| C—4. | Pull the other two students from class to discuss the picture<br><br>No<br><br>The school counselor cannot assume to know who the other two individuals in the picture are and should not pull additional students out of class to discuss the actions of the other in this case. The principal's investigation may call for this, but it would not be an appropriate responsibility of the school counselor. | |
| C—5. | Contact the student's parents<br><br>No<br><br>The principal will make this determination after talking with the student. | |

| C—6. | Contact local police |
|---|---|
| | No |
| | The principal will make this determination after talking with the student. |

| C—7. | Contact Child Protective Services |
|---|---|
| | No |
| | The principal will make this determination after talking with the student. Child Protective Services is generally involved in cases of abuse, neglect, and suicide threat or ideation that implicate the parent or guardian. |

## Section D: School Violence

The following day, you call the home of the student, who has been suspended, to offer the parent counseling resources for her son. In conversation, the parent notes that she could give those to her son, who has just left with his two friends to come to the school to get some books he needs to complete some assignments while on the 3-day suspension. You confirm the names of his friends and let the parent know that suspended students are not allowed on school property during the suspension period, so you will be letting the principal know. Although the parent appears unalarmed, you checked attendance on the other two students to find that they have been reported absent by the teachers. What action should you take at this point?

    (Select ONLY ONE in this section.)

| D—1. | No action required |
|---|---|
| | No |
| | Action on your part is absolutely required because this information indicates a violation of suspension and could indicate a school-wide threat. |

| D—2. | Call the parents of the other two students to report their absences |
|---|---|
| | No |
| | Although this would be appropriate, it is not the most appropriate action at this time. |

| D—3. | Go directly to the truancy officer<br><br>No<br><br>This would not be the most appropriate action at this time, and generally truancy officers get involved after a specific number of unexcused absences. |
|---|---|
| D—4. | Notify the resource officer<br><br>No<br><br>This would not be the most appropriate action at this time, because the principal/assistant principals determine actions related to suspension and school threat. |
| D—5. | Go directly to the school principal to report this information<br><br>Yes<br><br>This is the most appropriate action to take at this time. The principal should determine the next course of action. |
| D—6. | Call the local police<br><br>No<br><br>The principal will make this determination. |

## Section E: School Violence

The resource officer sees two students letting the suspended student in the hall door that is locked. He recognizes the three students and sees a suspiciously bulky zipped jacket. He quickly notifies the principal via the two-way radio, who immediately calls a lockdown. The resource officer yells to the students while the lockdown is being called, but the students dart down the halls in separate directions. After some gunfire throughout the halls of the school, the police swarm the school, apprehend the three students, and secure the school. As the school counselor, what intervention would you consider after such an incident has occurred?

(Select ONLY ONE in this section.)

| E—1. | Begin meeting with small groups of students until you have met with all students school wide<br><br>No<br><br>There are many students who will not need intervention and would rather not participate in counseling. |
|---|---|

| E—2. | No action required at this time by the school counselor<br><br>No<br><br>The school counselor needs to be proactive in reaching out to students who may need counseling to process what they experienced. |
|---|---|
| E—3. | Just have teachers report any behavioral changes in students<br><br>No<br><br>Although it is important for teachers to report such changes in behavior to the school counselor as a possible indicator for counseling, this action is not enough, because some students may not overtly display stress reactions. |
| E—4. | Visit all classes in the building to invite students to see the school counselor to talk about what they experienced<br><br>Yes<br><br>This would be the most appropriate action at this time. This would allow the school counselor to identify students in need of counseling services based on overt emotional reactions while also encouraging and offering counseling for others experiencing distress. |
| E—5. | Encourage students to resume their normal activities so as not to draw attention to the incident<br><br>No<br><br>Ignoring the emotional reaction will not make it go away and promotes dysfunction. Although resuming daily functioning and activities is the ultimate goal and may be just fine for some students immediately following a stress-inducing incident, it is important to offer the assistance needed and allow students to decide when they are ready to resume daily routines. |

# Scenario 3 Answers: Esther

## Brief Case Description

You are an elementary school counselor. A parent refers her third-grade daughter to you. She says she does not have the money to pay for counseling right now and understands that you meet with students for a limited number of individual sessions. This year, Esther, her daughter, began picking her arms so badly that they bled. She took her daughter to the family physician, and he said it did not appear to be allergies or a rash but seemed to be more emotionally driven. When she asked Esther what was wrong, she said, "I don't know." The parent adds that Esther's grades have continued to be good, and the problem does not seem to be related to friendship issues, because Esther has positive relations with peers at home and at school.

## Section A: Esther

What information might be useful from the parent at this time?
    (Select as many as you consider indicated in this section.)

| | |
|---|---|
| A—1. | Frequency of behavior<br>Yes<br>Frequency of behavior is important to assessing the severity of the issue. |
| A—2. | Student's diet<br>No<br>This is not indicated at this time, because the student has already seen a physician. |
| A—3. | Duration of behavior<br>Yes<br>Duration of behavior is important to assessing the severity of the issue. |
| A—4. | Medical history<br>No<br>The student has already visited the physician. The school counselor might suggest that the parent consider a second opinion by a medical doctor. |

| A—5. | Onset of behavior<br>Yes<br>Onset of the behavior may help to identify precipitating events or triggers that may be causing or contributing to the behavior. |
|---|---|
| A—6. | Family events<br>Yes<br>Family events may help to identify life changes or triggers that may be causing or contributing to the behavior. |
| A—7. | School events<br>Yes<br>School events may help to identify life changes or triggers that may be causing or contributing to the behavior. |
| A—8. | Student–family relations<br>Yes<br>Changes in relationships can have a significant impact on functioning and behavioral patterns. |
| A—9. | Mother's relationship with father<br>Yes<br>Changes in marital relationships impact family dynamics, functioning, and behavior. |
| A—10. | Student's hobbies<br>No<br>Exploring the student's hobbies is not indicated at the present time. The student's physician would have explored exposure to skin irritants. |
| A—11. | Living arrangements<br>Yes<br>It is important to gain an understanding of the student's environment in order to better understand the student. |
| A—12. | Time spent on the computer<br>No<br>Time spent on the computer would not offer insight into Esther's behavior at this time. |

## Section B: Esther

You meet with Esther and notice that she is a small third grader and very shy. You ask a few open-ended questions related to friends and family, but

Esther just gives a quick response that offers you no substantial insight. What approach might be the best to use with Esther at this time?

(Select ONLY ONE in this section.)

| | | |
|---|---|---|
| B—1. | **Strengths-based counseling**<br>No<br>Promoting Esther's strengths is certainly useful; however, it is difficult to identify and access those strengths without counselor–client communication. | |
| B—2. | **Cognitive behavioral counseling**<br>No<br>The CBT focus on thought processes could be useful in this case, but the school counselor must first promote counselor–client communication and build trust with this student. | |
| B—3. | **Play therapy**<br>Yes<br>Play therapy is an excellent choice at this time for Esther because play often promotes communication and relationship building between the client and counselor. This is also particularly helpful in cases where the child is reluctant to express thoughts and emotions and is in the initial stages of counseling. | |
| B—4. | **Gestalt**<br>No<br>Gestalt is certainly a good choice for helping students to resolve current life issues to become more self-aware and offers practical techniques for daily living. However, the school counselor will need to first establish communications with Esther. | |
| B—5. | **REBT**<br>No<br>Perhaps Esther's issues are related to faulty thinking or irrational beliefs, but REBT would not be indicated at this time. | |

## Section C: Esther

During the second session, Esther enters the room and walks over to the toys, and selects a female doll and a plastic shark off your toy shelf. Esther sits on the mat on the floor and proceeds to have the shark eat the head off the female doll. What might be the most appropriate communication by you in order to gather needed information about this behavior?

(Select as many as you consider indicated in this section.)

| | |
|---|---|
| C—1. | Esther, you seem to be angry at that doll.<br><br>No<br><br>The school counselor does not want to presume this emotion without exploring how the student perceived the action. |
| C—2. | Esther, do you like sharks?<br><br>No<br><br>Focus on the action and what may be implied by the action in the child's world. |
| C—3. | Esther, who is that doll?<br><br>Yes<br><br>This will help the school counselor to understand who the doll represents in the child's world. |
| C—4. | Esther, what is that shark doing?<br><br>Yes<br><br>This is a good choice, as it will help the school counselor to interpret the child's thoughts and emotions. |
| C—5. | Esther, that is a mean shark, why did you choose to play with it?<br><br>No<br><br>Focus on the action and what may be implied by the action in the child's world. |
| C—6. | Esther, why are you angry?<br><br>No<br><br>The school counselor does not want to presume this emotion without exploring how the student perceived the action. |
| C—7. | Esther, who is that shark?<br><br>Yes<br><br>This will help the school counselor to understand who or what the shark signifies in the child's world. |

## Section D: Esther

During the third session, Esther expresses her anger toward her mother, stating, "Mom doesn't love me, all she cares about is my getting good grades." Which counseling approach might be the most useful at this time to help Esther confront this irrational thought?

(Select ONLY ONE in this section.)

| | | |
|---|---|---|
| D—1. | Reality | |
| | No | |
| | Reality counseling is a great approach for examining how current behaviors are meeting or not meeting client needs, but this may or may not be related to irrational thoughts. | |
| D—2. | Solution-focused | |
| | No | |
| | It is important to focus on solutions to the problem, but at the present time addressing Esther's irrational belief would be appropriate. | |
| D—3. | Strengths-based | |
| | No | |
| | Focusing on Esther's strengths to encourage self-help is important, but she had expressed an irrational thought that the school counselor would be wise to address before moving on. | |
| D—4. | Behavioral | |
| | No | |
| | Behavioral counseling, which focuses on learned behaviors, is not indicated at this time. | |
| D—5. | REBT | |
| | Yes | |
| | REBT will provide the school counselor with the approach needed to debunk Esther's irrational belief. | |
| D—6. | Person-centered | |
| | No | |
| | Although the nurturing and warm approach of person-centered counseling is useful in Esther's case, it is not the best choice for countering irrational beliefs. | |

## Section E: Esther

As Esther enters your office for her fourth session, you notice that her arms are really picked and she is picking at her arms as she walks into your office. You ask her if she realizes that she is picking her arms. She says, "Yes." You ask her what she has been thinking about today. She says, "My test." You realize that this morning third-grade students took an important standardized test. You asked, "What are you thinking about the test?"

She responds, "I am so scared that I did not make an A, so Mom is going to take away my birthday party this summer." You ask, "Have you talked about this with your mother?" Esther says, "No, I'm afraid she will get mad and yell at me." What might be the best course of action at this time?

(Select ONLY ONE in this section.)

| E—1. | Friendship group<br>No<br>Peer relationship issues have not been identified. |
|---|---|
| E—2. | Self-esteem building<br>No<br>Although Esther is shy, her issues are not presented as related to self-esteem. Esther's issues are more likely related to her lack of candid communication with her parent and her respect for her parent's feelings. |
| E—3. | Encourage and role-play communication with mother<br>Yes<br>Esther is having difficulty communicating with her mother. Empowering Esther to communicate her thoughts and emotions with her parent is critical to continued family communications. Esther's behavior appears to be related to stress associated with the performance pressure she perceives from her mother. |
| E—4. | Strategies for reducing test-taking anxiety<br>No<br>This is not the immediate course of action, but the school counselor may want to consider this intervention after communication between Esther and her mother. |
| E—5. | Study-skills group<br>No<br>This is not the immediate course of action, but the school counselor may want to consider this intervention after communication between Esther and her mother. |
| E—6. | Encourage and role-play communication with teacher<br>No<br>Esther has not identified communications issues with her teacher. |

# Scenario 4 Answers: Early Intervention

## Brief Case Description

You are a middle school counselor. Your principal comes to you concerned about the disproportionately high number of students identified as special education and students with a 504 plan as compared with other schools in the district of similar size and population. He asks for suggestions that could reduce the number of students identified as special needs in your school while still providing students with the assistance that is needed to be successful. The principal also expresses his concern with the lack of referrals to the school-wide early intervention team, which you chair.

## Section A: Early Intervention

You provide the principal with the following suggestion:
   (Select ONLY ONE in this section.)

| | |
|---|---|
| A—1. | Require that teachers refer students to the early intervention team prior to referral to the 504 or child study teams, unless a parent objects<br><br>Yes<br><br>This would be the best course of action at this time, allowing for early and least restrictive intervention that may be all the student needs to be successful. |
| A—2. | Pay teachers for the time they spend in early intervention team meetings<br><br>No<br><br>Attending school-related meetings to help students to be successful is the responsibility of the educator. |
| A—3. | Require a minimum number of early intervention team meetings each academic year<br><br>No<br><br>This would create unwarranted team meetings to meet a quota. |
| A—4. | Require teachers and parents to refer students to the early intervention team prior to referral to a 504 or child study committee<br><br>No<br><br>Parents of children in the public schools have a legal right to make referrals to these committees and at any time. |
| A—5. | Require particular grade levels to go through the early intervention team prior to going through child study or the 504 team<br><br>No<br><br>This is not equitable access to educational programs. |

## *Section B: Early Intervention*

Joshua, a sixth-grade student, has been referred to the early intervention team for academic difficulties. His teacher expresses that he is well liked by other students and he is cooperative, and that she has not noticed any other concerns apart from academic performance. What type of information or data would be important to acquire from the teacher and parents during the initial team meeting to assess Joshua's issues?

(Select as many as you consider indicated in this section.)

| | |
|---|---|
| B—1. | Hobbies and interests<br>No<br>This would not be useful to assess Joshua's issues related to academic difficulties. |
| B—2. | Past and present social functioning<br>Yes<br>Interpersonal relations impact diverse areas of life. |
| B—3. | Sleeping habits<br>Yes<br>Sleep impacts daily functioning and performance. |
| B—4. | Medical information<br>Yes<br>There may be a medical explanation for Joshua's academic difficulties. |
| B—5. | Behavioral records<br>No<br>Behavior is not identified as a concern. |
| B—6. | Family income<br>No<br>Family income will not provide insight into the student's academic difficulties. |
| B—7. | Past and present academic performance<br>Yes<br>This will help the school counselor to identify the onset of academic difficulties and patterns in academic strengths and weaknesses. |
| B—8. | Subjects with which the student is struggling<br>Yes<br>It is important to know the academic areas of difficulty in order to target strategies for remediation. |

| B—9. | Past and present emotional functioning<br><br>No<br><br>Emotional disturbance is not identified as a concern. |
|---|---|
| B—10. | Student's eating habits<br><br>No<br><br>Student's eating habits would not offer insight into his academic difficulties at this time. |
| B—11. | Environmental factors<br><br>Yes<br><br>A change in environment may impact academic functioning. |

## Section C: Early Intervention

During the team meeting, an individualized intervention plan is established to target Joshua's areas of academic difficulty. After the early intervention team meeting, as the team's chair you would do the following:

(Select ONLY ONE in this section.)

| C—1. | Distribute a copy of the intervention plan to all the members of the team, the student's teachers, the parents, and to the student's record<br><br>Yes<br><br>The intervention plan needs to be shared with all those who work with the student, and it becomes a part of the student's permanent school record. |
|---|---|
| C—2. | Provide only the intervention team members and parents with a copy of the intervention plan<br><br>No<br><br>The plan needs to go to all those who work with the student and become a part of the student's academic record. |
| C—3. | Meet with the principal regarding the meeting outcome<br><br>No<br><br>The principal does not have time to meet and discuss the outcome of every education meeting that takes place in their building. |
| C—4. | Ensure that the intervention plan does not become a part of the student's educational record<br><br>No<br><br>The intervention plan is to become part of the student's educational record. |

## Section D: Early Intervention

Two weeks later, the team reconvenes at the request of the teacher, who reports that although Joshua's academics have improved slightly, Joshua is displaying behavioral issues such as agitation and bullying of other students, which is out of character for Joshua according to his teacher. During the meeting, the parent shares that she and her husband are going through a divorce, which began just about the time that Joshua's academic performance declined. Based on this new information, Joshua's intervention plan was modified to include participation in a small group on divorce. The following permissions must be obtained:
(Select ONLY ONE in this section.)

| D—1. | Informed consent from the parents of all group members<br>Yes<br>Although school counselors are not legally obligated to obtain parental permission prior to counseling, unless there is a federal or state statute to the contrary, considering that most school divisions do require parental permission for ongoing individual and small group counseling and considering the sensitive nature of the topic and age of the student, parental permission should be secured. |
|---|---|
| D—2. | Because small groups are a primary method of school counseling program delivery, parental consent is assumed<br>No<br>School counselors do not assume parental consent for student participation in group counseling. |
| D—3. | Informed consent of parents of all group members and participants<br>No<br>Students can give verbal consent, while the school counselor seeks written consent from parents. |
| D—4. | Informed consent only from Joshua's parent, because the activity is connected to an intervention plan<br>No<br>School counselors should secure written consent from parents for student participation in group counseling. |
| D—5. | No informed consent is required<br>No<br>Although school counselors are not legally obligated to obtain parental permission prior to counseling, unless there is a federal or state statute to the contrary, most school divisions require parental permission for ongoing individual and small group counseling and when meeting with students on sensitive topics. |

## Section E: Early Intervention

During your first group session, one of the most important issues you want to discuss with these adolescents relates to:
(Select ONLY ONE in this section.)

| E—1. | Goals<br>No<br>Not the most important among the choices. |
|------|----------------------------------------------------------|
| E—2. | Topic<br>No<br>Not the most important among the choices. |
| E—3. | Member rights<br>No<br>Not the most important among the choices. |
| E—4. | Confidentiality<br>Yes<br>It is critical to discuss with students the limits of confidentiality in group work during the first group session. |
| E—5. | Informed consent<br>No<br>Informed consent should be secured prior to the first session of the group. |
| E—6. | Termination<br>No<br>Termination is not generally discussed until the final stages of the group. |
| E—7. | Process<br>No<br>Not the most important among the choices. |
| E—8. | Emergency contact information<br>No<br>Generally, emergency contact information is on file in the school already. |

## Section F: Early Intervention

During the third group session, one of the group members becomes very angry and says, "I never even got to tell the jerk what I thought of him before he left us." Which counseling techniques might be useful at this time to mediate the student's emotional distress and work through the issue presented?

(Select as many as you consider indicated in this section.)

| F—1. | Clarifying<br>No<br>This will not help to mediate the student's emotional distress or help the student to work through the distressing experience. |
|---|---|
| F—2. | Empty chair<br>Yes<br>This is an excellent gestalt enacting dialogue technique to assist the student in appropriately experiencing the unresolved issues with his father. |
| F—3. | Paraphrasing<br>No<br>This will not help to mediate the student's emotional distress or help the student to work through the distressing experience. |
| F—4. | Relaxation techniques<br>Yes<br>This will help the student to self-regulate. |
| F—5. | Guided imagery<br>Yes<br>An excellent cognitive behavioral technique that will teach the student to use mental pictures to self-regulate. |
| F—6. | Stress inoculation<br>Yes<br>An excellent cognitive behavioral technique for teaching skills that head off stress and identify triggers to stress. |
| F—7. | Behavior contract<br>No<br>Behavioral interventions are not indicated for this student at this time. |

# Scenario 5 Answers: Academic Achievement

## Brief Case Description

You are a school counselor at a large, pluralistic elementary school. Twenty percent of the student body is special education and ESL students. Nearly half of the student body receives free or reduced lunch. Your school did not make AYP last year, so everyone is academic-focused and implementing programs that will result in the immediate improvement of standardized test scores.

## Section A: Academic Achievement

What information do you need in order to begin planning strategies to improve academic achievement?

(Select as many as you consider indicated in this section.)

| | | |
|---|---|---|
| A—1. | Parent support<br>Yes<br>Parents are resourceful and excellent sources of manpower and creativity. | |
| A—2. | Student interests<br>No<br>Knowledge of the students' interests will not aid in planning strategies for academic achievement. | |
| A—3. | Past successes<br>Yes<br>Draw upon what has worked before within the school and with your unique student population. | |
| A—4. | School and community resources<br>Yes<br>Knowing what resources are available to you is helpful in the planning process. | |
| A—5. | Target populations<br>Yes<br>School counselors need to know who is to receive the intervention. | |

| A—6. | Students' favorite subjects<br><br>No<br><br>Knowing which subjects students like best will not, generally, be helpful in planning strategies for academic achievement. However, teaching styles and methods of instruction preferred by students could be helpful. |
|---|---|
| A—7. | Subject areas of weakness<br><br>Yes<br><br>School counselors need to know the subjects for which students need intervention. |
| A—8. | Subject areas of strength<br><br>No<br><br>School counselors need to identify subject areas of weakness for intervention planning. |

## Section B: Academic Achievement

Which data sources would provide useful information for creating classroom guidance lessons to target specific grade levels and subjects?

(Select as many as you consider indicated in this section.)

| B—1. | Standardized test score reports<br><br>Yes<br><br>Standardized test score reports can identify specific students, groups of students, subject areas, content specific to subject areas, and teachers. |
|---|---|
| B—2. | School report card<br><br>Yes<br><br>Data from school report cards can serve as an indicator of systems-level student needs in specific academic areas. |
| B—3. | School-wide attendance patterns<br><br>Yes<br><br>Schools with poor student attendance will likely experience low academic performance because the two have been found to be correlated. |
| B—4. | Individual disciplinary records<br><br>No<br><br>Behavior can be an obstacle to academic performance; however, it would be time-consuming to review every student's disciplinary record and is not indicated for a systems-focused intervention. |

| B—5. | Family structure<br>No<br>Knowing students' family structure would not be particularly useful in planning systems-focused strategies for academic achievement. |
|---|---|
| B—6. | Each student's academic record<br>No<br>This will allow for individualized intervention; however, it can be time-consuming to review every student's academic record and is not indicated for systems-focused intervention planning. |

## Section C: Academic Achievement

Data analysis reveals grade three math and grade five English as areas of specific weakness, particularly among the special education and ESL populations and African American males. Which intervention would be most useful for providing responsive services for these struggling students?
   (Select ONLY ONE in this section.)

| C—1. | Small group on study skills<br>No<br>This would be a useful responsive service for these students; however, it is not the best choice among those listed. |
|---|---|
| C—2. | Classroom guidance lesson on study skills that crosswalks school counseling standards and core academic standards<br>No<br>Study skills would be useful for this population; however, the target subjects are math and English, which may not be the core subjects covered in this classroom guidance lesson. |
| C—3. | Small group on study skills that crosswalks school counseling standards and math and English standards<br>Yes<br>Small groups would provide a systems-focused responsive service that targets the two specific areas of need for these students. |
| C—4. | Small group on test taking that crosswalks school counseling standards and core academic standards<br>No<br>Test-taking skills would be useful for this population; however, the target subjects are math and English, which may not be the core subjects covered in this classroom guidance lesson. |

| C—5. | Classroom guidance lesson on test-taking skills that crosswalks school counseling standards and core academic standards |
|---|---|
| | No |
| | Test-taking skills would be useful for this population; however, the target subjects are math and English, which may not be the core subjects covered in this classroom guidance lesson. |
| C—6. | Small group on test taking |
| | No |
| | This would be a useful responsive service for these students; however, it is not the best choice among those listed. |

## Section D: Academic Achievement

While chatting with your school's test coordinator, you discover that many special education students have not been given special accommodations during standardized testing. When you voice your concern to the test coordinator, she says that as long as examiners and proctors are in short supply and because teachers are not always giving these students the accommodations during the school year, then she is not going to worry about it at testing time. What is the best course of action to take at this time?

(Select ONLY ONE in this section.)

| D—1. | Let the test coordinator know that you will be making the principal aware of these unlawful instructional and standardized testing practices |
|---|---|
| | Yes |
| | The principal needs to be made aware that the special education students are not receiving their accommodations as written on the legally binding IEP. |
| D—2. | Let the test coordinator know that you will be making the principal aware of these questionable instructional and standardized testing practices |
| | No |
| | These practices are not only questionable but unlawful, because they clearly deprive special education students of their rights to testing accommodations. |
| D—3. | Let the test coordinator know that if this continues you will need to notify the principal |
| | No |
| | School counselors are student advocates and advocates for social justice. Also, knowing and not doing anything about it can make the school counselor liable as well. |

| D—4. | Call a meeting of the teachers, test coordinator, and principal about these practices <br><br> No <br><br> This is the responsibility of the principal/designated school administrator. |
|---|---|
| D—5. | Voice your concerns to the test coordinator and trust her to correct the standardized testing practices <br><br> No <br><br> This is an unlawful practice that must be brought to the attention of the school administrator for immediate correction and possible exploration into past testing impacts and action. |
| D—6. | Notify the school division's testing administrator about these questionable standardized testing practices <br><br> No <br><br> School counselors should follow the chain of command by reporting this information to the school principal. |

## Section E: Academic Achievement

The actions of the teachers and test coordinator concern you, so you review some of the special education students' IEPs to find that several students were given special accommodations only on standardized tests, not on classroom tests. When you speak to one of the teachers of these students, he says that this was an IEP team decision that included the principal and that the decision was based on the lack of manpower during the school day. What is the best course of action to take at this time?

(Select as many as you consider indicated in this section.)

| E—1. | Talk to the principal about ways that these students can get the accommodations during the school day, not just on standardized testing days <br><br> Yes <br><br> School counselors use their leadership skills to partner with school administrators. |
|---|---|
| E—2. | Contact the school division's test administrator <br><br> No <br><br> School counselors partner with their building principals to effect change. |

| E—3. | Discuss with the principal your concern about setting the students up for failure on standardized testing days if they have not been pulled out of the class the entire year for testing<br>Yes<br>Helping the principal to understand the adverse impact that this practice can have on student performance during standardized testing would be beneficial. |
|---|---|
| E—4. | Contact the State Department of Education<br>No<br>School counselors can best serve students by working within the school's policies, and because this is an IEP team decision, it is not an unlawful or unethical practice that warrants going over the head of the building principal. |
| E—5. | Let the principal know that if he does not do something about this, then you are going to contact the Department of Education<br>No<br>Although the situation may adversely impact student scores, the situation is not unlawful and was based on a team decision, which included the parent. |
| E—6. | Contact your school division's supervisor of instructional practices so that he or she can talk to the principal about these practices<br>No<br>This action could harm your relationship with your principal, and thus your ability to provide optimal services to students. |
| E—7. | Request to be a part of the IEP meetings, so that you can have a voice in the creation of students' IEPs<br>Yes<br>School counselors can advocate for students by taking part in child study, IEP, and other academic-related meetings. |

# Scenario 6 Answers: Assessment

## Brief Case Description

You are a high school counselor. Terrance is a junior at the high school whose mother has requested that you pull his record and go over the grades and assessments with her so that she might better understand his academic status and level of functioning. She wants to know if he has the grades and intelligence to get into a 4-year college and to be successful in college. She says Terrance has identified seven colleges that offer majors in communication, which is his area of interest.

## Section A: Assessment

The first assessment you come to is the WAIS-II. You explain that Terrance has a verbal IQ score of 95 and a performance IQ score of 85, giving him a full-scale IQ of 90. Terrance's mother responds, "I don't know what that means." What information would you share with the student's mother?

(Select as many as you consider indicated in this section.)

| | |
|---|---|
| A—1. | Most individuals have an IQ score between 85 and 115 <br> Yes <br> This is accurate and helpful information to give the parent. |
| A—2. | Because the assessment uses a 95 percent confidence level, Terrance's score could, at any given time, fall within 5 points in either direction <br> Yes <br> This will help the parent to understand how the score might be captured on other similar assessments. |
| A—3. | Terrance's IQ score indicates genius <br> No <br> This is not an accurate interpretation of Terrance's score. |
| A—4. | Terrance has an average IQ <br> Yes <br> This is an accurate interpretation of Terrance's score. |
| A—5. | Terrance has a very low IQ <br> No <br> This is not an accurate interpretation of Terrance's score. |

| A—6. | Terrance's IQ indicates mild retardation |
|------|------------------------------------------|
|      | No |
|      | This is not an accurate interpretation of Terrance's score. |

## Section B: Assessment

Terrance's mother also says that Terrance told her that he got a 34 on his ACT test. She begins to cry, stating that her son would "never get into college with such low scores on his college entrance exams." You look at Terrance's score report from ACT and see that, indeed, Terrance's score on the ACT was 34. What information would you share with this parent?

(Select as many as you consider indicated in this section.)

| B—1. | The average score of the ACT is 21 |
|------|-------------------------------------|
|      | Yes |
|      | This is accurate information that will help the parent to understand the meaning of her son's score. |
| B—2. | The average score on the ACT is 71 |
|      | No |
|      | This is not accurate; the average score on the ACT is 21. |
| B—3. | Because the high score is 75, Terrance did not do well |
|      | No |
|      | This is not accurate; the high score on the ACT is 36. |
| B—4. | ACT scores range from 1 to 36 |
|      | Yes |
|      | This is accurate and will help Terrance's mother to understand his score. |
| B—5. | ACT scores range from 25 to 75 |
|      | No |
|      | This is not accurate information; the ACT score range is 1 to 36. |
| B—6. | Because the high score is 36, Terrance did very well |
|      | Yes |
|      | This is an accurate interpretation of Terrance's ACT score. |

## Section C: Assessment

As you go through Terrance's record you notice that there are no SAT scores. His mother says he is not taking the SAT because he took the ACT. What advice would you give to the parent at this point?
(Select ONLY ONE in this section.)

| C—1. | The ACT is all he needs |
|---|---|
| | No |
| | It is best to take the one that the college of your choice requires. Many will take either test, but both are encouraged because each tests you in a different way. |
| C—2. | The SAT is the most widely used college entrance exam in the country although many colleges accept either the ACT or SAT |
| | Yes |
| | This is accurate information. Students should also be advised to take the test required by the college of their choice. |
| C—3. | The ACT measures the same thing as the SAT |
| | No |
| | This is not accurate information. |
| C—4. | The SAT is not used very often for college entrance; however, it is a good measure of achievement |
| | No |
| | The SAT is the most widely used college entrance exam in the country. |
| C—5. | The SAT is the only assessment that should be taken for college entrance |
| | No |
| | Students who do not wish to take both the ACT and the SAT should take the test required by the college of their choice. |

## Section D: Assessment

Terrance's mother says that she is still a bit concerned about Terrance's choice of major. She worries that it will not be a good match. She adds that she knows Terrance is interested in communication, but she is not sure about his skills and abilities or that the work environment would fit his personality. The school counselor suggests that the career counselor administer the following career interest inventory:

(Select ONLY ONE in this section.)

| D—1. | ASVAB<br>No<br>The ASVAB is an aptitude test. |
|---|---|
| D—2. | Kaufman<br>No<br>The Kaufman is an assessment of cognitive development and not generally used as a career decision-making tool. |
| D—3. | SDS<br>Yes<br>The SDS will match Terrance's skills and interests to specific careers. |
| D—4. | Super's model of career development<br>No<br>This is a career development model not a career assessment. |
| D—5. | WAIS<br>No<br>This is an intelligence test and is not generally used to make career decisions. |
| D—6. | Vineland<br>No<br>This assessment measures adaptive behavior. |

## Section E: Assessment

Terrance's mother thanks you for your time and asks, "What do we need to do next, because it is already the spring of Terrance's junior year?" The following information would be useful for the parent at this time:

(Select as many as you consider indicated in this section.)

| E—1. | FAFSA deadlines<br>Yes<br>This form should be completed in January of the student's senior year. |
|---|---|
| E—2. | SAT information and deadlines<br>Yes<br>Students are encouraged to take both the SAT and the ACT, unless their school(s) of choice specifies one or the other. |

| E—3. | ACT information and deadlines <br> No <br> The student already took the ACT and scored well. |
|---|---|
| E—4. | PSAT information and deadlines <br> Yes <br> Although this test is generally taken in the ninth and 10th grade years, it is sometimes taken in the 11th grade year for scholarship awards and as a practice test for the SAT. |
| E—5. | College fair dates <br> Yes <br> This would be beneficial to Terrance, who has not identified a specific college. |
| E—6. | GED Official Practice Test information and deadlines <br> No <br> This is an alternative education route for students who do not desire to graduate from high school or who are at risk of dropping out of high school. |
| E—7. | Scholarship websites <br> Yes <br> This is useful information for college-bound students. |
| E—8. | Financial aid website <br> Yes <br> This is useful information for college-bound students. |

# Scenario 7 Answers: Julianna

## Brief Case Description

Julianna is a fifth-grade African American student diagnosed with ADHD, and you are the elementary school counselor at her school. The teacher and parent report that Julianna consistently presents as hyperactive, restless, argumentative, and impulsive. Julianna's mother reports that the medication Julianna is taking does not appear to be working because Julianna continues to experience academic, social, and behavioral issues. Julianna's mother is a single parent and admits that she does not have much time to spend with Julianna and her other two children to help with their studies because she works two jobs. A 504 committee meeting was just held, and Julianna qualified for a 504 plan due to the academic and social impact related to Julianna's ADHD.

## Section A: Julianna

During the 504 meeting, you identified the following strategies and approaches to help Julianna and her family:

(Select as many as you consider indicated in this section.)

| A—1. | Homeschooling<br>No<br>Julianna can benefit from the social interaction and structure of school. |
|---|---|
| A—2. | Social skills development<br>Yes<br>Students with ADHD often experience interpersonal relationship issues. |
| A—3. | Reduced television time<br>No<br>A reduction in television time is not indicated at this time. |
| A—4. | Parenting skills training<br>Yes<br>It is important to help parents to acquire the skills needed to help their children with ADHD. |

| A—5. | Family counseling |
| | Yes |
| | ADHD is a challenge that impacts the entire family. |
| A—6. | Reduced computer time |
| | No |
| | A reduction in computer time is not indicated at this time. |
| A—7. | Change in diet |
| | Yes |
| | There is much research to support the effectiveness of diet in mediating the symptoms of ADHD. This is an option worthy of further investigation. |
| A—8. | Increased time spent with friends |
| | No |
| | An increase in the amount of time spent with friends is not indicated at this time. Additionally, more time with friends does not equal enhanced social skills. It is possible that more time with friends will lead to more rejection until proper social skills are developed. |
| A—9. | Counseling |
| | Yes |
| | A combination of counseling and medication has been found to be effective in mediating the symptoms of ADHD. |
| A—10. | Reduced length of academic work |
| | Yes |
| | This is a 504 plan accommodation that has been found to be helpful for students with ADHD. |
| A—11. | Increased length of academic work |
| | No |
| | Lengthening academic work and the time required to complete such assignments is frustrating for a child with ADHD, who is already having difficulty focusing on the workload assigned. |
| A—12. | Providing choices (academic and home tasks) |
| | Yes |
| | Allowing choices for students with ADHD will help them to select a "means to the end" that is best suited for them and helps them to stay on task. |

## Section B: Julianna

Julianna's mother asks about what other things she can do at home to improve Julianna's behavior and increase cooperation. In addition to organization and maintaining a consistent schedule, you name the following:

(Select as many as you consider indicated in this section.)

| | |
|---|---|
| B—1. | Positive reinforcement<br>Yes<br>Positive reinforcement for following rules at home and school has been used successfully with children and adolescents with ADHD. |
| B—2. | Loss of privileges<br>Yes<br>Loss of privileges has been used successfully as a mild consequence to undesired behaviors for children with ADHD. |
| B—3. | Allow more computer time<br>No<br>Increasing computer time is not indicated. |
| B—4. | Negotiated rewards<br>Yes<br>Allowing choices and negotiating rewards helps children with ADHD to participate in their own behavioral plan. |
| B—5. | Contracts<br>Yes<br>Behavior contracts have been found to be useful in mediating the negative behaviors associated with ADHD and provide a clearly defined process of rewards and consequences. |
| B—6. | Resist setting goals<br>No<br>Goals are useful for children with ADHD, aiding in directing behavior. |
| B—7. | Mild consequences<br>Yes<br>Mild consequences are enough to shape behavior. |
| B—8. | Give specific behavioral feedback<br>Yes<br>Specific feedback allows for specific change and clear understanding. |

## Section C: Julianna

What counseling theory might be most useful when working with Julianna?
    (Select ONLY ONE in this section.)

| C—1. | Gestalt counseling<br>No<br>This is not the best counseling approach among those listed here for children with ADHD. |
|---|---|
| C—2. | Behavioral counseling<br>Yes<br>Behavioral counseling is the approach most widely used with children with ADHD. |
| C—3. | Reality counseling<br>No<br>This is not the best counseling approach among those listed here for children with ADHD. |
| C—4. | Person-centered counseling<br>No<br>This is not the best counseling approach among those listed here for children with ADHD. |
| C—5. | Adlerian counseling<br>No<br>This is not the best counseling approach among those listed here for children with ADHD. |
| C—6. | Cognitive behavioral counseling<br>No<br>This is not the best counseling approach among those listed here for children with ADHD. |

## Section D: Julianna

Several months into the 504 plan, the teacher and parent report that Julianna's behavioral and peer relations problems have increased, and her academic performance has declined. Julianna is now having full-blown temper tantrums at home, at school, and in the community. She is disobedient and blames others for her actions. The school counselor strongly encourages the following actions to help Julianna and her family: (Select as many as you consider indicated in this section.)

| D—1. | Referral to child study for possible testing and special education services |
| --- | --- |
| | Yes |
| | It is a good idea to explore possible coexisting conditions. |
| D—2. | Homeschooling |
| | No |
| | The structure provided by attending school and the social interactions with age-appropriate others is beneficial for children with ADHD. |
| D—3. | Participation in Governor's School |
| | No |
| | Governor's School is for students who have been identified as gifted. |
| D—4. | Medical examination by the child's physician |
| | Yes |
| | It is important to rule out medical conditions that may be a contributing factor. |
| D—5. | Less time with peers |
| | No |
| | Less time with peers is not indicated as this time. |
| D—6. | Appointment with a child psychiatrist |
| | Yes |
| | An appointment with a child psychiatrist is indicated based on presenting behaviors and current diagnosis. |
| D—7. | More time with peers |
| | No |
| | More time with peers is not indicated. |
| D—8. | Family counseling |
| | Yes |
| | The entire family is impacted by the behavioral conditions of a family member. |
| D—9. | Resources related to helping children with disruptive behavior issues/disorders |
| | Yes |
| | School counselors provide parents with information and resources related to behavioral and emotional issues. |

## Section E: Julianna

Julianna's mother returns to you a few weeks later and says that the psychiatrist has diagnosed Julianna with oppositional defiance disorder and recommended ongoing individual counseling for Julianna and the family. She asks if you would be Julianna's counselor over the next couple of years. Your response is:
   (Select ONLY ONE in this section.)

| | |
|---|---|
| E—1. | Of course<br><br>No<br><br>Julianna's counseling needs are beyond the scope of school counseling. |
| E—2. | I would like to, as I have enjoyed working with Julianna very much. However, I just do not have time as the only school counselor in the building<br><br>No<br><br>Time is not the primary issue. |
| E—3. | Julianna's needs are beyond the scope of school counseling, but I have a list of counseling resources, which may be helpful in identifying a counselor<br><br>Yes<br><br>School counselors do not provide individuals with ongoing counseling for chronic behavioral, emotional, and mental health issues. This type of long-term counseling is beyond the scope of school counseling. |
| E—4. | I would not be able to do this during the school day, as it is beyond the scope of school counseling. However, I can provide counseling services to Julianna outside of school hours at your home or mine for a minimal charge<br><br>No<br><br>This is a dual relationship and an ethical violation. |
| E—5. | Oppositional defiance disorder is not really my area of expertise, but I will work with Julianna because she and I already have a positive relationship<br><br>No<br><br>Practicing outside of your areas of expertise is an ethical violation and could become a legal issue as well |

# Appendix I: ASCA Ethical Standards for School Counselors[1]

(adopted 1984, revised 1992, 1998, 2004, 2010, 2016)

## Preamble

The American School Counselor Association (ASCA) is a professional organization supporting school counselors, school counseling students/interns, school counseling program directors/supervisors and school counselor educators. School counselors have unique qualifications and skills to address preK–12 students' academic, career and social/emotional development needs. These standards are the ethical responsibility of all school counseling professionals.

School counselors are advocates, leaders, collaborators and consultants who create systemic change by providing equitable educational access and success by connecting their school counseling programs to the district's mission and improvement plans. School counselors demonstrate their belief that all students have the ability to learn by advocating for an

---

education system that provides optimal learning environments for all students.

All students have the right to:

- Be respected, be treated with dignity and have access to a comprehensive school counseling program that advocates for and affirms all students from diverse populations including but not limited to: ethnic/racial identity, nationality, age, social class, economic status, abilities/disabilities, language, immigration status, sexual orientation, gender, gender identity/expression, family type, religious/spiritual identity, emancipated minors, wards of the state, homeless youth and incarcerated youth. School counselors as social-justice advocates support students from all backgrounds and circumstances and consult when their competence level requires additional support.
- Receive the information and support needed to move toward self-determination, self-development and affirmation within one's group identities. Special care is given to improve overall educational outcomes for students who have been historically underserved in educational services.
- Receive critical, timely information on college, career and postsecondary options and understand the full magnitude and meaning of how college and career readiness can have an impact on their educational choices and future opportunities.
- Privacy that should be honored to the greatest extent possible, while balancing other competing interests (e.g., best interests of students, safety of others, parental rights) and adhering to laws, policies and ethical standards pertaining to confidentiality and disclosure in the school setting.
- A safe school environment promoting autonomy and justice and free from abuse, bullying, harassment and other forms of violence.

# PURPOSE

In this document, ASCA specifies the obligation to the principles of ethical behavior necessary to maintain the high standards of integrity, leadership and professionalism. The ASCA Ethical Standards for School Counselors were developed in consultation with state school counseling associations, school counselor educators, school counseling state and district leaders and school counselors across the nation to clarify the norms, values and beliefs of the profession.

The purpose of this document is to:

■ Serve as a guide for the ethical practices of all school counselors, supervisors/directors of school counseling programs and school counselor educators regardless of level, area, population served or membership in this professional association.
■ Provide support and direction for self-assessment, peer consultation and evaluations regarding school counselors' responsibilities to students, parents/guardians, colleagues and professional associates, schools district employees, communities and the school counseling profession.
■ Inform all stakeholders, including students, parents/guardians, teachers, administrators, community members and courts of justice of best ethical practices, values and expected behaviors of the school counseling professional.

# A. RESPONSIBILITY TO STUDENTS

## A.1. Supporting Student Development

**School counselors:**

a. Have a primary obligation to the students, who are to be treated with dignity and respect as unique individuals.
b. Aim to provide counseling to students in a brief context and support students and families/guardians in obtaining outside services if the student needs long-term clinical counseling.
c. Do not diagnose but remain acutely aware of how a student's diagnosis can potentially affect the student's academic success.
d. Acknowledge the vital role of parents/guardians and families.
e. Are concerned with students' academic, career and social/emotional needs and encourage each student's maximum development.
f. Respect students' and families' values, beliefs, sexual orientation, gender identification/expression and cultural background and exercise great care to avoid imposing personal beliefs or values rooted in one's religion, culture or ethnicity.

g. Are knowledgeable of laws, regulations and policies affecting students and families and strive to protect and inform students and families regarding their rights.
h. Provide effective, responsive interventions to address student needs.
i. Consider the involvement of support networks, wraparound services and educational teams needed to best serve students.
j. Maintain appropriate boundaries and are aware that any sexual or romantic relationship with students whether legal or illegal in the state of practice is considered a grievous breach of ethics and is prohibited regardless of a student's age. This prohibition applies to both in-person and electronic interactions and relationships.

## A.2. Confidentiality

**School counselors:**

a. Promote awareness of school counselors' ethical standards and legal mandates regarding confidentiality and the appropriate rationale and procedures for disclosure of student data and information to school staff.
b. Inform students of the purposes, goals, techniques and rules of procedure under which they may receive counseling. Disclosure includes informed consent and clarification of the limits of confidentiality. Informed consent requires competence, voluntariness and knowledge on the part of students to understand the limits of confidentiality and, therefore, can be difficult to obtain from students of certain developmental levels, English-language learners and special-needs populations. If the student is able to give assent/consent before school counselors share confidential information, school counselors attempt to gain the student's assent/consent.
c. Are aware that even though attempts are made to obtain informed consent, it is not always possible. When needed, school counselors make counseling decisions on students' behalf that promote students' welfare.
d. Explain the limits of confidentiality in developmentally appropriate terms through multiple methods such as student handbooks, school counselor department websites, school counseling brochures, classroom curriculum and/or verbal notification to individual students.

e. Keep information confidential unless legal requirements demand that confidential information be revealed or a breach is required to prevent serious and foreseeable harm to the student. Serious and foreseeable harm is different for each minor in schools and is determined by students' developmental and chronological age, the setting, parental rights and the nature of the harm. School counselors consult with appropriate professionals when in doubt as to the validity of an exception.

f. Recognize their primary ethical obligation for confidentiality is to the students but balance that obligation with an understanding of parents'/guardians' legal and inherent rights to be the guiding voice in their children's lives. School counselors understand the need to balance students' ethical rights to make choices, their capacity to give consent or assent, and parental or familial legal rights and responsibilities to make decisions on their child's behalf.

g. Promote the autonomy of students to the extent possible and use the most appropriate and least intrusive method to breach confidentiality, if such action is warranted. The child's developmental age and the circumstances requiring the breach are considered, and as appropriate, students are engaged in a discussion about the method and timing of the breach. Consultation with peers and/or supervision is recommended.

h. In absence of state legislation expressly forbidding disclosure, consider the ethical responsibility to provide information to an identified third party who, by his/her relationship with the student, is at a high risk of contracting a disease that is commonly known to be communicable and fatal. Disclosure requires satisfaction of all of the following conditions:
   1) Student identifies partner, or the partner is highly identifiable
   2) School counselor recommends the student notify partner and refrain from further high-risk behavior
   3) Student refuses
   4) School counselor informs the student of the intent to notify the partner
   5) School counselor seeks legal consultation from the school district's legal representative in writing as to the legalities of informing the partner

i. Request of the court that disclosure not be required when the school counselor's testimony or case notes are subpoenaed if the release of confidential information may potentially harm a student or the counseling relationship.

j. Protect the confidentiality of students' records and release personal data in accordance with prescribed federal and state laws and school board policies.

k. Recognize the vulnerability of confidentiality in electronic communications and only transmit student information electronically in a way that follows currently accepted security standards and meets federal, state and local laws and board policy.

l. Convey a student's highly sensitive information (e.g., a student's suicidal ideation) through personal contact such as a phone call or visit and not less-secure means such as a notation in the educational record or an e-mail. Adhere to state, federal and school board policy when conveying sensitive information.

m. Advocate for appropriate safeguards and protocols so highly sensitive student information is not disclosed accidentally to individuals who do not have a need to know such information. Best practice suggests a very limited number of educators would have access to highly sensitive information on a need-to-know basis.

n. Advocate with appropriate school officials for acceptable encryption standards to be utilized for stored data and currently acceptable algorithms to be utilized for data in transit.

o. Avoid using software programs without the technological capabilities to protect student information based upon currently acceptable security standards and the law.

# A.3. Comprehensive Data-Informed Program

**School counselors:**

a. Collaborate with administration, teachers, staff and decision makers around school improvement goals.

b. Provide students with a comprehensive school counseling program that ensures equitable academic, career and social/emotional development opportunities for all students.

c. Review school and student data to assess needs including, but not limited to, data on disparities that may exist related to gender, race, ethnicity, socio-economic status and/or other relevant classifications.

    d. Use data to determine needed interventions, which are then delivered to help close the information, attainment, achievement and opportunity gaps.

    e. Collect process, perception and outcome data and analyze the data to determine the progress and effectiveness of the school counseling program. School counselors ensure the school counseling program's goals and action plans are aligned with district's school improvement goals.

    f. Use data-collection tools adhering to confidentiality standards as expressed in A.2.

    g. Share data outcomes with stakeholders.

## A.4. Academic, Career and Social/Emotional Plans

**School counselors:**

    a. Collaborate with administration, teachers, staff and decision makers to create a culture of postsecondary readiness

    b. Provide and advocate for individual students' preK–postsecondary college and career awareness, exploration and postsecondary planning and decision making, which supports the students' right to choose from the wide array of options when students complete secondary education.

    c. Identify gaps in college and career access and the implications of such data for addressing both intentional and unintentional biases related to college and career counseling.

    d. Provide opportunities for all students to develop the mindsets and behaviors necessary to learn work-related skills, resilience, perseverance, an understanding of lifelong learning as a part of long-term career success, a positive attitude toward learning and a strong work ethic.

## A.5. Dual Relationships and Managing Boundaries

**School counselors:**

    a. Avoid dual relationships that might impair their objectivity and increase the risk of harm to students (e.g., counseling one's family members or the children of close friends or associates). If a dual relationship is unavoidable, the school counselor is responsible for taking action to eliminate or reduce the potential for harm to the student through use of safeguards, which might include informed consent, consultation, supervision and documentation.

b. Establish and maintain appropriate professional relationships with students at all times. School counselors consider the risks and benefits of extending current school counseling relationships beyond conventional parameters, such as attending a student's distant athletic competition. In extending these boundaries, school counselors take appropriate professional precautions such as informed consent, consultation and supervision. School counselors document the nature of interactions that extend beyond conventional parameters, including the rationale for the interaction, the potential benefit and the possible positive and negative consequences for the student and school counselor.

c. Avoid dual relationships beyond the professional level with school personnel, parents/guardians and students' other family members when these relationships might infringe on the integrity of the school counselor/student relationship. Inappropriate dual relationships include, but are not limited to, providing direct discipline, teaching courses that involve grading students and/or accepting administrative duties in the absence of an administrator.

d. Do not use personal social media, personal e-mail accounts or personal texts to interact with students unless specifically encouraged and sanctioned by the school district. School counselors adhere to professional boundaries and legal, ethical and school district guidelines when using technology with students, parents/guardians or school staff. The technology utilized, including, but not limited to, social networking sites or apps, should be endorsed by the school district and used for professional communication and the distribution of vital information.

# A.6. Appropriate Referrals and Advocacy

**School counselors:**

a. Collaborate with all relevant stakeholders, including students, educators and parents/guardians when student assistance is needed, including the identification of early warning signs of student distress.

b. Provide a list of resources for outside agencies and resources in their community to student(s) and parents/guardians when students need or request additional support. School counselors provide multiple referral options or the district's vetted list and are careful not to indicate an endorsement or preference for one counselor or practice. School counselors encourage parents to interview outside professionals to make a personal decision regarding the best source of assistance for their student.

c. Connect students with services provided through the local school district and community agencies and remain aware of state laws and local district policies related to students with special needs, including limits to confidentiality and notification to authorities as appropriate.

d. Develop a plan for the transitioning of primary counseling services with minimal interruption of services. Students retain the right for the referred services to be done in coordination with the school counselor or to discontinue counseling services with the school counselor while maintaining an appropriate relationship that may include providing other school support services.

e. Refrain from referring students based solely on the school counselor's personal beliefs or values rooted in one's religion, culture, ethnicity or personal worldview. School counselors maintain the highest respect for student diversity. School counselors should pursue additional training and supervision in areas where they are at risk of imposing their values on students, especially when the school counselor's values are discriminatory in nature. School counselors do not impose their values on students and/or families when making referrals to outside resources for student and/or family support.

f. Attempt to establish a collaborative relationship with outside service providers to best serve students. Request a release of information signed by the student and/or parents/guardians before attempting to collaborate with the student's external provider.

g. Provide internal and external service providers with accurate, objective, meaningful data necessary to adequately evaluate, counsel and assist the student.

h. Ensure there is not a conflict of interest in providing referral resources. School counselors do not refer or accept a referral to counsel a student from their school if they also work in a private counseling practice.

# A.7. Group Work

**School counselors:**

a. Facilitate short-term groups to address students' academic, career and/or social/emotional issues.
b. Inform parent/guardian(s) of student participation in a small group.
c. Screen students for group membership.
d. Use data to measure member needs to establish well-defined expectations of group members.
e. Communicate the aspiration of confidentiality as a group norm, while recognizing and working from the protective posture that confidentiality for minors in schools cannot be guaranteed.
f. Select topics for groups with the clear understanding that some topics are not suitable for groups in schools and accordingly take precautions to protect members from harm as a result of interactions with the group.
g. Facilitate groups from the framework of evidence-based or research-based practices.
h. Practice within their competence level and develop professional competence through training and supervision.
i. Measure the outcomes of group participation (process, perception and outcome data).
j. Provide necessary follow up with group members.

# A.8. Student Peer-Support Program

**School counselors:**

a. Safeguard the welfare of students participating in peer-to-peer programs under their direction.
b. Supervise students engaged in peer helping, mediation and other similar peer-support groups. School counselors are responsible for appropriate skill development for students serving as peer support in school counseling programs. School counselors continuously monitor students who are giving peer support and reinforce the confidential nature of their work. School counselors inform peer-support students

about the parameters of when students need to report information to responsible adults.

# A.9. Serious and Foreseeable Harm to Self and Others

**School counselors:**

a. Inform parents/guardians and/or appropriate authorities when a student poses a serious and foreseeable risk of harm to self or others. When feasible, this is to be done after careful deliberation and consultation with other appropriate professionals. School counselors inform students of the school counselor's legal and ethical obligations to report the concern to the appropriate authorities unless it is appropriate to withhold this information to protect the student (e.g., student might run away if he/she knows parents are being called). The consequence of the risk of not giving parents/guardians a chance to intervene on behalf of their child is too great. Even if the danger appears relatively remote, parents should be notified.

b. Use risk assessments with caution. If risk assessments are used by the school counselor, an intervention plan should be developed and in place prior to this practice. When reporting risk assessment results to parents, school counselors do not negate the risk of harm even if the assessment reveals a low risk as students may minimize risk to avoid further scrutiny and/or parental notification. School counselors report risk assessment results to parents to underscore the need to act on behalf of a child at risk; this is not intended to assure parents their child isn't at risk, which is something a school counselor cannot know with certainty.

c. Do not release a student who is a danger to self or others until the student has proper and necessary support. If parents will not provide proper support, the school counselor takes necessary steps to underscore to parents/guardians the necessity to seek help and at times may include a report to child protective services.

d. Report to parents/guardians and/or appropriate authorities when students disclose a perpetrated or a perceived threat to their physical or mental well-being. This threat may include, but is not limited to, physical abuse, sexual abuse, neglect, dating violence, bullying or sexual harassment. The school counselor follows applicable federal, state and local laws and school district policy.

# A.10. Underserved and At-Risk Populations

**School counselors:**

a. Strive to contribute to a safe, respectful, nondiscriminatory school environment in which all members of the school community demonstrate respect and civility.

b. Advocate for and collaborate with students to ensure students remain safe at home and at school. A high standard of care includes determining what information is shared with parents/ guardians and when information creates an unsafe environment for students.

c. Identify resources needed to optimize education.

d. Collaborate with parents/guardians, when appropriate, to establish communication and to ensure students' needs are met.

e. Understand students have the right to be treated in a manner consistent with their gender identity and to be free from any form of discipline, harassment or discrimination based on their gender identity or gender expression.

f. Advocate for the equal right and access to free, appropriate public education for all youth, in which students are not stigmatized or isolated based on their housing status, disability, foster care, special education status, mental health or any other exceptionality or special need.

g. Recognize the strengths of students with disabilities as well as their challenges and provide best practices and current research in supporting their academic, career and social/emotional needs.

# A.11. Bullying, Harassment and Child Abuse

**School counselors:**

a. Report to the administration all incidents of bullying, dating violence and sexual harassment as most fall under Title IX of the Education Amendments of 1972 or other federal and state laws as being illegal and require administrator interventions. School counselors provide services to victims and perpetrator as appropriate, which may include a safety plan and reasonable accommodations such as schedule change, but school counselors defer to administration for all discipline issues for this or any other federal, state or school board violation.

b. Report suspected cases of child abuse and neglect to the proper authorities and take reasonable precautions to protect the privacy of the student for whom abuse or neglect is suspected when alerting the proper authorities.

c. Are knowledgeable about current state laws and their school system's procedures for reporting child abuse and neglect and methods to advocate for students' physical and emotional safety following abuse/neglect reports.

d. Develop and maintain the expertise to recognize the signs and indicators of abuse and neglect. Encourage training to enable students and staff to have the knowledge and skills needed to recognize the signs of abuse and neglect and to whom they should report suspected abuse or neglect.

e. Guide and assist students who have experienced abuse and neglect by providing appropriate services.

## A.12. Student Records

**School counselors:**

a. Abide by the Family Educational Rights and Privacy Act (FERPA), which defines who has access to students' educational records and allows parents the right to review and challenge perceived inaccuracies in their child's records.

b. Advocate for the ethical use of student data and records and inform administration of inappropriate or harmful practices.

c. Recognize the difficulty in meeting the criteria of sole-possession records.

d. Recognize that sole-possession records and case notes can be subpoenaed unless there is a specific state statute for privileged communication expressly protecting student/school counselor communication.

e. Recognize that electronic communications with school officials regarding individual students, even without using student names, are likely to create student records that must be addressed in accordance with FERPA and state laws.

f. Establish a reasonable timeline for purging sole-possession records or case notes. Suggested guidelines include shredding paper sole-possession records or deleting electronic sole-possession records when a student transitions to the next level, transfers to another school or graduates. School counselors do not destroy sole-possession records that may be needed by a court of law, such as notes on child abuse, suicide, sexual harassment or violence, without prior review and approval by school district legal counsel. School counselors follow district policies and procedures when contacting legal counsel.

## A.13. Evaluation, Assessment and Interpretation

**School counselors:**

a. Use only valid and reliable tests and assessments with concern for bias and cultural sensitivity.
b. Adhere to all professional standards when selecting, administering and interpreting assessment measures and only utilize assessment measures that are within the scope of practice for school counselors and for which they are licensed, certified and competent.
c. Are mindful of confidentiality guidelines when utilizing paper or electronic evaluative or assessment instruments and programs.
d. Consider the student's developmental age, language skills and level of competence when determining the appropriateness of an assessment.
e. Use multiple data points when possible to provide students and families with accurate, objective and concise information to promote students' well-being.
f. Provide interpretation of the nature, purposes, results and potential impact of assessment/evaluation measures in language the students and parents/guardians can understand.
g. Monitor the use of assessment results and interpretations and take reasonable steps to prevent others from misusing the information.
h. Use caution when utilizing assessment techniques, making evaluations and interpreting the performance of populations not represented in the norm group on which an instrument is standardized.
i. Conduct school counseling program evaluations to determine the effectiveness of activities supporting students' academic, career and social/emotional development through accountability measures,

especially examining efforts to close information, opportunity and attainment gaps.

# A.14. Technical and Digital Citizenship

**School counselors:**

a. Demonstrate appropriate selection and use of technology and software applications to enhance students' academic, career and social/emotional development. Attention is given to the ethical and legal considerations of technological applications, including confidentiality concerns, security issues, potential limitations and benefits and communication practices in electronic media.
b. Take appropriate and reasonable measures for maintaining confidentiality of student information and educational records stored or transmitted through the use of computers, social media, facsimile machines, telephones, voicemail, answering machines and other electronic technology.
c. Promote the safe and responsible use of technology in collaboration with educators and families.
d. Promote the benefits and clarify the limitations of various appropriate technological applications.
e. Use established and approved means of communication with students, maintaining appropriate boundaries. School counselors help educate students about appropriate communication and boundaries.
f. Advocate for equal access to technology for all students.

# A.15. Virtual/Distance School Counseling

**School counselors:**

a. Adhere to the same ethical guidelines in a virtual/distance setting as school counselors in face-to-face settings.
b. Recognize and acknowledge the challenges and limitations of virtual/distance school counseling.
c. Implement procedures for students to follow in both emergency and nonemergency situations when the school counselor is not available.

d. Recognize and mitigate the limitation of virtual/distance school counseling confidentiality, which may include unintended viewers or recipients.

e. Inform both the student and parent/guardian of the benefits and limitations of virtual/distance counseling.

f. Educate students on how to participate in the electronic school counseling relationship to minimize and prevent potential misunderstandings that could occur due to lack of verbal cues and inability to read body language or other visual cues that provide contextual meaning to the school counseling process and school counseling relationship.

# B. RESPONSIBILITIES TO PARENTS/GUARDIANS, SCHOOL AND SELF

## B.1. Responsibilities to Parents/Guardians

**School counselors:**

a. Recognize that providing services to minors in a school setting requires school counselors to collaborate with students' parents/ guardians as appropriate.

b. Respect the rights and responsibilities of custodial and noncustodial parents/guardians and, as appropriate, establish a collaborative relationship with parents/guardians to facilitate students' maximum development.

c. Adhere to laws, local guidelines and ethical practice when assisting parents/guardians experiencing family difficulties interfering with the student's welfare.

d. Are culturally competent and sensitive to diversity among families. Recognize that all parents/guardians, custodial and noncustodial, are vested with certain rights and responsibilities for their children's welfare by virtue of their role and according to law.

e. Inform parents of the mission of the school counseling program and program standards in academic, career and social/emotional domains that promote and enhance the learning process for all students.

f. Inform parents/guardians of the confidential nature of the school counseling relationship between the school counselor and student.

g. Respect the confidentiality of parents/guardians as appropriate and in accordance with the student's best interests.

h. Provide parents/guardians with accurate, comprehensive and relevant information in an objective and caring manner, as is appropriate and consistent with ethical and legal responsibilities to the student and parent.

i. In cases of divorce or separation, follow the directions and stipulations of the legal documentation, maintaining focus on the student. School counselors avoid supporting one parent over another.

## B.2. Responsibilities to the School

**School counselors:**

a. Develop and maintain professional relationships and systems of communication with faculty, staff and administrators to support students.

b. Design and deliver comprehensive school counseling programs that are integral to the school's academic mission; driven by student data; based on standards for academic, career and social/emotional development; and promote and enhance the learning process for all students.

c. Advocate for a school counseling program free of non-school-counseling assignments identified by "The ASCA National Model: A Framework for School Counseling Programs" as inappropriate to the school counselor's role.

d. Provide leadership to create systemic change to enhance the school.

e. Collaborate with appropriate officials to remove barriers that may impede the effectiveness of the school or the school counseling program.

f. Provide support, consultation and mentoring to professionals in need of assistance when in the scope of the school counselor's role.

g. Inform appropriate officials, in accordance with school board policy, of conditions that may be potentially disruptive or damaging to the school's mission, personnel and property while honoring the confidentiality between the student and the school counselor to the extent feasible, consistent with applicable law and policy.

h. Advocate for administrators to place in school counseling positions certified school counselors who are competent, qualified and hold a master's degree or higher in school counseling from an accredited program.

i. Advocate for equitable school counseling program policies and practices for all students and stakeholders.

j. Strive to use translators who have been vetted or reviewed and bilingual/multilingual school counseling program materials representing languages used by families in the school community.

k. Affirm the abilities of and advocate for the learning needs of all students. School counselors support the provision of appropriate accommodations and accessibility.

l. Provide workshops and written/digital information to families to increase understanding, improve communication and promote student achievement.

m. Promote cultural competence to help create a safer more inclusive school environment.

n. Adhere to educational/psychological research practices, confidentiality safeguards, security practices and school district policies when conducting research.

o. Promote equity and access for all students through the use of community resources.

p. Use culturally inclusive language in all forms of communication.

q. Collaborate as needed to provide optimum services with other professionals such as special educators, school nurses, school social workers, school psychologists, college counselors/admissions officers, physical therapists, occupational therapists, speech pathologists, administrators.

r. Work responsibly to remedy work environments that do not reflect the profession's ethics.

s. Work responsibly through the correct channels to try and remedy work conditions that do not reflect the ethics of the profession.

# B.3. Responsibilities to Self

**School counselors:**

a. Have completed a counselor education program at an accredited institution and earned a master's degree in school counseling.

b. Maintain membership in school counselor professional organizations to stay up to date on current research and to maintain professional competence in current school counseling issues and topics. School counselors maintain competence in their skills by utilizing current interventions and best practices.

c. Accept employment only for those positions for which they are qualified by education, training, supervised experience and state/national professional credentials.

d. Adhere to ethical standards of the profession and other official policy statements such as ASCA Position Statements and Role Statements, school board policies and relevant laws. When laws and ethical codes are in conflict school counselors work to adhere to both as much as possible.

e. Engage in professional development and personal growth throughout their careers. Professional development includes attendance at state and national conferences and reading journal articles. School counselors regularly attend training on school counselors' current legal and ethical responsibilities.

f. Monitor their emotional and physical health and practice wellness to ensure optimal professional effectiveness. School counselors seek physical or mental health support when needed to ensure professional competence.

g. Monitor personal behaviors and recognize the high standard of care a professional in this critical position of trust must maintain on and off the job. School counselors are cognizant of and refrain from activity that may diminish their effectiveness within the school community.

h. Seek consultation and supervision from school counselors and other professionals who are knowledgeable of school counselors' ethical practices when ethical and professional questions arise.

i. Monitor and expand personal multicultural and social-justice advocacy awareness, knowledge and skills to be an effective culturally competent school counselor. Understand how prejudice, privilege and various forms of oppression based on ethnicity, racial identity, age, economic status, abilities/disabilities, language, immigration status, sexual orientation, gender, gender identity expression, family type, religious/spiritual identity, appearance and living situations (e.g., foster care, homelessness, incarceration) affect students and stakeholders.

    j.  Refrain from refusing services to students based solely on the school counselor's personally held beliefs or values rooted in one's religion, culture or ethnicity. School counselors respect the diversity of students and seek training and supervision when prejudice or biases interfere with providing comprehensive services to all students.

    k.  Work toward a school climate that embraces diversity and promotes academic, career and social/emotional development for all students.

    l.  Make clear distinctions between actions and statements (both verbal and written) made as a private individual and those made as a representative of the school counseling profession and of the school district.

    m. Respect the intellectual property of others and adhere to copyright laws and correctly cite others' work when using it.

# C. SCHOOL COUNSELOR ADMINISTRATORS/ SUPERVISORS

**School counselor administrators/supervisors support school counselors in their charge by:**

    a.  Advocating both within and outside of their schools or districts for adequate resources to implement a comprehensive school counseling program and meet their students' needs.

    b.  Advocating for fair and open distribution of resources among programs supervised. An allocation procedure should be developed that is nondiscriminatory, informed by data and consistently applied.

    c.  Taking reasonable steps to ensure school and other resources are available to provide appropriate staff supervision and training.

    d.  Providing opportunities for professional development in current research related to school counseling practice and ethics.

    e.  Taking steps to eliminate conditions or practices in their schools or organizations that may violate, discourage or interfere with compliance with the ethics and laws related to the profession.

    f.  Monitoring school and organizational policies, regulations and procedures to ensure practices are consistent with the ASCA Ethical Standards for School Counselors.

# D. SCHOOL COUNSELING INTERN SITE SUPERVISORS

**Field/intern site supervisors:**

a. Are licensed or certified school counselors and/or have an understanding of comprehensive school counseling programs and the ethical practices of school counselors.

b. Have the education and training to provide clinical supervision. Supervisors regularly pursue continuing education activities on both counseling and supervision topics and skills.

c. Use a collaborative model of supervision that is ongoing and includes, but is not limited to, the following activities: promoting professional growth, supporting best practices and ethical practice, assessing supervisee performance and developing plans for improvement, consulting on specific cases and assisting in the development of a course of action.

d. Are culturally competent and consider cultural factors that may have an impact on the supervisory relationship.

e. Do not engage in supervisory relationships with individuals with whom they have the inability to remain objective. Such individuals include, but are not limited to, family members and close friends.

f. Are competent with technology used to perform supervisory responsibilities and online supervision, if applicable. Supervisors protect all electronically transmitted confidential information.

g. Understand there are differences in face-to-face and virtual communication (e.g., absence of verbal and nonverbal cues) that may have an impact on virtual supervision. Supervisors educate supervisees on how to communicate electronically to prevent and avoid potential problems.

h. Provide information about how and when virtual supervisory services will be utilized. Reasonable access to pertinent applications should be provided to school counselors.

i. Ensure supervisees are aware of policies and procedures related to supervision and evaluation and provide due-process procedures if supervisees request or appeal their evaluations.

j. Ensure performance evaluations are completed in a timely, fair and considerate manner, using data when available and based on clearly stated criteria.

k. Use evaluation tools measuring the competence of school counseling interns. These tools should be grounded in state and national school counseling standards. In the event no such tool is available in the school district, the supervisor seeks out relevant evaluation tools and advocates for their use.

l. Are aware of supervisee limitations and communicate concerns to the university/college supervisor in a timely manner.

m. Assist supervisees in obtaining remediation and professional development as necessary.

n. Contact university/college supervisors to recommend dismissal when supervisees are unable to demonstrate competence as a school counselor as defined by the ASCA School Counselor Competencies and state and national standards. Supervisors consult with school administrators and document recommendations to dismiss or refer a supervisee for assistance. Supervisors ensure supervisees are aware of such decisions and the resources available to them. Supervisors document all steps taken.

# E. MAINTENANCE OF STANDARDS

When serious doubt exists as to the ethical behavior of a colleague(s) the following procedures may serve as a guide:

a. School counselors consult with professional colleagues to discuss the potentially unethical behavior and to see if the professional colleague views the situation as an ethical violation. School counselors understand mandatory reporting in their respective district and states.

b. School counselors discuss and seek resolution directly with the colleague whose behavior is in question unless the behavior is unlawful, abusive, egregious or dangerous, in which case proper school or community authorities are contacted.

c. If the matter remains unresolved at the school, school district or state professional practice/standards commission, referral for review and appropriate action should be made in the following sequence:
   ■ State school counselor association
   ■ American School Counselor Association (Complaints should be submitted in hard copy to the ASCA Ethics Committee, c/o the Executive Director, American School Counselor Association, 1101 King St., Suite 310, Alexandria, VA 22314.)

# F. ETHICAL DECISION MAKING

When faced with an ethical dilemma, school counselors and school counseling program directors/supervisors use an ethical decision-making model such as Solutions to Ethical Problems in Schools (STEPS) (Stone, [2001,] 2013):

    a. Define the problem emotionally and intellectually
    b. Apply the ASCA Ethical Standards for School Counselors and the law
    c. Consider the students' chronological and developmental levels
    d. Consider the setting, parental rights and minors' rights
    e. Apply the ethical principles of beneficence, autonomy, nonmaleficence, loyalty and justice
    f. Determine potential courses of action and their consequences
    g. Evaluate the selected action
    h. Consult
    i. Implement the course of action

# GLOSSARY OF TERMS

**Advocate**
a person who speaks, writes or acts to promote the well-being of students, parents/guardians and the school counseling profession. School counselors advocate to close the information, opportunity, intervention and attainment gaps for all students.

**Assent**
to demonstrate agreement when a student is not competent to give informed consent to counseling or other services the school counselor is providing.

**Assessment**
collecting in-depth information about a person to develop a comprehensive plan that will guide the collaborative counseling and service provision process.

**Boundaries**
something that indicates or affixes an extent or limits.

## Breach
disclosure of information given in private or confidential communication such as information given during counseling.

## Competence
the quality of being competent; adequacy; possession of required skill, knowledge, qualification or capacity.

## Confidentiality
the ethical duty of school counselors to responsibly protect a student's private communications shared in counseling.

## Conflict of Interest
a situation in which a school counselor stands to personally profit from a decision involving a student.

## Consent
permission, approval or agreement; compliance.

## Consultation
a professional relationship in which individuals meet to seek advice, information and/or deliberation to address a student's need.

## Conventional Parameters
general agreement or accepted standards regarding limits, boundaries or guidelines.

## Cultural Sensitivity
a set of skills enabling you to know, understand and value the similarities and differences in people and modify your behavior to be most effective and respectful of students and families and to deliver programs that fit the needs of diverse learners.

## Data Dialogues
inquiry with others around student information to uncover inequities, promote informed investigations and assist in understanding the meaning of data and the next steps to have an impact on data.

## Data Informed
accessing data, applying meaning to it and using data to have an impact on student success.

**Developmental Level/Age**
the age of an individual determined by degree of emotional, mental and physiological maturity as compared with typical behaviors and characteristics of that chronological age.

**Disclosure**
the act or an instance of exposure or revelation.

**Diversity**
the inclusion of individuals representing more than one national origin, gender/gender identity, color, religion, socio-economic stratum, sexual orientation and the intersection of cultural and social identities.

**Dual Relationship**
a relationship in which a school counselor is concurrently participating in two or more roles with a student.

**Emancipated Minor**
a minor who is legally freed from control by his or her parents or guardians, and the parents or guardians are freed from any and all responsibility toward the child.

**Empathy**
the action of understanding, being aware of, being sensitive to and vicariously experiencing the feelings, thoughts and experience of another without having the feelings, thoughts and experience fully communicated in an objectively explicit manner.

**Encryption**
process of putting information into a coded form to control and limit access to authorized users.

**Ethics**
the norms and principles of conduct and philosophy governing the profession.

**Ethical Behavior**
actions defined by standards of conduct for the profession.

**Ethical Obligation**
a standard or set of standards defining the course of action for the profession.

**Ethical Rights**

the fundamental normative rules about what is allowed of people or owed to people, according to some legal system, social convention or ethical theory.

**Feasible**

capable of being done, effected or accomplished.

**Gender Expression**

the ways in which students manifest masculinity or femininity in terms of clothing, communication patterns and interests, which may or may not reflect the student's gender identity.

**Gender Identity**

One's personal experience of one's own gender. When one's gender identity and biological sex are not congruent, the student may identify as transsexual or transgender.

**Harassment**

the act of systematic and/or continued unwanted disturbing or troubling persecution.

**Informed Consent**

assisting students in acquiring an understanding of the limits of confidentiality, the benefits, facts and risks of entering into a counseling relationship.

**Intervention**

to provide modifications, materials, advice, aids, services or other forms of support to have a positive impact on the outcome or course of a condition.

**Legal Mandates**

a judicial command or precept issued by a court or magistrate, directing proper behavior to enforce a judgment, sentence or decree.

**Legal Rights**

those rights bestowed onto a person by a given legal system.

**Mandatory Reporting**

the legal requirement to report to authorities.

**Minors**

persons under the age of 18 years unless otherwise designated by statute or regulation.

**Peer Helper**

peer-to-peer interaction in which individuals who are of approximately the same age take on a helping role assisting students who may share related values, experiences and lifestyles.

**Peer Support**

programs that enhance the effectiveness of the school counseling program while increasing outreach and raising student awareness of services.

**Perception**

A mental image or awareness of environment through a physical sensation. A capacity for understanding or a result of an observation.

**Privacy**

the right of an individual to keep oneself and one's personal information free from unauthorized disclosure.

**Privileged Communication**

conversation that takes places within the context of a protected relationship, such as that between an attorney and client, a husband and wife, a priest and penitent, a doctor and patient and, in some states, a school counselor and a student.

**Professional Development**

the process of improving and increasing capabilities through access to education and training opportunities.

**Relationship**

a connection, association or involvement.

**Risk Assessment**

a systematic process of evaluating potential risks.

**School Counseling Supervisor**

a qualified professional who provides guidance, teaching and support for the professional development of school counselors and school counseling candidates.

**Serious and Foreseeable**

when a reasonable person can anticipate significant and harmful possible consequences.

**Sole-Possession Records**
exempted from the definition of educational records and the protection of
FERPA, are records used only as a personal memory aid that are kept in the
sole possession of the maker of the record and are not accessible or
revealed to any other person except a temporary substitute for the maker
of the record and provide only professional opinion or personal
observations.

**Stakeholder**
a person or group that shares an investment or interest in an endeavor.

**Supervision**
a collaborative relationship in which one person promotes and/or evaluates
the development of another.

**Title IX of the Education Amendments of 1972**
a law that demands that no person in the United States shall, on the basis
of sex, be excluded from participation in, be denied the benefits of or be
subjected to discrimination under any education program or activity
receiving federal financial assistance.

**Virtual/Distance Counseling**
counseling by electronic means.

# Appendix II: ASCA School Counselor Competencies[1]

## I. School Counseling Programs

School counselors should possess the knowledge, abilities, skills and attitudes necessary to plan, organize, implement and evaluate a comprehensive, developmental, results-based school counseling program that aligns with the ASCA National Model.

### I-A: KNOWLEDGE

ASCA's position statement, The Professional School Counselor and School Counseling Preparation Programs, states that school counselors should articulate and demonstrate an understanding of:

I-A-1.  The organizational structure and governance of the American educational system as well as cultural, political and social influences on current educational practices

I-A-2.  The organizational structure and qualities of an effective school counseling program that aligns with the ASCA National Model

---

I-A-3.  Barriers to student learning and use of advocacy and data-driven school counseling practices to close the achievement/ opportunity gap

I-A-4.  Leadership principles and theories

I-A-5.  Individual counseling, group counseling and classroom instruction ensuring equitable access to resources promoting academic achievement, career development and personal/social development for every student

I-A-6.  Collaborations with stakeholders such as parents and guardians, teachers, administrators and community leaders to create learning environments that promote educational equity and success for every student

I-A-7.  Legal, ethical and professional issues in pre-K–12 schools

I-A-8.  Developmental theory, learning theories, social justice theory, multiculturalism, counseling theories and career counseling theories

I-A-9.  The continuum of mental health services, including prevention and intervention strategies to enhance student success

## I-B: ABILITIES AND SKILLS

An effective school counselor is able to accomplish measurable objectives demonstrating the following abilities and skills:

I-B-1.  Plans, organizes, implements and evaluates a school counseling program aligning with the ASCA National Model

I-B-1a. Creates a vision statement examining the professional and personal competencies and qualities a school counselor should possess

I-B-1b. Describes the rationale for a comprehensive school counseling program

I-B-1c. Applies the school counseling themes of leadership, advocacy, collaboration and systemic change, which are critical to a successful school counseling program.

I-B-1d. Describes, defines and identifies the qualities of an effective school counseling program

I-B-1e. Describes the benefits of a comprehensive school counseling program for all stakeholders, including students, parents, teachers, administrators, school boards, department of education, school

counselors, counselor educators, community stakeholders and
business leaders

I-B-1f. Describes the history of school counseling to create a context for
the current state of the profession and comprehensive school
counseling programs

I-B-1g. Uses technology effectively and efficiently to plan, organize,
implement and evaluate the comprehensive school counseling
program

I-B-1h. Demonstrates multicultural, ethical and professional competencies
in planning, organizing, implementing and evaluating the
comprehensive school counseling program

I-B-2. Serves as a leader in the school and community to promote and
support student success

I-B-2a. Understands and defines leadership and its role in comprehensive
school counseling programs

I-B-2b. Identifies and applies a model of leadership to a comprehensive
school counseling program

I-B-2c. Identifies and demonstrates professional and personal qualities and
skills of effective leaders

I-B-2d. Identifies and applies components of the ASCA National Model
requiring leadership, such as an advisory council, management tools
and accountability

I-B-2e. Creates a plan to challenge the non-counseling tasks that are
assigned to school counselors

I-B-3. Advocates for student success

I-B-3a. Understands and defines advocacy and its role in comprehensive
school counseling programs

I-B-3b. Identifies and demonstrates benefits of advocacy with school and
community stakeholders

I-B-3c. Describes school counselor advocacy competencies, which include
dispositions, knowledge and skills

I-B-3d. Reviews advocacy models and develops a personal advocacy plan

I-B-3e. Understands the process for development of policy and procedures
at the building, district, state and national levels

I-B-4. Collaborates with parents, teachers, administrators, community
leaders and other stakeholders to promote and support student
success

I-B-4a. Defines collaboration and its role in comprehensive school
counseling programs

I-B-4b. Identifies and applies models of collaboration for effective use in a
school counseling program and understands the similarities and
differences between consultation, collaboration and counseling and
coordination strategies.

I-B-4c. Creates statements or other documents delineating the various rols
of student service providers, such as school social worker, school
psychologist and school nurse, and identifies best practices for
collaborating to affect student success

I-B-4d. Understands and knows how to apply a consensus-building process
to foster agreement in a group

I-B-4e. Understands how to facilitate group meetings to effectively and
efficiently meet group goals

I-B-5. Acts as a systems change agent to create an environment promoting
and supporting student success

I-B-5a. Defines and understands system change and its role in
comprehensive school counseling programs

I-B-5b. Develops a plan to deal with personal (emotional and cognitive)
and institutional resistance impeding the change process

I-B-5c. Understands the impact of school, district and state educational
policies, procedures and practices supporting and/or impeding
student success

## I-C: ATTITUDES

School counselors believe:

I-C-1. Every student can learn, and every student can succeed

I-C-2. Every student should have access to and opportunity for a high-
quality education

1-C-3. Every student should graduate from high school and be prepared
for employment or college and other post-secondary education

I-C-4. Every student should have access to a school counseling program

I-C-5. Effective school counseling is a collaborative process involving
school counselors, students, parents, teachers, administrators,
community leaders and other stakeholders

I-C-6. School counselors can and should be leaders in the school and
district

I-C-7. The effectiveness of school counseling programs should be
measurable using process, perception and outcome data

# II: Foundations

School counselors should possess the knowledge, abilities, skills and attitudes necessary to establish the foundations of a school counseling program aligning with the ASCA National Model.

## *II-A: KNOWLEDGE*

School counselors should articulate and demonstrate an understanding of:

II-A-1. Beliefs and philosophy of the school counseling program that align with current school improvement and student success initiatives at the school, district and state level

II-A-2. Educational systems, philosophies and theories and current trends in education, including federal and state legislation

II-A-3. Learning theories

II-A-4. History and purpose of school counseling, including traditional and transformed roles of school counselors

II-A-5. Human development theories and developmental issues affecting student success

II-A-6. District, state and national student standards and competencies, including ASCA Student Standards and other student standards that may complement and inform the comprehensive school counseling program

II-A-7. Legal and ethical standards and principles of the school counseling profession and educational systems, including district and building policies

II-A-8. The three domains of academic achievement, career planning and personal/social development

## *II-B: ABILITIES AND SKILLS*

An effective school counselor is able to accomplish measurable objectives demonstrating the following abilities and skills:

II-B-1. Develops the beliefs and philosophy of the school counseling program that aligns with current school improvement and student success initiatives at the school, district and state level

II-B-1a. Examines personal, district and state beliefs, assumptions and philosophies about student success, specifically what they should know and be able to do

II-B-1b. Demonstrates knowledge of a school's particular educational philosophy and mission

II-B-1c. Conceptualizes and writes a personal philosophy about students, families, teachers, school counseling programs and the educational process consistent with the school's educational philosophy and mission

II-B-2. Develops a school counseling mission statement aligning with the school, district and state mission

II-B-2a. Critiques a school district mission statement and identifies or writes a mission statement aligning with beliefs

II-B-2b. Writes a school counseling mission statement that is specific, concise, clear and comprehensive, describing a school counseling program's purpose and a vision of the program's benefits for every student

II-B-2c. Communicates the vision and mission of the school counseling program to all appropriate stakeholders

II-B-3. Uses student standards, such as ASCA Student Standards, and other appropriate student standards such as district or state standards, to drive the implementation of a comprehensive school counseling program

II-B-3a. Crosswalks the ASCA Student Standards with other appropriate standards

II-B-3b. Prioritizes student standards that align with the school's goals

II-B-4. Applies the ethical standards and principles of the school counseling profession and adheres to the legal aspects of the role of the school counselor

II-B-4a. Practices ethical principles of the school counseling profession in accordance with the ASCA Ethical Standards for School Counselors

II-B-4b. Understands the legal and ethical nature of working in a pluralistic, multicultural and technological society.

II-B-4c. Understands and practices in accordance with school district policy and local, state and federal statutory requirements.

II-B-4d. Understands the unique legal and ethical nature of working with minor students in a school setting.

II-B-4e. Advocates responsibly for school board policy and local, state and federal statutory requirements in students' best interests

II-B-4f. Resolves ethical dilemmas by employing an ethical decision-making model appropriate to work in schools

II-B-4g. Models ethical behavior

II-B-4h. Continuously engages in professional development and uses resources to inform and guide ethical and legal work

II-B-4i. Practices within the ethical and statutory limits of confidentiality

II-B-4j. Continually seeks consultation and supervision to guide legal and ethical decision making and to recognize and resolve ethical dilemmas

II-B-4k. Understands and applies an ethical and legal obligation not only to students but to parents, administration and teachers as well

## *II-C: ATTITUDES*

School counselors believe:

II-C-1. School counseling is an organized program for every student and not a series of services provided only to students in need

II-C-2. School counseling programs should be an integral component of student success and the overall mission of schools and school districts

II-C-3. School counseling programs promote and support academic achievement, personal and social development and career planning for every student

II-C-4. School counselors operate within a framework of school and district policies, state laws and regulations and professional ethics standards

# III: Delivery

School counselors should possess the knowledge, abilities, skills and attitudes necessary to deliver a school counseling program aligning with the ASCA National Model.

## *III-A: KNOWLEDGE*

School counselors should articulate and demonstrate an understanding of:

III-A-1. The concept of a guidance curriculum

III-A-2. Counseling theories and techniques that work in school, such as solution-focused brief counseling, reality therapy, cognitive-behavioral therapy

III-A-3. Counseling theories and techniques in different settings, such as individual planning, group counseling and classroom guidance

III-A-4. Classroom management

III-A-5. Principles of career planning and college admissions, including financial aid and athletic eligibility

III-A-6. Principles of working with various student populations based on ethnic and racial background, English language proficiency, special needs, religion, gender and income

III-A-7. Responsive services

III-A-8. Crisis counseling, including grief and bereavement

## III-B: ABILITIES AND SKILLS

An effective school counselor is able to accomplish measurable objectives demonstrating the following abilities and skills.

III-B-1.  Implements the school guidance curriculum

III-B-1a. Crosswalks ASCA Student Competencies with appropriate guidance curriculum

III-B-1b. Develops and presents a developmental guidance curriculum addressing all students' needs, including closing-the-gap activities

III-B-1c. Demonstrates classroom management and instructional skills

III-B-1d. Develops materials and instructional strategies to meet student needs and school goals

III-B-1e. Encourages staff involvement to ensure the effective implementation of the school guidance curriculum

III-B-1f. Knows, understands and uses a variety of technology in the delivery of guidance curriculum activities

III-B-1g. Understands multicultural and pluralistic trends when developing and choosing guidance curriculum

III-B-1h. Understands the resources available for students with special needs

III-B-2.  Facilitates individual student planning

III-B-2a. Understands individual student planning as a component of a comprehensive program

III-B-2b. Develops strategies to implement individual student planning, such as strategies for appraisal, advisement, goal-setting, decision-making, social skills, transition or postsecondary planning

III-B-2c. Helps students establish goals, and develops and uses planning skills in collaboration with parents or guardians and school personnel

III-B-2d. Understands career opportunities, labor market trends, and global economics, and uses various career assessment techniques to assist students in understanding their abilities and career interests

III-B-2e. Helps students learn the importance of college and other post-secondary education and helps students navigate the college admissions process

III-B-2f. Understands the relationship of academic performance to the world of work, family life and community service

III-B-2g. Understands methods for helping students monitor and direct their own learning and social/emotional and career development

III-B-3. Provides responsive services

III-B-3a. Understands how to make referrals to appropriate professionals when necessary

III-B-3b. Lists and describes interventions used in responsive services, such as consultation, individual and small-group counseling, crisis counseling, referrals and peer facilitation

III-B-3c. Compiles resources to utilize with students, staff and families to effectively address issues through responsive services

III-B-3d. Understands appropriate individual and small-group counseling theories and techniques such as rational emotive behavior therapy, reality therapy, cognitive-behavioral therapy, Adlerian, solution-focused brief counseling, person-centered counseling and family systems

III-B-3e. Demonstrates an ability to provide counseling for students during times of transition, separation, heightened stress and critical change

III-B-3f. Understands what defines a crisis, the appropriate response and a variety of intervention strategies to meet the needs of the individual, group, or school community before, during and after crisis response

III-B-3g. Provides team leadership to the school and community in a crisis

III-B-3h. Involves appropriate school and community professionals as well as the family in a crisis situation

III-B-3i. Develops a database of community agencies and service providers for student referrals

III-B-3j. Applies appropriate counseling approaches to promoting change among consultees within a consultation approach

III-B-3k. Understands and is able to build effective and high-quality peer helper programs

III-B-3l. Understands the nature of academic, career and social/emotional counseling in schools and the similarities and differences among school counseling and other types of counseling, such as mental health, marriage and family, and substance abuse counseling, within a continuum of care

III-B-3m. Understands the role of the school counselor and the school counseling program in the school crisis plan

III-B-4. Implements system support activities for the comprehensive school counseling program

III-B-4a. Creates a system support planning document addressing school counselor's responsibilities for professional development, consultation and collaboration and program management

III-B-4b. Coordinates activities that establish, maintain and enhance the school counseling program as well as other educational programs

III-B-4c. Conducts in-service training for other stakeholders to share school counseling expertise

III-B-4d. Understands and knows how to provide supervision for school counseling interns consistent with the principles of the ASCA National Model

## III-C: ATTITUDES

School counselors believe:

III-C-1. School counseling is one component in the continuum of care that should be available to all students

III-C-2. School counselors coordinate and facilitate counseling and other services to ensure all students receive the care they need, even though school counselors may not personally provide the care themselves

III-C-3. School counselors engage in developmental counseling and short-term responsive counseling

III-C-4. School counselors should refer students to district or community resources to meet more extensive needs such as long-term therapy or diagnoses of disorders

# IV: Management

School counselors should possess the knowledge, abilities, skills and attitudes necessary to manage a school counseling program aligning with the ASCA National Model.

## *IV-A: KNOWLEDGE*

School counselors should articulate and demonstrate an understanding of:

IV-A-1. Leadership principles, including sources of power and authority, and formal and informal leadership

IV-A-2. Organization theory to facilitate advocacy, collaboration and systemic change

IV-A-3. Presentation skills for programs such as teacher in-services and results reports to school boards

IV-A-4. Time management, including long- and short-term management using tools such as schedules and calendars

IV-A-5. Data-driven decision making

IV-A-6. Current and emerging technologies such as use of the Internet, Web-based resources and management information systems

## *IV-B: ABILITIES AND SKILLS*

An effective school counselor is able to accomplish measurable objectives demonstrating the following abilities and skills:

IV-B-1. Negotiates with the administrator to define the management system for the comprehensive school counseling program

IV-B-1a. Discusses and develops the components of the school counselor management system with the other members of the counseling staff

IV-B-1b. Presents the school counseling management system to the principal, and finalizes an annual school counseling management agreement

IV-B-1c. Discusses the anticipated program results when implementing the action plans for the school year

IV-B-1d. Participates in professional organizations

IV-B-1e. Develops a yearly professional development plan demonstrating how the school counselor advances relevant knowledge, skills and dispositions

IV-B-1f. Communicates effective goals and benchmarks for meeting and exceeding expectations consistent with the administrator-counselor agreement and district performance appraisals

IV-B-1g. Uses personal reflection, consultation and supervision to promote professional growth and development

IV-B-2. Establishes and convenes an advisory council for the comprehensive school counseling program

IV-B-2a. Uses leadership skills to facilitate vision and positive change for the comprehensive school counseling program

IV-B-2b. Determines appropriate education stakeholders who should be represented on the advisory council

IV-B-2c. Develops meeting agendas

IV-B-2d. Reviews school data, school counseling program audit and school counseling program goals with the council

IV-B-2e. Records meeting notes and distributes as appropriate

IV-B-2f. Analyzes and incorporates feedback from advisory council related to school counseling program goals as appropriate

IV-B-3. Collects, analyzes and interprets relevant data, including process, perception and results data, to monitor and improve student behavior and achievement

IV-B-3a. Analyzes, synthesizes and disaggregates data to examine student outcomes and to identify and implement interventions as needed

IV-B-3b. Uses data to identify policies, practices and procedures leading to successes, systemic barriers and areas of weakness

IV-B-3c. Uses student data to demonstrate a need for systemic change in areas such as course enrollment patterns; equity and access; and the achievement, opportunity and information gap

IV-B-3d. Understands and uses data to establish goals and activities to close the achievement, opportunity and information gap

IV-B-3e. Knows how to use and analyze data to evaluate the school counseling program, research activity outcomes and identify gaps between and among different groups of students

IV-B-3f. Uses school data to identify and assist individual students who do not perform at grade level and do not have opportunities and resources to be successful in school

IV-B-3g. Knows and understands theoretical and historical bases for assessment techniques

IV-B-4. Organizes and manages time to implement an effective school counseling program

IV-B-4a. Identifies appropriate distribution of school counselor's time based on delivery system and school's data

IV-B-4b. Creates a rationale for school counselor's time to focus on the goals of the comprehensive school counseling program

IV-B-4c. Identifies and evaluates fair-share responsibilities, which articulate appropriate and inappropriate counseling and non-counseling activities

IV-B-4d. Creates a rationale for the school counselor's total time spent in each component of the school counseling program

IV-B-5. Develops calendars to ensure the effective implementation of the school counseling program

IV-B-5a. Creates annual, monthly and weekly calendars to plan activities to reflect school goals

IV-B-5b. Demonstrates time management skills including scheduling, publicizing and prioritizing time and task

IV-B-6. Designs and implements action plans aligning with school and school counseling program goals

IV-B-6a. Uses appropriate academic and behavioral data to develop guidance curriculum and closing-the-gap action plan and determines appropriate students for the target group or interventions

IV-B-6b. Identifies ASCA domains, standards and competencies being addressed by the plan

IV-B-6c. Determines the intended impact on academics and behavior

IV-B-6d. Identifies appropriate activities to accomplish objectives

IV-B-6e. Identifies appropriate resources needed

IV-B-6f. Identifies data-collection strategies to gather process, perception and results data

IV-B-6g. Shares results of action plans with staff, parents and community

## IV-C: ATTITUDES

School counselors believe:

IV-C-1. A school counseling program and guidance department must be managed like other programs and departments in a school

IV-C-2. One of the critical responsibilities of a school counselor is to plan, organize, implement and evaluate a school counseling program

IV-C-3. Management of a school counseling program must be done in collaboration with administrators

# V: Accountability

School counselors should possess the knowledge, abilities, skills and attitudes necessary to monitor and evaluate the processes and results of a school counseling program aligning with the ASCA National Model.

## V-A: KNOWLEDGE

School counselors should articulate and demonstrate an understanding of:

V-A-1. Basic concept of results-based school counseling and accountability issues

V-A-2. Basic research and statistical concepts to read and conduct research

V-A-3. Use of data to evaluate program effectiveness and to determine program needs

V-A-4. Program audits and results reports

## V-B: ABILITIES AND SKILLS

An effective school counselor is able to accomplish measurable objectives demonstrating the following abilities and skills.

V-B-1. Uses data from results reports to evaluate program effectiveness and to determine program needs

V-B-1a. Uses formal and informal methods of program evaluation to design and modify comprehensive school counseling programs

V-B-1b. Uses student data to support decision making in designing effective school counseling programs and interventions

V-B-1c. Measures results attained from school guidance curriculum and closing-the-gap activities

V-B-1d. Works with members of the school counseling team and with the administration to decide how school counseling programs are evaluated and how results are shared

V-B-1e. Collects process, perception and results data

V-B-1f. Uses technology in conducting research and program evaluation

V-B-1g. Reports program results to professional school counseling community

V-B-1h. Uses data to demonstrate the value the school counseling program adds to student achievement

V-B-1i. Uses results obtained for program improvement

V-B-2. Understands and advocates for appropriate school counselor performance appraisal process based on school counselor competencies and completion of the guidance curriculum and agreed-upon action plans

V-B-2a. Conducts self-appraisal related to school counseling skills and performance

V-B-2b. Identifies how school counseling activities fit within categories of performance appraisal instrument

V-B-2c. Encourages administrators to use performance appraisal instrument reflecting appropriate responsibilities for school counselors

V-B-3. Conducts a program audit

V-B-3a. Completes a program audit to compare current school counseling program implementation with the ASCA National Model

V-B-3b. Shares the results of the program audit with administrators, the advisory council and other appropriate stakeholders

V-B-3c. Identifies areas for improvement for the school counseling program

## *V-C: ATTITUDES*

School counselors believe:

V-C-1. School counseling programs should achieve demonstrable results

V-C-2. School counselors should be accountable for the results of the school counseling program

V-C-3. School counselors should use quantitative and qualitative data to evaluate their school counseling program and to demonstrate program results

V-C-4. The results of the school counseling program should be analyzed and presented in the context of the overall school and district performance

# Glossary

**Academic development**: one of three developmental domains within a comprehensive school counseling program, promoting skills, relating learning to life, and enhancing academic success and a positive attitude toward school and learning.

**Academic-focused**: the school counselor's focus on academic development and academic achievement and the removal of barriers toward that end. While priority is given to the role of counselor, school counselors embrace the dual role of educator, which is the role that sets our counseling speciality apart from others and defines our profession.

**Accommodation**: adjustments made to instruction, homework, testing, and the physical environment in order to promote the success of students with special needs (e.g., special education, 504, and ESL students), as well as students with temporary conditions (e.g., illness, injury).

**Accountability**: practices that are data-driven, standards-based, research-supported, evaluated for effectiveness and ongoing program improvement, and demonstrate *how* school counselors make a difference in the lives of students.

**Achievement gap**: the disparity in educational performance that exists between specific populations of students, primarily low-income and minority students when compared with peers on a variety of educational measures, namely standardized tests.

**Action plan**: written plans that describe specific programming and how programming will achieve stated objectives, including closing the achievement gap activities. SCOPE, the School Counseling Operational Plan for Effectiveness, is an example of an ASCA-recommended action plan.

**Action research**: research conducted for the purpose of enhancing the effectiveness of one's practices and/or measuring program outcomes.

**Active listening**: a basic counseling skill and communication skill that attends to the student's verbal and nonverbal behaviors.

**Addiction**: psychological and/or physiological dependence on a substance or activity.

**Advisory council**: a committee of stakeholders, established by the school counselor, to direct and assist the school counseling program. ASCA recommends an advisory committee as part of the school counseling program management system to promote program success.

**Advocacy**: a function of the school counselor that involves acting and speaking on behalf of others to support equity and access to programming and to promote student, family, school, and community relations and development.

**Aggression**: verbal, physical, and psychological behaviors intended to cause harm, threat, or pain.

**Americans with Disabilities Act (ADA)**: national legislation that prohibits discrimination against persons with a disability in employment, public institutions, public transportation, and telecommunications. A *qualified individual with a disability* is entitled to reasonable accommodations.

**Anorexia**: an eating disorder that is characterized primarily by a consistent and extreme restriction of food intake and a refusal to maintain minimum normal body weight for age and height.

**Antisocial behavior**: behavior, covert and overt, that disregards the rights and privacy of others and the norms, laws, and standards of a society.

**Appraisal** (also see **assessment**): approaches and/or measures (standardized and nonstandardized) used to gain a greater understanding of a student's functioning (e.g., intellectual, educational, mental, emotional, social, physical, or occupational).

**ASCA National Model**: the only national model for the profession of school counseling designed to serve as a framework from which to implement a comprehensive, developmental, and primarily preventative school counseling program.

**ASCA National Standards**: national standards (a foundational component of the ASCA National Model) that depict what students should know and be able to do as a result of a comprehensive school counseling program in three broad developmental areas: career, academic, and personal–social.

**Assessment** (also see **appraisal**): approaches and/or measures (standardized and nonstandardized) used to gain a greater understanding of a student's functioning (e.g., intellectual, educational, mental, emotional, social, physical, or occupational).

**Behavior contract**: a plan of action used for general education students to reduce or eliminate specific, observable, and measurable undesirable behaviors by applying specific interventions and rewards.

**Behavior intervention plan**: a plan of action, often part of an IEP for special education students, aimed at reducing or eliminating specific, observable, and measurable undesirable behaviors by applying individualized interventions and rewards.

**Behavioral rehearsal**: practicing new skills and behaviors for application outside of the counseling environment.

**Bibliotherapy**: the use of books/literature in counseling toward established counseling goals.

**Bulimia**: an eating disorder that is characterized primarily by reoccurring episodes of bingeing and purging (e.g., vomiting, laxatives) and a preoccupation with body weight.

**Bullying** (also see **cyberbullying**): any verbal, nonverbal, or physical behavior intended to intimidate, threaten, harm, or cause physical, emotional, and/or psychological pain.

**Career awareness**: the focus on career development at the elementary level that promotes students' knowledge of the world of work.

**Career counseling**: counseling aimed at career development at a specific time and across the lifespan.

**Career development**: one of three developmental domains of a comprehensive school counseling program that promotes students' identification of, and preparation for, desired post-high school occupations, education, and training and relating school and the world of work.

**Career development inventories**: instruments used to enhance a student's knowledge pertaining to occupational choices, self-knowledge (e.g., interests, values, skills), and education and training related to specific careers.

**Career exploration**: a focus at the middle school level that enhances students' understanding of career opportunities and the link between school and work, developing an academic plan to meet postsecondary career choices.

**Career planning**: a focus at the high school level that encourages students to continue to update and follow through on established career and academic plans for career readiness.

**Child abuse**: harm toward a child caused by neglect or exploitation and/or physical, emotional, psychological, or sexual mistreatment.

**Child neglect**: failure to provide for the social, psychological, emotional, and biological needs of a child; failure to prevent suffering or to act on behalf of the child that places the child in imminent danger; behaviors that place the child in harm's way.

**Child study**: a team approach to identifying and understanding the needs of a student who is not achieving academically in comparison with peers, or who is demonstrating physical, emotional, verbal, or psychological issues that are interfering with daily functioning.

**Closed group**: group that is no longer open to new membership once group facilitation begins.

**Collaboration**: a function of the school counselor that involves working cooperatively with others toward a common goal.

**Computer-assisted career guidance systems**: electronic systems designed to promote career readiness.

**Conflict resolution**: the process by which students resolve conflict peacefully by engaging a variety of skills (e.g., problem solving, empathy, clarification, questioning, communication, and negotiation).

**Consultation**: a function of the school counselor that involves providing services in their area of expertise to other stakeholders (e.g., teachers, parents, and school administrators).

**Crisis**: traumatic or extremely stressful situations that require immediate action to secure the safety and well-being of students and others (e.g., suicide or homicide risk, post-student suicide, homicide, accidental death, terrorism, natural disaster, and child abuse/neglect).

**Cyberbullying** (also see **bullying**): any electronic (e.g., via texting, Internet, email, chat rooms, or social networks) behavior intended to intimidate, threaten, harm, or cause physical, emotional, and/or psychological pain.

**Data analysis**: an examination of information that aids school counselors in identifying stakeholder needs, targeting programming, and determining program effectiveness and areas for improvement.

**Data driven**: programs, practices, and activities that are created based on an analysis of data.

**Diagnostic test**: an assessment used to identify areas of academic competencies and areas of deficit.

**Disability**: a cognitive/psychological, behavioral, and/or physical impairment that limits one or more daily living functions.

**Educational diagnostician**: an individual employed by school divisions to assess levels of student academic functioning and to suggest interventions to meet individual student needs; often a member of child study teams.

**Emancipated minor**: a minor who has been granted by the courts the decision-making power of an adult with regard to their own affairs. Emancipated minors do not need parental consent to engage in counseling services.

**Encapsulation**: ignorance of one's cultural background and how culture impacts one's total being.

**English as a second language**: students whose primary or native language is not English.

**Equity and access**: equal opportunity to rigorous curriculum and school and community programs.

**Extrinsic motivation**: motivation that is achieved with external rewards (e.g., stickers, certification, treats, or praise).

**Family Educational Rights and Privacy Act (FERPA)**: legislation enacted to protect the privacy of students' academic records and to allow parents and students to inspect academic records and petition for the removal of information perceived as inaccurate. FERPA is also known as the Buckley Amendment.

**504 plan**: a written document that identifies special accommodations afforded to students with qualifying conditions pursuant to Section 504 of the Rehabilitation Act of 1973.

**Free and appropriate public education**: legislation that ensures individualized curriculum that meets unique student needs and prepares students for post-high school education, careers, and independent living.

**General equivalency diploma (GED)**: an alternative to a high school diploma and completion of high school, the GED established mastery of high school core course content and may be obtained during the high school years through alternative educational programs or post-high school for those adults who "dropped out" of high school.

**Guidance counselor**: an outdated title for the counselor in the PK–12 school setting, depicting only one component of the many functions of the contemporary school counselor that is associated primarily with more directive approaches and education and career planning.

**High stakes testing**: standardized testing used to determine passing or failure of select core courses and graduation from high school; it also drives the type of diploma received.

***In loco parentis***: a common-law doctrine that allows educators to act as parents, protecting students and their rights while under their care at school.

**Inclusion classroom**: a general education classroom that provides additional supports and accommodations for special education student participation.

**Individual-focused**: school counseling practices that are more focused on intervention for a select individual than on prevention and intervention services for all students.

**Individualized education program**: a written document that identifies specific and individualized strategies for the personal–social, academic, and career success of students with a qualifying disability under IDEA as part of special education services.

**Individuals with Disabilities Education Act (IDEA)**: national legislation that ensures that the educational needs of students with disabilities are met.

**Intelligence quotient**: a score from standardized intelligence tests, which represents one's level of intelligence.

**Intelligence test**: standardized tests intended to assess an individual's cognitive abilities and yield an intelligence quotient score.

**Intervention**: activities and strategies applied with the purpose of reducing or eliminating specific thoughts, actions, or situations.

**Intrinsic motivation**: motivation that is achieved with internal rewards (e.g., specific positive feedback, or earned recognition through accomplishment).

**Leadership**: the ability to inspire, influence, and persuade others to follow or act.

**Learning profile**: a comprehensive conceptualization that considers an individual's learning styles, predisposition toward specific intelligences (see **multiple intelligences**), as well as cultural and gender differences.

**Least restrictive environment**: special education students are to receive educational services that promote success in the least restrictive manner while receiving accommodations and supports as outlined in the student's IEP; the least restrictive environments in the public school setting are the general education classrooms (also see **inclusion classroom**).

**Limited English proficient (LEP)**: individuals whose first language is not English and who therefore are restricted in their English-speaking ability.

**Medical plan**: used in schools for students with medical conditions that may warrant special accommodations for a specified amount of time.

**Modeling**: observing and imitating others.

**Motivation**: a force, energy, desire, or state of being that directs thoughts and behavior.

**Multicultural counseling**: counseling that is sensitive to the needs of all people and their unique worldviews grounded in gender, race, ethnicity, culture, social status, economic status, sexual orientation, and religion.

**Multiple intelligences**: eight independent cognitive and affective intelligences working interactively for a holistic understanding of human intelligence.

**Needs assessment**: formal and informational measures that result in the identification of stakeholder needs.

**Negative reinforcement**: removal of a stimulus in an effort to increase a desired behavior or response.

**New vision school counseling**: the current movement to transform school counseling into an academic- and systems-focused paradigm.

**No Child Left Behind**: legislation that supports standards-based education and the measurement of goals to enhance academic outcomes and to close achievement gaps between specific classes and racial groups of students.

**Nontraditional occupation**: occupations in which few individuals of a specific gender generally work. For example, occupations historically dominated by females would be nontraditional occupations for males (e.g., nurse), and occupations historically dominated by males would be nontraditional for females (e.g., mechanic).

**Occupational Information Network**: national database for career information, exploration, assessment, and career decision making.

***Occupational Outlook Handbook***: nationally recognized source for career information and career decision making.

**Open group**: groups that allow new membership once group facilitation begins.

**Outcome evaluation**: program evaluation that determines the effectiveness of a program or intervention in meeting established goals and objectives.

**Paraphrasing**: a basic counseling technique that involves the school counselor restating what a student has shared to communicate understanding.

**Peer helping/peer support**: programs that involve students helping students (e.g., peer tutoring, peer mentoring, or **peer mediation**).

**Peer mediation**: a process by which students help students to resolve conflict peacefully by engaging a variety of skills (e.g., problem solving, empathy, clarification, questioning, communication, and negotiation). Peer mediation involves more than two individuals.

**Personal–social development**: one of three developmental domains within a comprehensive school counseling program that promotes total student well-being through the application of counseling theory and techniques and teaches skills for living (e.g., safety, problem solving, decision making, conflict resolution, and communication).

**Play therapy**: the use of directive and nondirective play facilitated by the school counselor as a therapeutic medium for emotional expression and communication.

**Positive reinforcement**: application of a stimulus in an effort to increase a desired behavior or response.

**Prevention**: activities and strategies applied with the purpose of averting specific thoughts, actions, or situations.

**Primary prevention**: programming that focuses on prevention and wellness for a large population (e.g., the entire student body), who may or may not be potentially at risk for a specific targeted behavior or problem.

**Process evaluation**: program evaluations that assess the program's strengths and weaknesses for program improvement.

**Professional associations**: school counseling-related associations that support the profession with resources, professional development opportunities, unification, and advocacy.

**Professional school counselor**: the title that replaced that of guidance counselor due to our emphasis on comprehensive counseling services and holistic student development.

**Program evaluation**: an ongoing component of accountable school counseling practices that results in data that demonstrates program outcomes and answers the question "How do school counselors make a difference in the lives of students?"; also provides information for program improvement.

**Reciprocal determinism**: a term coined by Albert Bandura to describe how behavior is determined by the shared relationship (one acting upon the other) between a person and the environment.

**Reinforcement/reinforcer** (also see **positive/negative reinforcement**): a concept used in operant conditioning to refer to a stimulus, positive or negative, to increase the likelihood of desired behaviors or reduce or eliminate undesired behaviors.

**Research-based**: school counseling practices and programming that are supported by research.

**Resilience**: the capacity of an individual to cope with stress and harsh conditions.

**Response-to-intervention**: an intervention process used to help struggling students to improve behavior and achieve academically.

**Responsive services**: services that meet the immediate needs and distressing issues of students.

**Results report**: written reports that describe the outcomes of specific programming as outlined in action plans, including closing the achievement gap activities. SCORE, the School Counseling Operational Report of Effectiveness, is an example of an ASCA-recommended results report.

**Risk factors**: any physical, personal, social, familial, environmental, or economical condition that places students at a disadvantage and serves as an obstacle to well-being, academic achievement, and healthy student development.

**School counselor**: current (as of 2016) contemporary title for the counselor in the PK–12 school setting, depicting a comprehensive counseling specialty that shares the dual roles of educator and counselor and practices using a comprehensive developmental model that attends to the whole child/adolescent/young adult.

**School nurse**: an individual employed by school divisions to attend to student injury, coordinate medical care with physicians, psychologists, and parents, and administer medications during the school day; often a member of child study teams.

**School psychologist**: an individual employed by school divisions to assess levels of student psychological functioning and to suggest interventions to meet individual student needs; often a member of child study teams.

**School social worker**: an individual employed by school divisions to assess levels of student social and family functioning and to suggest interventions to meet individual student needs; often a member of child study teams.

**School-to-Work Opportunities Act**: legislation that seeks to ensure that students will be well prepared to succeed in our multifaceted and technologically advanced workforce.

**Secondary prevention**: programming aimed at mediating a specific behavior or problem that has been identified as a potential threat among a particular population or subgroup of students.

**Section 504**: A part of the ADA, also known as the Rehabilitation Act of 1973, that protects individuals with disabilities from discrimination and allows for equal access to services and the provision of reasonable accommodations related to the disability.

**Social justice**: the ideology that each individual is equally valued, respected, and deserving of equal treatment and equal opportunity.

**Social responsibility**: an ethical ideology that is grounded in the principles of equality, unity, and respect for human rights and acting on behalf of the good of society.

**Special needs students**: students who are limited English proficient or have a 504 plan or IEP.

**Stakeholder**: any individual or organization that impacts or is impacted by the school.

**Standards**: statements that delineate what students should know and be able to do.

**Strengths-based counseling**: a counseling approach that emphasizes the value of protective factors in combating risk factors and enhancing resilience.

**Substance abuse**: repeated use of a chemical substance that may or may not include dependence.

**Substance use**: repeated use of a chemical substance without dependence.

**Suicide assessment**: screening an individual to determine their risk for suicide.

**Suicide ideation**: thinking about taking one's own life.

**Summarizing**: a basic counseling technique whereby the school counselor condenses into a few brief statements that which the student has conveyed over a period of time during the counseling session.

**Systems-focused**: school counseling practices that are more focused on prevention and intervention services for all students rather than a select few.

**Teaming**: joining together with other stakeholders to accomplish a common goal.

**Tertiary prevention**: programming that targets a specific population who are already engaging in the at-risk behavior or experiencing a specific problem, in order to reduce or eliminate the problem or behavior and improve quality of life.

***Transforming school counseling initiative***: the movement to change the paradigm of school counseling to one that is academic- and systems-focused.

**Universal Academic Achievement**: academic achievement for all students.

**Wellness**: a sense of personal, social, emotional, physical, and spiritual well-being.

**Worldview**: how an individual conceptualizes and interprets the world, views their relationship with the world, and interacts with the world that is grounded in presupposition, beliefs, and values.

**Zeitgeist**: the thought or spirit of the time in a specified time period or generation.

# References

Adler, A. (1925). *The practice and theory of individual psychology* (P. Radin, Trans., rev. ed., 1929). London: Routledge.

Akos, P. (2002). Student perceptions of the transition from elementary to middle school. *Professional School Counseling, 5*, 339–345.

Akos, P., Cockman, C. R., & Strickland, C. A. (2007). Differentiating classroom guidance. *Professional School Counseling, 10*, 455–463.

American Counseling Association. (2003). *ACA taskforce on counselor wellness and impairment*. Retrieved October 1, 2010, from www.counseling.org/wellness_taskforce/index.htm.

American Counseling Association. (2014). *Code of ethics and standards of practice*. Alexandria, VA: Author.

American School Counselor Association. (2012a). *The ASCA national model: A framework for school counseling programs* (3rd ed.). Alexandria, VA: Author.

American School Counselor Association. (2012b). *ASCA school counselor competencies*. Retrieved March 6, 2017, from www.schoolcounselor.org.

American School Counselor Association. (2014). *Mindsets and behaviors for student success: K–12 college- and career-readiness standards for every student*. Alexandria, VA: Author.

American School Counselor Association. ([2010]2016a). *Ethical standards for school counselors*. Alexandria, VA: Author.

American School Counselor Association. (2016b). *The ASCA national model: Implementation guide*. Alexandria, VA: Author.

American School Counselor Association. (2017). *ASCA position statements*. Retrieved March 6, 2017, from www.schoolcounselor.org.

Anderman, L. H., & Leake, V. S. (2005). The ABCs of motivation: An alternative framework for teaching preservice teachers about motivation. *The Clearing House, 78*, 192–197.

Anderson, L. W., & Krathwohl, D. R. (Eds.). (2001). *A taxonomy for learning, teaching, and assessing: A revision of Bloom's taxonomy of educational objectives*. New York, NY: Longman.

Association for Assessment in Counseling and Education. (1998). *Competencies in assessment and evaluation for school counselors*. Retrieved September 3, 2009, from http://aace.ncat.edu.

Association for Counselor Education and Supervision. (2007). ACES technology competencies for counselor education students. Retrieved November 10, 2010, from, http://files.acesonline.net/doc/2007_aces_technology_competencies.pdf.

Bandura, A. (1969). *Principles of behavior modification*. New York, NY: Holt, Rinehart & Winston.

Bandura, A. (1977). *Social learning theory*. Englewood Cliffs, NJ: Prentice Hall.

Bauman, S. (2008). *Essential topics for the helping professional*. Boston, MA: Allyn & Bacon.

Beck, A. (1979). *Cognitive therapies and emotional disorders*. New York, NY: International Universities Press.

Bell, S. K., Coleman, J. K., Anderson, A., Whelan, J. P., & Wilder, C. (2000). The effectiveness of peer mediation in a low-SES rural elementary school. *Psychology in the Schools, 37*, 505–516.

Bernard, J. M., & Goodyear, R. K. (2004). *Fundamentals of clinical supervision* (3rd ed.). Boston, MA: Allyn & Bacon.

Bernard, J. M., & Luke, M. (2015). A content analysis of 10 years of clinical supervision articles in counseling. *Counselor Education and Supervision, 54*(4), 242–257.

Berne, E. (1961). *Transactional analysis in psychotherapy*. New York, NY: Grove Press.

Birkeland, S., Murphy-Graham, E., & Weiss, C. (2005). Good reasons for ignoring good evaluation: The case of the drug abuse resistance education (DARE) program. *Evaluation and Program Planning, 28*, 247–256.

Bloom, B. S. (1953). Thought processes in lectures and discussions. *Journal of General Education, 7*, 160–169.

Brown, D. (2015). *Career information, career counseling, and career development* (11th ed.). Boston, MA: Pearson.

Cameron, S., & Turtle-Song, I. (2002). Learning to write case notes using the SOAP format. *Journal of Counseling & Development, 80*(3), 286.

Campbell, C. A., & Dahir, C. A. (1997). *Sharing the vision: The national standards for school counseling programs*. Alexandria, VA: American School Counselor Association Press.

Capp, G. (2015). Our community, our schools: A case study of program design for school-based mental health services. *Children & Schools, 37*(4), 241–248.

Capuzzi, E., & Stauffer, M. D. (2015). *Foundations of addictions counseling* (3rd ed.). Boston, MA: Pearson.

Cashwell, C. S., Young, J. S., Fulton, C. L., Willis, B. T., Giordano, A., Daniel, L. W., Crockett, J., Tate, B. N., & Welch, M. L. (2013). Clinical behaviors for addressing religious/spiritual issues: Do we practice what we preach? *Counseling & Values, 58*(1), 45–58.

Child Welfare Information Gateway. (2013). *What is child abuse and neglect: Recognizing signs and symptoms.* United States department of health and human services children's bureau. Retrieved March 5, 2017, from www.childwelfare.gov/pubPDFs/whatiscan.pdf#page=1&view= Introduction.

Cochran, L. (1997). *Career counseling: A narrative approach.* Newbury Park, CA: Sage.

Cohen, G. J., & Weitzman, C. C. (2016). Helping children and families deal with divorce and separation. *Pediatrics, 138*(6), 103–111.

Corey, G. (2015). *Theory and practice of group counseling* (9th ed.). Belmont, CA: Thomson Brooks/Cole.

Council for Accreditation of Counseling and Related Educational Programs. (2012). *CACREP accreditation manual.* Alexandria, VA: Author.

Council for Accreditation of Counseling and Related Educational Programs. (2016). *CACREP standards.* Alexandria, VA: Author.

Council for the Accreditation of Educator Preparation (2010). *Knowledge, skills, and professional dispositions.* Retrieved January 22, 2017, from https://mwsu.edu/academics/education/ncate-transition.

Cronley, C., & Evans, R. (2017). Studies of resilience among youth experiencing homelessness: A systematic review. *Journal of Human Behavior in the Social Environment, 27*(4), 291–310.

Dalgas-Pelish, P. (2006). Effects of a self-esteem intervention program on school-age children. *Pediatric Nursing, 32*, 341–349.

de Shazer, S. (1985). *Keys to solution in brief therapy.* New York, NY: Norton.

Donne, J. (n.d.). *Quotes.net.* Retrieved May 12, 2011, from www.quotes.net/quote/3018.

Dougherty, M. (2013). *Psychology consultation and collaboration in school and community settings* (6th ed.). Belmont, CA: Brooks/Cole.

Dupere, V., Leventhal, T., Dion, E., Crosnoe, R., Archambault, I., & Janosz, M. (2015). Stressors and turning points in high school and dropout. *Review of Educational Research, 85*(4), 591–629.

Education Trust, The (1997, February). *The national guidance and counseling reform program.* Washington, DC: Author.

Elijah, K. (2011). Meeting the guidance and counseling needs of gifted students in school settings. *Journal of School Counseling, 9*, 1–19.

Ellis, A., & Dryden, W. (1997). *The practice of rational emotive behavior therapy.* New York, NY: Springer.

Ellis, A., & Harper, R. A. (1997). *A guide to rational living* (3rd ed.). Hollywood: Wilshire.

Erford, B. T. (2014). *Transforming the school counseling profession* (4th ed.). Boston, MA: Pearson.

Erikson, E. H. (1950). *Childhood and society*. New York, NY: Norton.

Erikson, E. H. (1959). *Identity and the life cycle*. New York, NY: International Universities Press.

Forester-Miller, H., & Davis, T. E. (1996). *A practitioner's guide to ethical decision making*. Alexandria, VA: American Counseling Association.

Fowler, J. (1981). *Stages of faith: The psychology of human development and the quest for meaning*. New York, NY: HarperCollins.

Gardner, H. (1983). *Frames of mind: The theory of multiple intelligences*. New York, NY: Basic Books.

Gardner, H., & Moran, S. (2006). The science of multiple intelligences theory: A response to Lynn Waterhouse. *Educational Psychologist, 41*(4), 227–232.

Gilchrist-Banks, S. (2009). *Choice theory: Using choice theory and reality therapy to enhance student achievement and responsibility*. Alexandria, VA: American School Counselor Association.

Glasser, W. (1998). *Choice theory*. New York, NY: HarperCollins.

*Goals 2000: Educate America Act*, H.R. 1804. (1994). Retrieved September 8, 2009, from www.ed.gov/legislation/GOALS2000/TheAct/index.html.

Goodman-Scott, E., Betters-Bubon, J., & Donohue, P. (2015). Aligning comprehensive school counseling programs and positive behavioral interventions and supports to maximize school counselor efforts. *Professional School Counseling, 19*(1), 57–67.

Gottfredson, L. S. (1981). Circumscription and compromise: A developmental theory of occupational aspirations. *Journal of Counseling Psychology, 28*(6), 545–579.

Grothaus, T., Lorelle, S., Anderson, K., & Knight, J. (2011). Answering the call: Facilitating responsive services for students experiencing homelessness. *Professional School Counseling, 14*(3), 191–201.

Havighurst, R. J. (1972). *Developmental tasks and education*. New York, NY: McKay.

Hobson, S. M., Fox, R. W., & Swickert, M.L. (2000). School counselor shortages: A statewide collaborative effort in counselor education. Ypsilanti, MI: Eastern Michigan University (ERIC Document Reproduction Service No. ED454484).

Holcomb-McCoy, C. C. (2004). Assessing the multicultural competence of school counselors: A checklist. *Professional School Counseling, 7*, 178–183.

Holcomb-McCoy, C. C. (2007). School counseling to close the achievement gap: A social justice framework for success. Thousand Oaks, CA: Corwin Press.

Holland, J. L. (1966). *The psychology of vocational choice*. Waltham, MA: Blaisdell.

Holland, J. L. (1974). *Self-directed search*. Palo Alto, CA: Consulting Psychologists Press.

Holland, J. L. (1985). *Making vocational choices: A theory of personalities and work environments* (2nd ed.). Englewood Cliffs, NJ: Prentice Hall.

Huda, M., Jasmi, A. K., Hehsan, A., Mustari, I. M., Shahrill, M., Basiron, B., & Gassama, S. K. (2017). Empowering children with adaptive technology skills: Careful engagement in the digital information age. *International Electronic Journal of Elementary Education, 9*(3), 698–708.

Kaffenberger, C., & Young, A. (2013). *Making DATA work* (3rd ed.). Alexandria, VA: American School Counselor Association.

Kagan, J. & Snidman, N. (1991). Temperamental factors in human development. *American Psychologist, 46*, 856–862.

Kerr, M. M. (2016). *School crisis prevention and intervention*. Long Grove, IL: Waveland Press.

Kimbel, T., & Schellenberg, R. (2014). Meeting the holistic needs of students: A proposal for spiritual and religious competencies for school counselors. *Professional School Counseling, 17*(1), 76–85.

Kitchener, K. S. (1984). Intuition, critical evaluation, and ethical principles: The foundation for ethical decisions in counseling psychology. *Counseling Psychologist, 12*(3), 43–55.

Kohlberg, L. (1967). Moral and religious education in the public schools: A developmental view. In T. R. Sizer (Ed.), *The roles of religion in public education* (pp. 164–183). Boston, MA: Houghton Mifflin.

Kohlberg, L. (1969). *Stages in the development of moral thought*. New York, NY: Holt, Rinehart & Winston.

Kottman, T., & Meany-Walen, K. (2015). *Partners in play: An Adlerian approach to play therapy* (3rd ed.). Alexandria, VA: American Counseling Association.

Krumboltz, J. D. (1994). Improving career development theory from a social learning theory perspective. In M. L. Savickas & R. W. Lent (Eds.), *Convergence in career development theory* (pp. 9–32). Palo Alto, CA: CPP Books.

Kubler-Ross, E., & Kessler, D. (2014). *On grief and grieving: Finding the meaning of grief through the five stages of loss*. New York, NY: Scribner.

Kuder, G. F. (1964). *Kuder general interest survey: Manual*. Chicago, IL: Science Research Associates.

Lazarus, A. A. (1976). *Multimodal behavior therapy*. New York, NY: Springer.

Leary, M. A., Schreindorfer, L. S., & Haupt, A. L. (1995). The role of self-esteem in emotional and behavioural problems: Why is low self-esteem dysfunctional? *Journal of Social and Clinical Psychology, 14*, 297–314.

Lewis, J., Arnold, M., House, R., & Toporek, R. (2003). *Advocacy competencies*. Retrieved March 7, 2011, from www.counseling.org/resources.

Marzano, R. J. (2004). *Building background knowledge for academic achievement: Research on what works in schools*. Alexandria, VA: Association for Supervision and Curriculum Development.

Maslow, A. H. (1970). *Motivation and personality* (2nd ed.). New York, NY: Harper & Row.

Mason, E. M., Ockerman, M., & Chen-Hayes. (2013). Change-agent-for-equity (CAFÉ) model: A framework for school counselor identity. *Journal of School Counseling, 11*, 1–25.

Matsumoto, D., & Juang, L. (2016). *Culture and psychology* (6th ed.). Belmont, CA: Wadsworth Publishing.

McClelland, D. C. (1961). *The achieving society*. Princeton, NJ: Van Nostrand.

McClelland, D. C. (1985). *Human motivation*. Glenview, IL: Scott, Foresman.

McWhirter, J. J., & McWhirter, B. T. (2012). *At-risk youth: A comprehensive response* (5th ed.). Pacific Grove, CA: Brooks/Cole.

Moldovan, O. D. (2014). Intrinsic and extrinsic motivation to primary school children. *Journal Plus Education/Educatia Plus, 10*(1), 203–211.

Morrison, J. (2016). *Diagnosis made easier: Principles and techniques for mental health clinicians* (2nd ed.). New York, NY: Guilford Press.

Moyer, M., & Nelson, K. W. (2007). Investigating and understanding self-mutilation: The student voice. *Professional School Counseling, 11*, 42–48.

Moyer, M., & Yu, K. (2012). Factors influencing school counselors' perceived effectiveness. *Journal of School Counseling, 10*, 1–23.

National Board for Professional Teaching Standards. (2012). *School counseling standards*. Retrieved January 21, 2017, from www.nbpts.org.

National Career Development Association. (2009). *Multicultural career counseling minimal competencies*. Retrieved July 1, 2010, from http://associationdatabase.com/aws/NCDA/pt/sp/guidelines.

National Center for Educational Statistics (2014). *Digest of education statistics*. Retrieved March 6, 2017, from https://nces.ed.gov/programs/digest/d15/tables/dt15_219.70.asp.

Nelson, M. D., Tarabochia, D. W., & Koltz, R. L. (2015). PACES: A model of student well-being. *Journal of School Counseling, 13*(19), 1–25.

Nye, R. D. (1975). *Three psychologies: Perspectives from Freud, Skinner, and Rogers*. Pacific Grove, CA: Brooks/Cole.

Ockerman, M. S., Patrikakou, E., & Hollenbeck, A. F. (2015). Preparation of school counselors and response to intervention: A profession at the crossroads. *Journal of Counselor Preparation & Supervision, 7*, 161–184.

Page, B., Pietrzak, D., & Sutton, J. (2001). National survey of school counselor supervision. *Counselor Education and Supervision, 41*, 142–150.

Parr, A., & Bonitz, V. S. (2015). Role of family background, student behaviors, and school-related beliefs in predicting high school dropout. *Journal of Educational Research, 108*(6), 504–514.

Parsons, F. (1909). *Choosing your vocation*. Boston, MA: Houghton Mifflin.

Perls, F. S. (1969). *Gestalt therapy verbatim*. Moab, UT: Real People Press.

Phillips, S. D., Christopher-Sisk, E., & Gravino, K. L. (2001). Making career decisions in a relational context. *The Counseling Psychologist, 29*, 193–213.

Piaget, J. (1932). *The moral judgment of the child*. London: Routledge & Kegan Paul.

Piaget, J. (1963). *The origins of intelligence in children*. New York, NY: Norton.

Porfeli, E. J., Hartung, P. J., & Vondracek, F. W. (2008). Children's vocational development: A research rationale. *Career Development Quarterly, 57*, 25–37.

Remley, T., & Herlihy, B. (2015). *Ethical, legal, and professional issues in counseling* (5th ed.). Upper Saddle River, NJ: Pearson.

Roberts, R. (2002). *Self esteem and early learning* (2nd ed.). Thousand Oaks, CA: Sage.

Roe, A. (1957). Early determinants of vocational choice. *Journal of Counseling Psychology, 4*, 212–217.

Rogers, C. (1961). *On becoming a person: A therapist's view of psychotherapy*. New York, NY: Houghton Mifflin.

Rogers, C. (1969). *Freedom to learn*. Columbus, OH: Merrill Publishing.

Ross, C. E., & Broh, B. A. (2000). The roles of self-esteem and the sense of personal control in the academic achievement process. *Sociology of Education, 73*, 270–285.

Rothrauff, T. C., Cooney, T. M., & Shin An, J. (2009). Remembered parenting styles and adjustment in middle and late adulthood. *The Journals of Gerontology, 64b*, 137–147.

Santrock, J. (2014). *Life-span development* (15th ed.). New York, NY: McGraw-Hill Education.

Savickas, M. L. (1997). Constructivist career counseling: Models and methods. *Advances in Personal Construct Psychology, 4*, 149–182.

Savickas, M. L. (2000). Renovating the psychology of careers for the twenty-first century. In A. Collin & R. A. Young (Eds.), *The future of career* (pp. 53–68). New York, NY: Cambridge University Press.

Schaan, V., & Vogele, V. (2016). Resilience and rejection sensitivity mediate long-term outcomes of parental divorce. *European Child & Adolescent Psychiatry, 25*(11), 1267–1269.

Schellenberg, R. (2000). Aggressive personality: When does it develop and why? *Virginia Counselors Journal, 26*, 67–76.

Schellenberg, R. (2007). Standards blending: Aligning school counseling programs with school academic achievement missions. *Virginia Counselors Journal, 29*, 13–20.

Schellenberg, R. (2008). *The new school counselor: Strategies for universal academic achievement*. Lanham, MD: Rowman Littlefield Education.

Schellenberg, R. (2013). *A new era in school counseling: A practical guide*. Lanham, MD: Rowman Littlefield Education.

Schellenberg, R., & Grothaus, T. (2009). Promoting cultural responsiveness and closing the achievement gap with standards blending. *Professional School Counseling, 12,* 440–449.

Schellenberg, R., & Grothaus, T. (2011). Using culturally competent responsive services to improve student achievement and behavior. *Professional School Counseling, 14,* 222–230.

Schellenberg, R., Parks-Savage, A., & Rehfuss, M. (2007). Reducing levels of elementary school violence with peer mediation. *Professional School Counseling, 10,* 475–481.

School-to-Work Opportunities Act, P.L. 103–239. (1994). Retrieved October 1, 2010, from www.fessler.com/SBE/act.htm.

Search Institute, The. (2007). *Developmental assets lists.* Retrieved September 12, 2010, from www.search-institute.org/developmental-assets/lists.

Seligman, L. (2004). Diagnosis and treatment planning in counseling. *Professional School Counseling, 2,* 244–247.

Shoffner, M. F., & Williamson, R. D. (2000). Engaging preservice school counselors and principals in dialogue and collaboration. *Counselor Education and Supervision, 40,* 128–141.

Skinner, B. F. (1971). *Beyond freedom and dignity.* New York, NY: Vintage Books.

Smith, L., Beck, K., Bernstein, E., & Dashtguard, P. (2014). Youth participatory action research and school counseling practice: A school-wide framework for student well-being. *Journal of School Counseling, 12*(21), 1–31.

Stone, C. (2013). *School counseling principles, ethics, and law.* Alexandria, VA: American School Counseling Association.

Strong, E. K., & Campbell, D. P. (1974). *Strong-Campbell interest inventory.* Stanford, CA: Stanford University Press.

Sue, D. W. & Sue, D. (2015). *Counseling the culturally diverse: Theory and practice* (7th ed.). Hoboken, NJ: Wiley.

Super, D. E. (1949). *Appraising vocational fitness.* New York, NY: Harper & Brothers.

Super, D. E. (1970). *Work values inventory.* Boston, MA: Houghton Mifflin.

Super, D. E. (1980). A life-span, life-space approach to career development. *Journal of Vocational Behavior, 16,* 282–298.

Tiedeman, D. V. (1961). Decision and vocational development: A paradigm and its implications. *Personnel and Guidance Journal, 40,* 15–21.

Turner, S. L. (2007). Introduction to special issue: Transitional issues for K–16 students. *Professional School Counseling, 10,* 225–226.

United States Department of Education. (2000). *Education for Homeless Children and Youth Program title VII, subtitle B of the McKinney-Vento Homeless Assistance Act: Report to congress, fiscal year 2000.* Retrieved October 1, 2009, from www.ed.gov/programs/homeless/resources.html.

United States Department of Education. (2001). *No Child Left Behind Act of 2001*. Retrieved October 1, 2009, from www.ed.gov/policy/elsec/leg/esea02/index.html.

United States Department of Education. (2003). *Guidance on constitutionally protected prayer in public elementary and secondary schools*. Retrieved October 11, 2010, from www2.ed.gov/policy/gen/guid/religionandschools/prayer_guidance.html.

United States Department of Education. (2004). *Individuals with Disabilities Act*. Retrieved October 18, 2009, from www.wrightslaw.com/idea/law/idea.regs. subparte.pdf.

United States Department of Education. (2008). *Family Educational Rights and Privacy Act of 1974*. Final Rule. Retrieved May 3, 2009, from www.ed.gov/legislation/FedRegister/finrule/2008-4/120908a.pdf.

United States Department of Education. (2009). *Rehabilitation Act of 1973, section 504*. Retrieved October 11, 2010, from www2.ed.gov/about/offices/list/ocr/504faq.html.

United States Department of Housing and Urban Development (2014). *The 2014 annual homeless assessment report (AHR) to congress.* Retrieved March 6, 2017, from www.hudexchange.info/resources/documents/2014-AHAR-Part1.pdf.

Vygotsky, L. S. (1934). *Thought and language*. Cambridge, MA: Massachusetts Institute of Technology Press.

Vygotsky, L. S. (1978). *Mind and society*. Cambridge, MA: Harvard University Press.

Wedding, D., & Corsini, R. J. (2013). *Current psychotherapies* (10th ed.). Itasca, IL: Brooks Cole.

Whiston, S. C., Tai, W. L., Rahardja, D., & Eder, K. (2011). School counseling outcome: A meta-analytic examination of interventions. *Journal of Counseling & Development, 89*, 37–55.

Wigfield, A. & Eccles, J. S. (2000). Expectancy-value theory of achievement motivation. *Contemporary Educational Psychology, 25*, 68–81.

Willard, N. E. (2006). *Cyberbullying and cyberthreats: Responding to challenge of online cruelty, threats, and distress* (2nd ed.). Eugene, OR: Center for Safe and Responsible Internet Use.

Wolf, J. T. (2004). Teach, but don't preach: Practical guidelines for addressing spiritual concerns of students. *Professional School Counseling, 7*, 363–366.

Wright, K., & Stegelin, D. A. (2002). *Building school and community partnerships through parent involvement* (2nd ed.). Upper Saddle River, NJ: Merrill/Prentice Hall.

Young, A., Dollarhide, C. T., & Baughman, A. (2015). The voices of school counselors: Essential characteristics of school counselor leaders. *Professional School Counseling, 19*(1), 36–45.

Youngs, B. B. (1992). *The six vital ingredients of self-esteem: How to develop them in your students*. Torrance, CA: Jalmar Press.

# Index